John Osborne

STUDIES IN MODERN DRAMA
KIMBALL KING, *Series Editor*

THEATRE UNDER
DECONSTRUCTION?
A Question of Approach
by Stratos E. Constantinidis

THE PINTER ETHIC
The Erotic Aesthetic
by Penelope Prentice

BARNESTORM
The Plays of Peter Barnes
by Bernard F. Dukore

NEW THEATRE VISTAS
*Modern Movements
in International Theatre*
edited by Judy Lee Oliva

DAVID MAMET'S
*GLENGARRY GLEN ROSS
Text and Performance*
edited by Leslie Kane

PAST CRIMSON, PAST WOE
*The Shakespeare-Beckett
Connection*
edited by Anne Marie Drew

MODERN DRAMATISTS
*A Casebook of Major British,
Irish, and American Playwrights*
edited by Kimball King

THE THEATRE OF TONY
KUSHNER
Living Past Hope
by James Fisher

ALAN BENNETT
A Critical Introduction
by Joseph O'Mealy

HOLLYWOOD ON STAGE
*Playwrights Evaluate
the Culture Industry*
edited by Kimball King

BLACK WOMEN PLAYWRIGHTS
Visions on the American Stage
edited by Carol P. Marsh-Lockett

READING STEPHEN SONDHEIM
A Collection of Critical Essays
edited by Sandor Goodhart

PEERING BEHIND THE
CURTAIN
*Disability, Illness, and the Extra-
ordinary Body in Contemporary
Theater*
edited by Thomas Fahy and
Kimball King

JOHN OSBORNE
VITUPERATIVE ARTIST
A Reading of His Life and Work

By Luc Gilleman

ROUTLEDGE
NEW YORK & LONDON
2002

Published in 2002 by
Routledge
29 West 35th Street
New York, NY 10001

Published in Great Britain by
Routledge
11 New Fetter Lane
London EC4P 4EE

Routledge is an imprint of the Taylor & Francis Group.

10   9   8   7   6   5   4   3   2   1

Library of Congress Cataloging-in-Publication Data

Gilleman, Luc M. (Luc Maurice)
   John Osborne: vituperative artist / by Luc Gilleman.
      p.   cm. — (Garland reference library of the humanities; v. 1963. Studies in
   modern drama; v. 11)
   Includes bibliographic references (p.) and index.
   ISBN 0–8153–2201–1 (acid free paper)
      1. Osborne, John 1929—Criticism and interpretation. 2. Invective in literature.
I. Title. II. Garland reference library of the humanities; vol. 1963. III. Garland
reference library of the humanities. Studies in modern drama; v. 11.

PR6029.S39 Z637 2001
822'.914—dc21   00–061736

Printed on acid-free, 250-year-life paper
Manufactured in the United States of America

Contents

Preface   vii

Acknowledgments   x

References to Osborne's Works   xi

1. Osborne's Phallic Art   1

Part I

2. Rise to the Top, 1956–1963   29

3. *Look Back in Anger* (1956): Of Bears and Traps   45

4. *The Entertainer* (1957): The Use of Despair   63

5. *Luther* (1961): The Negative Way of Anger   85

Part II

6. At the Top, 1964–1971   109

7. *Inadmissible Evidence* (1964): The Birthing of the Self   123

8. *A Patriot for Me* (1965): Society and the Hidden Self   141

Part III

9. The Long Descent, 1972–1994   163

10. *A Sense of Detachment* (1972): The Limits of Authenticity   177

11. *Watch It Come Down* (1976): A Most Necessary Failure   197

12. *Déjàvu* (1992): Elegy for Lost Origins   213

A Note on Further Reading   234

Notes   235

Index   255

Preface

What to do with John Osborne? He is as much an anomaly today as he was in 1956 when he began his career as a young and unknown actor/playwright. Reviewers responded to him then with enthusiasm, but also with distrust, praising the energy and flair of his unique voice, while lamenting its stubborn refusal to bend to customary aesthetic constraints; but these were cavils that Osborne refused to heed. He continued on his defiant course and created a richly diverse, though often frustratingly complex body of work.

Why, then, is there not more interest in Osborne's work? Distrust, it seems, has been followed by indifference. Though *Look Back in Anger* still stands as a milepost in the history of drama, recent anthologies rarely contain any of Osborne's plays. Dramatic criticism, of course, follows its own fashions. Not too long ago, questions of a work's possible offensiveness simply were not considered academically respectable. Now the question of representation, especially of minority groups, is often a central critical concern, and academics routinely wonder whether a work perpetuates or interrogates a cultural stereotype. What can be done, then, with the work of a man like Osborne, who all his life said the wrong things at the wrong time?

There is something uplifting in the works of playwrights who espouse worthwhile causes. In many liberal institutions, it is far easier to teach Caryl Churchill, David Henry Hwang, or Tony Kushner than John Osborne. For Osborne, there are no good brave causes—only people who muddle on in life, who hurt, and often hurt in return. Deeply steeped in personal neurosis, Osborne's work demands the kind of painstaking and loving exegesis an analyst is expected to give to a patient's troubling dream. What makes this difficult, however, is that often his work is so vexing as to invite an almost instant and vehement response. I have never seen so many angry young women as when I introduced Osborne to my classes at Smith College; but this also means that Osborne's work is still alive and well and that a reappraisal of it is more than timely.

This study deals with Osborne's complete oeuvre, yet only works that I consider major have been subjected to an in-depth, chapter-length analysis. As Osborne always was experimenting with form and technique, his plays invite a wide array of critical approaches. As often as possible, I have engaged the critical questions that are most relevant today, notably, the relationship between life and work, the function of the gaze, and the construction of gender. Because Osborne's relationship with critics has been particularly turbulent, I have traced the evolution of his reception by turning to critical reviews at the beginning of each major chapter.

Chapters are grouped in three parts to reflect the course of Osborne's career. *Look Back in Anger, The Entertainer,* and *Luther* punctuate his quick rise to the top. *Inadmissible Evidence* and *A Patriot for Me*, written when critics finally conceded to his lasting importance, are his most mature works. *A Sense of Detachment, Watch It Come Down,* and *Déjàvu* signal the slow and painful descent of his career.

Writing is lonely work. At least it seems so, until one writes acknowledgments and realizes to what extent a book is the result of collaboration. A great number of people helped me to complete this work. Smith College offered me a much needed sabbatical leave as well as research and travel grants for work in London and Austin, Texas. In 1997 and 1998, I was also the grateful recipient of a Jean Picker Fellowship, funding course release and research in London.

Much of the research for this book was done at the Theatre Museum in London, the archives of the Royal National Theatre, and the British Film Institute. I would like to thank Anne Mayer, Press Manager of the Royal Court Theatre; Janet Birkett and her staff at the Theatre Museum in Covent Garden; Vanessa Choudbury, Press Officer, and Nicola Scadding, Archivist, at the Royal National Theatre. I am extremely grateful to Luke Kernan from the National Film and Television Archive at the British Film Institute for providing me with a complete list of Osborne's television appearances and television plays. I also thank Kathleen Dickson and the staff of the BFI for helping me in my work.

My research also led me to examine an important collection of Osborne's personal papers housed at the Harry Ransom Humanities Research Center at the University of Texas at Austin. I thank Research Librarian Tara Wenger and her staff for their kindness and advice.

A number of Smith students contributed to this book by sorting and cataloguing secondary sources. I am especially grateful to Leonora Knapp and Judith Shatzky, who did most of that tedious work.

Colleagues and friends have supported me with advice or have read and edited chapters. I thank Douglas Patey who answered practical questions concerning book publishing and Bruce Dalhberg, professor emeritus at Smith College, who gave me valuable bibliographic information on Luther. I am eternally indebted to Sarah Grover who stood by me and read, reread, and commented on every chapter. Without her help, this work would not have seen the light. The better book, I believe, is still in her mind. I am grateful to Gilbert Debusscher from the Université Libre de Bruxelles for a meticulous annotation of the chapter on *A Patriot for Me*. Elizabeth Harries, my colleague at Smith's English Department, was more than generous with her time, reading and commenting on almost the entire manuscript. For this and for sharing with me the joys of eating Sushi, my thanks. And I simply cannot find words to express my gratitude to another colleague, William Oram, who followed this project from start to finish, reading and returning chapters to me in record time, even at moments of busy work in class and committees. He is not only a model colleague but a steadfast friend in times of trouble. I have, of course, been unable to incorporate everyone's suggestions, and it goes without saying that shortcomings or errors in this manuscript are entirely mine.

I would also like to thank Timothy Wiles and Albert Wertheim, professors at my alma mater, Indiana University, who guided me in my first steps as a drama critic, and in particular, Stephen Watt, who suggested that I write this book for Kimball King's series. James Morgan and Maria Zamora of Garland Press, Anne Davidson and William Germano from Routledge, and Tom Wang from Taylor & Francis cracked the whip when I needed it most. Kimball King, editor of the series in which this book appears, was a supportive, almost fatherly presence. To this true gentleman, my heartfelt thanks. I also thank Joris Duytschaever from the Universitaire Instelling Antwerpen for taking a keen interest in my work on drama and for having offered several opportunities for seeing my work into publication, and Nina Korotkova for having witnessed the genesis of this work and for offering suggestions on the final manuscript. Thanks also to my parents for their unwavering support. I dedicate this book to them.

This book is not a hagiography; it is simply a work born of fascination. In case anyone could still be in doubt after looking through this book, let me state here explicitly what I think of Osborne. I believe he was a true artist — that is, a man whose very flaws are interesting. As a human being, he clearly had an unpleasant side. So do most of us; the difference is that we will remember his—and perhaps even with some fondness. The struggle with himself, he exposed in his plays and was therefore deeply hurt by the mockery of critics. If this is a sin, it is shared by many artists. Not all of his plays are a joy to watch or read, but none is without its rewards for the attentive reader or spectator. In approaching Osborne's work, one must resist the temptation to call for the scissors and glue, to insist on pruning and reorganizing in the name of improvement. Throughout my analyses, I have focused especially on these excesses which, together with moments of exaggerated economy, always prove to be the most revealing. The play lives where it sloshes loosely in its mold or spills over its confines. That is where, for me, the recalcitrant spirit of Osborne will remain alive.

Acknowledgments

The author and publisher gratefully acknowledge the cooperation of Mrs. Helen Osborne, who permitted quotations from the following plays by John Osborne used in this work: *Déjàvu, A Patriot for Me, A Sense of Detachment, Watch it Come Down, Inadmissible Evidence, The End of Me Old Cigar*, and *Epitaph for George Dillon*. See "References to Osborne's Works" for editions used.

We further acknowledge permission to reprint excerpts from the following works by John Osborne: *Look Back in Anger*. Copyright 1982 by Penguin Books. Reprinted by permission of S.G. Phillips, Inc., John Osborne, and Faber and Faber, Ltd. *Déjàvu*. Copyright 1991 by Faber and Faber. Reprinted by permission of John Osborne and Faber and Faber, Ltd. *The Entertainer*. Copyright 1958 by Criterion Books. Reprinted by permission of S.G. Phillips, Inc., John Osborne and Faber and Faber, Ltd. *Luther*. Copyright 1961 by John Osborne. Copyright renewed 1989 by John Osborne. Reprinted by permission of Dutton Signet, a division of Penguin Putnam, Inc.; David Higham Associates: Osborne / 20 March 2001; John Osborne; and Faber and Faber, Ltd. *A Patriot for Me*. Copyright 1965 by Faber and Faber, Ltd. Reprinted by permission of John Osborne and Faber and Faber, Ltd. *Inadmissible Evidence*. Copyright 1965 by Grove. Reprinted by permission of John Osborne and Faber and Faber, Ltd. *Epitaph for George Dillon*, by John Osborne and Anthony Creighton. Copyright 1958 by Criterion Books. Reprinted permission of John Osborne and Faber and Faber, Ltd. Every effort has been made to obtain permission to reproduce material. If any proper acknowledgment has not been made, we would invite copyright holders to inform us of the oversight.

References to Osborne's Works

Almost a Gentleman: An Autobiography. Vol II: 1955–1966. London: Faber, 1991.

A Better Class of Person: An Autobiography. Vol I: 1929–1956. London: Faber, 1981.

The Blood of the Bambergs. Plays for England: The Blood of the Bambergs *and* Under Plain Cover. London: Evans Brothers Limited, 1963.

Damn You, England: Collected Prose. London: Faber, 1994.

Déjàvu. London: Faber, 1991.

The End of Me Old Cigar. The End of Me Old Cigar *and* Jill and Jack. London: Faber, 1975.

The Entertainer. New York: Criterion Books, 1958.

Epitaph for George Dillon. By John Osborne and Anthony Creighton. New York: Criterion Books, 1958.

The Father. Strindberg's The Father *and Ibsen's* Hedda Gabler. Adapted by John Osborne. London: Faber, 1989.

God Rot Tunbridge Wells. A Better Class of Person *and* God Rot Tunbridge Wells. London: Faber, 1985.

Hedda Gabler. Adapted by John Osborne. London: Faber, 1972.

The Hotel in Amsterdam. Chicago: Dramatic Publishing Co., 1974.

Inadmissible Evidence. New York: Grove, 1965.

Jill and Jack. The End of Me Old Cigar *and* Jill and Jack. London: Faber, 1975.

Look Back in Anger. New York: Penguin Books, 1982.

Luther. New York: Signet Books, 1963.

A Patriot for Me. London: Faber, 1965.

The Picture of Dorian Gray: A Moral Entertainment. Adapted by John Osborne from the novel by Oscar Wilde. London: Faber, 1973.

A Place Calling Itself Rome. London: Faber, 1973.

The Right Prospectus. London: Faber, 1970.

A Sense of Detachment. London: Faber, 1973.

Time Present. West of Suez. West of Suez, A Patriot for Me, Time Present, The Hotel in Amsterdam. Four Plays by John Osborne. New York: Dodd, Mead, & Company, 1973.

Tom Jones. A Film Script by John Osborne. Ed. Robert Hughes. New York: Grove, 1964.

Under Plain Cover. Plays for England: The Blood of the Bambergs *and* Under Plain Cover. London: Evans Brothers Limited, 1963.

Very Like a Whale. London: Faber, 1971.

Watch It Come Down. London: Faber, 1975.

West of Suez. West of Suez, A Patriot for Me, Time Present, The Hotel in Amsterdam. Four Plays by John Osborne. New York: Dodd, Mead, & Company, 1973.

The World of Paul Slickey: A Comedy of Manners with Music. London: Faber, 1959.

CHAPTER 1

Osborne's Phallic Art

POLITICS

"People are more out of sympathy with me now than they were, say, twenty years ago," Osborne said in a 1976 interview. About his plays, he said, "the older people hate them and then the young loathe them."[1] In 1992, to another interviewer, an even more disgruntled Osborne referred to himself as "yesterday's man": "no one has any interest in me any more. I don't know why you've come."[2] Yet at his death on Christmas Eve 1994, the man who had so often complained of being ill respected, indeed largely forgotten, received surprisingly warm and generous accolades in the press. In his eulogy at the memorial service, David Hare alluded to "the heartfelt and often guilty appreciation which followed on his death."[3] To have been so little liked became in retrospect proof of integrity rather than nastiness. "We all need a sense of outrage to keep us alive," said John Mortimer in an obituary that thanked Osborne for having supplied us with the necessary vexations. As a young playwright he had done so by attacking venerable institutions, referring to, for instance, the monarchy as the "gold filling in a mouthful of decay."[4] Where many had been appalled, others had been exhilarated by what Osborne liked to call spirited "kicks against the pricks." Clearly even in his later public role as old curmudgeon, Osborne had continued to exert a certain appeal. His cantankerous diatribes against ever increasing bureaucratization, his tireless advocacy of old humanitarian values, and his unabashed patriotism had been sympathetically received by growing numbers who feared the fast changes in England's identity. Interestingly, many of these new sympathizers from the right had started out as leftists—very much indeed the way Osborne had.

In the late fifties and early sixties, Osborne had been so outspokenly leftist that on several occasions the management of the English Stage Company had sought to distance itself from him.[5] So much the better for Osborne who

1

thought of socialism mainly in terms of outrage and scandal. Socialism to Osborne was never a well-planned political doctrine but an attitude, a way of looking at the world. It meant to "stand up, say what you think about whom and what you don't like in our society, and to hell with making a fool of yourself—and the more enemies you make the better." In this he followed his grandfather for whom a socialist was "a man who doesn't believe in raising his hat."[6] Socialism, in other words, was all about feelings—and these were also the writer's concern: "a writer can demonstrate feeling. It takes an extraordinary human being to demonstrate action as well."[7] Once in a while, however, he did act upon his feelings: he made the occasional guest appearance on television in Labour election programs, actively supported the cultural boycott against South Africa,[8] and, on one much publicized occasion, was arrested during a CND demonstration on Trafalgar Square. But his heart was not in such actions. He disliked mass protests, the feeling of having one's identity swallowed up by a group. He had no interest in or patience with the political game, with planning, organization, and compromise. "Socialism," Osborne wrote in 1957, "is about people living together, and the sooner the leaders of the Labour Party stop arguing about sugar and cement and wake up to the fact the better. . . . The Labour Party has concerned itself too much with order papers, and ignored human behaviour. It should turn its attention to the things that matter, to the things that make people feel."[9]

At a time when the welfare state was still being built, this was a strangely inappropriate remark. Supplying sufficient amounts of sugar and cement or finding ways of funding free sets of teeth for a population that had never enjoyed the benefits of adequate dentistry were definitely "things that matter." But Labour, he thought, did wrong to appeal so much to people's "cupidity." It sought technological and technocratic solutions for what was, in effect, a spiritual hunger. Typically, Osborne found it neither improper nor inconsistent to inveigh against the materialism of others at a time when he was so particularly well provided for himself. The man who had once lived with his mother in Fulham on less than one pound a week had seen his weekly income increase to £3,500 after just eighteen months of fame and was now thought to be "one of the most prosperous living playwrights of the century."[10] Money, he said, only mattered in so far as it provided security. Rather than compromising him, affluence ensured his integrity in the sense that he could now vent his anger more freely.

He did this most notoriously in 1961, when in reaction to the Berlin crisis that nearly triggered a third World War, he sent a particularly vehement open "Letter to My Fellow Countrymen" to the socialist newspaper the *Tribune*. Usually referred to as "Damn You, England," the letter is now memorable mainly for its hysterical intensity; the word hate or hatred appears some thirteen times in the span of its very short text. It accuses the British government of being so spellbound by the superpowers that it would readily gamble away peace and endanger the survival of the planet. Osborne later explained that he felt prompted to write the letter after he saw how poorly the public had received Bertrand Russell's well-reasoned article on the same subject. Intent on shaking up a nation indifferent to its own fate, Osborne had decided to aim the flamethrower of his rhetoric at it.

Unlike Russell's well-argued contribution, Osborne's letter is that of a fuming and ranting Old Testament prophet. The most striking aspect of this public letter concerning an affair of supranational importance is its tone of personal grievance. When Macmillan's Conservative ruling party and Gaitskell's Labour opposition allowed for the manufacture and testing of the first British hydrogen bomb, it was Osborne's life that was being threatened: "I fear death. I dread it daily. I cling wretchedly to life, as I have always done. I fear death, but I cannot hate it as I hate you. It is only you I hate, and those who let you live, function and prosper." In revenge, the people that had wounded him thus, most notably Gaitskell and Macmillan, had to die: "there is murder in my brain, and I carry a knife in my heart for every one of you." The diatribe ends somewhat melodramatically with Osborne signing the letter "in sincere and utter hatred."[11]

Shortly after its publication in the *Tribune,* the letter appeared in national and international newspapers and had an even stronger effect than Osborne had hoped. Indeed, Osborne was slightly taken aback by the storm he had unleashed. His attack had been so sweeping and his disgust so naked that the letter arose in even the most apathetic readers the strongest of sentiments. What followed was a public outcry of such insane hysteria, it easily matched Osborne's. At one point, Major Colin de Vere Gordon-MacLean marched up to Osborne to demand his apologies on behalf of England. But what irritated many and amused even more was that Osborne had sent the letter from a luxurious hideaway in the South of France. A cartoon in the *Daily Mail* depicts a cigar smoking Osborne, lazily stretched out under a parasol, two bottles of champagne chilling at his side. A book on his lap reads "How To Cure Indigestion," by Martin Luther, a mocking reference to Osborne's emphasis on digestive problems in his play *Luther,* which was then in rehearsal. Two middle-aged British women tourists comment, "Look, dear, there's that *poor* Mr. Osborne 'clinging wretchedly to life as he always has done.'"[12] The article under the cartoon attempts to undermine Osborne's credibility and integrity further by painting the Angry Young Man's lavish lifestyle and by detailing the "considerable fortune" he was still expecting to amass from *Luther* and from his film company's successful production of Alan Sillitoe's *Saturday Night and Sunday Morning.* In its coarse suggestiveness, the article implied that a politics so loftily unaware of its own material allegiances was not worth serious consideration.

Osborne, as always, seemed nonplussed by such reactions. Though "Damn You, England" expressly demands not to be read as sheer rhetoric

("No, this is not the highly paid 'anger' or the 'rhetoric' you like to smile at"), he later referred to it as "a very melodramatic exercise,"[13] a sort of vituperative "poem,"[14] and ascribed the offense it had caused to people's literal-mindedness: "I happened to write in an overheated oratorical strain and I put it that way because I thought it would have the most impact. I wanted to arouse feeling, but the bourgeois, philistine, anti-art population of England took every word of that journalistic device literally."[15] It never occurred to him that some might have found it distasteful that he presented himself as if at the center of a problem of worldwide scope, involving the fate of millions. He had absolutely no patience with people who thought it absurd for a man to talk about personal victimization at the hands of a society that had so richly rewarded him. To Osborne, the opposite was true. If his anger had been motivated by immediate material need, it would merely have amounted to spite. In general, he believed his aesthetics to be existentially, not materially, predicated. Its wellspring was personal suffering, the badge of his particular kind of artistic sensitivity; and being an artist meant endowing that personal pain with a general, that is social, validity. In short, at the basis of his aesthetics was an egoism so intense, but also so grand, that it could convince less acutely self-involved mortals that they in fact felt the same. For such an artist the difference between the personal and the public ceases to exist, and aesthetics become quite naturally political; and to the extent that politics involves the shaping of forms of life out of human material, it clearly *is* a kind of aesthetics and therefore the artist's business. The artist's political function, however, is not to outline a program or propose an argument but to set a tone or define a feeling. In "They Call It Cricket," he made that point perfectly clear:

> I shall not try and hand out my gospel version of the Labour Party's next manifesto to prop up any journalist who wants a bit of easy copy or to give some reviewer another smart clue for his weekly written-up crossword game. I shall simply fling down a few statements—you can take your pick. They will be what are often called "sweeping statements," but I believe we are living at a time when a few "sweeping statements" may be valuable. It is too late for caution. (65)

While it was wrong of Labour to allow money and possessions to govern people's imagination and desires, neither should Labour stimulate the rampant greed and envy, in short, the philistinism, that had animated this attack on Osborne's fortune. That would in fact be a Tory strategy; and Tory, for Osborne, was the most obscene four-letter word he knew. It was the party of "'restraint,' 'good taste,' 'healthy caution'."[16] So yes, under present conditions to insist on the importance of feelings, as he did, may seem excessive, but, then excess was a political response against the moderation preached by the dominant classes.

It was curious logic for a socialist, but consistent in a high-handed, patronizing way. Its self-centeredness undoubtedly expressed a good measure of arrogance but also a political disaffiliation that many shared. Support of the hydrogen bomb and subservience to American values and policies had cost Labour traditional followers. These were the people that recognized their own plight in Osborne's angry voice. Suspicious of progress for its own sake, some of them turned to apparently timeless values such as patriotism and tradition and, as David Edgar's *Maydays* (1983) so strikingly illustrates, often became outspokenly conservative. In 1967, Osborne wrote: "Friends who were never friends call me blimp. To hell with them. It is harder than they will ever know." When in 1968, a year of international political upheaval, Kenneth Tynan asked him whether he had "moved toward a right-wing position," Osborne insisted that he had "always had leftist, radical sympathies" and that this had not changed. What had changed, however, was the nature of leftism itself: "a lot of left-wing feeling nowadays strikes me as instant mashed-potato radicalism. It hasn't been felt through and worked through. I find it easy and superficial and tiresome."

At the time of the interview, student protests at the Sorbonne had para-lyzed the French government. Significantly, the impetus had shifted from the working class to the sons and daughters of the middle class. Leftism was tak-ing a turn, emphasizing the political importance not of workers, who suppos-edly had sold out to the comforts of capitalism, but of minorities and women. As an individualist, Osborne disapproved of such group leftism: "now they're all 'we-ing' all over the place. And acting as groups, which I find both unin-teresting and ugly." 1968, moreover, was celebratory and narcissistic—and hence distasteful to a writer who professed to think of "life as a long process of disappointment."[17] Neither of the two major components of 1968 political philosophy, mindless pacifism or militant activism, appealed to him. The Flower People, he said, were "soft and sloppy-minded." As a writer, he believed in discipline and that made him "inevitably a conservative rather than an anarchist."[18] Suspicious of other people's anger, he thought of the more militant new leftists as "a lot of people exploiting other people." Osborne nev-ertheless continued to vote Labour until well into the seventies, though he became increasingly disgusted with that party's compromising over issues of principle. He soon came to hold Labour "responsible for the moral slum and squalid climate we have created since the heady days of 1945," and if he con-tinued for the time being to cast his vote for it, it was out of nostalgia and with little conviction.[19] He distanced himself from his own past involvement in left-ist activism, minimal as that had been, and spoke out sharply against the social and political causes that dominated the late sixties and early seventies.[20]

The socialist of the late fifties had apparently turned conservative, or at least he displayed the emotional attitudes commonly associated with it. He expressed dismay at the Garrick Club's decision to admit women,[21] lamented the EEC-prohibition on unfiltered Turkish cigarettes,[22] defended a monarchy he had once mocked, and vigorously campaigned against the Chunnel and the Alternative Service Book.[23] Where he had once been interested in issues—the fight against South African apartheid, French atrocities in the Algerian war, Portuguese dictatorship and human rights abuses—when being passionate about such issues was thought to be boorish, now he was the first to poke fun at them when they became a fashionable outlet for middle-class self-righteousness. When everyone condemned South African apartheid, as he had once done, he started to speak admiringly of the Afrikaners.[24] When he thought political correctness had taken hold of press and education, he loudly contested it as "fascist liberalism," all the while enjoying the endless possibilities of outrage the new puritanism afforded him. He could now make the most imbecilic comments ("I have two of God's greatest gifts—to be born English and heterosexual"[25]) and be certain that someone would receive it with equally preposterous indignation. But, never having been a doctrinaire socialist, now he did not embrace the Tory party line either. He had no sympathy with Margaret Thatcher's neo-conservatism,[26] though he allowed himself to think kindly of her successor, the often derided, more centrist John Major.[27] In later age, he denied all political affiliation.[28]

Political definitions of what constitutes the Left and the Right evolved over the years, but Osborne's philosophy remained basically unchanged.[29] Like Alceste of Molière's *Misanthrope,* Osborne simply made sure he stood on the wrong side of every issue. Happily for him, the apparently unpopular side had its own following. The younger middle-class spectators of the fifties and sixties readily empathized with a degree of seductive waywardness if it could help them to define their individuality in an age that threatened it. What was attractive was that Osborne supplied the attitudes and voice of rebellion without demanding forfeiture of newly gained comforts. Floating on a surfeit of style, one could apparently safely sail the "egalitarian" waters of the "American century." Painstaking analysis and rigorous argumentation were unnecessary and had, in any case, proven to be ineffective; what was needed was more "feeling." Osborne thereby unwittingly paved the way for the post–'68 world he would so heartily detest.

Conceiving of language as the clay out of which individuals mold their most intimate feelings, while simultaneously designating feeling as a political concern, sooner or later produces a conflict of interest. Osborne was unable to resolve it and ended up fulminating against a problem largely of his own making. His insistence that politics ought to be concerned with style, with aesthetics, rather than with economics, with the material conditions of life, echoes the postmodern conviction that inequality and injustice can be solved ideologically by erasing the boundaries between education, therapy, and politics. His belief that politics has to concern itself less with "order papers" and more with "the way people live together" comes all too close to the postmodern slogan that "the personal is the political." That slogan made it any radical's duty to instill desired attitudes, censor language, and regulate personal behavior—in other words, to lay siege to the sovereignty of the individual. Approaching politics only by way of its discursive roots threatened what Osborne identified as the seat of individuality itself.

In the latter part of his career, Osborne appealed mainly to those who feared the consequences of thinking about politics in a way he had helped to promote. Eager to assert their own integrity, they empathized with Osborne's virulent dislike of hypocrisy and his rabid pursuit of the mealy-mouthed social engineering brigade of jeans-clad bishops and social workers. In this way, Osborne indeed managed to be "a lifelong satirist of prigs and puritans, whether of the Right or of the Left," as self-proclaimed socialist David Hare put it.[30] That Osborne's satire revolved angrily around its own contradictions and suffered, most painfully, from its own kind of priggishness, he politely left unmentioned.

SELF-IMAGE

How strange, one interviewer remarked of Osborne, that a man who so often offends others is so often and easily offended himself. She also confessed to being troubled by his "indifference to other people's feelings" and noticed rightly that "while being almost disablingly sensitive himself, he can't believe for a minute that anyone else can be hurt."[31] Examples of this abound. Osborne took journalists to court for referring to him as "the original Teddy Boy"[32] yet built his notoriety out of infinitely worse abuse of journalists, calling them "vicious," "wheedling" creatures with "squalid, seedy sex lives."[33] Not satisfied with vilifying them in interviews and publications, he sent them obscene postcards, plainly counting on their being too perversely flattered to press charges. "I don't really mind being called a dumb cunt ," said Francis King of the *Sunday Telegraph* in a personal letter to Osborne, dated 27 September 1978; "but, if you wish to send further such obscenities through the post, would it be too much trouble to use an envelope?"[34] Osborne's excuse was that he had been treated far worse. In fact, it would appear the world had been created expressly to vex him, so long is the list of his pet peeves; and high up on that list is people's objection to being called names. "You're not allowed to call anyone a cripple or a dwarf," Osborne complained, referring to the current climate of political correctness. "You can't even call them a *girl*. That, that, I will *resist*. I find it deeply depressing when people so easily go around being wounded about things that are said about them. I mean, if they'd had to put up with what *I* have! My entire *life* I've been abused and reviled." Then later in the same interview, when shown some of the inconsistencies of this stance, he rather disarmingly admitted to the fault of being "hideously spontaneous."

Calling one's cruelty a form of hideous spontaneity may, of course, be a flattering way of conceding to an inability or unwillingness to conceive of others as sensitively as one conceives of oneself. Granted, such egocentrism often typifies the artist. It is nevertheless also true that it will be accepted as the prerogative of a special susceptibility only if it produces art that is as generously sensitive as the artist is mean. Apparently unsure of the value of his work, Osborne took care to obfuscate the boundaries between his oeuvre and his life. His works are deeply, and often confusingly, autobiographical, and he carefully cultivated his image as artist, effectively turning himself into his own major work of art. This had obvious advantages. As the pronouncements of an artist are primarily artistic, they are both real and unreal, deeply truthful because inspired, yet also false because endowed with a measure of poetic license. Hence, he felt justified when dragging others to court, but hurt when literal-minded others did the same to him.

The prospect of having to meet the famous "angry" writer must have been daunting to interviewers because many report their surprise at encountering instead a soft-spoken, rather shy, and perfectly courteous man.[35] Much suggests that Osborne enjoyed thwarting people's expectations, aware of the confusion it would create. Contradiction, inconsistency, and excess were to him means of instilling a sense of irreducible individuality. His example in that respect was Dr. Johnson, whom he deeply admired and read avidly, and whom he described in terms that he would clearly have loved to hear applied to himself:

> He's an extraordinarily sensitive character, and terribly courageous, and on the outside he seems very often rather brutal and a bit of a show-off. In a way I think he's the prime example of a person who eludes the modern idea of the interview, where you can get someone in depth ... in some way strip a human personality down.... Of course it's not really possible, because I think the human personality is irreducible, and I think someone like Johnson is the perfect literary example of it. Because if you were to interview him, anyone, you still wouldn't get Dr. Johnson.[36]

Affable yet brutal, sensitive yet cruel, Osborne spent a lifetime defining himself in opposition to what he thought were people's received opinions of him and of the world; and out of such contradictions emerges indeed a fascinatingly irreducible and eminently theatrical figure.

The theatricality of Osborne's self-image had the added advantage of being strikingly out of touch with the age. While he is credited with having launched the postwar trend of plays that deal with contemporary issues in contemporary idiom, Osborne differs from his successors in that he never aspired to exchange the old-fashioned image of *artiste* and *homme de théâtre* for that of social researcher. Much like Noel Coward, author of middle-class dramas that Osborne's theatre was said to have made superfluous, he always appeared

immaculately dressed, flaunting remarkable poise and faintly raffish elegance.[37] An actor's training had taught him to control the nasal whine and pip-
ing sound of his original voice. In interviews he uttered the most outrageous
opinions in a deliberately low and lazy voice, with a slight lisp and a rather
affected drawl. Sporting natty white suits and colorful silk scarves, blowing bil-
lows of black smoke from unfiltered Turkish cigarettes, and sipping champagne from morning till evening, he led a consciously theatrical life and
visibly enjoyed its effect on others. Even his final exit he stage-managed himself. This time, though, he had foreseen that drastic cuts would be necessary,
since in its initial conception, the funeral would have lasted up to six hours.[38]
The ceremony, in keeping with his plays, remained nevertheless typically
excessive (or "undisciplined," to use the critics' favorite word), exhibiting
rather too much pomp and circumstance. There was bite even to that final gesture: at the memorial service on 2 June 1995, names of people barred from the
ceremony were listed as prominently as Luther's Ninety-Five Theses. Among
the names were those of old colleagues and erstwhile well-wishers Arnold
Wesker and Sir Peter Hall.[39]

Given Osborne's great talent for antagonizing people, as well as for making friends, it is not surprising that the author was constantly being confused
with his equally wayward heroes. Jimmy Porter, Bill Maitland, Archie Rice,
and Luther were obviously emanations of himself, exhibiting personality traits
he had also been publicizing in other, less immediately theatrical ways.
Though Osborne strongly objected to naive readings that take a character's
pronouncements for those of the author, he in fact promoted them by styling
himself after his heroes, becoming chubbier with *Luther,* for instance, or
growing a dapper mustache with *A Patriot for Me.* It is especially difficult not
to see later plays as podiums from which Osborne vented private frustrations.
In *Déjàvu,* for instance, there is no noticeable difference between J.P.'s and
Osborne's customary cynicisms about icons of liberalism—except that the latter received a more public hearing through interviews and television appearances than the former did in that relatively poorly attended play. Osborne, the
public voice of a deeply private anger, was in many respects a more successful creation than J.P.

FRIEND AND FOE

Like his heroes who feel besieged by the whole world and flail about wildly
in their ranting speeches, Osborne projects a self-image of a man desperately
fighting from an embattled position. The list of his enemies is long and
diverse. It contains among others, "grasping" wives, "smothering" mothers,
"strident" feminists, "trendy" vicars, social workers, apathetic audiences,
Japanese tourists, Australians and Canadians who live in England and speak
with the wrong accent, gay and lesbian activists, the European Community,

the twenty-first century, the Chunnel, low flying airplanes, people who object to dog excrement on city pavement, and miners who insist on greater handouts from the welfare state. Enemies can change, adjectives remain of the same order—reducible to the three choice epithets Jimmy applies to Alison's upper-class family in *Look Back in Anger:* sycophantic, phlegmatic, and pusillanimous (I, 21). Pusillanimous, Jimmy cries, grabbing the dictionary, means "wanting of firmness of mind, of small courage, having a little mind, mean spirited, cowardly, timid of mind. From the Latin pusillus, very little, and animus, the mind" (I, 22). Mockingly he addresses his wife as the "Lady Pusillanimous" before abbreviating it into the coarse cry, "Hey Pusey."

Smallness in any sense then—of spirit, of vision, of mind—is the most fundamental ill from which the whole compendium of Osbornian sins can be derived. Greediness, envy, narrow-mindedness, lack of imagination, stridency, militancy, pettiness, and cold-heartedness are all sins of smallness. Osborne's enemies are what Matthew Arnold called "philistines," a biblical word of which Osborne is particularly fond. For Arnold, the philistines were those who lacked "sweetness and light"—in effect, the cultural capital one acquires through a broad liberal education. For Osborne, modern philistines lack not school education but life experience and vitality. So in the late fifties and early sixties, the better educated higher classes were more likely to be the philistines. The authority with which they preached morality to the lower classes derived from a sense of privilege, not from suffering, of which, to Osborne's thinking, they had but little experience, being far too sheltered from life. From the seventies onward, however, when the welfare state assumed definite shape (only to be nearly immediately dismantled), the philistines were the welfare ideologists who preached the new morality of liberalism—and did so with a self-righteousness often instilled by liberal education.[40] With their minds caught in a straitjacket of theoretical notions, they shared with the philistines of an earlier age an inability to conceive of humans as evolving, complex, often contradictory beings.

The opposite, largeness, Osborne values in any of its manifestations: largesse, magnanimity, generosity, courage, ardor, impetuosity, broadmindedness (of the kind not predicated on indifference), love—in one word, "enthusiasm." It was not the American-style, mindless, wide-eyed wonderment that Osborne had in mind, but an existential quality, based on experience and choice, and touched by despair and tragedy. Madeline, the older woman Jimmy was in love with before he met Alison, had the gift of enthusiasm; so had the homosexual Webster, that is before he became militant, as we learn in *Déjàvu,* and insisted on preaching the gay gospel.[41] Enthusiasm is a sort of ebullience of spirit associated with a child's reckless abandon to play. Osborne's Luther, for instance, constantly longs for the "innocent body of a child," an image that to him represents liberation from paralyzing self-consciousness, physically expressed in his constipation. Later, looking back on the most creative and inspiring moments of his life, moments that also shaped history, Luther recalls having felt most like a child.

GENDER POLITICS AND AESTHETICS

This strict dichotomy of values endows Osborne's style with its typical, puritanical thrust, evident in its use of adjectives expressing disapprobation: avid, craven, grasping, overweening, precious, plodding, dismal, sordid, shabby, shrill, strident, sanctimonious, captious, vindictive, dissembling, and so on. The sometimes tedious return of these adjectives constitutes the most distinctive feature of Osborne's style. Inevitably, such sharply polarized prose also engages the troubled oppositions of gender ideology. Not surprisingly, since the seventies epithet "misogynist" has weaseled itself into critical appraisals, it has stubbornly fastened itself onto Osborne's tarnished reputation. Grating with the sound of semi-official condemnation, it has taken the place of that more fanciful appellation "cad" that middle-aged male reviewers used to apply to Osborne and his heroes in the late fifties.

If gendered readings are so often moralistic, it is because gender pertains to a value system rather than to biological sex. Feminine and masculine are terms that summarize a complementary number of positive and negative qualities that provide the necessary polarized tension around which an argument can be built. A tolerance for ambiguity, for instance, is commonly perceived to be a feminine characteristic: postmodern theorists like to refer to the *jouissance* that can be derived from an *écriture féminine,* a writing that through ambiguity, contradiction, and paradox encourages the endless play of its signifiers. Masculine, as Virginia Woolf argues in *A Room of One's Own* (1929), stands for a preference for rigid categories, linear thinking, hierarchies. But one can easily gather enough examples to revert such arbitrary gender assignations without loss of argumentative plausibility. The same can be done with the common view that social conscience is a feminine characteristic, while individualism at the expense of society is more typically masculine. For purposes of consistent argumentation, the important part of a dichotomy is the tension it creates, not the way its variables are precipitated in opposing categories. Reversing a commonly accepted dichotomy often appears particularly insightful, if only because the counter-intuitive requires more thought. This, of course, is Osborne's strategy. "Above all," he declares, "[woman] is the enemy of the group." Biological imperatives impose on her a pragmatic and selfish realism: "her roots are so deep in sexuality that she is the natural enemy of the visionary, the idealist." In an interview with Helena Matheopoulos, pompously entitled "This Is What I Expect of a Woman," he affirms perversely that "men are vague" while "women always crave for clear-cut situations or definitions," adding: "they are more geometrical and have tidier brains."

This reversal enables Osborne to consider generosity, broad-mindedness, and other virtues of largeness, as more typically masculine, and sins of small-ness (greed, envy, narrow-mindedness, etc.) as feminine. Of course, women may be unstinting in their generosity (as is the case with Mrs. Tanner in *Look Back in Anger*), and men dogmatically intolerant (as Alison's brother Nigel in the same play). However, apart from a mere allusion to the adventuresome Madeline in *Look Back in Anger,* it is hard to find an example of a woman in Osborne's oeuvre who possesses the virility of mind and demeanor that Osborne finds attractive. His positive portrayals of women—as can be found, for instance, in *The End of Me Old Cigar*—usually emphasize responsiveness toward male desire, empathy with a male's performance anxiety, and a trust-ing willingness to reveal lack of self-confidence.

Whenever a woman breaks out of her customary supporting role, Osborne regards her with suspicion. A strident woman may seem mannish, says Osborne, but has only assimilated what is small and mean in men. As he puts it in a preachy *Daily Mail* piece entitled "What's Gone Wrong with Women?" (14 November 1956), "gleaming with the colours of the male arrogance, [woman] becomes an iron butterfly."[42] To these "iron butterflies," to harsh, ungenerous womanhood, Osborne ascribes all current political ills. The heady years of socialist welfare state building were marked by virile boldness of con-ception, but the Tory victories that followed in the fifties, and the adulteration of the welfare state ideal into a policy of small consumerism and social con-trol, resulted from the increasing feminization of society. Present society, Osborne says, is dominated by "the characteristic female indifference to any-thing but immediate, personal suffering." Conveniently eliding the gender-sex difference, he adds: "the new conservatism, the atmosphere of caution, fatigue and malaise, the attitude of 'this-doesn't-touch-me, why-should-I-pay-for-the-next-man', on every level stems from woman." Missing a real man's broad vision and idealism, woman tends to be conservative in politics: "most women want to retain the death penalty and 'bring back the cat'. Go to any Tory con-ference, let anyone even dare to discuss the abolition of capital punishment, and watch these overdressed bullies with blue hair leap to their feet and bay their lungs out like a herd of outraged seals." When a woman finds herself on the other side of the political divide, as was the case with actress Vanessa Red-grave, she tends to rush toward her militant goals with as much blind uncon-cern for those who stand in her way as a locomotive—or rather as a Big Van, Osborne's term for the woman he disliked intensely.[43]

Osborne's men are more complex. They are not machismo figures, as a strict gender dichotomy would suggest, but mixtures of strength and weak-ness, generosity and small-mindedness, proving that what Osborne considers as the dominant pole of the two categories comprises its opposite. The open-ing stage direction of *Look Back in Anger* paints the portrait of Jimmy Porter in contrasting colors of "sincerity" and "malice," "tenderness" and "cruelty"

(I, 9). Nobody would contest Jimmy's gift of friendship; few however would disagree with Helena that he is also a most "unpleasant" young man (II, i, 50). Though Jimmy's robust heterosexual appetite is emphasized throughout the play, his manliness is nevertheless sufficiently unconventional for the time to have met with some derision. Some reviewers suggested boot camp or a duck in the horse pond as cure for his sissyness.[44] Did not Jimmy himself admit he could at times be as "hysterical" as a girl? (II, i, 59). Jimmy's constant scuffles with Cliff did nothing to alleviate suspicions about the true nature of his sexuality, neither did his quips that he was "tired of being hetero" and envied, what he called, the "Michelangelo Brigade" (II, 1, 50). Subsequent Osborne plays, nearly without exception, continued to present male heroes whose sexual allegiances were, to say the least, questionable. With *A Patriot for Me* (1965), Osborne became one of the first to challenge theatre censorship by introducing a homosexual hero.

Osborne's heroes were not the only ones who defied accepted notions of masculinity; so did Osborne himself through his camp behavior and foppish dress. There is, he explained proudly for the benefit of a possible American reader, an "epicene tradition in the English temperament, as constant to soldiery and poetry as it is to the playhouse."[45] This did not prevent his own sexual orientation from remaining subject to much speculation. Instead of setting the record straight, Osborne kept the impertinently curious in suspense. In a 1992 interview, Lynn Barber pointed out how percentages keep shifting, from 20 to 35 and even 45 percent, in Osborne's different versions of his anecdotal reply to Noel Coward's query about the degree of his homosexuality. She then prissily added that Osborne "has never actually had sex with a man."[46] For Walter Wager, the question was important enough to serve as a rather incongruous introduction to an article about Osborne's writing methods: "for those concerned about recent controversies over the alleged homosexual domination of the British theatre, Osborne is neither a homosexual nor a particular defender of their rights."[47] The first part of that statement must have met with some skepticism. Before his success with *Look Back in Anger,* the parents of his first wife-to-be, Pamela Lane, were sufficiently suspicious of the true nature of his sexuality to have him shadowed by a detective. With the latter part of the statement, many would agree and would in fact insist that Osborne went out of his way to insult homosexuals. Athony Page, who directed several Osborne plays, states quite boldly that "the homophobia recurs throughout Osborne's writing."[48] To Nicholas de Jongh, who found it expedient to "out" the playwright shortly after his death by revealing his affair with fellow actor and collaborator Anthony Creighton, Osborne is an "inveterate despiser and mocker of homosexuals."[49] He pointed out that Osborne had, in his autobiographies, exposed Anthony Creighton and Tony Richardson's homosexuality without asking for their permission, all the while cravenly hiding his own similar proclivities.

Osborne, in his autobiographies, can certainly be as mean and unjust as he can be generous and warm-hearted; but there are no contradictions in Osborne's attitude toward homosexuality, regrettable as it may have been in some of its cruder expressions. It is fully consistent with his value system. He did not in the least disapprove of homosexuality. Jimmy Porter, speaking of the homosexual Webster, could not put it more clearly—nor more bluntly: "as if I give a damn which way he likes his meat served up" (I, 36). What irritated Osborne was the current ideological exploitation of homosexuality. Once a taboo, it had become the password of a new liberal philistinism. To hold up one's sexual identity as a badge of honor and bully others into abject acknowl-edgment of it was arrogant and small. A measure of reserve in such matters was preferable. So he mocked actor Sir Ian McKellen for advocating his homo-sexuality but praised Tony Richardson for trying to uphold the fiction that he was dying from leg cancer instead of AIDS. In matters of personal politics or sexuality, judicious restraint is more becoming than embarrassing exhibition-ism. Art executes a delicate balancing act between veiling and unveiling. To stand absolutely naked is to be artless.[50] And Osborne had still other reasons for disliking the myth of "coming out." With the subject basking in the light of sexual truth, is the proverbial closet, that dark place where the secret self spins its artful lies, irrevocably emptied? That anyone would be willing to define the complexity of their being by reducing it to their sexual preference defied his imagination. Why would anyone want to circumscribe sexuality so rigorously in the first place? Homosexuality, to him, was "a place of tremen-dous pain for people" but also "a fascinating metaphor for human ambiguity": "where does friendship end and where do people become queer?"[51] No need to settle such issues. Their very ambiguity is rich with dramatic potential.

No ambiguity, however, is entirely free from bias, and the kind Osborne had in mind is no exception. Though the kind of man he admires may express his sexual being ambiguously, he is not androgynic, in the sense of possessing an equal and mutually enhancing balance of feminine and masculine charac-teristics. In Osborne's system, the masculine constitutes the larger category that encompasses the feminine. Whereas a woman may find it hard to express herself in masculine ways without losing her femininity and becoming an "iron butterfly," a man radiates his virility more triumphantly when he holds the feminine at his core. A measure of effeminacy in a man then may prove his virility, in the sense that he feels sufficiently confident to allow himself such behavior. Music-hall artist Max Miller appears in Osborne's eulogy as a pri-apic god, positively scintillating with masculine energy and lust. That he was also supremely effeminate in appearance and behavior did not discredit the myth of his heterosexual libertinage: "this steely suggestion of ambivalence," Osborne recalls, "was very powerful and certainly more seductive than the common run of manhood then. He even made his fleshy, round shoulders seem like the happy result of prodigious and sophisticated sexual athletics—the only form of exercise he acknowledged."[52] Far from diminishing his masculine sex appeal, Max Miller's white face and effeminate make up heightened the promise of his sexual, invariably heterosexual, prowess.

This was the model of masculinity Osborne strove to emulate in his own life. In case anyone might confuse a show of decadent elegance with lack of virility, Osborne often refers to the unbridled libido that marked his youthful years (when the highest score of his amorous accomplishment was a legendary nine in one morning) and hints at how favorably he compared in size to the apparently less well-endowed Laurence Olivier.[53] The absurdity of such phallic overcompensation becomes sadly evident in the glee with which Osborne recounts how he once managed to make Lynn Reid Banks, feminist and author of *The L-Shaped Room*, bite into a sandwich stuffed with a used condom. He will never forget, he says, her horrified expression. Witnessing one of Edmund Kean's superior performance feats could not have been more satisfying.[54]

This then is the punishment for those who are revolted by the "greasy pole" of "male squalor." The same thinking—or lack of it—must have led Osborne to choose as epigraph for the second volume of his autobiography a quotation he attributes to St. Augustine, "A Stiff Prick hath no Conscience." Such pranks, some might argue, do not testify of a wide and generous imagination. Betraying the sexist fantasies of the West Fulham boy Osborne once was, they go immediately to the sexual heart of the matter and express themselves tellingly in the crudest of symbolisms. It seems then that the broad-minded and generous may at times function on a petty level without having their moral ascendancy seriously questioned. In other words, the large contains the small and, just as the masculine comprises the feminine, the warm-hearted may occasionally resort to base tactics when it suits their purpose. Face to face with his natural counterpart, the hot-blooded vituperator becomes quite simply a mean little prick, an abundant, if squalid, source of mean insults. But, as Osborne declares, better to be a bully than a hypocrite.[55] Anything is better than indifference, the only thing that can truly destroy the artistic sensibility.[56]

"O HAPPY POET! BY NO CRITIC VEXT!" [57]

In a well-known sketch by Breughel, a bespectacled critic peers over an artist's shoulder at the latter's canvas. Whereas the artist's gaze is open, clear, and bold, the critic's is fixed and restrained by its obsessive attention to detail. Both men's bodies bespeak difference in every respect: that of the artist is straight and robust, that of the critic is stooped and shriveled. What comes to mind—irreverently, of course—is an obscene satirical drawing by Félicien Ropps, "Le droit au travail, le droit au repos," depicting a proudly tumescent phallus in a jacket, followed by his flaccid counterpart, drably drooping in a gray raincoat. The energetic virility, the "cockiness," of Breughel's artist stands in similar, striking contrast to the thin-lipped, spinsterish appearance of the critic, whose spent look betrays uncomprehending envy for the phallic power that creates art.

An uncharitable and, let us hope, unjust picture of the critic, but one that surely looked right to Osborne on whom critical reviews had the dispiriting effect of postcoital discussions. Why are they so eager to pull the soaring artist back to earth? Critics are a mean lot, spoil sports who refuse to get into the spirit of a thing, who insist on remaining onlookers rather than participants—and the kind of onlookers that maliciously wave burning cigarettes amid throngs of festive balloons. Criticism seems all too eager to deflate the ridiculous tumidity of rhetoric and reduce it to a flabby set of paltry motivations. Art is affirmation, criticism is negation; art is seduction whereas criticism's first impulse is refusal. Art, in other words, is masculine; criticism is feminine, in the sense that it connotes the absence of a virile, expansive, visionary principle.

Critics who are unable to grasp that art requires a wide vision, broad gestures, sweeping emotions, and who instead pedantically insist on the rules of good composition or narrow morality, suffer from a form of small-mindedness.[58] Apparently it is not only their minds that are small; their shortcomings have a physical counterpart. "There's something deeply and abjectly wrong with them," Osborne told Robert Chesshyre. In a television interview, he put it rather more bluntly: "a lot of them are cripples, quite literally. They got surgical boots or skin diseases or things they've inherited or picked up from other people." The picture that emerges is that of so many Quasimodos shuffling through the theatre, gnashing their teeth with envy for the creator of such unbearable beauty. The critic's frustration is that of the *artiste manqué* and all too often translates into a sneering and condescending disposition toward "real" artists. They are "always stunned," Osborne says, "when you turn around and kick them in the groin."[59] This is Osborne's ungentlemanly way of pointing at the culprit, because he indeed believes that this is the very spot where the "lack" manifests itself most clearly. Of scholars—whom he lumps together with journalists, reviewers, and critics under the category of sterile scribblers who produce copy that lacks the thrust and vigor of manly prose[60]—Osborne has said that they "fasten their German-English on to the merest rustle of activity, like Lady Chatterley's husband training binoculars on the gamekeeper."[61]

This is Osborne at his best—smart, irreverent, and, one hopes, totally unfair. The simile is also revealing, aptly summarizing the essence of his vision in suggesting that what draws critic to artist is a perverse eroticism. The critic is an emasculated creature who seeks out the virility of the artist with a longing as dangerous to the artist as that of castrating woman to phallic man. In other words, Osborne's distaste for critics has the same origin as his "misogyny." The "natural enemy of the visionary, the idealist," woman is incessantly and meanly intent on diminishing whatever remains beyond her reach. "Why, why, why, why do we let these women bleed us to death?"

Jimmy wails in *Look Back in Anger*. "Have you ever had a letter, and on it is franked 'Please Give Your Blood Generously'? Well, the Postmaster-General does that, on behalf of all the women of the world" (III, i, 84).

In the aptly titled *The End of Me Old Cigar* (1975), Regine and Stella do to the phallus what Brueghel's critic does to the work of art: they take a good close look at it and gleefully reduce the myth to its pitiful reality—in other words, they discover the penis in the phallus.

> REGINE: See it dangle, dingle dangle, jingle jangle in its usual petulant pendulance. A sorry, blue-veined pork sword looking like an unripe, yellowish Stilton. Lying against its horse-hair sack, wee bag, of a million million pestilent tadpoles looking for a muddy pool to rest in. Throbbing for all the world's distaste like a turkey's gobbling neck.
>
> STELLA: No wonder they call it a 'gobble job.'
>
> REGINE: Erect, well now, that's a sight, if they can get it up without your thumbs splitting and fingers enflamed with corns, more horn than they could ever manage with that. Erect as an Irish volunteer, blind, hopeless, eyeless in girls' Gaza. These footling frail inches of phallus, trying to ascend Everest like a Mick navvy without enough scaffolding.
>
> STELLA: Perhaps that's what Disraeli meant by 'the greasy pole of politics.'
>
> REGINE: Rather keen on poles, aren't they? Well, that flag won't fly much longer. It's coming down. In all its tatters and tyranny. We will be the mast, the mast, mast of woman, flying our flag. Greasy indeed! Mrs. Disraeli must have known the real truth behind that bit of front bench grandiloquence. (I, 23)

Driven by a merciless reality principle, woman can only be bored by man's flights of fancy: "if only they knew how they sickened us with their schooldays, memories, endless, endless memories. Their peacock regimentals, their desperate fetishes and paltry pornography" (I, 22). Things shrivel rather than stiffen under this Medusa's gaze. In the eyes of woman, the emperor never has any clothes: the nude becomes the naked; the pornographic, the ridiculously graphic; and revolutionary ardor, a little boy's temper tantrum. In a sense, Osborne's plays prove woman right. Alison in *Look Back in Anger* may fondly believe that her Jimmy is a revolutionary born too late, but it takes only one motherly slap from Helena to reduce him to a whimpering boy (II, ii, 73–74). Jimmy's verbal bravura is not borne out by bold actions or by a manly hold on reality. Bogged down in a sort of restless passivity, he is Lord and King over only a sweetstall. The virility of his speech is therefore as detached from reality, as disinterested, as pure art. If woman is attracted to the myth, as even Helena is, it is exactly because she senses the pitiful reality underneath. Osborne's men intimidate no one. Indeed what they elicit is either contempt or an unhappy love for the hidden weakness, the lack that their defiant verbal erections are meant to hide.

GENESIS

Osbornian anger follows a similar phallic pattern, throbbing with excited conviction of its own sovereignty and invincibility only to suddenly tumble back into impotent despair. To distinguish itself from sterile literary devices and to qualify as the animating presence of life in art, anger had to sprout from reality. To prove its authenticity, Osborne published autobiographical writings which were to accompany his plays throughout his further career, the earliest ("They Call It Cricket") appearing nearly simultaneously with the production of his first successful play, *Look Back in Anger* (1956). He evidently understood that continued success would depend on his ability to convey a personal mythology that would root his anger in real childhood and youth experiences—experiences later reinforced by a series of betrayals, especially by the women who shared his life. When in 1957, the journalist Tom Maschler gave a number of angry young writers the chance to explain their philosophies, Osborne contributed an article primarily about his family. Two full-fledged autobiographies later the mythology had taken firm shape.

John Osborne was born on 12 December 1929, to Nellie Beatrice Grove, a barmaid who preferred to think of herself as a "victualler's assistant," and Thomas Godfrey Osborne, a commercial copywriter who spent most of his short life on sick leave. Osborne describes his family background as upperworking class, though it was quite solidly lower-middle class, considering his father's occupation and his family's aspirations to genteelness.[62] Families on both sides had been publicans, and actors visiting their pubs had been their only connection with the stage.[63] After his father's death from tuberculosis in 1941, John's education and health needs were taken care of by the company for which his father had worked. Dependence on such charity instilled in John lasting resentment for the little indignities of cheap respectability. He spent most of his childhood years either in third-rate sanatoria or at home, sick with a particularly debilitating form of rheumatic fever, and was later sent to a minor public school (Belmont College, a boarding school in Devon), from which he was expelled at the age of fifteen and a half after hitting the headmaster. This would become a self-defining anecdote, proof of a budding, bristling cockiness that later helped turn John into an icon of the "angry" postwar generation.[64]

The child Osborne, we are told, is silent witness to the clash of opposing forces represented by his mother's and father's families—the former, selfrespecting working-class; the latter, genteel lower-middle class. The Groves were simple, boisterous loudmouths; the Osbornes treacherous and chilly masters of the art of deflection and absorption. Both were equally averse to hope or enthusiasm. In fact, as Osborne recalls in the first and best volume of his autobiography, they thrived on despondency. When the two parties crossed arms, the Osbornes invariably came out victorious. Nellie Beatrice always lost nerve when the Osbornes, distracted by her interference from their own quarrel, closed ranks and silently watched as she grew nervous and stumbled over her words. They had a way of conveying their superiority so that she felt ridiculous and ineffectual.[65] Play after play, Osborne would demonstrate the trembling impotence of anger against the "power of negation," economically expressed in a shrug of the shoulder, a cold stare, or the crackle of an iron.

The boy John sympathizes neither with the hotheaded Groves nor with the chilly Osbornes, sensing a life-denying quality in both. His sympathy goes rather to the vulnerability trapped in between, his father, whose spirit was destroyed by a mother who despised her son's physical weakness and by a wife who felt cheated, discovering she had married a "feverish failure of a man" (*Look Back II*, i, 58). When Osborne witnesses his mother's lack of compassion for his dying father and later her disgust for his corpse, he experiences for the first time a hatred for his mother that will accompany him through life.[66] In reaction, he symbolically ruptures the umbilical cord, referring to his mother from then on only by her first name, Nellie Beatrice. Having rejected his mother, he now cherishes to the point of devotion the memory of the lank figure of a father in tweedy dressing gown, sensitive, almost feminine, with manicured pale hands. Not in the loud, blustering voice of his mother, but rather in the memory of the gentle, Welsh modulations of his father does Osborne locate authenticity. John is ten when his father dies; the latter's idealized figure is a dream—but a dream that comes as if from the womb itself, reconstructed, as Osborne says, from hazy yet blissful memories. Wishing to be the child of masculine beauty and delicateness, he wants to dispense of the mother, an unbearable reminder of man's insufficiency, the fate of his being "of woman born." Echoing King Lear's "yet thou art my flesh, . . . or rather a disease that's in my flesh,/Which I must needs call mine" (II, iv), Osborne thinks of his mother as the source of his own sickness, a congenital affliction that cannot be eradicated since it lurks in the very marrow of his bones.[67]

The image that haunts him in later life is that of his father's pale, naked figure, standing, in the last stages of deathly sickness, erect, trembling, and blind on the landing before falling headlong down the stairs at his mother's feet.[68] Tender solicitude for such frail exposure mounts as Osborne imagines the indifference and contempt with which it must have met. In the eyes of any of Osborne's self-sufficient and despising women, like Regine in *The End of me Old Cigar*, such a naked Christ must be as preposterous as the phallus standing "erect as an Irish volunteer, blind, hopeless, eyeless," "throbbing for all the world's distaste like a turkey's gobbling neck." John will not have to wait long for his father's humiliation to be avenged. It comes in the form of a German bomb that sends the house atremble, chasing his dazed mother out of the lavatory onto the landing, knickers at her feet.

Osborne's description of the event is humorous yet also cruelly detached. For his mother, it is a horrifying moment of dread and shame, during which she stumbles out of the lavatory to the stairs—arms out, mouth open, underwear around the ankles—only to meet the ridicule of her son. For Osborne, it is an act of heavenly justice, retribution for his father's humiliation at the top of these self-same stairs. Arms wide and knees bent—the comparison could not be more perfect. This aging female, comically exposed in her sagging underwear, is without knowing it grotesquely aping Christ! Osborne recalled it later as the most preposterous and amusing sight of his mother, one he would cherish the rest of his life as a well-spring of laughter. Only his mother's sexual humiliation could vindicate the dignity of his father's nakedness. The blast had at least momentarily wiped his mother's famous Black Look off her face and replaced it with one of incomprehension and fear.[69] Osborne assimilated these moments in his creations by making the story of masculine vulnerability, defiantly facing the headlong tumble that will inevitably follow, emblematic to his art.

For Osborne, anger is the courage of weakness. Turning out well-honed yet sharply abrasive phrases became his way of constructing masculinity, a condition that is supposed to be natural but that in Osborne is always problematic. In his autobiography, he recounts how, as a much bullied boy at school, he dreaded nothing more than the prospect of being sexually humiliated by a gang of rapacious young females. They would hold some unhappy boy down, while their leader, Daphne—no nymph but a perverse young Valkyrie—would squat on his face, choking him while her minions pulled down his shorts. John, a lonely boy, knows he is their ideal victim but manages to escape.[70] Deficient in physical strength, he hones his verbal skills and learns to defend himself by flexing the muscles of his mouth.[71] Later, he takes up boxing in school and finds that a display of excessive energy in a weaker fighter can often intimidate a stronger opponent.[72] As an actor, he would frequently have to resort to such desperate daring to master his stage fright and to startle or impress bored and hostile audiences. Always, such daring carried a note of tremulous sexual challenge. Drama, to him, was the art of indecent exposure. Force feeding his verbal ejaculations to a priggish audience and watching the repulsion on their faces gave Osborne an undeniably sexual thrill.

PHALLIC ART

Art as an act of aggression: Osborne readily admits that his talent is to vex rather than to entertain, though he would love to achieve the latter by virtue of the former. But when in the process of creation, he writes not for an audience but against an audience. Every one of his plays seeks its justification in itself and takes, in one way or another, its genesis as its implicit or explicit subject. A play such as *Epitaph for George Dillon* (1957), co-authored with Anthony Creighton, deals specifically with the plight of the artist and with the nature, prerogatives, and duties of artistic talent. Another such as *Luther* (1961), explores the transformation of private anguish into public anger. Still another, such as *A Patriot for Me* (1965), portrays the painful birthing of a self-image. In other words, nearly all Osborne's plays deal in one way or another with creativity or creation in relation to the construction of masculinity. Woman apparently does not create; she gives birth. In her child she acknowledges her loss of sovereignty, her subjection to reality principle. The erect and lonely phallus, on the other hand, bodily expresses the vulnerable sovereignty of desire and imagination, ridiculed by those better reconciled with the limitations of humdrum reality.

"All art is organized evasion," Osborne declares. But what Osborne's art evades most desperately is its own lack of sovereignty. Like the phallus, it wants to believe that it depends on no one, that it has erected itself on virgin ground merely by the strength of its own desire. For the scriptwriter Laurie in *The Hotel in Amsterdam* (1968), creation happens *ex nihilo* : "what I do, I get out of the air. Even if it's not so hot always, I put my little hand out there in that void, there, empty air. Look at it. It's like being a bleeding conjurer with no white tie and tails. Air . . ." (38). To endeavor to stand up by sole virtue of inner tension—or, as Regine says about the phallus, "to ascend Everest like a Mick navvy without enough scaffolding"—is Osborne's definition of what art attempts to do. When he first saw *Mother Courage,* performed in London by Bertolt Brecht and Helene Weigel's Berliner Ensemble in August 1956, he was struck by that play's major prop, a horseless carriage. To him it was the symbol of a theatre that had managed to find its own principle of inner vitality: "it may seem to stink and fume, but it *is* faster, more convenient, and somehow, the inescapable fact is that it *works*."[73] Such theatre, it seemed to him, did not have to be pulled in motion by a plot; it had managed to shake off the harness of the well-made play, that cumbersome external structure still all too visible in his own *Look Back in Anger.*

Osborne bridled at critics' suggestion that he borrowed from Brecht for his plays *The Entertainer* (1957) and *Luther* (1961). The Brechtian alienation technique made sense within the German cultural tradition; the English, however, had their own rich resources for dramatic renewal. If only plays could be driven by their own momentum, organized implicitly according to the structure of emotion itself. Osborne's answer was not German-style alienation but its opposite, English vitality, to be found in the theatre from Shakespeare to the music hall. *Hamlet* was, in a strictly critical sense, a flawed play. It was, in fact, what the critics like to say about Osborne's plays, "undisciplined"—too long, embracing far too many ideas, indulging in too many subplots with too many characters; but few critics would dare to deny that *Hamlet* works on the stage as well as on the page. Again and again, plays manage to break out of externally imposed constraints simply by a power emanating from within, from the beauty of the inspired word.

Writing combines passion and craft; good writing, however, communicates passion but hides its craft. The impulse to write can be strong, overwhelming, but a thousand constraints soon freeze the hand, block the spontaneity of thought. Vituperative sentences such as "she's as rough as a night in a Bombay brothel, and as tough as a matelot's arm" ("arse," as the uncensored text read) require assonance, alliteration, and a solid dose of perverse imagery. The resulting forcefulness of utterance, however, renders us oblivious to the laborious search for style—what Osborne refers to as his halting, tentative mode of composition (*Look Back II*, i, 52).[74] More to the point, in contrast to the statement's undeniable pungency, any misgivings about its offensive or nonsensical imagery sound irrelevant or petty. The effect Osborne searched for was that of a spark struck out of stone. In the final instance, the spark illuminates nothing. The crankiness and random cruelties are there for their own sake. To be vital, they have to be gratuitous, undeserved, and out of all proportion to the crime.

For Osborne, vituperation was to effect the miracle of self-levitation by which a genuinely vital art would come to stand free from a constraining narrative trellis. Intense feeling, he hoped, would produce a style that, rather than coming in aid of meaning, would become meaning. This proved to be quite challenging for audiences. What happens when you divest Jimmy's language from its materiality—that is, when you paraphrase it? Any analysis of an Osborne play that starts by separating form from content and aims at evaluating ideas rather than rhetoric or "poetry" will end up dismissing it as a tangle of contradictions. This is not always typical of other realistic plays—of the plays of Bernard Shaw, for example (which Osborne disliked). There, critical translation is inculcated into the very make-up of the play and occasionally reveals itself in long, argumentative speeches. In contrast, in Osborne's plays, ideas are bandied about but rarely fully developed, sometimes resulting in thematic inconsistency or vagueness. But then the theatre, as Osborne points out, is "not a schoolroom." It is not a place for discussion and examination; if there are any lessons to be taught, they should be "lessons in feeling."

Much like a musical score, the written text of a play is a blueprint of affects. Characters in an Osborne play flaunt their inconsistencies and relish the crudity of their own remarks in set speeches called "arias." His heroes, like their creator himself, are far more interested in the energizing or depleting effect of ideas than in the ideas themselves. We see Jimmy Porter scanning the Sunday papers in search of anything that can raise his hackles, from the Bishop of Bromley's antiquated views of the working classes to the story of the murderous stampede after a religious festival. People are judged in similar ways, for their draining or invigorating effect. Alison saps Jimmy's vitality whereas Madeline, an older woman Jimmy used to be in love with, possessed the gift of energy: "even to sit on the top of a bus with her was like setting out with Ulysses" (I, 19). And so does Webster, Alison's homosexual friend: "when he comes here, I begin to feel exhilarated," Jimmy says. "He doesn't like me, but he gives me something, which is more than I get from most people." And that something is enthusiasm: "oh, brother, it's such a long time since I was with anyone who got enthusiastic about anything" (I, 15). Osborne succeeds when he can create a moment of high intensity that even in its stupidity or sentimentality, communicates itself to the audience. Kenneth Tynan complained of the "painful whimsey" of the bear-squirrel game the two lovers play in *Look Back in Anger.* Far from being a mistake, such scenes are the essence of Osborne's drama.

Drama, to Osborne, is the art of exaggeration. Any kind of calm consideration or good judgment could take the wind out of a play's rhetorical sails. "Like Dr. Johnson," Osborne says, "I think one prejudice is worth twenty principles."[75] A thought not yet neutralized—or, rather, not yet neutered—by sound judgment has retained its "virility." Only a strong, impulsive thought, fuelled by private neurosis, can deliver the momentum necessary to carry the personal voice into the public arena. There, the artist's voice will sound more real in its blatant expression of prejudice than that of its more cautious audience and for its sheer intensity will perhaps be allowed to speak for it. Bias is not then what art sometimes fails to escape; it is its very essence. If Osborne comes across as "prejudiced" in a number of ways (homophobic, xenophobic, misogynist, racist, etc.), it is because he has understood the role prejudice plays in art.

Osborne's prejudices, however, come with wings. He believes, quite simply, in inspiration, in "the great white dove that appears to me in the sky"[76] and in language ("I have a great allegiance to words"). Such a romantic vision of creativity is a curious anachronism in a playwright credited with having introduced contemporary themes to early postwar drama. Osborne has explicitly distanced himself from later playwrights whom he accuses of having turned the stage into a laboratory for social research: "there was always the danger of writing becoming sociology or journalism. All those plays on telly about labourers on building sites and Irishmen. They're journalistic pieces, very skilful [*sic*] but not A-R-T."[77] The dramatist should still be in the first place a poet, an inspired wordsmith. Osborne's great literary models range from Luther and Shakespeare to such eighteenth-century giants as Dr. Johnson and Henry Fielding, writers who combine earthy realism with a quasi-baroque enjoyment of word sculpture. Osborne's notebooks accordingly abound with pithy statements that derive power of conviction from style rather than thought.[78] Osborne's drama shares none of the linguistic minimalism popularized in his time by the theatre of the absurd. Unlike Beckett, early Bond, Pinter, or Simpson, he does not use inarticulate characters to explore the intricacies of miscommunication. Osborne harks back to an older tradition in presenting characters that express themselves far better than their audience could ever dream.[79]

Osborne calls words "the last link with God,"[80] but the Spirit literally comes down to earth in the words Osborne pens on the page; the words should reek of reality itself. "When writing is going well," Osborne claims, "it is the most glorious thing in the world. It's greater than sex."[81] Greater, quite possibly, because inspired writing is not supposed to have any of the compromising, the give and take, of an actual sexual encounter. The thrill of inspiration, however, is real; the physical metaphors multiply as Osborne tries to describe it. Words should erupt onto the page, like a "brutal, volcanic flow of scalding vituperation." The model Osborne holds up for emulation here is *Bondage of the Will*, in which Luther responds to Erasmus' cautious, rarefied prose with words that fume with the sweat and squalor of man. Osborne relishes the thought of Luther's big-fisted words delivering blows under the belt. Not a pretty picture, he agrees, but how exciting![82] With initial distaste turning into sudden excitement, Osborne's ideal reader reacts to such manly vigor like a not less idealized virgin bride.

Art, for Osborne, seduces not through sophistication but through dazzle, and its secret is not cunning but insolence: "all genius is cheek," he says in his essay on Max Miller. "You get away with your nodding little vision and the world holds its breath or applauds."[83] Anyone can receive proper praise for saying the right things. The point is to receive a standing ovation for saying outrageous things because only then have you mastered the secret of style. "His impeccable contempt is his energy," Osborne writes of Jeffrey Bernard, fellow writer and accomplice in concerted attacks on the fig leaf of common decency. "Whenever anyone tells me that a scene or a line in a play of mine goes too far in some way then I know my instinct has been functioning as it should."[84] Nearly all Osborne's plays suggest that the making of a public voice requires a similar, initial strong resistance. Jimmy Porter (*Look Back in Anger*), Archie Rice (*The Entertainer*), Luther (*Luther*), Bill Maitland (*Inadmissible Evidence*), and other Osbornian characters are self-dramatizing heroes who communicate their tragic self-concept to resisting others. They are essentially artists who suffer an artist's anxiety at the thought of talking in a vacuum. Unlike politicians and propagandists, they do not seek to simply exchange a private voice for a brazenly public one; they rather aim, as artists do, at inverting the claustrophobically intimate into the universal. The presupposition is that even the most private of pains is lined with a despair recognizable to all, but that the inversion necessary to turn the private into the public requires a strength of feeling attainable by but a few. In other words, not content but strength of feeling endows the deeply personal with general validity, turns private obsession into art. The artist may be wrong, yet will be forgiven if he is magnificently wrong. In fact, the true artist makes his audience fall for heroes that are objectionable to them—in the way expert seducers exert their dangerous spell, not in spite of, but thanks to their ugliness—and end up inspiring the most abject of loving devotions the more passionately they were rejected at first.

The prig's presence has therefore to be assumed in Osborne's drama for anger to attain its required gleeful pitch. That also means that success has to be measured on a scale of failure—something not without consequences for a dramatic artist whose income depends on the instant popularity garnered up by a performance. If the audience is supposed to be philistine, only failure can in the last instance prove the artist's mettle and integrity. Osborne, assured of his seductive charms by a string of commercial successes, allowed himself to reminisce with special fondness about the plays that flopped most spectacularly, *The World of Paul Slickey* (1959), *A Sense of Detachment* (1972), and *Watch It Come Down* (1975).

In *A Better Class of Person*, Osborne asserts that negative audience reaction is almost a guarantee of quality. If that were the case, one would have to conclude that Osborne's mastery received much public recognition. He admits himself that record numbers of people have walked out of his plays, banging their seats and yelling at the actors. No other modern playwright would pride himself, as Osborne does, on having been ambushed by incensed spectators and pursued by a howling pack up Charing Cross Road. With his habitual defiance, Osborne affirms he particularly relished the booing from the better heeled audience in the stalls, and he reports with pride that for *A Sense of Detachment* spectators gave vent of their revulsion almost precisely where the script had asked for it. When they realized they were fulfilling the role Osborne had already written for them, their anger could be awe-inspiring.[85] The whole idea behind the enterprise was to let his critics know that *their* prigishness was part of *his* set-up so that he could say: "you are MY object. I am not yours. You are my vessel, you are MY hatred. That is my final identity."[86]

Part I

CHAPTER 2

Rise to the Top, 1956–1963

ROYAL COURT THEATRE

Expelled from school, the young John Osborne entered the professional world with only a couple of O-levels to fend for himself. He found a job as a reporter for trade magazines and at night took dancing lessons and played in an amateur theatre company. He joined the theatre first in a non-theatrical capacity, as a teacher and minder of actors' children. When a school inspector discovered he lacked the requisite certifications, the traveling company retained him as a stage assistant and occasional understudy. Then started the uncertain life of an artist touring the provinces. For a time he was a partner in Anthony Creighton and Clive St. George's small theatre company, playing a seasonal repertoire of well-tested plays in resort towns. Then came long spells of unemployment during which he found time to try his hand at writing plays. His first play *The Devil Inside* (1949) was written with fellow actress Stella Linden. Later followed two plays co-written with Anthony Creighton, *Personal Enemy* (1955) and *Epitaph for George Dillon*. The first two plays went largely unnoticed; the third met with some acclaim in 1957, when it was produced in the wake of *Look Back in Anger* and *The Entertainer*'s tremendous success.

Like that of countless other minor actors and aspiring playwrights, Osborne's life could have continued its uncertain course if it were not for the foundation of the English Stage Company (ESC), brainchild of a poet, Ronald Duncan; an aristocrat, Lord Harewood; and a schoolteacher, J.E. Blacksell. Neville Blond, chairman of the company, was a successful Manchester businessman who provided the team with £50,000 from a fortune he had made exporting textiles. George Devine, an accomplished Shakespearean actor, was appointed artistic director.[1] In, 1956, the company settled into the Royal Court Theatre (RCT) which, having suffered severe bomb damage during the war, had reopened only four years earlier. Few remembered that its original stage dated back to 1871 and, under Barker-Vedrenne management (1904–07), had seen innovative productions of Bernard Shaw's plays.

George Devine's goal was to create a writer's theatre as it existed on the continent, especially in France, in the hope of reviving London's theatre industry.[2] Its proximity to the West End ensured that the Royal Court Theatre could play an inspiring role. West End theatres revolved virtually exclusively around star actors and were rapidly losing contact with modern theatrical developments. Powerful theatre managers such as "Binkie" Beaumont of H.M. Tennent maintained a repertoire of light and commercially successful entertainment, produced by a bevy of aging popular playwrights. Appealing mainly to pre-war middle-class audiences, Somerset Maugham (1874–1965), J.B. Priestley (1894–1984), Noel Coward (1899–1973), Graham Greene (1904–1991), and Terence Rattigan (1911–1977) seemed eerily out of touch with modern reality. Maugham's most popular dramas—*Lady Frederick* (1907), *Circle* (1921), and *The Constant Wife* (1926)—either predated WW I or followed closely after. Coward, as evidenced by his tremendously successful *Hay Fever* (1925) and *Private Lives* (1930), was at his best when reporting on the tedium of opulent lives during the interbellum. With *The Deep Blue Sea* (1952) and *Separate Tables* (1954), Rattigan introduced more contemporary themes, but the language and construction of these essentially romantic plays still recalled the world of Coward. As far as the social problem play was concerned, no important playwrights carried on the work of Bernard Shaw after his death in 1950. The play of ideas, so strongly represented in France by Sartre and Anouilh, had as British practitioners of importance only Priestley and Greene. With the exception of *An Inspector Calls* (1946), most of Priestley's psychological, magic-realistic dramas were written in the thirties. And Greene, who only occasionally turned his hand to playwriting, explored moral ambiguities and crises of faith much more skillfully in his novels than in his plays (for example, *The Living Room* (1952)).

"Serious" drama was of course still being produced. In, 1951, the Festival of Britain drew attention to the then ongoing revival of verse drama by T.S. Eliot (*Murder in the Cathedral* (1935), *The Cocktail Party* (1949), *The Confidential Clerk* (1953)) and Christopher Fry (*The Lady's Not For Burning* (1948)). Real theatrical excitement and innovation, however, were to be found abroad. France was a true font of experimentation, with existentialist drama by Jean-Paul Sartre (*Huis-Clos* (1944; London, 1946), *Les Mouches* (1942; London, 1951), *Nekrassov* (1955; London, 1956)) and "theatricalist" creations by Jean Anouilh (*L'Invitation au château* (1947; London, 1950)). The end of WW II also saw the emergence of the Theatre of the Absurd, presented in France mainly by foreign-born playwrights: Eugène Ionesco (*La Cantatrice Chauve* (1949; London, 1956), *La Leçon* (1951; London, 1955), *Les Chaises* (1952; London, 1957)), Arthur Adamov (*Le Professeur Taranne, Tous contre tous* (1953), *Le Ping-Pong* (1955; London, 1959)), and Samuel Beckett

(*En Attendant Godot* (1953; London, 1955)). These playwrights were as obsessively preoccupied with depicting the modern condition as they were with finding new means to express it. The same was true for Bertolt Brecht in Germany. The Berliner Ensemble he had founded in 1949 visited London in 1956, the year of his death, with productions of *Mother Courage* and *The Caucasian Chalk Circle*. In London, these foreign plays met with guarded curiosity or bewilderment, and it was only after Osborne's *Look Back in Anger* had created a new openness to experimentation that they exerted their full effect on British drama. The Theatre of the Absurd became particularly influential, inspiring F.N. Simpson (*A Resounding Tinkle* (1957) and *One Way Pendulum* (1959)) and Harold Pinter (*The Room* and *The Dumbwaiter* (1957), *The Birthday Party* (1958)). Brechtian staging and acting techniques were equally inspiring, if only because they showed yet another way out of the structural straitjacket of the well-made play. The American playwright David Rabe has described the well-made play as

> that form which thinks that cause and effect are proportionate and clearly apparent, that people know what they are doing as they do it, and that others react accordingly, that one thing leads to another in a rational, mechanical way, a kind of Newtonian clock of a play, a kind of Darwinian assemblage of detail which would then determine the details that must follow, the substitution of the devices of logic for the powerful sweep of pattern and energy that is our lives.[3]

Plot rather than character driven, the well-made play stands out by a tight and economic construction that guarantees maximum suspense and, since every event or idea is accounted for in the end, minimal audience frustration. Pinero, Coward, and Rattigan were deft practitioners of the genre, and in the early part of Osborne's career, the well-made play was still popular in West End - theatres—plays, for instance, by Hugh and Margaret Williams. "The Williams well-maders," Osborne said of their plays, "work in so far as they succour and flatter a bewildered, disinherited middle-class audience bawling after a decadent and dummy tradition":

> One day I expect Mr Williams will be on stage opening a jar from Fortnums and snarling some forced banter about au-pair girls or Pol Roger, and he will suddenly find himself in the midst of an Ionesco nightmare. The entire audience will rise out of their seats, invade the proscenium arch and demand that they be allowed to live there. With Hugh Williams. I think they would deserve squatters' rights.[4]

With other playwrights of his generation, Osborne was convinced that contemporary life was too complex to be reduced to any handy plot formula.

What influenced young British playwrights most was the emotionally vibrant theatre of the United States: Lillian Hellman (*The Little Foxes* (1939;

London, 1942)), Arthur Miller (*All My Sons* (1947; London, 1948), *Death of a Salesman* (1949), *The Crucible* (1953; London, 1956)), Tennessee Williams (*The Glass Menagerie* (1945; London, 1948), *A Streetcar Named Desire* (1947; London, 1949)), and Thornton Wilder (*The Matchmaker* (1938; Edinburgh, 1954)). Among the customary English fare of genteel drawing-room comedies, the work of these playwrights stood out by sheer emotional intensity and directness of language. British theatre still reverted to the traditions of a more circumspect age, fiercely guarded by the Lord Chamberlain's censorship office. Banned in Britain, Tennessee Williams's *Cat on a Hot Tin Roof* (1954) could only be seen in a 1958 private production. Turning theatres into private clubs and requiring audiences to become members became the usual way of circumventing censorship. The English Stage Company would have to resort to the same subterfuge for productions of Edward Bond's shocking play *Saved* (1965) and Osborne's *A Patriot for Me* (1965).

Under Devine's artistic leadership, the English Stage Company actively searched for writers, soliciting new scripts from aspiring playwrights and inviting novelists and poets to try their hand at writing for the stage. Among its first productions were plays by novelists Angus Wilson, whose *The Mulberry Bush* inaugurated the RCT's first season, and Nigel Dennis (*Cards of Identity* (1956), and later, *The Making of Moo* (1957)). During its opening season, the RCT also presented *The Death of Satan,* by Ronald Duncan, one of the founding members of the ESC, who had already known some success with his verse drama *This Way to the Tomb* (1947).

None of these first productions, however, made an impact comparable to that of Osborne's *Look Back in Anger*, staged on 8 May, 1956.[5] Whatever its intrinsic merits and shortcomings, its success, and the public debate about society and the arts that it sparked, created a new openness to experiment. A wave of new playwrights flooded the stage: John Arden, N.F. Simpson, Brendan Behan, Shelagh Delaney, John Mortimer, Robert Bolt, Arnold Wesker, Bernard Kops, Henry Livings, David Turner, Harold Pinter, and many more. After having delighted for years in middle-class settings and voices, the audience now acquired a taste for grim lower-class situations and accents.[6] John Arden's *Live Like Pigs* (1958), Edward Bond's *The Pope's Wedding* (1962), Arnold Wesker's *Chicken Soup with Barley* (1958) and *The Kitchen* (1959) presented characters that were often barely articulate and in settings so dismal that such drama gave rise to the appellation "kitchen-sink realism." Theatre was moving and changing, but in the general excitement this created were also worry and fear. Gareth Lloyd Evans, a traditional critic, heard in these plays only "the huge grunts of mankind as it satisfies its animal instincts," and complained that "immediacy has taken the place of dimension—we seem to be taking everything out of language, thoughts, feelings even, except the ingredient of instant response. Memory, comparison, context are 'lost leaders' and form is broken and untended."[7]

Yet by disrupting established conventions of composition and dramatic language, these plays acquired the texture and sound of contemporary life. Emerging conventions required new production, directing, and acting methods. A number of young directors, William Gaskill, John Dexter, and Tony Richardson, started their careers at the Royal Court Theater before moving on to other venues. The new theatre of directness required faster responses. What was being said was often less important than how and why it was being said. Actors had to become more sensitive to the give and take of language, to the way language games shift and develop in patterns that are never fully controlled by their participants. Whereas previously superb middle-class diction and the ability to give caricatured renditions of the working-class idiom had been the requisites for a career in dramatic arts, movie and stage actors now proudly sported fake or genuine lower-class accents.[8] In this general climate of experimentation, productions of the traditional repertoire also underwent a sea change. At the Old Vic and Stratford's Memorial Theatre, home of the Royal Shakespeare Company, older directors such as Michael Benthall and Glen Byam Shaw made way for more daring experimenters such as Peter Hall, Peter Brook, and Peter Wood.

To ascribe all these changes to the 1956 production of *Look Back in Anger*, as is routinely done, is mainly a matter of convenience, but the play did serve as focal point for people's excitement and anger and its author as figurehead for the changes in British dramatic art. It was important, moreover, that the play and its author proved the commercial viability of such changes. Osborne's success did not lose momentum. With *The Entertainer* (1957) and *Luther* (1961) he proved himself a dramatist of lasting importance and, financially speaking, an absolute godsend for the English Stage Company. "Without Osborne's solid successes," the *Sunday Times* reported in, 1962, "the Royal Court would probably not have lasted for more than six months." Most of the RCT's income had come from "transfers to the West End, tours and film rights" and half of that exclusively from Osborne plays, from *Look Back* to *Luther*.[9]

TOM JONES

Osborne became a successful entrepreneur. Together with director Tony Richardson, he co-managed Woodfall Films, a company whose productions gave lasting shape to our vision of postwar British life and that triggered a short-lived renaissance of the British movie. Many of its productions were film adaptations of Osborne's work: Tony Richardson directed the film version of *Look Back in Anger* (1959) and *The Entertainer* (1960), Anthony Page that of *Inadmissible Evidence* (1968). It also produced work by women: Shelagh Delaney's *A Taste of Honey* (1961; dir. Tony Richardson) and novelist Edna O'Brien's *The Girl with Green Eyes* (1963; dir. Desmond Davis). Both films presented Rita Tushingham in what was for that time an uncharacteristically plain portrait of young womanhood. *Saturday Night and Sunday Morning*

(1960; dir. Tony Richardson), after a novel by Alan Sillitoe, who also wrote the script, and *Tom Jones* (1963; dir. Tony Richardson), scripted by Osborne after the well-known Henry Fielding novel, were the company's financially most rewarding movies. Henry Fielding's roguish plot supplemented by Osborne's customary energy proved a formula for success. In 1964, Osborne was awarded one of the four Oscars the movie and its makers earned, the others going to Tony Richardson (Best Director), John Addison (Best Composer), and the movie itself (Best Picture).

The plot adheres closely to the original story: Tom Jones, illegitimate son of Jenny Jones and Partridge the barber, is raised to young manhood by Squire Allworthy. Tom proves to be a good-natured rogue, interested only in hunting pheasants and women, well on his way to fulfilling the prophecy that he "was born to be hanged." His companion on nightly poaching and prowling raids is Black George and on frolicking expeditions George's daughter, Molly. Problems arise when bastard son Tom, whose jolly nature conquers every decent heart, enters into conflict with the priggish and malignant Blifil, nephew of Tom's adoptive father. The object of their contention is Sophie, Squire Western's daughter. It is this conflict that propels Tom from Edenic youth into adulthood. But this *Bildung* requires time, and its goal, the girl and the fortune, will only be reached many adventures later. One of Tom's many amorous dalliances, for instance, is with Mrs. Waters—who, we later learn, is in fact Jenny Jones, his mother. Yet that disturbing moment of incestuous pleasure proves illusory: in the end we discover that Tom is really Bridget's, Mr. Allworthy's sister's, son, thus becoming the only heir to Allworthy's fortune.

The movie's immense success was not as unpredictable as traditional accounts maintain.[10] Despite its eighteenth-century setting, its themes are thoroughly contemporary, not to say "Osbornian." This is the story after all of yet another one of England's bastard sons who hits his unruly head against a ceiling of unwelcome restraints. The hero is a working class lad who by happenstance finds himself among his superiors. His unbounded energy and enthusiasm clash with the moral censures of the degenerates among that class—censures presented by Fielding as aberrations, as a meanness of spirit and a perversion of the honest, upright nature of such true aristocrats as Squires Allworthy and Western. Tom is in fact the true heir to their unbridled English spirit, and he is even more so in Osborne's script than he appears in the movie where sexual initiative, for instance, is often passed from Tom to the women. As Robert Hughes states: "Tom, it seems, was directed and played as a somewhat more passive creature than Mr. Osborne (and Mr. Fielding) wrote him. He doesn't initiate much; he 'gets laid,' as that telling Americanism has it, by Molly, Mrs. Waters, and Lady Bellaston" (190).[11]

This is a curious decision on the part of Richardson but not in disagreement with the general tenor of the movie. In Fielding, the women are mainly plot devices. They have to be married off to fulfill the men's financial or libidinal requirements. The movie uses women for an additional purpose, as eyes through which the spectator gazes at Tom—in other words, as a means of directing and defining the spectator's view. For instance, when Sophie succumbs to the masculine heat of the hunting scene, Osborne invites us to cast admiring glances at our hero through that young woman's eyes: "admiration and desire crawl their way around Sophie's eyes and mouth as she watches Tom" (44). Even Sophie's chambermaid, Mrs. Honor, casts a lascivious eye over Tom's body, saying to her mistress, "That he is, the most handsomest man I ever saw in my life, and as you say, ma'am, I don't know why I should be ashamed of looking at him though he is my better" (49). It is with Tom, not Sophie or Molly, we are supposed to fall in love, and even the heterosexual male spectator is invited to do so safely through the filter of feminine desire.

Tom Jones was attractive to Osborne as a story of quintessential Englishness, and this at a time when Osborne freely professed his nationalist sentiments in the newspapers. Osborne's vision of England's past is a not uncommonly romantic one: once upon a time, men were men and women were women, and all of them lived an upright yet passionate life. It is a fable, of course, one Osborne is not so naive as to believe yet nevertheless clearly enjoys retelling. This nostalgia for a past that never was appears as early as *Look Back in Anger*, where Jimmy Porter demonstrates his fondness for Vaughan Williams' musical expressions of national identity or for the certainties of Edwardian Imperialism, and increases as Osborne grows older, leading to diatribes against the EEC, ruminations about England's ancient heroes, and defenses of fox hunts and other English traditions. It is onto the past that Osborne projects the self-determination and regional sovereignty he longs for when faced with modern integrationist tendencies. It is therefore with Squire Western's bold rejection of modernity that Osborne sympathizes, especially when the former directs himself at his more refined sister: "and I despise your citified claptrap; I'd rather be anything than a courtier or a Presbyterian, or a crawler round those damned German kings, as I believe some people are" (66).

No rule of compromise or niggling calculation governs Osborne's vision of the past. This is a world of tumescent virility exploding uninhibitedly in moments of joyous carnage. Osborne clearly delights in Fielding's unashamedly masculine enjoyment of sexuality and highlighted it in his script. A fight among enraged women, for instance, is described with voyeuristic relish: "Tom puts an end to the fight by taking his horsewhip to the mob. Molly tries to hold together her torn dress. Tom goes to her and they embrace" (34). One of the more effective scenes portrays a hunting party. The event is so central to the general atmosphere of the story that in Osborne's script it triggers the following descriptive passage of purple prose:

> The hunt is no pretty Christmas calendar affair but a thumping dangerous
> vicious business, in which everyone takes part so wholeheartedly that it

seems to express all in the raw, wild vitality that is so near to the surface of
their lives. It is passionate and violent. Squire Western howls dementedly as
he flogs his horse over the muddy earth. The curate kicks his beefy heels in
the air, bellowing with blood and pleasure. Big, ugly, unlovable dogs tear at
the earth. Tom reels and roars on his horse, his face ruddy and damp, almost
insensible with the lust and the cry and the gallop, with the hot quarry of flesh
in the crisp air, the blood and flesh of men, the blood and fur of animals.
Everyone is caught up in the bloody fever. (44)

Needless to say such a description goes far beyond the requirements of a movie
script. It stands out, for instance, by the sensuous joy of alliterative play ("bellowing with blood and pleasure," "reels and roars"), the obsessive repetition
of the word "blood" or "bloody," the accumulation of adjectives and adverbs
that nearly on their own carry the whole sensuous impact of the passage
(thumping, dangerous, vicious, raw, wild, passionate, violent, dementedly,
muddy, beefy, big, ugly, unlovable, ruddy, damp, hot . . .). In *Almost a Gentleman,* Osborne confessed to often feeling constrained by the demands for
precision in scriptwriting, which left all too little scope for verbal exuberance
of this kind. Ironically, nothing of the tenor of his description survived in the
movie. What in Fielding and Osborne is wild abandon becomes caricatured in
Richardson's and his cameraman Walter Lassally's rendition so that the scene
becomes an indictment rather than a celebration of hunting.

EPITAPH FOR GEORGE DILLON

Much of *Tom Jones*'s success depended on its splendid cast of actors: Hugh
Griffith, Edith Evans, Susannah York, and Joan Greenwood—all of whom had
successful careers on stage. Tom Jones himself was played by Albert Finney,
who had made his first major film appearance in the Woodfall film production
of *Saturday Night and Sunday Morning* and who in 1961, at the Théâtre des
Nations in Paris, had been nominated "best actor of the season" for his leading role in Osborne's *Luther.* His humorous rendition of Tom Jones further
ensured his future as major film and stage actor. For a writer such as Osborne,
however, working for the big screen did not exert the same appeal.[12] After he
found that Richardson had mangled his script for the next major Woodfall production, *The Charge of the Light Brigade* (1968), he resolutely returned to the
stage, finding only there the respect and sovereignty his particular talent
required.[13]

   Look Back in Anger (1956), *The Entertainer* (1957), and *Luther* (1961)
are complex works that deserve to be carefully analyzed, as will be done in the
chapters that follow. Though no work of Osborne is uninteresting, some plays
however may be allowed to speak virtually for themselves, being technically
or conceptually less challenging. A possible exception is *Epitaph for George*

Dillon, a full-length play of some complexity that will, however, be only briefly discussed here because it cannot be wholly ascribed to Osborne.

Epitaph for George Dillon was produced on 11 February, 1958, in the deep and turbulent wake of Osborne's first huge successes, at a time when the Royal Court Theatre was eager to fulfill the audience's demand for more Osborne plays. The play had been written four years earlier, in collaboration with Anthony Creighton, with whom Osborne had also written *Personal Enemy,* a play that enjoyed a short and unexceptional run in Harrogate in 1955. Originally, *Epitaph for George Dillon* was constructed as a series of flashbacks, but Osborne revised it, placing all action in the present. He then shortened the play for its West End and Broadway productions, re-titling it *George Dillon.* It was generally thought that Creighton wrote the more conventional, plot-driven parts and that Osborne was responsible for George Dillon's longer speeches.

George Dillon starts like a boarding room farce, with rather caricatural sketches of lower-middle class life, but develops into a quite interesting study in failure—a topic close to Osborne's heart. As with Jimmy Porter in *Look Back in Anger*, most reviewers saw in George Dillon a thinly disguised portrait of Osborne, the artist. Some in fact noticed the physical resemblances between Robert Stephens' impersonation of Dillon and Osborne himself: "his hunched shoulders and nasal twang are modelled so faithfully after John Osborne's own physical characteristics that any resemblance between author and hero can hardly be co-incidental";[14] "there is in his voice a cawing note that may even have been modeled on Mr. Osborne himself. This is the roundest portrait I have seen of a certain kind of neurotic artist."[15]

Harold Hobson compared George Dillon to Louis Dubedat, the artist and swindler in Shaw's *A Doctor's Dilemma,* but pointed out that Osborne's play poses a different kind of question. Shaw was obsessed with the problem of the genuiness of Dubedat's talent—because only that would redeem that character despite his fickleness, treachery, and cruelty. In contrast, Osborne and Creighton are interested in the artist's relationship to his self: "the question they ask is not, does George Dillon deceive others, but the much more interesting one, because so rarely posed, is he deceiving himself?" For Hobson, who bases this on a theory from the Spanish critic Gonzalo Torrente Ballester, such a shift moves modern drama away from its subservience to bourgeois morality where the basic question always turns around the contractual obligation, the quid pro quo, and on toward a theatre preoccupied with existential questions.[16]

George Dillon is an unemployed actor/playwright who careens violently between vanity and self-doubt. His story is that of an artistically talented young man who sponges off a lower-middle class family that has invited him into their midst to take the place of a dead son. For a long time George's main talent consists in maintaining high expectations as his scripts continue to be rejected. This is the starting point for a well-worn Faustian motive. Only when George sells his artistic soul and allows an unscrupulous theatre manager to butcher one of his plays does he become a "success": but the price is too high. By then he is so disgusted with himself that he no longer possesses the energy to leave the family behind. In other words, at the height of his success, when he is celebrated by the family as a future son-in-law and successful artist, he is "overcome with failure. Eternal bloody failure" (III, ii, 86). He has become what he has feared most, "just another caricature" (II, 60).

In the tenor of its dialogue, the conventionality of its construction, and the use of symbolism, *George Dillon* seems very much the kind of traditional, romantic play Terence Rattigan could have written. It is special and interesting, however, in its curious self-awareness of theatrical conventions, posing a question that will continue to fascinate Osborne in later work: how can a theatre bogged down in clichés and conventions come alive and be convincingly authentic? What, in other words, is the relationship between convention and authenticity? His answer: authenticity is a flame that only briefly yet violently rises from the ashes of clichés.

George believes himself to be such a flame, one of the very few who are truly alive and live conflicts intensely. Others, in his opinion, are mere caricatures: "put any of them on a stage," he says, "and no one would take them seriously for one minute! They think in clichés, they talk in them, they even feel in them—and, brother, that's an achievement!" (II, 58). Of one character, for instance, he says that she "doesn't even exist—she's just a hole in the air!" (II, 60). The common run of people cannot even fathom the tragedy of sheer existence: "They've no curiosity. There are no questions for them, and, consequently, no answers" (II, 61). "Their existence," says George, "is one great cliché that they carry about with them like a snail in his little house—and they live in it and die in it!" (II, 59).

It is important for Dillon to believe that he, in contrast, is special. "Say what you like: I have a mind and feelings that are all fingertips," while that of the others is "all thumbs, thumbs that are fat and squashy—like bananas, in fact, and rather sickly" (II, 59). George belongs to an elite, whereas Josie, the girl he makes pregnant, belongs to the masses; in fact, "Josie is that mass, all rolled into one" (II, 59). One woman in the family, however, stands up to him, as his equal in intelligence and rather his superior in experience. Ruth realizes Dillon has to belittle others in order to erect himself on the ruins of their being. Though tempted and seduced by Dillon's flaming anger and despair, Ruth is also aware of his hollowness: "oh, a good delivery, George. You're being brilliant, after all. They're very easy people to score off, but, never mind, go on!" (II, 59).

Ruth is fascinated by George but wise enough to resist her own fascination. Her role for him is to provide the resistance he requires in order to shine. She pulls him down, deflates his rhetoric. That perversely excites him and for a moment, he triumphs: "why haven't we talked like this before," Ruth says, almost convinced. "A few moments ago you made me feel old. Now, I suddenly feel younger" (II, 61). "You're a good audience," he replies. "Even if I do have to beat you down. That's all I need—an audience" (II, 62). Beating down the audience is necessary to create moments of reality and intensity. In other words, both actor and audience have their roles to play, being united in a complex contest of seduction and refusal.

Afterward however, George collapses: "he takes a deep breath, and sits down quickly, suddenly drained. She watches him, fascinated" (II, 62). Ruth has understood the source of George's energy. His splendid moments of originality, authenticity, vitality arise *ex nihilo,* out of nothing tangible, fired on by despise, by hate, and especially by the effort to overcome guilt at having despised in others what he secretly knows to be part of himself. In these moments, George not only feels contempt for the people around him but denies what he has in common with them. Time and time again, George rises himself from nothingness and bursts into a colorful display of "Life"; yet always, afterward, when the curtain falls, he sinks back into the grey mass out of which he has erected himself. When "up" George feels special, a leader of people, a god; when "down," he is the most despicable among them. Once the energy has been expended, reality returns and with it the consciousness of his own limitations. Ruth is fascinated by the quick change: "these agonizing bubbles of personality, then phut! Nothing. Simply tiredness and pain" (II, 62).

George's talent is a disease: "you're sick with [talent]," says Ruth; but, as George says, what if he only suffers the symptoms of talent but not the real disease? "What is worse is having the same symptoms as talent, the pain, the ugly swellings, the lot—but never knowing whether or not the diagnosis is correct" (II, 62). The stakes are high, given the self-loathing that always follows his brief moments of triumph. One slight mistake and what was splendidly tragic becomes farcical—and how eager people are to see greatness deflated because, as much as they may admire it, true greatness, true art, makes their own life unbearable:

> Just a trip on the stage-cloth, and Lear teeters on, his crown round his ears, his grubby tights full of mothholes. How they all long for those tights to fall down. What a relief it would be! Oh, we should all use stronger elastic. And the less sure we are of our pathetic little divine rights, the stronger the elastic we should use. You've seen the whole, shabby, solemn pretence now. (III, ii, 87)

Ironically, when George truly "falls," no one but Ruth notices. Finally, at the end of the play, having sold his talent for quick money to make a smash hit, he will commit what in his eyes is the equivalent of artistic suicide: he will allow himself to be buried by mediocrity. George is already considering this move when he asks Ruth, "Do you think there may be some kind of euthanasia for that? Could you kill it by burying yourself here—for good?" (II, 62). The epitaph that George Dillon composes for himself is that of failed promise: "he achieved nothing he set out to do. He made no one happy, no one look up with excitement when he entered the room" (III, ii, 87). Even that sentiment, though the fruit of his personal suffering, is not original: "even his sentimental epitaph is probably a pastiche of someone or other, but he doesn't quite know who" (III, ii, 87).

MINOR WORK

With his next play, Osborne's figurative tights did indeed fall down. As Charles Hussey put it, *The World of Paul Slickey* (1959) "brought [Osborne] to the distinction of being the only dramatist in recent history to have been booed personally at the stage door after the curtain had come down."[17] Osborne's only musical, it is somewhat of a curiosity. On his first trip to New York for the Broadway production of *Look Back,* Osborne was wildly enthusiastic about the vibrant energy generated by a modern musical such as *West Side Story.* He immediately decided to try his hand, and as it proved unsuccessfully, at a musical of his own. Unlike *West Side Story, The World of Paul Slickey* deals not with youth but with the smallness of contemporary British life—a rather less congenial topic to inspire an exciting score, the more so since Osborne's lyrics proved fairly tame. *Paul Slickey* is meant as a spoof on the kind of journalism that had made Osborne rich and famous by keeping him a frequent front page figure, but that also had all too crudely intruded upon his privacy and cheapened his views. The play, though, also professes to have a wider aim, namely to expose the hypocrisy, greed, and debasement of modern life in general. With characteristic Osbornian distaste, it is dedicated to "those who daily deal out treachery . . . and . . . betray my country [. . . .], to their boredom, their incomprehension, their distaste." In any case, Osborne declared in a pre-emptive strike, which would become a habit in later plays, that such people would not profit from the play because they were congenitally unable to listen and understand. As the Royal Court Theatre showed no interest in the musical, Osborne directed and partially financed it himself. It premièred at the Pavilion Theatre in Bournemouth on 14 April, 1959.

"I created Paul Slickey as a monster," Osborne recalled in 1994.[18] The figure that emerges from the play, however, is a more complex creation than its creator dared to admit. Played by Dennis Lotis, then the English equivalent of Frank Sinatra, Slickey is at once charming, vain, and corrupt. He first appears to us in silhouette, like a gumshoe in a *série noire* ("When he is not embracing a GIRL—he uses a cigarette-holder" (I, i, 11)), his shadow projected onto a cloth representing his gossip column. The smallness of his profession stands in contrast to the esteem in which Slickey holds himself. While regarding his talents equal to those of any playwright/novelist, Slickey applies them for purely destructive purposes: "we can't build your boat, but we'll make damn sure you sink it!" For that, he is regally paid ("In my cashmere coat and my seat at the Caprice.") In his title song, he proudly claims to remain superbly unaffected by anything: "anybody, anything ... leaves me ... newspaper neatly/quite, quite cold" (I, i, 18). The fault, ultimately, is not Slickey's but that of the people who eagerly feed on his gossip. This, after all, "is the age of the common man," and the common man is a herd animal, "always on the band wagon, never in the cart" (I, i, 15).

A musical comedy of manners, with some fairly good jokes and tolerably well managed farcical situations, the play proved at first to be moderately entertaining. Jack Oakham, alias Paul Slickey, is asked to investigate the dark financial dealings of an estate that happens to belong to his wife's family, a situation that offers Osborne the opportunity to parody upper class manners and hypocrisy as well. A series of increasingly improbable events culminates in a chemically induced and miraculously speedy sex change. In modern society, Osborne implies, the difference between the sexes is in any case virtually nonexistent. "We all know that the line dividing male and female is little more than a vague shadow," says one female character: "if men have become sloppy, boneless and emasculated, it's their own fault entirely. [. . .] And power, political power, like everything else, is passing into the hands of the women. [. . .] If you want to make certain of being a success in politics, there is only one realistic solution: become a woman!" (II, x, 78).

When the play transferred to the Palace Theatre in London, it met with extraordinary hostility, not because it was offensive but because it was insufficiently entertaining. Audiences booed, and the next day critics launched a concerted attack on it. Their glee at Osborne's "failure" was so tangible that critic Harold Clurman, in a more thoughtful assessment, openly deplored what he called the reviewers' "gratuitous venom." Osborne, he thought, had simply not yet fully mastered the technical difficulties of the genre: "the lyrics are . . . too complex, and the prosody . . . painfully awkward for clean musical delivery"; the dances did not contribute to the play and therefore seemed "mere choreographic exercises."[19]

Osborne was only slightly more successful with his first attempt at writing for television, perhaps because he had a low opinion of the medium and the genre. "Any fool can write a television play," he once said. "I just do the odd one occasionally when I get a one-shot idea."[20] *A Subject of Scandal and Concern* is a low-key docudrama about the socialist George Holyoake, the last man to be imprisoned for blasphemy in 1842. Directed by Tony Richardson, it was broadcast by BBC Television on 6 November 1960. In a rather strenuous attempt to endow the play with modern relevance, Osborne had it introduced by a present-day lawyer visiting a client in prison. From the onset, the narrator's dismissive attitude implies that the case will be lost on its audience. Television spectators seek only to be entertained and when faced with anything of serious intent demand that the moral be spelled out. The narrator concludes his grim story by accusing the audience of selling their souls and conscience for material comforts: "that's all. You may retire now. And if a mini car is your particular mini dream, then dream it" (III, 47). That last statement will be repeated, almost verbatim, by Bill Maitland in *Inadmissible Evidence* five years later.

A Subject of Scandal and Concern is Osborne's first attempt to deal with the birthing of a voice, a topic he will return to in *Luther* and in *Inadmissible Evidence*. Holyoake is a stammering school teacher who delivers lectures on socialism—a speaker who cannot speak and who, one day, is tricked into publicly revealing his atheism and his low opinion of institutionalized religion. In a hypocritical world, Holyoake is that rare man who speaks from an inner conviction, without pride, driven by the sole desire to be truthful to himself. Richard Burton portrays the character most effectively, as a man uneasy in body and speech, a man seen frequently looking down, as if to gather thoughts that have tumbled to his feet, then shifting his glasses nervously onto his nose. At once humble and stubborn, Holyoake defends his ideas, and when tried for blasphemy, he bravely insists on taking up his own defense.

Only through hardship and betrayal, when his convictions are tested in a public court, will Holyoake find his true voice. Holyoake's voice, says the narrator, had become "notably stronger and his impediment astonishingly improved" (II, 37). While in prison, friends denounce and abandon him; even his family turns away from him, bitter at his foolhardiness. At the depth of his suffering, he learns that his best friend, imprisoned for sedition, has died not only recanting his beliefs but cursing Holyoake as well. When his daughter dies, Holyoake orders his wife to have the burial conducted without the ministrations of the Church. The more he isolates himself from others through such acts, the more clearly delineated become his personality and ideas.

But Holyoake's victory is at once his defeat, and he loses his tongue once again. "When you leave this place," his wife tells him bitterly, "you will walk over the grave of your own child. Well? Where is your tongue now, Mr. Holyoake?" Abandoned by everyone and subjected to the chaplain's relentless praying, Holyoake for the first time finds no solace in the dignified resolution with which he has adhered to his convictions and his rights. The camera, taking in the Chaplain's unassailable position in the pulpit, peers down pitilessly at Holyoake, who, small and insignificant, eyes wide open, shakes his head. Descending from his pulpit, the chaplain kneels in front of Holyoake, beseeching him to speak. Holyoake "makes an animal effort to speak but nothing will happen" (III, 46).

"There was a general sneer of relief from most of the British press when [*A Subject of Scandal and Concern*] was seen to be little more than a documentary lecture of small merit," said Charles Hussey.[21] Of even less import was *Plays for England,* a theatrical diversion, all too clearly an exercise for the left hand. It consists of two one-hour plays, one a satirical charade on royalty worship, the other on the cruel scandal mongering of the Yellow Press. Together, they form a perfect double-bill of comedies to fill an agreeable evening at the theatre. Both were produced for the first time at the Royal Court Theatre on 19 June 1962. *The Blood of the Bambergs,* subtitled "A Fairy Story," was directed by John Dexter, known for his successful Royal Court Theatre productions of Arnold Wesker plays. *Under Plain Cover* was Jonathan Miller's directorial debut. Miller, who held a degree in medicine from Cambridge, was then known mainly for his contributions as writer and comic actor in the 1960 revue *Beyond the Fringe.* An absurdist comedy about sexual perversion, *Under Plain Cover* found in Miller its ideal director.

The Blood of the Bambergs uses a well-worn plot to solicit some predictable laughter. A Royal Wedding is in full preparation when news arrives of the princely bridegroom's death. Instead of canceling the wedding, an Australian look-alike of the prince, in fact an illegitimate offspring of the same royal branch, is cajoled and blackmailed into standing in for the dead prince. This then allows Osborne to poke fun at the inanity of a costly but empty ritual. *Under Plain Cover* portrays a young couple's total absorption in acting out their innocent sexual fantasies until a journalist informs them they are in fact brother and sister. Their enforced separation, the young woman's hasty marriage to a more suitable partner, and finally the siblings' reunion are orchestrated by the press, which reduces these harrowing events to sentimental cliché. At the end of the play, the journalist responsible for cruelly breaking in on their privacy dies apparently from sheer self-disgust ("STANLEY collapses, drunk and miserable. Dead possible" (85)). Given Jean Genet's far more inventive use of ritual, play-acting, and fetishism, these plays are neither very interesting nor original and were dismissed by reviewers as "clumsy," "laborious,"[22] "dull and flat," and altogether "unexceptional."[23]

ANGRY YOUNG MEN

In a span of seven years Osborne had written three box office successes, several minor plays, and a string of scripts and articles. His consistent productivity and ability to hold the audience's interest with often challenging plays showed him to be a dramatist of lasting importance; but he was also an artist who, especially in his early years, was able to shape the receptivity his work required. George Devine and the English Stage Company had given him a helping hand when he most needed it. Once in the saddle, Osborne maintained his grip, cleverly playing on the media's thirst for scandal and renewal. About the origin of the term "Angry Young Man," there was considerable dispute, some claiming it was taken from Leslie Young's 1951 autobiography of that title. Osborne ascribed it to George Fearon, the Royal Court's Press agent at the time of *Look Back in Anger,* who supposedly used it to express his dislike of Osborne's work and personality.[24] The term received wide recognition after journalist Tom Maschler assembled essays from various upcoming writers in a volume entitled *Declaration* (1957).[25] The book aimed at becoming the manifesto of a new literary movement, though the authors brought together in this way (Doris Lessing, Colin Wilson, John Osborne, John Wain, and Bill Hopkins were among them) shared no common program and in fact did not even like each other.[26] What united this non-movement was the authors' interest in contemporary issues, belief in the importance of passion rather than reason, and trust in direct and vigorous speech. The writers were young in the sense that they had written their major works in the years following WW II.[27] They were also angry in the sense that they rejected both the old and the new world, the hypocrisy of the middle-class establishment but also the drabness of the welfare state. Their works dealt realistically with the life of young, usually male heroes in contemporary society.[28] Though an important number of women were often counted in the movement (Shelagh Delaney, Ann Jellicoe, and Lynn Reid Banks, for instance) a more gender-neutral term such as "Angry Young Artists" was never used.

As Harry Ritchie explains in his book *Success Stories,* Osborne may have expressed his virulent dislike of the term, but also knew how to make use of it in order to ensure attention.[29] He soon became known as the angriest of angry authors, and only after *Look Back in Anger* did the term "Angry Young Man" gain widespread recognition. An important number of "angry" works, however, predate *Look Back*—among them, John Wain's *Hurry on Down* (1953), Iris Murdoch's *Under the Net* (1954), Kingsley Amis's *Lucky Jim* (1954) and *That Uncertain Feeling* (1955). Following close on *Look Back in Anger* come Colin Wilson's *The Outsider* (1956), John Braine's *Room at the Top* (1957), and David Storey's *This Sporting Life* (1960).

What enhanced the term's media appeal while simultaneously exposing it to criticism was its affinity with the American youth cult represented by the Marlon Brando ideal of the "rebel without a cause" and the Jack Kerouac model of the "beat generation." Movies of the period, *The Wild Ones* (1954; with a terse, leather-clad Brando), *East of Eden* and *Rebel Without a Cause* (1955; both with a restive, febrile James Dean) provided young males with a complete set of attitudes to emulate. The ideal male character conveyed a blend of romanticism and cynicism. Most attractive was a certain air of premature disenchantment, especially with the world of adults—a turning away in disgust from what actually had made the youth cult possible, namely cold reality principle and the world of business. With his jazz trumpet and a reputation for sexual voracity, Jimmy Porter in *Look Back in Anger* was very much the product of that American age, though he also laments it with a British snootiness that certainly predates it. By having his hero effortlessly alternate between jazz trumpet solo and Flanagan and Allen routines, Osborne sought to preserve the most vital elements of British lower-class culture, simply by wedding them to American ones. Even then *Look Back* did not become a success overnight and on its own merits but had first to be recognized as a "phenomenon" indicative of the dangerous transitory nature of the fifties.

CHAPTER 3

Look Back in Anger (1956)
Of Bears and Traps

RECEPTION

Look Back in Anger was fated to become Osborne's flagship, though an older, reminiscing Osborne would put it far less grandly: it "fixed me like a butterfly in a glass cage." Journalists and critics could not resist coining titles that punned either on "look back" or on "anger" and preferably on both: "Angry Old Blimp," "Look Forward in Fear," "Look Back in Candour," "Britain's Fiery Dramatist," "Most Angry Fella," etc. This was irksome for a young playwright eager to spread his wings. "You became an object rather than a human being," Osborne complained. "It was like being called the Walls Ice-cream Man."[1] Yet he also readily admitted that the play and the appellation of Angry Young Man had served him well as the trademark that saved him from penury and in fact "paid the rent" for the rest of his life.[2]

Success, however, had not been assured from the start. After all, Osborne was an unemployed actor who sent an often rejected manuscript to the Royal Court Theatre, after reading in *The Stage* that George Devine was looking for new plays. He received an advance of £ 25 for his play, but had to wait almost a year to see it staged.[3] At first the play drew little critical attention, and only after an extract was shown on television, did the weekly reviews in the "posh papers" appear and make all the difference.[4] A young and upcoming left-wing critic, Kenneth Tynan, hailed Osborne as "the first spokesman for post-war youth." The play, he said, may well respond to a minority taste; "what matters, however, is the size of the minority. I estimate it at roughly 6, 733, 000, which is the number of people in this country between the ages of twenty and thirty."[5] He famously added that he doubted if he "could love anyone who did not wish to see *Look Back in Anger*." Not everyone agreed with that assessment. Two headlines capture the climate of excited dissension that greeted the play when it moved from London to the provinces: " 'Look Back in Anger' Was an

'Insult'," cried the reviewer of the *Northern Daily Mail* (31 October 1957); "'Look Back in Anger' is electrifying," responded the dramatic critic of the *Salisbury Times* (1 November 1957). Such polarization of opinion ensured that for many years to come the play would remain the center of a lively debate about theatre, youth, and the state of the nation.

After playing for eighteen months in London and the provinces, *Look Back in Anger* was transferred to Broadway where it was an immediate hit.[6] Already accustomed to the emotional fireworks of O'Neill, Williams, Miller, and Odets, Americans more easily appreciated the raciness of Osborne's dialogue.[7] *Look Back in Anger,* they declared, was "the most virile and exciting play to come out of London in a long, long time."[8] Before *Look Back in Anger,* theatres in London had apparently suffered from "a bad case of virginity," to borrow one of Jimmy Porter's expressions. Critics who championed Osborne's work made it seem as if action on the pre-Osbornian stage had consisted entirely of young men swinging tennis rackets and women with huge bouquets of flowers entering through French windows. This was an exaggeration, but a useful one because it highlighted Osborne's contribution. The "heyday of nobility revivals," as Osborne called it, supposedly came to an end only when *Look Back in Anger* boldly rent the veil of decency that had stifled dramatic creativity.[9] *Look Back in Anger,* says fellow playwright Arnold Wesker, joining others in resorting to an image of masculine sexual aggression, served as a "battering ram": "the door was kicked open and an angry flood of writing and social protest poured through."[10]

The play also conquered the European continent where newspapers were soon debating the phenomenon of the "Boze Jonge Lieden" or the "Zornige Junge Männer."[11] Critical discussions, both abroad and at home, invariably centered on "the crisis of masculinity" which, supposedly, was at the center of the play. "Weaned by the Welfare State," ran one headline: "from pontificating unchallenged at the fireplace, [the male ego] has been downgraded to obsequiousness in the kitchen. From being the fighter and provider it has nose-dived to passive petulance in coffee bars." *Look Back in Anger,* continued the nameless reviewer, portrayed the "British male's nagging fears of his own futility."[12] Anger was a sort of compensation, or as the *Surrey Times* called it, using a revealingly sexual trope, a form of "verbal indecent exposure" that served as defiant reassertion of threatened manliness.[13] Some male critics felt exhilarated. Kenneth Tynan hastened to buy himself a trumpet so as to lay hands on that gleaming attribute of Jimmy's masculinity.[14] The American critic Walter Kerr went embarrassingly agog at the thought of Jimmy's irresistible masculine force: "you are asked to believe . . . that two women not only love this volcano of random, ceaseless, spluttering venom but that the more abused of them, will, literally, crawl on her knees and elbows to beg him back. You believe it. The truth about this conscienceless sadist is that he is absolutely alive."[15]

Yet this apparent icon of masculinity made on many critics quite the opposite impression. They felt discomfited by Jimmy's "infantile wail" or "boyish vulnerability" and thought that his emotional instability would have been more plausible in a woman.[16] An anonymous reviewer took issue with such criticism but confirmed the impression nonetheless: "nobody would doubt if the nagging was being done by a woman. Why doubt it, therefore, because in this case the fault-finder is a man?"[17] Jimmy, of course, represented a new ideal of masculinity, derived largely from American models that emphasized the hero's sexual unease. It valued "raw intensity" rather than the self-control propagated in traditionally British models of middle-class masculinity. Osborne was convinced that "the stiff upper lip" was "a physical deformity." "It's a myth that the British . . . are reserved," he said. "You just go into a pub and talk to ordinary people. They'll start pouring out their hearts to you after a beer or two."[18] For many British reviewers, however, such behavior was too lower class and far too outspoken for the stage. Papers reported on well-known titled personages who had walked out of the play, protesting that its language was "typical of a brawl that might happen in one of the slum areas of Glasgow."[19] That the action is set in the Midlands rather than in London certainly did not help to endear the play to such spectators. Heroes like Jimmy Porter, Somerset Maugham famously declared, were nothing but scum.[20] Jimmy was a boor and a cad, and his behavior toward his wife was inexcusable in real life and as unacceptable on the stage. In their eyes, Jimmy's violent energy had the throb not of masculine resolve but of effeminate hysteria. Far from being too masculine, he was not masculine enough and needed toughening up. Quite a few reviewers, in fact, listed wholesome disciplinary measures that would guarantee results.

From the beginning, *Look Back in Anger* was a source of confusion that did not end with disputes about the sexuality of its hero. Every aspect of the play seemed open to a variety of interpretations. Was the play, for instance, truly as innovative as it seemed? Structurally, it seemed an old-fashioned three-acter, with rather forced entrances and exits and a dramatic curtain. In many ways, it still harked back to the conventions of the well-made play, though it seemed imbalanced because of one character's dominance.[21] Everyone agreed that it stood out because its language was contemporary in its sauciness and irreverence.[22] It also distinguished itself by raising expectations it never fulfilled. In many ways, the play seemed conventional enough, yet it sinned against every principle of economy, counting, for instance, some twenty-six off-stage characters. It was as if the play had set itself the boundaries of a specific theatrical genre only to be able to break them.

Today, confusion still surrounds the play. On the surface, *Look Back in Anger* appears to be a social problem or state of the nation play, dealing with the inertia and lack of resolve that were said to be typical of the welfare state. Its many topical references are indeed meaningful only to an audience of the late 1950s. Yet the play is still occasionally revived, having established itself

firmly in the canon as a work that signals the transition toward increased directness in the language of the postwar British stage. Young male actors remain
appreciative of its long and challenging set speeches, which allow them to
demonstrate their skill and mettle, but modern directors find it hard to dispel
an impression of datedness, which is especially evident in the play's portrayal
of gender relationships. As one female critic put it, "The overwhelming impression now is one of rampant misogyny and pervasive sexism."[23] So despite the
changes in critical idiom, the main objection is still Jimmy's caddishness, for-
merly a sore spot only to old-fashioned defenders of the masculine ideal of the
gentleman. Other present-day critics continue to worry about the play's
"dowdy plot and its intolerable lapses into cuddliness."[24] If despite these apparent structural shortcomings and sins against current sensibilities, the play is
still sometimes successfully produced,[25] it is because some directors realize
that its irresistible energy is not generated by Jimmy's arrogant certainties, but
by a more fundamental and lastingly unsettling ambiguity for which the welfare state serves then only as the most topical trope.

LANGUAGE AND ENERGY

The play pulses with energy. Jimmy and Alison are a warring couple, and in a
short time span, the emotional space between them dilates, contracts, and
dilates again. Act I demonstrates that mechanism, reaching its apogee when
Jimmy, in an excess of physical action, smashes into Alison's ironing board. She
burns her arm, and her scream of pain and disgust chases him out of the room.
"There's hardly a moment when I'm not—watching and wanting you," Jimmy
says afterwards in explanation. "I've got to hit out somehow" (I, 33). A love
game ensues during which she becomes his beautiful squirrel and he her gruff
and awkward super-bear. They reach a moment of unparalleled closeness which
nearly inspires Alison with the necessary confidence to confide to her husband
that she is pregnant with his child, but the news of Helena's arrival drives them
apart again. Jimmy disapproves of her friend. At once Jimmy and Alison
become arch enemies. In an apotheosis of apparently random cruelty, Jimmy
expresses a wish he does not know could come true in the months to follow. This
is marvelous drama. The world it presents is far from admirable, but one does
not have to have lived much to recognize that it has an honest feel to it.

   After it has been established that the couple's cruelty is a form of closeness, Alison obeys the biological imperative of her ill-fated pregnancy by leaving Jimmy at the end of Act II. Yet this does not abrogate the pulsating
movement. It will be completed by her return in Act III. That last act opens on
a tableau identical to that of the first: a woman stands at the ironing board,
wearing one of Jimmy's shirts, while Jimmy and friend Cliff read the newspapers. The woman, however, is now Helena, who has remained with Jimmy
after Alison's departure. This "repetition with a difference" technique is com-

mon in musical composition and in comedy and farce, but such mirroring of one scene by another is usually found too mechanical for realistic plays. Evidently, the play prefers to pursue a pleasing musical regularity even to the extent of straining verisimilitude.

Musical rhythms are also evoked by Jimmy's infatuation with jazz and his way of spontaneously switching into vaudeville song-and-dance routines which he executes with the help of friend Cliff. It becomes clear then that the play has been constructed not so much with a view of exploring themes and ideas but rather as an orchestration of psychologically plausible emotional affects. The opening stage direction moreover resorts to musical terminology to explain the different personalities in the play. Alison, it says, is "the most elusive personality to catch in the uneasy polyphony of these three people" and her "well-bred malaise . . . is often drowned in the robust orchestration of the other two" (I, 10).

Act II adds Helena's alto to Alison's soprano, Jimmy's tenor, and Cliff's *basso continuo.* It starts with a *recitativo,* perfectly plausible on the musical stage, but in terms of realistic drama, awkwardly strained as exposition in which the two women delineate for the audience the forces of attraction and repulsion in the couple's exhausting love dance, in which Cliff apparently plays the role of dancing master. Rather than engaging in a conversation, the two women are involved in a straightforward question-answer session in which Helena adopts the role of stern interrogator. This recitative is punctuated by angry bursts on the jazz trumpet, as Jimmy practices next door. At times the lyricism of strongly alliterative sentences exceeds their realistic intent, as when Alison refers to the bear-squirrel game she plays with Jimmy as "a silly symphony for people who couldn't bear the pain of being human beings any longer" (II, i, 47).

In this symphony of despair, we never lose sight of the playwright-conductor who all too visibly wields the baton. Osborne later poked fun at the overbearing presence of explicit stage directions in his early plays. At the time, they were necessary because his plays require a then unconventional acting style, acutely demanding in terms of timing and movement.[26] Actors needed to develop an ear for the give and take of language, for the logic of the language game. Since characters now rarely meant what they said, in fact, used language mainly strategically, actors had to pay more attention to swiftly changing interactional dynamics. The "how" and "why" of language sometimes became more important than the "what." Once audience and performers had assimilated the new acting and dialogue conventions, Osborne's stage directions became less conspicuously present. Even then, however, they remained remarkably prominent, suggesting that far from a necessary evil, they play a crucial role in orchestrating the music of affects. The extent to which stage directions, in fact, create the scene over and above the dialogue is easily demonstrated by omitting the latter altogether:

Silence. His rage mounting within.

[Alison] recognising an onslaught on the way, starts to panic. [But] the wild note in her voice has re-assured him. His anger cools and hardens. His voice is quite calm when he speaks. He clutches wildly for something to shock Helena with. [He] kicks [the] cistern. Sits on it, beats [it] like bongo drums. [He is] capable of anything now. Cliff and Helena look at Alison tensely, but she just gazes at her plate. (stage directions II, i, 51–53)

The stage directions convey in themselves the scene's meaning (see appendix). This is choreographed emotion, not so much in emulation as in excess of Osborne's model Tennessee Williams. All we need to know about the scene is already imparted through movement, intensity, and intonation. In other words, the *how* and the *to whom* of the dialogue are more important than the *what*.

So in Osborne's drama, it is context not content that dominates exchange. Like "negative space," meaning has to be excavated from in between stage directions.[27] Words delineate rather than articulate an emotion, circumscribing a space occupied usually by longing or regret. Osborne therefore derides literal-minded critics who take a character's most salient utterance, such as Jimmy's famous "there aren't any good, brave causes left" (III, i, 84) as key to his personality: "they were incapable of recognizing the texture of ordinary despair, the way it expresses itself in rhetoric and gestures that may perhaps look shabby, but are seldom simple."[28] This, of course, exasperated critics who, led astray by the "well-made" aspect of the play, could not be expected to regard language with such reservations.

Osborne, moreover, adapts a similar technique to create a sense of character. The opening stage direction presents character mainly in terms of an emotional range, which, in Jimmy's case, is unhelpfully wide: "he is a disconcerting mixture of sincerity and cheerful malice, of tenderness and freebooting cruelty; restless, importunate, full of pride, a combination which alienates the sensitive and insensitive alike" (I, 9–10). This may be accurate but does not help the critic understand the logic of that character's behavior. Osborne, in fact, establishes character mainly negatively. Its reality immaterializes, so to speak, within a cloud of other names. Osborne is said to have possessed a drawing with the twenty-six or so characters that never appear but are constantly referred to in *Look Back in Anger,* serving as the imaginary coordinates of Jimmy and Alison's existences.[29]

This general vagueness is particularly frustrating for critics, or as Osborne calls them, the "deluded pedants," "fashionable turnips," "death's heads of imagination and feeling" who watch a play with the grim determination to master by understanding it. "I offer no explanations to such people," Osborne says dismissively. And, in any case, "they . . . have no ear at all."[30] The play, however, is undeniably effective on an emotional or musical level, especially for those audience members who do not have to make a living by paraphrasing plays in terms of meaning and motivation. One more roundabout way, however, of explaining what generates the dynamics of the play is through an examination of its superficial certainties and central ambiguities. The place to start is simply at the surface level, which consists of topical references to the welfare state.

THE WELFARE STATE

Though Jimmy is working class, he has profited from the "free education for all" schemes that were introduced after the war. He recently graduated from one of the newer universities (not even "red brick" but "white tile," as he says). The object of his anger is his upper-class wife Alison and everything that makes her attitude of silent withdrawal typical of her class and of society at large. "All this time, I have been married to this woman, this monument to non-attachment, and suddenly I discover that there is actually a word that sums her up," Jimmy says (I, 21). The context in which he makes this accusation is a marriage firmly cemented in unhappiness and enduring because each of the partners is trapped into the other's neurosis. Beyond that, however, it is the "Brave New-nothing-very-much-thank-you" world, the British welfare state, gutted of its ideals and stuffed with American-style consumerism ("it's pretty dreary living in the American age," Jimmy says, "unless you're an American of course"), a country already five years under conservative rule and still to remain so for another three successive elections until 1964. In that year, Bill Maitland, another Osbornian hero, will take the stage in *Inadmissible Evidence* and roundly denounce the welfare state for having encouraged a lower-middle class materialism and philistinism. It had made people calculating and smug, or, as Bill Maitland put it, it had turned the minicar into everyone's minidream.

Most people would agree that Jimmy is not an easy man to live with and that his much pestered wife is not to be envied. Yet the "word that sums her up," according to Jimmy, is not reticent, modest, or endlessly forbearing, but "pusillanimous." It is the blanket epithet Jimmy casts over all he dislikes: wife; establishment figures like Alison's brother Nigel, "the Platitude from Outer Space"; and society at large. It sums up not only his wife's attitude but the state of mind the welfare state had helped to promote. Those Five Shining Years after 1945, when Labour laid the foundations of the welfare state had been bold and virile in conception. Things had started to go wrong, however, as soon as emphasis shifted from ideas to actualization, and dreaming made way for the give and take of politics. Between 1948 and 1951, $ 2.7 billion in American Marshall plan loans had been funneled into the welfare state, adulterating, some claimed, the vision of the just society on which the new world was being built. By 1951, Labour had lost the impetus of its reforms, and the Conservative Party ("Dame Alison's mob," as Jimmy's friend Hugh calls them) returned to power. "We accepted the revolution of 1832 and governed England for a considerable part of the nineteenth century in consequence," said Robert Boothby, voicing the Conservative Party's views on the welfare state. "We have accepted the revolution of 1945 and are looking forward to governing England again for a good part of the rest of this century."[31] Once out of power, Labour lost touch with the essence of socialism, which, according to Osborne, is defiance. More pragmatic socialists such as Hugh Gaitskell and, in the mid-sixties, Harold Wilson, increasingly equated welfare with mass consumerism and the promise of technology.[32] Even a leftist critic such as Raymond Williams came to fear that the welfare state had been a Trojan horse through which an American-style materialism had entered the country. According to Osborne, what had finally conquered the nation was not visionary enthusiasm but the grocer's mentality of balanced accounts.

The welfare state—or to use a then popular oxymoron, "People's Capitalism"—so obviously was not the "third way," the humane alternative to communism and capitalism. It may have "put an end to capitalism as we know it," as Bryan Magee phrased it in his 1962 socialist tract *The New Radicalism,* but only so as to inaugurate a new and more subtly dangerous development of it. All over the Western industrial world, free capitalism was making way for organized capitalism, and the welfare state appeared to be the particular form this transition had assumed in Britain. With it came the contradictions and "mystifications" that social philosophers of the Frankfurt School, Habermas and Marcuse in particular, would warn against.[33] An unelected technocracy masked its insidious and intrusive power behind an ideology of service and caring. Economic decisions, some with profound political impact, were declared too technical to be subjected to public debate. This produced a "legitimation crisis," as Habermas calls it, that deepened the public's sense of alienation and political disaffection. Most importantly, the welfare state replaced the "us versus them" dichotomy, the basis of dualistic class antagonisms that had fueled the hunger marches of the 1930s, with a system of interdependence and complicity that blurred exploitative structures and sapped revolutionary ardor.

The stronger beat the pulse of the welfare state's utopian idealism, the more inevitable became the accompanying sense of betrayal. The dominant mood of the time is perhaps best described by Harry Hopkins in his popular social study *The New Look:*

> In the middle-aged, dismay was heightened by poignant memories of the Thirties, suffused with the bright orange promise of Mr. Gollancz's Left Book Club, still lit by the afterglow of the Russian Revolution, and the heroic achievement of "the Socialist Sixth of the World." The young had felt then that they held in their hands the keys to a Better World. All they had to do was to get to the doors and insert them.
>
> But now, alas, the doors were open. And they were seen to be small prosaic doors leading to television sets and washing machines. As for the keys, they were in the care of the economists and technicians.[34]

The good news was that the state was becoming less reactionary but mainly because the people management ideal had proven to be more effective than forceful repression—something industrial psychologists working for large American companies demonstrated daily. What Marcuse called "repressive tolerance"[35] would in the sixties so successfully cut off all means of acting upon social reality in socially constructive ways, that the welfare state gave rise to an unprecedented flowering of narratives that displaced stunted social affects onto an aesthetic level in an attempt to symbolically work through some of the frustrations and anxieties experienced by the disoriented individual. Between the fifties and the seventies, there were comic renditions of frustration as in Kingsley Amis's *Lucky Jim,* parables of powerless defiance as in Alan Sillitoe's *The Loneliness of the Long Distance Runner,* cautionary tales of passion and betrayal as in John Braine's *Room at the Top,* fantasies of total state control and anarchistic revolt as in Anthony Burgess's *A Clockwork Orange,* and tales of socially induced psychosis as in Doris Lessing's *Briefing for a Descent into Hell.* Women, whose condition was most spectacularly improved by Welfare measures, chose this time of increased maternity care to write harrowing stories about the emotional deprivation of single mothers—as, for instance, in Margaret Drabble's *The Millstone,* Shelagh Delaney's *A Taste of Honey,* or Lynn Reid Banks's *The L-Shaped Room.* Apparently, all was not what it seemed; under welfare state conditions, appearances were more than ever deceptive. As Doris Lessing put it in *The Four-Gated City:*

> Great business entities fought: but they worked together behind the scenes, and employed the same firms, or people. The newspapers that remained might call themselves Right, Left, or Liberal, but the people who wrote for them were interchangeable, for these people wrote for them all at the same time, or in rapid succession. The same was true of television: the programmes had on them the labels of different companies, or institutions, but could not be told apart, for the same people organized and produced and wrote and acted in them. The same was true of the theatre. It was true of everything.[36]

THE QUEST FOR CERTAINTY

In this climate Jimmy Porter raises his Messianic cry, "either you're with me or against me" (III, i, 86). Everywhere he finds proof of the workings of a dangerously equalizing force: "even the book reviews seem to be the same as last week's. Different books—same reviews" (I, 10). Differences that once were deemed essential, such as those of culture and language, are rapidly disappearing. He complains that half of the book reviews of the English novel are now written in French. In this cultural mix, national identity is threatened with extinction: "we get our cooking from Paris . . . our politics from Moscow, and our morals from Port Said" (I, 17). Where then is the individual to find the parameters by which to measure personal identity and development? "Always the same. We never seem to get any further, do we? Always the same ritual. Reading the papers, drinking tea, ironing. . . . Our youth is slipping away" (I, 15).

Against the pull of depressing sameness, Jimmy can only pitch his energy and vigilance. He constantly tries to convince himself and others that he is nobody's fool, that he knows what is going on and can see what people are about. He can measure up the Bishop of Bromley, who denies the existence of class distinctions (I, 13); he knows the type represented by Alison's brother, Nigel, the "chinless wonder from Sandhurst" who ought to be given a medal for "Vaguery in the Field" (I, 20); he can see through the "Marquess of Queensberry manner" of Alison's parents and knows "they'll kick you in the groin while you're handing your hat to the maid" (I, 21); he knows that Miss Drury may look like a "mild old gentlewoman" but that she is in fact just "an old robber" (I, 25); and he is not taken in by Helena, that "saint in Dior's clothing" as he knows very well that she's just "a cow" (II, i, 55). The list goes on. In fact, life is as deceptive as a chocolate meringue: "sweet and sticky on the outside, and sink your teeth in it, . . . inside, all white, messy and disgusting" (II, i, 49). Thoroughly sickened by modernity, he dreams of how solid life must have seemed for the affluent classes in the Edwardian era. He has no illusions, though, realizing that the way he pictures Edwardian life is "romantic" and "phoney" (I, 17). When Alison finally leaves him with a letter expressing her "deep, loving need" of him, he positively rages with misery and disgust: "oh, how could she be so bloody wet! Deep loving need! That makes me puke! . . . She couldn't say 'You rotten bastard! I hate your guts, I'm clearing out, and I hope you rot!' No, she has to make a polite, emotional mess out of it!" (II, ii, 72). To avoid such messiness, he insists that people stop "sitting on the fence" and declare their allegiances: "well, she can talk, can't she? You can talk, can't you? You can express an opinion. Or does the White Woman's Burden make it impossible to think?" (I, 11).

Alison, however, has good reason to suspect Jimmy's insistence and to pull back into herself. If Jimmy urges her to respond, it is not so much to hear her thoughts as to take the soundings of his own being. Jimmy, of course, has good reason to suspect Alison's silence and passivity. It is her way of resisting him and of saving her selfhood. Love, for Jimmy, cannot be satisfied with anything less than complete surrender—this perhaps in protest against his mother's deeply ingrained mercantilism. He recounts with much bitterness how his mother came to despise her husband, who was dying of wounds suffered in one of the last "good brave causes" of the century, the Spanish civil war, when she realized "that she had allied herself to a man who seemed to be on the wrong side in all things" (II, i, 57). Jimmy therefore expects from his own wife, as Alison explains to Helena, absolute allegiance "to himself and all the things he believes in, his present and his future, but his past as well. All the people he admires and loves, and has loved. The friends he used to know, people I've never even known—and probably wouldn't have liked. His father, who died years ago. Even the other women he's loved" (II, i, 42). Only a soldier, such as Alison's father, Colonel Redfern, can understand such notions of total, unstinting loyalty that may never expect to be rewarded (II, ii, 65). Jimmy does not promise material comforts and he can hardly be said to offer much emotional support. It is for what he fails to give her that she should love him: "I may be a lost cause," he says, "but I thought if you loved me, it needn't matter" (III, ii, 95).

Such love devours and threatens to annihilate its object. Jimmy is indeed a master devourer who is from the beginning of the play portrayed mainly in terms of consumption. Rather than taking part in the world, he obsessively consumes it in the form of newspapers and magazines. The opening scene shows Jimmy and Cliff sprawled out under newspapers, the room littered with reading matter ranging from the gossip papers to literary magazines. With Jimmy constantly calling out for tea, food, and tobacco, life in the attic room is characterized by an almost fetal dependency in which Alison's role is that of a much harassed mother patiently doing her boys' ironing. Such claustrophobic coziness is to Jimmy both enjoyable and threatening. When the pealing of church bells reminds him of another kind of smothering oppressiveness, this time of religion, he cries out, "Stop ringing those bells! There's somebody going crazy in here" (I, 25).

When tension in that "cozy zoo" mounts too high, Jimmy and Alison become bear and squirrel, executing a dance of mutual admiration on the refrain that "bears and squirrels *are* marvellous" (I, 34). Being "all love, and no brains," as Alison explains to Helena, these creatures can always count on finding each other on the level of "dumb, uncomplicated affection" (II, i, 47). Whenever Jimmy fails to see a "beautiful, great-eyed squirrel" in his Alison, however, he is faced quite simply with a woman, someone as able to consume as to be consumed—equipped, moreover, with the kind of sexual charms that sap the very vitality that makes Jimmy go in search of them: "it is not that she hasn't her own kind of passion," Jimmy grumbles. "She has the passion of a python. She just devours me whole every time, as if I were some over-large rabbit" (I, 37).[37] This accusation sets a pattern for all Jimmy's hateful remarks about women, in that they would make perfect sense if only he were to make them about himself. It is hard to imagine a love more devouring than his own since it leaves virtually no independent existence to his wife, and it is particularly ironic to hear Jimmy, the habitual noisy trespasser on his companions' silent thoughts, complain loudly about "the eternal flaming racket of the female" (I, 25). If he attacks women, it is for what their bodies symbolize to him. Love is nowhere better equated with ingestion and assimilation than in woman's capacity to become pregnant. It is onto his wife's belly, which unbeknown to him carries his own child, that Jimmy projects his fear of entrapment: "that's me. That bulge around her navel—if you're wondering what it is—it's me. Me, buried alive down there, and going mad, smothered in that peaceful looking coil" (I, 38).

All women, in fact, appear to him as mothers, either actual or potential, all too ready to smile down or frown upon their man-child. "Really, Jimmy, you're like a child," Alison pleads when Jimmy becomes positively unbearable—which makes him snap back, "Don't try and patronise me" (I, 24). Mrs. Tanner is the only good mother in the play. She has spent a lifetime scrubbing floors to protect the dreams of son and husband whose visionary enthusiasm is topped only by their complete practical incompetence. With similar self-abnegating devotion, she has set up Jimmy in his sweet stall, an occupation befitting this Peter Pan figure who may hate the smothering yet "peaceful looking coil" in which he has ensconced himself, but who nevertheless does not want to be born into the real world with its necessity for compromise. Mrs. Tanner's death in the middle of the play presents an ill omen for our times: "the injustice of it is almost perfect!" Jimmy says later. "The wrong people going hungry, the wrong people being loved, the wrong people dying!" (III, ii, 94).

The other women simply infuriate Jimmy as they stand between man and the certainties of his desire. Alison's mother, the "female rhino," had to be "pole-axed" before Jimmy could carry off her daughter; Helena's "matriarchal authority" is said to "arouse all the rabble-rousing instincts of his spirit"; and lastly, the silent endurance of Griselda-like Alison inspires her rambunctious husband-boy to unparalleled heights of hysteria. In his feverish mind, Alison becomes the Lady Pusillanimous, "some fleshy Roman matron," on her way to the Games with her poor husband Sextus who, despite his promising name, all too evidently fails to satisfy her in any way. These women, then, are the windmills that send Jimmy back onto his "old charger . . . all tricked out and caparisoned in discredited passions and ideals" for a desperate but rousing joust for manly self-assertion, fought only with the whiplash of his tongue, as here in his attack on Alison's mother:

> I say she ought to be dead. . . . My God, those worms will need a good dose of salts the day they get through her! Oh what a bellyache you've got coming to you, my little wormy ones! Alison's mother is on the way!. . . She will pass away, my friends, leaving a trail of worms gasping for laxatives behind her—from purgatives to purgatory. (II, i, 53)

DOUBLE-BINDING RELATIONSHIPS

Not satisfied with anything less than total allegiance to his being, Jimmy attacks every part of his wife in which he does not recognize himself and is particularly vicious toward people that could reasonably be expected to lay some other claim on her, Alison's family, for instance, and Helena, a friend of hers of whom he disapproves. Under such conditions, betrayal becomes the natural corollary of love, a belief that Osborne found confirmed in the story of Judas that he always hoped to turn into a play. It was never written, but its dramatic possibilities and relevance to Osborne's thinking are obvious since, apart from featuring a love kiss that spells betrayal, it equates love with assimilation or devouring (Judas is present at the Last Supper when Jesus offers his body and blood to his disciples) and assimilation, in turn, with betrayal (in John 13:27, it is Christ's offer of his body that effectively turns Judas into a traitor). Jimmy's conviction that he is being betrayed makes him search his wife's belongings "to see if there is something of me somewhere, a reference to me" (I, 36). He furiously rifles her handbag ("I want to know if I'm being betrayed" (I, 36)) and reads her letters in search of himself: "she writes long letters back to Mummy, and never mentions me at all, because I'm just a dirty word to her too" (I, 36–37).

Hurt by her husband's relentless aggression, Alison retreats further into herself. Osborne claimed to have created the role of Alison as "a study of the tyranny of negation," adding, "Alison's brutal power lay in the puny crackle of her iron." Osborne might have thought of Strindberg's *The Stronger,* a play in which a bold character loses her footing and finally stumbles because the woman she addresses maintains an icy silence. But *Look Back in Anger* is much more attentive to reciprocity, to ways in which both characters stimulate each other to respond in ways they both dislike. "That girl there can twist your arm off with her silence," Jimmy cries, doubling his efforts to make her express an opinion and of course driving her ever further away from him. Cliff, who refers to himself as a "no-man's land" in this ongoing battle, plays an active role in keeping the couple together. "If I hadn't been here," he says, "everything would have been over between these long ago" (II, i, 60). Ironically, that nothing is ever truly over is the most maddening feature of this relationship. The few times Alison braves a response, it is met with anger or derision. She cannot even signal her agreement, as she knows Jimmy will think she is simply trying to appease him. "I knew just what he meant," Alison says to Cliff. "I suppose it would have been easy to say, 'Yes, darling, I know just what you mean. . . . It's those easy things that seem to be so impossible with us" (I, 28).

The couple is in fact engaged in one of those double-binding relationships where, to put it plainly, you are damned if you do and damned if you don't— the kind of conflict without solution and without clear winners or losers that politically inspired anti-psychiatrists in the sixties singled out as the private expression of the prevailing social condition of futility and helplessness.[38] Technological society, R.D. Laing claimed in his 1967 tract *The Politics of Experience,* resembles a servomechanism—an automatic, autonomous device, powerfully geared toward maintaining an inner equilibrium. He referred to it as a "captivity that man has somehow imposed upon himself."[39] In *Knots,* a booklet of playful patterns of maddening yet beautiful complexity, he demonstrated the many ways in which human interaction can acquire the qualities of such a homeostatic mechanism, often violent when experienced from within, from an individual participant's point of view, yet from without perfectly and exasperatingly stable. In the sixties, such relationships would come to symbolize the ways in which the welfare state had perfected its subtle, treacherous forms of control. In *Look Back in Anger,* the double-binding circle of anger and despair not only produces a similar sense of prevailing futility and helplessness but also serves as an ironic commentary on the origin and limits of Jimmy's quest for certainty.

THE END OF ALL CERTAINTIES

In fact, while insisting on the importance of drawing clear boundaries, Jimmy simultaneously emphasizes its impossibility because life, he says, is irrevocably messy. One of his many songs, he says, starts off with "there are no dry cleaners in Cambodia" (III, i, 50), and he proclaims that love "takes muscle and guts": "and if you can't bear the thought . . . of messing up your nice, clean soul, . . . you'd better give up the whole idea of life, and become a saint. . . . Because you'll never make it as a human being" (III, ii, 93–94). If Helena finally leaves, while confessing her enduring love for Jimmy, it is because she is unable to live up to that reality: she has never been able to forget the "book of rules" and clings to her belief in "right and wrong" and consequently "can't take part—in all this suffering" any longer (III, ii, 88, 89, 93).

Such "timidity of mind," however, is not the right attitude, the play asserts. The opposite of pusillanimity and a cure for the nation as a whole, we learn from *Look Back in Anger,* is enthusiasm. "Oh heavens, how I long for a little ordinary human enthusiasm," Jimmy sighs. "I want to hear a warm, thrilling voice cry out Hallelujah! . . . Hallelujah! I'm alive!" (I, 15). And he will indeed hear a voice cry out—not in joy, though, but in pain. It will be that of his wife Alison, who, driven to distraction by his incessant taunts, will hurl a cup onto the floor and beg Jimmy for a moment of peace. He will not let her have it until, as he says, a child will grow in her and die so that she herself may be born as a true human being, someone as "corrupt and futile" as himself, someone he can love in the only way he values, as a "lost cause" (I, 37).

When that wish turns out to have been a prophecy, and Alison returns to him humbled and defeated, Jimmy abandons his usual masculine bravura. He is unable to "splash about" in Alison's tears, as in one vicious moment he had said he would. He no longer insists on certainties and confesses to his self-doubts: "was I really wrong to believe that there's a—a kind of—burning virility of mind and spirit that looks for something as powerful as itself?" The question remains tellingly unanswered, but it at least invites us to take a closer look at the attributes of Jimmy's virility. The bear, his alter-ego, is at once a symbol of masculine self-sufficiency ("There's no warm pack, no herd to comfort him" (III, ii, 94)) and, being a child's toy, of infantile dependence. The same can of course be said of the trumpet with which Jimmy vents his masculine energy, directing it mainly against Helena, in what she calls "an oddly exciting" way (II, i, 41). On women, however, rests the burden of reading the signs in a way congruent with Jimmy's desire for certainty. Alison fell in love because, unlike other women, she did not feel "contempt" for that "odd creature" that arrived at the party on a bike, having oil splattered "all over his dinner jacket" but saw instead "a knight in shining armour" (II, i, 45). Now, at the end of the play, when Alison comes back defeated and in pain, it is again from her that he expects reassurance: "that voice that cries out doesn't *have* to be a weakling's, does it?" (III, ii, 94).

It is, in fact, a weakling's voice, the play concludes. The couple reverts to their private fantasy world of bears and squirrels, but rather than just admiring each other's strength or beauty, these furry creatures now admit to being in need of each other's constant support: the squirrel will help maintain the bear's fur and claws just as the bear will look out for his "none too bright" squirrel. Now finally, the man who so vehemently derided the prevalent "timidity of mind" acknowledges that he and his wife are both "very timid little animals" afraid of the "cruel steel traps" that lie everywhere around (III, ii, 96). As Matt Wolf puts it perceptively: "a harrowing play, famed for making an adult of the British stage, turns out to be about two very scared, overgrown children."[40]

What does the play then tell us? Feeling and reason, enthusiasm and pusillanimity, masculine and feminine, socialism and conservatism require the tension of constant vigilance and expenditure of anger to be kept apart. Again and again, the play demonstrates how extremes mutually define one another—how, for instance, enthusiasm provokes timidity of mind and vice versa. Jimmy's quest for certainty is an emotional necessity, a response to the threat of sameness, a threat heightened by social and political conditions typical of the welfare state. Structurally and conceptually, though, the play assumes the fundamental interconnectedness of reality that makes such a certainty a practical impossibility. Jimmy's vituperative vitality, in other words, amounts to a sort of Grand Refusal, all the more admirable precisely because it is based not on certainty but on the knowledge of its own futility.

It can hardly be expected that an Osbornian play would balance all its accounts so neatly, though it certainly does its very best to give that impression. The sentimentality of the closing scene, what Kenneth Tynan referred to as the "painful whimsey" of the bear-squirrel game, may seduce the viewer into overlooking the simple fact that at least one trap has been permanently removed for Jimmy. Alison has not only lost her child, thereby fulfilling Jimmy's ill-conceived wish, but also, in excess of all plot requirements, the ability to ever become a mother again. The final words of the play, "Oh, poor, poor bears!" said by Alison as she tenderly embraces Jimmy, are not meant to sound ironic, but, of course, should to anyone who were to remember that Alison has been hurt far more than Jimmy by the steel trap of life. This is all too clearly not what the play wants us to do: "it was my child too, you know," Jimmy reminds Helena. "But . . . it isn't my first loss" (III, ii, 92). The play equates Alison's loss of her child and womb with Jimmy's of his father at the age of ten, when he learned all about "love . . . betrayal . . . and death" (II, i, 58). So a play that started by calling for a celebration of life in the end stands revealed not just as a humble acceptance of the complexity of existence but as a ritual exorcism of female fertility and motherhood.

APPENDIX

The predominance of stage directions is nowhere more striking than in the second half of Act Two, Scene One, and it is only by omitting the dialogue that one realizes to what extent the play's action consists almost entirely of emotional affects—in other words of movement, rhythm, and intonation conveyed through stage directions. Notice the alternation of dilating and contracting movements, of increases and decreases in rhythm and emotional pitch. Printed in bold are punctuating moments in Jimmy's mood swings.

Cliff and Helena carry on with their meal. [Jimmy] starts eating. The silent hostility of the two women has set him off on the scent, and he looks quite cheerful, although the occasional, thick edge of his voice belies it. [He] savour[s] every word [and] offer[s] [the] teapot sweetly to Helena. He smiles, and pours out a cup for her.

[He] turn[s] to Alison suddenly. He turns very deliberately [to Helena], delighted that she should rise to the bait so soon—**he's scarcely in his stride yet.** [He] turn[s] [back] to Alison. A slight pause as his delight catches up with him. **He roars with laughter.** He returns to his meal, but his curiosity about Alison's preparations at the mirror won't be denied any longer. He turns round casually, and speaks to her.

He crosses to the table, and sits down C. He leans forward, and addresses her again. He has been prepared for some plot, but he is genuinely surprised by [her reply] as Cliff was a few minutes earlier.

Silence. **His rage mounting within.**

[Alison] recognising an onslaught on the way, starts to panic. The wild note in her voice has re-assured him. **His anger cools and hardens.** His voice is quite calm when he speaks. He clutches wildly for something to shock Helena with. **[He] kicks [the] cistern. Sits on it, beats [it] like bongo drums.** [He is] capable of anything now. Cliff and Helena look at Alison tensely, but she just gazes at her plate.

Cliff gets up quickly, and takes his arm. Jimmy pushes him back savagely, and [Cliff] sits down helplessly, turning his head away on to his hand. [Jimmy] brakes for a fresh spurt later. **He's saving his strength for the knock-out.**

[He speaks] in what he intends to be a comic declamatory voice. He smiles down at Alison, but still she hasn't broken. Cliff won't look at them. Only Helena looks at him. Denied the other two, he addresses her. He can feel her struggling on the end of his line, and he looks at her rather absently. [Helena] think[s] patient reasonableness may be worth a try. [Alison] turn[s] her face away L. He looks at her in surprise, but he turns back to Helena. Alison can have her turn again later. [Alison] start[s] to break. [She] put[s] her hands over her ears.

He crosses down to the armchair, and seats himself on the back of it. He addresses Helena's back. The comedy of this strikes him at once, and he laughs. [He] com[es] out of his remembrance suddenly [and addresses] Alison. **He can smell blood again, and he goes on calmly, cheerfully.** [He speaks] to Alison, [. . .] articulating with care.

[He addresses] Cliff [and] rises. His imagination is racing, and the words pour out.

[He] moves up L., facing them, [then] crosses to above table. He moves round the table, back to his chair R. He leans across the table at [Helena]. He waits for her to reply.

[Helena replies] quite calmly. They look into each other's eyes across the table. He moves slowly up, above Cliff, until he is beside her. She makes a move to rise [but] remains seated, and looks up at him. [Helena replies in a voice] like ice. He looks down at her, a grin smouldering round his mouth. [He] bring[s] his face close to hers [and speaks] gently. His grin widens.

His good humour of a moment ago deserts him, as he begins to remember. He moves R. [and] turns to the window. [He] look[s] out. He moves up C. again [and speaks] with a kind of appeal in his voice. He moves L., behind the armchair. He leans forward on the back of the armchair [then] moves around the chair [and] sits. They all sit silently. Presently, Helena rises. Alison nods. [Helena] crosses to door.

A slight pause.

[Jimmy] not looking at [Alison], almost whisper[s]. Her back stiffens. **His axe-swinging bravado has vanished, and his voice crumples in disabled rage. Alison suddenly takes hold of her cup, and hurls it on the floor. He's drawn blood at last.** She looks down at the pieces on the floor, and then at him. Then she crosses, R., takes out a dress on a hanger, and slips it on. As she is zipping up the side, she feels giddy, and she has to lean against the wardrobe for support. She closes her eyes [and speaks] softly. [Jimmy is] hardly able to get his words out. [Alison] crosses to the bed to put on her shoes. Cliff gets up from the table, and sits in the armchair R. He picks up a paper, and looks at that. **Jimmy has recovered slightly, and manages to sound almost detached.** He gets up and faces Cliff, who doesn't look up from his paper. But inspiration has deserted him by now.

Cliff is still looking down at his paper. [Jimmy] moves up C., watching her look for her gloves. Helena enters, carrying two prayer books [and] after a moment [starts to speak]. [Jimmy] turn[s] [and] goes out. [Helena] nods [and] turn[s] on Cliff. [He] look[s] up slowly. He looks at her steadily, and adds simply [a few words]. But she goes on simply to avoid his reply.

[Helena is] in command now [while] Alison [is] numbed and vague by now. Helena looks at her, and realizes quickly that everything now will have to depend on her own authority. She tries to explain patiently. [Helena speaks] very gently. [Alison] pause[s]. [Helena] [is] relieved, saying the word almost with difficulty. [Alison] puts down one of the prayer books on the table.

Enter Jimmy. He comes down C., between the two women. Jimmy [addresses] Alison. [There is a] slight pause. Jimmy sits on the bed [and] rubb[s] his fist over his face.

He crosses to the door, and stops. Helena looks quickly at Alison. Cliff exit[s].

[Jimmy] looks at [Alison]. She is standing by the dressing table, her back to him. She kneels down, and hands [his shoes] to him. [He] look[s] down at his feet [and] shrugs. He looks into her eyes, but she turns away, and stands up. Outside, the church bells start ringing. Helena moves up to the door, and waits watching them closely. Alison stands quite still, **Jimmy's eyes burning into her.** Then, she crosses in front of him to the table where she picks up the prayer book, her back to him. She wavers, and seems about to say something, but turns upstage instead, and walks quickly to the door. [Alison] [is] hardly audible. She goes out, Helena following. **Jimmy gets up, looks about him, unbelievingly**, and leans against the chest of drawers. The teddy bear is close to his face, and he picks it up gently, looks at it quickly, and throws it downstage. It hits the floor with a thud, and it makes a rattling, groaning sound—as guaranteed in the advertisement. **Jimmy falls forward on to the bed, his face buried in the covers.**

CHAPTER 4

The Entertainer (1957)
The Use of Despair

> *What's the use of despair,*
> *If they call you a square?*
>
> —ARCHIE, *THE ENTERTAINER*

RECEPTION

In the late fifties and early sixties, the world of theatre and literature was in upheaval, and names were made and unmade with astonishing rapidity. Shelagh Delaney and Colin Wilson would come and go, but Osborne, the man who had spearheaded that upheaval with *Look Back in Anger*, managed to stay. He reacted promptly to media attention, retaining public prominence by personal eccentricity and hard work. *The Entertainer* (1957) proved yet another tremendous box-office success, not the least because Sir Laurence Olivier played the bravely pathetic music-hall artist Archie Rice.

The cooperation between Britain's most famous and best established actor and its most angry young son was for many reviewers the most newsworthy feature of the play. Olivier, it was reported, had been intrigued rather than impressed by *Look Back in Anger,* but Arthur Miller, who had taken him to see it, understood its importance and advised Olivier to act in the next Osborne play.[1] Olivier's willingness, even insistence, to play "with a lot of newcomers" was widely debated. The *Daily Mail* reported that he had turned down a Hollywood fee of £100,000 in order to slum at the Royal Court Theatre's going rate of less than £50 a week.[2] His fans shuddered at the thought of the god descending from his pedestal to play the part of a failure, written by someone who, despite his recent *succès de scandale,* seemed all too uncomfortably close to failure himself. They were convinced that what had prompted Olivier to accept the role was not Osborne's talent but Olivier's fear of being left behind by recent developments in theatrical taste and fashion. "Fear is the only rational explanation for a great and sensitive actor co-operating in his own belittle-ment," Derek Monsey thought.[3]

Even without Olivier, the play was bound to have drawn attention. The symbolic overtones of character, conflict, and setting resonated strongly in the then current atmosphere of anxiety about national identity. By the end of October 1956, Britain and France had embarked on an ill-fated military campaign against Egypt to recapture the recently nationalized Suez canal and to wrest power away from Egypt's militant leader Colonel Nasser. It was generally understood that this was Britain's desperate attempt to reassert its international prestige and, at first, it indeed quickened the heartbeat of many a frustrated patriot. "Let the crybabies howl! It's GREAT Britain again," ran a newspaper headline. People wrote letters to the papers, saying "how good it is to hear the British Lion's roar ...'; but when the superpowers called Britain to order and the military campaign failed, public humiliation fol-lowed: "The truth has to be faced now. The 'Lion's Roar' that had proved so gratifying to the reader of the *Daily Telegraph* was all too plainly that poor beast's last!"[4] Barely six months later, one character in Osborne's *The Enter-tainer* would express a bafflement at Britain's position in the world that many shared: "What d'you make of all this business out in the Middle East? People seem to be able to do what they like with us. Just what they like. I don't understand it. I really don't" (i, 17).

Before the Suez crisis, there had been other attempts to bolster national pride. The coronation ceremonies of Elizabeth II in 1953 evoked dreams of past glory and vain hopes for a new Elizabethan Age. Around the same time, national schemes for moral improvement were promoted by traditionalists in the Conservative Party such as Lord Hailsham. Without a concomitant sense of national achievement, however, all this was bound to fail. In his contribu-tion to Tom Maschler's *Declaration,* a collection of essays by "angry young" writers, Osborne declared that "my objection to the Royalty symbol is that it is dead; it is the gold filling in a mouthful of decay."[5] Now, in *The Entertainer,* he had one character similarly question whether the monarchy could still func-tion as a symbol sufficiently powerful to redeem people's suffering: "what's it all in aid of—is it really just for the sake of a gloved hand waving at you from a golden coach?" (x,77).

The combination of Osborne's notoriety and Olivier's fame proved irre-sistible. When the play premiered at the Royal Court Theatre on 10 April 1957, it was "booked out for the entire season."[6] On 10 September, it moved on to the music-hall size Palace Theatre, where it was immediately reported to be the "biggest money-spinner for advance booking that the Palace has had for years for a non-musical play."[7] After touring the provinces, it returned for another short spell to London's West End, before transferring to Broadway. "This was the 'Establishment's first bow to the 'angries,'" Kenneth Tynan asserted. "It meant that they had officially arrived."[8]

If that is truly so, then official recognition came at a high price. A surprising number of critics could not abide the idea that an upstart playwright could have spoken for the nation and tried to wrest from Osborne the laurels of his success. *The Entertainer,* they said, had little intrinsic value and was merely a vehicle for an actor. In fact, it was so poorly written, so lacking in discipline and rigor, that it would never have survived without Laurence Olivier's superb interpretation. They pointed out—and, as it happens, with good reason—that the last two scenes seemed too hastily written or unfinished. The dialogue nearing the end of the play indeed sounds stilted, and characters such as Graham and the protagonist's brother, Billy, who make their first appearance then, are types rather than complex human beings. A more generous assessment, however, would have conceded that this is exactly what Osborne had meant them to be, but the critics were not in the mood for generosity. They went so far as to dislike what is in fact the most interesting feature of the play, its rapid transitions between domestic and music hall scenes, made possible by having them both share the same set.[9] While fluid in terms of feeling and motion, such transitions may indeed be rather abrupt in terms of causal logic. This did not escape the critics' attention. While conceding that Osborne had mastered the language of despair, they criticized him for not sufficiently explaining and motivating action.[10] Some had in fact nothing good to say about the play and thought even the emotions were mismanaged: "Consider *The Entertainer* dispassionately," the *Birmingham Post* said, "and you will find that it is false, sentimental, and cheap."[11] All this could only have one effect: the darker was the critic's view of Osborne's contribution, the brighter shone Olivier's star.

Osborne had been upstaged by his principal actor. At a celebration after the first performance, Olivier gave the curtain speech, reminiscing about the history of the Royal Court Theatre where he first played in 1928. He then danced across the stage with his wife Vivien Leigh.[12] In the papers, brief mention goes to the "beaming" twenty-seven year old author, who is overheard murmuring "it's a dream."[13] Only one reviewer states that at the première the audience also clamored for John Osborne.[14] All in all, *The Entertainer* was not Osborne's but "Sir Laurence Olivier's New Triumph," as a headline read in the *Manchester Guardian.*[15] When the play later appeared in print, one reviewer expressed astonishment at discovering that Laurence Olivier had not been improvising but had used Osborne's lines.[16]

By linking his fame to that of *The Entertainer,* Olivier bestowed on the play the kiss of death.[17] In fact, in 1989, *The Entertainer* became, so to speak, his tombstone, Archie's signature line "Why should I care" being used in the news to announce the great actor's death.[18] Before and after, whenever *The Entertainer* was revived, with other actors stepping into Olivier's shoes, attention focused less on the play's intrinsic value than on the comparative merits of its leading actor. Two revivals stand out prominently: the 1974 production at the Greenwich Theatre, directed by John Osborne himself, featuring Max Wall in the principal role, and the 1993 BBC-2, televised performance, directed by Nicholas Renton, with Michael Gambon as Archie. The latter may have been the best, though as adaptation rather than revival. By 1974, the play's reputation as a famous "oldie," enhanced by Tony Richardson's 1960 screen version with Olivier and most of the original cast, had weakened its message of defiance. It was a venerable fossil—as much so, in fact, as its new principal actor, Max Wall, one of the last remaining genuine music-hall artists. Even while deploring the play's cult aspect, critic Ronald Bryden, like so many others, could not but marvel at its stubborn power. His verdict today still stands: "In spite of its period flaws and fundamental uncertainties, *The Entertainer* set out to mirror post-imperial Britain as a whole and succeeded in doing so, as much by its internal contradictions as by its aggressively stated, slightly overstated protestations."[19] These contradictions are the subject of the present analysis, but first let us raise the curtain on the play itself.

CHARACTERS

Foreign sounds fill the auditorium; people are fighting; a woman screams: a purely auditory scene opens the play. This violent and alien communality contrasts sharply with the dignified loneliness of the figure that now appears and listens. First to take center stage is not Archie, the play's protagonist, but his seventy-year old father, Billy. In many ways, Billy is an endearing figure, and it is not surprising that Laurence Olivier asked for the role of Billy before agreeing to play the bumbling vaudeville actor Archie. Billy represents old England, proud of its independent ways and leading position in the world, but also inured to criticism and therefore rather self-satisfied. The first thing Billy does is to clamor for silence—and he does so in an imposing voice, trained by a long career in the music hall. The response is immediate, delivered with Irish flair and temper: "Why don't you shut your great big old gob, you poor, bloody old fool!" (i, 12). Billy, imperturbable, sings a hymn, creating an island of Englishness in a sea of foreignness. In these surroundings, his solitary dignity may be pathetic yet is not without a certain charm.

The setting, a house in a "large coastal resort," alludes to past prosperity and present decline. It is "one of those tall ugly monuments" to the past that exudes an air of elegiac poetry. Built "by a prosperous business man at the beginning of the century," it has long lost its former importance and centrality. Though not too far from the front, the promenade along the sea shore, it is nevertheless situated in a place where tourists never venture. Its neighborhood can only be defined in terms of lack, of what it is not, no longer, or just barely: "It is not residential, it is hardly industrial. It is full of dirty blank spaces, high black walls, a gas holder, a tall chimney, a main road that shakes with dust and lorries" (11). This is an England we have come to know from Woodfall productions. The drabness of these surroundings reflects not only the emotional and financial bankruptcy of the people who live there but of the country as a whole.

The domestic scenes involve three generations. The Edwardian past, a time of certainties, is represented by Billy; the shoddy present, with its undignified scramble for survival, by Archie and Phoebe; the uncertain future, by their children Mick, Frank, and Jean. The heavy toll the present exacts is nowhere more evident than in the suffering of Archie's wife, Phoebe. When not already bogged down in alcoholic stupor, Phoebe hides in the darkness of a movie theatre, attempting to escape the unbearable company of her self-absorbed father-in-law and the equally unbearable absence of her unfaithful husband. She often stays to watch the beginning of the main show over again, not because she loves the movie, the title or actors of which she rarely recalls, but to muster the necessary strength to face the light of reality. Even this no longer alleviates her suffering. Her mood veering constantly between extremes of happy excitement and despair, she cannot escape the feeling that everything in life is going downhill, the gin and the movies included. Still, she clings to Archie, insisting until the end that "he's always been good to me. Whatever he may have done. Always" (x, 78). For Archie, she is a "poor, pathetic old thing." Pity and guilt dominate his feelings for her, prompting him to prove himself once and for all free of such painful emotions. "She's getting old," he says to his family in her presence," and she's worried about who's going to keep her when she can't work any longer. She's afraid of ending up in a long box in somebody else's front room in Gateshead, or was it West Hartlepool?" (vi, 54–55).

In their separate ways, all of these characters have reason to fear what fate has in store for them. Each of the three children personifies a different attitude toward the present and a different road toward the future. Mick is the dutiful son who, like Archie's successful brother, does what is demanded of him. The problems in the Middle East, where he is taken hostage while fulfilling his national service, symbolize England's changing international status. The fact that Mick is killed unheroically on the eve of his liberation intimates that traditional forms of patriotism have lost their redemptive power. His brother Frank is the neurotic one, the weakling, who on occasion shows surprising mettle, as when his refusal to serve in the army lands him in prison. Usually, he shuns conflict and commitment. Frank has nothing to contribute; he feels no loyalty toward his country and is intent on emigrating to Canada. Jean is Archie's daughter, not Phoebe's—as she is all too often told. She is a determined, intelligent, angry young woman who never acts without examining the moral consequences of her action and then only when prompted by justified rage over loss of values and the rule of expediency. At the beginning of the play, the celebration and quarrels that greet her unexpected homecoming introduce the spectator to the various sources of the family's despair, and the rest of the play is concerned with sorting out different responses to the solid weight of the past, the drab reality of the present, and the fear of the future.

CONFLICTS

Three interrelated conflicts organize the action. Jean has returned home because she is thinking of breaking off her engagement with Graham, a young man with, as she has only recently realized, a temperament and beliefs radically different from her own. Increasingly impatient with political defeatism, Jean has become actively involved in local programs for social improvement and in the Campaign for Nuclear Disarmament. In contrast to that troubled, searching character, Graham seems to have been born ready-made, in a three-piece suit with attaché case in hand. "There are plenty of these around," Osborne tells us, "well dressed, assured, well educated, their emotional and imaginative capacity so limited it is practically negligible. They have an all-defying inability to associate themselves with anyone in circumstances even slightly dissimilar to their own" (xii, 83). So these two characters present opposing attitudes toward present reality. Jean is what Archie calls a "sentimentalist," though one desperately seeking a way out of her pain through political resolve and action. Graham, on the other hand, suffers from not much more than greedy and confident expectation of future comfort and power. Two deaths and several liquor-ridden nights later, Jean will radically break with Graham and with what he calls the "better, more worthwhile things in life" and turn resolutely toward the people with whom he claims she has nothing in common (xii, 83–84).

In the meantime, a telegram has revealed the second conflict, the news that Sergeant Mick has been taken prisoner. Hopes for a settlement and the soldier's heroic return are confirmed by the papers, and the family already basks in their boy's fame; but as the tension of anxious anticipation mounts, the family's internal dissensions come to the fore. Phoebe is fond but also distrustful of Jean, annoyed at being pitied by the daughter of a woman whose place she has taken. Archie is all on his own, brooding over some new and desperate scheme to ensure his survival. Billy increasingly hides behind his old certainties, and Jean is more and more distraught at the family's self-preoccupation.

Though a mixture of love, compassion, guilt, and duty still holds the family together, each of its members is locked in his or her own troubles and eager to find a way out for "good old number one." Billy's way of pursuing his own little business amid all the surrounding mayhem reveals its less endearing side when Phoebe discovers he has taken a bite out of the welcoming cake that in the kitchen is awaiting Mick's return. Billy, in other words, may proudly proclaim his belief in the family's ability to form a mutually supportive front against the world, but his behavior shows that he is first of all concerned with his own needs. So Phoebe has good reason to inveigh against Billy for being such a "bloody *greedy* old pig" (vi, 57). When others stand by, awed at an anger that far exceeds its object, it is because they sense the depth of her frustration and suffering. Though Phoebe may be miserable, she clings desperately to the last vestiges of her self-respect, even if that means forcefully, meanly, and repeatedly reminding her father-in-law and stepdaughter of their dependent positions in the family.

Jean, in contrast, seems very much the reasonable one. She is patient, and generous—yet the play does not entirely embrace her point of view. It is true that she is to be commended for expressing her honest concern about the state of the nation and Phoebe's well-being, and for doing so not only in words but in action. She marches in demonstrations and, when offered the opportunity of a comfortable marriage or a business career overseas, she decides to stay and look after Phoebe. Yet, as Frank points out, Jean's judgment of others is sometimes too swift and radical and, as Archie and Phoebe suspect, to some extent inspired by a belief in her own moral superiority. You're better than a "dose of salts," Archie retorts mockingly, accusing her of striving not so much for others' happiness as for her own "inner cleanliness" (x, 82). What she is lacking, he claims, is the humility he wears so prominently on his own sleeve: "I *am* humble! I am very humble, in fact. I still have a little dried pea of humility rattling around inside me. I don't think *you* have" (x, 77).

Even so, Jean knows her father as well as he knows her. Archie may be humble; he is also sly. He is the kind of man who tells himself he "doesn't feel a thing" in order to do the things he should not be doing and who does them knowing all too well that in the long run they will not make the least difference: his show will not be a success, he will not be making it great. In the meantime, he would have betrayed Phoebe, Billy, and Jean—the remaining members of the little community of wash-outs that gives sense to his being. It is not true that Archie "doesn't feel a thing." To betray so callously what one loves so dearly requires much self-loathing; but one must love one's self-loathing to turn such betrayal into the splendid yet miserable act of defiance that is called "detachment," the fierce act of will through which Archie becomes the fascinated observer of his own drama. Jean is too intelligent not to realize that Archie's all too ready admission that he lacks feelings is a way of forestalling well-deserved rebuke, and that by disarmingly agreeing with her that he is a "bastard on wheels" he absolves himself of the need to abandon his selfish pursuits (x, 76).

In short, each of these characters may be socio-politically typical yet assumes nonetheless a measure of specificity by being seen through his or her own eyes as well as through the eyes of others. Specificity of character, in other words, cannot be accurately defined: a difference rather than an essence, it is the fiction through which an empathizing spectator accounts for a discrepancy between word and action, potentiality and actuality. A spectator who in this way constructs a character's uniqueness neither condemns nor justifies, but rather probes the depths of a character's humanity which, in the final instance, only reflect the intensity of the spectator's empathetic involvement. One truth Osborne thereby holds as unassailable, namely that as shabby as these characters may be, they are preferable to those well-adjusted citizens, Jean's successful fiancé and Archie's even more successful older brother.

The sudden news of Mick's murder plunges the family in an angry grief that further strains the bonds of allegiance that holds them together. "Those playing fields of Eton / Have really got us beaten" Frank sings in mourning (ix, 74). Mick's death does not so much invalidate the love of one's country ("But ain't no use agrievin' / 'Cos it's Britain we believe in" is only partially ironic) as destroy whatever little trust these people may still have had invested in their leaders, in the Establishment. Emigration is for Frank the only remaining alternative. By then, the third conflict has been set in motion. Archie, who has unwisely invested money in a road show, is trying to marry a rich, young, stage-struck girl, a "professional virgin," as Jean calls her, "Miss Nothing of 1957" (x, 80). When that fails, because Billy reveals his son's married state to the girl's family, Archie commits a final act of betrayal, blackmailing his old father into making a come-back that proves fatal to his already poor health. Even then, Archie, the crafty fox, is offered an escape. Older brother Billy promises to pay his debts in return for his prompt emigration. But Archie stays on and allows the tax man his triumph: after twenty years of successful tax evasion, Archie is finally hauled off to prison.

PAST GLORY, PRESENT PAIN

As is the case with the deceptively nostalgic *Look Back in Anger, The Entertainer* offers a critique of the present from a view of the past that in turn is heavily colored by that present. In other words, neither the present nor the past is portrayed objectively but, as is the case with the characters in the play, each is represented in the form of a mutually reflecting fiction. So, it is because the present is racked by domestic and international tensions that Billy can come to represent the idea of a country once united and at peace with itself. In turn, it is this fiction of the fullness of the past that ends up reinforcing the belief in history as an inexorable process of loss. When Billy speaks, Osborne explains, "it is with a dignified Edwardian diction—a kind of repudiation of both Oxford and cockney that still rhymes 'cross' with 'force,' and yet manages to avoid being exactly upper class or effete. Indeed, it is not an accent of class but of period. One does not hear it often now" (i, 13). Far from implying an erasure of difference, Billy's apparent classlessness, the way he combines dignity with folksiness, presupposes a trusting reliance on people's ability to make fine distinctions of accent and demeanor. It is therefore the loss of distinctions that Billy most regrets. In the past, he recalls, women were still women: "They were graceful, they had mystery and dignity. Why when a woman got out of a cab, she descended. Descended. And you put your hand out to her smartly to help her down" (v, 33). In fact, you called them "Ladies, and you took off your hat before you dared speak to them. Now! Why, half the time you can't tell the women from the men. Not from the back. And even at the front you have to take a good look, sometimes" (i, 18).

In the fifties, this socially validated, cohesive system of difference made way for a bewildering cultural jumble, as an influx of commonwealth immigrants supplemented the already established contingent of European war refugees. Foreigners ("Bloody Poles and Irish!" (i, 13)) have nestled in the once venerable houses of England's former bourgeoisie, piercing the peace with their strange sounds. A "black fellow" has settled down in Mick's vacant room (i, 16). These are the strange spoils of war—at least, such is the bitter opinion of common people who see their neighborhoods change beyond recognition. Archie reports that a woman on the bus attacked two colored boys with her umbrella, crying "I lost two boys in the war for the likes of you!" (i, 35). Such changes encroach upon Billy's universe, rendering ridiculous his careful balancing act between vulgarity and taste. The sound of the past, as we hear it in Billy's solemn hymn singing, risks being drowned in the noise of modernity, represented on stage by modern music, "the latest, the loudest, the worst" (i, 11). "Rock of Ages cleft for me / Let me hide myself in thee" is not without good reason Billy's preferred hymn. From the imagined certainties of the past, Billy can only condemn or pity the present: "I feel sorry for you people. You don't know what it's really like. You haven't lived, most of you. You've never known what it was like, you're all miserable really. You don't know what life can be like" (i, 23).

Billy had the good fortune of retiring from the music hall before it quite ceased to be the genuinely popular and vital form of entertainment it supposedly once was. Granted, the music hall had always been on the verge of toppling into vulgarity, but that was the very reason why the entertainer had to walk a fine line between self-respecting dignity and hearty folksiness. The music hall, however, has not been able to maintain that delicate position and has slid downward into the lower type of burlesque. Billy's son, Archie, is sliding down with it. It is the nudes that draw the audience now, not the gags. Archie's only role is to do the "bits" in between chorus numbers—and even then he is barely tolerated by an impatient or bored public. He tries to survive by giving the audience what they want, female impersonators, rock 'n roll; but rather than launching the fads, Archie keeps running behind them and so always ends up losing (vi, 47). In his latest venture, he attempts to surf the downward wave by investing money in a road show with nudes; but Archie has no business sense, and that venture too is doomed to fail (i, 18). The inevitability of failure is Archie's only remaining certainty, and so his life consists of continuous compromise and humiliation, a wild scampering for survival. No "Rock of Ages" for Archie, but only the Rockliffe, a pub where he seeks the company of young women, would-be actresses, chorus girls, and nudes in cabarets (i, 18). Billy calls it the "meat-market."

In that world, money is not the great equalizer, the font of opportunity, but the great homogenizer, the one value that makes all others superfluous. On Archie's stage, Britannia has become a nude in a helmet; and patriotism, a snarl of derision:

Those bits of red still on the map
We won't give up without a scrap.
What we've got left back
We'll keep—and blow you, Jack! (iv, 33)

Under such circumstances, patriotism no longer provides a way of transcending the personal for the communal but serves as yet another excuse for gratifying egotistic needs. When Archie sings "we're all out for good old number one," he means both "good old England" and everyone's own little person, the distinction having become immaterial. The idea promoted by the welfare state, of a "good old England" as a community of mutually supportive citizens, meets only with distrust. "I don't want no drab equality," Archie, the master tax-evader, states in a song that expresses dismay at seeing the National Health spend tax money on the free dispensation of wigs and spectacles (iv, 32).

Granted, Archie sings all this without heart, without conviction, giving his audience what they want to hear. They can hardly be blamed for distrusting the welfare state because, in their eyes, it offers a too abstract view of people's desires and needs. They want their England smaller so that they can keep track of who gets what from whom and why. To be assured of help in time of need is one thing; to be deprived of the power that a little charity bestows upon the giver is quite another. It is not the welfare state's generosity they resent, but its blindness. A charity proportionate to the recipient's moral value would be more acceptable to them—provided, of course, that welfare would look at the world through their own discriminating eye. Billy too prefers self-supporting communities to the newly installed, virtually automated redistribution schemes: "You've got to look after your own kind. No use leaving it to the bloody Government for them to hand out to a lot of bleeders who haven't got the gumption to do anything for themselves" (i, 21). So no one in the play is deceived by the welfare state's promise of a more just society. Surrounded by domestic misery, Jean remarks sarcastically, "They're all looking after us. We're all right, all of us. Nothing to worry about. *We're* all right. God save the Queen!" (iii, 31). Phoebe's unhappy memories of a deprived youth and a miserable marriage are quelled by Archie's pat rejoinder: "This is a welfare state, my darling heart. Nobody wants, and nobody goes without, all are provided for" (vi, 53).

Institutionalized caring has made people callous and conservative. One of Archie's numbers, "Why should I care. Why should I let it get me?" is as much a personal mantra, inoculating him against the daily humiliation he has to endure on stage, as a general reflection on a prevalent mood (ii, 25). As Frank, repeating his father's belief in "good old number one," puts it: "Oh, they may say they [care], and may take a few bob out of your pay packet every week and stick some stamps on your card to prove it, but don't believe it—nobody will give you a second look. They're all so busy, speeding down the middle of the road together, not giving a damn where they're going, as long as they're in the bloody middle!" (viii, 68).[20]

Yet these characters' critique of the welfare state's social program has to be measured against their own failure to respond adequately to each other's needs and, more importantly, has to be placed in the context of their present misery, which makes them regard history as a process of depreciation. Dissatisfied with the dreary present, they project upon the past a fullness of being they are craving for and feel justified in doing so because they are surrounded everywhere by evidence of past affluence and national self-assurance. For Billy, the past is not pollution, poverty, class struggle, revolution, and war but cheap beer and Yorkshire Pudding:

> BILLY: Last time I sang that was in a pub, some place in Yorkshire. If you bought
>   a pint of beer, you could get a plateful of Yorkshire Pudding then, as much
>   as you could eat. All for tuppence.
> ARCHIE: Come off it, Dad. Nobody ever gave away stuff like that, not even when
>   you remember.
> BILLY: I tell you, you got a plate of Yorkshire Pudding—
> ARCHIE: You're getting really old.
> BILLY: As much as you could eat. (viii, 65)

Archie may scoff at Billy, but his own idea of eternal bliss is not that different from Billy's nostalgic view of the past. "All my life I've been searching for something," he says in a drunken mood: "I've been searching for a draught Bass you can drink all the evening without running off every ten minutes, that you can get drunk on without feeling sick, and all for fourpence. Now, the man who could offer me all of that would really get my vote. He really would" (x, 76).

"TOWARD A SENTIMENTAL THEATRE"

Good cheer, Bass, and Yorkshire Pudding: it is a fantasy created by drunken, miserable minds longing for oblivion. Yet the play presents this idealized view of a lost world as more desirable than the certainty of financial success overseas. Phoebe's niece has started a lucrative hotel business in Canada and has invited the family to join in its management. Frank is eager to go and advises Jean to think about "number one . . . because nobody else is going to do it for you" (viii, 68). This is clearly not the course the play endorses. Jean will stay, bound by her love for and duty toward common people—especially the lost ones like Phoebe. Archie, whose debts and tax problems should serve as powerful incentives for emigration, is too sentimentally attached to England to start a new life elsewhere and, as the end of the play shows, prefers an English prison to a Canadian hotel. In the end, while Jean and Frank in their different ways have become more decisive and have gotten a better hold on the world, Archie, with Phoebe in tow, is more than ever adrift.

Yet it is Archie and the music hall that are allowed the final gesture. In fact, while unrolling the bundle of conflicts, Osborne has directed our sympathies increasingly away from Jean toward Archie. In the end, Jean is no longer lost, angry, and confused; she knows exactly who she is and what she ought to do. Her final speech, about man's solitude in a godless universe, is about loss but nevertheless ends on a declaration of resolve: "Somehow, we've just got to make a go of it. *We've only ourselves"* (xii, 85). As she becomes more res- olute, however, her identity closes in on itself and loses its most fascinating aspect, its indeterminacy. The gradual shaping of a self, as it adjusts its needs and desires in conformity with its chosen goals, is in dramatic terms uninter- esting, accompanied as it is by a contraction of the space available for empa- thetic involvement. As soon as we understand and applaud Jean's course of action, we are absolved of the need to sympathize with her plight.

Sorting Archie out is quite a different matter. As he explains to Jean, he is utterly detached in real life as well as on the stage:

> You see this face, you see this face, this face can split open with warmth and humanity. It can sing, and tell the worst, unfunniest stories in the world to a great mob of dead, drab erks and it doesn't matter, it doesn't matter. It does- n't matter because —look at my eyes. I'm dead behind these eyes. I'm dead, just like the whole inert, shoddy lot out there. It doesn't matter because I don't feel a thing, and neither do they (viii, 72).

Yet this denial of humanity is a little too emphatic to be convincing. The longer we know Archie, the more we wonder about the self that occasionally lights up behind the dead eyes. "Just now and then," says Osborne, "for a second or two, he gives the tiniest indication that he is almost surprised to find himself where he is" (vii, 59). Archie's life has been a continuous stripping away of every possible value, of everything in fact that endows life with weight, sense, and importance. Empathizing with this increasingly blurred self as it moves further away from its ideal demands an ever greater imaginative effort from the audience. Finally, when Archie is at his weakest, when his actions have made him a legitimate target for Jean's contempt, the audience's emotional complicity with that character may have deprived it of objective grounds for judgment or condemnation. Those who believe otherwise because they have resisted such involvement, who like Archie's bored audience have sat back with a smug "I defy yez to entertain me!", are at the end of the play confronted with their own inadequacy (viii, 72). Archie's final gesture, expressed in words as effective as an upward thrusting finger, must be the closest the music hall has ever come to Baudelaire's "hypocrite lecteur!—mon semblable—mon frère": "Let me know where you're working tomorrow night—and I'll come and see *YOU"* (xiii, 89).

When Archie leaves the stage for prison, a spotlight fixed onto the floor illuminates his absence. Then, hinting at the misery still ahead, "the little world of light snaps out, the stage is bare and dark." Darkness is what awaits not only Archie, but the dying music hall, and, beyond it, a lost England as well. "Don't clap too hard," says Archie during his final appearance. "We're all in a very old building" (xiii, 86). It was not difficult to conclude, as Milton Shulman did,

that "the crumbling edifice" of the music hall represents England, since
Osborne had made sure to emphasize that point in interviews and program
notes. To prepare Olivier for the role of Archie, Osborne took him on a nightly
exploration of the few remaining music halls in London. There they watched
performers vainly compete with more exciting forms of entertainment. "I have
been to the music halls all over the country," Osborne wrote, "where, during
an evening, you can see part of England dying before your eyes."[21] The part
that was dying was characterized by working class vitality, endurance, and
resistance, of a kind he illustrated in an admiring description of his grand-
mother, clearly the model for Mrs. Tanner in *Look Back in Anger*:

> She is a tough, sly old Cockney, with a harsh, often cruel wit, who knows
> how to beat the bailiffs and the money-lenders which my grandfather man-
> aged to bring on to her. Almost every working day of her life, she has got up
> at five o'clock to go out to work, to walk down what has always seemed to
> me to be the most hideous and coldest street in London. Sometimes when I
> have walked with her, all young bones and shiver, she has grinned at me, her
> face blue with what I thought was cold. 'I never mind the cold—I like the
> wind in my face.' She'd put her head down, hold on to her hat and *push*.[22]

When describing the last music-hall entertainers, Osborne likewise emphasized how determinedly they pushed on against the cold blast of chill reception. Olivier, who embraced Osborne's views on the music hall as a "great and
valuable part of English life" on the verge of extinction, recollected especially
"the gallantry of the lone figure on the stage set against the whole audience."[23]
A professional, as Billy in the play recalls, did not need a microphone or special effects then, just "an old backcloth behind him and he can hold them on
his own for half an hour" (x, 81).

"Let's pull ourselves together, and the happier we'll be!" (vi, 58). This, in
short, is the music hall's message, not different in fact from what one gets to
hear in a pub over a Bass and Yorkshire Pudding. During the heyday of the
music hall, the years leading up to WW I, shared laughter at predictable
moments and targets created a comforting impression of cultural unity. It was
a time, as Billy says, when "we were all English. What's more, we spoke English." The most rousing moments of the music hall consisted of what today
would be termed sexist jokes ("I turned 'em round and touched 'em up with
the end of me old cigar!" (viii, 61)), homophobic quips about being fancied by
the orchestra conductor who is "the only boy soprano in the Musicians' Union"
(ii, 24), obligatory affirmations of patriotism ("Good old England, you're my
cup of tea" (iv, 32)), unabashed exultation in imperialism ("What we've got
left back/ We'll keep—and blow you, Jack!" (iv, 33)), and only half-mocking
celebrations of mediocrity ("Thank God I'm normal!" and "I'm what you call
a moderate, I weigh all the pros, and the cons (ii, 25; vii, 60)). As popular entertainment, the music hall fulfilled three functions simultaneously: it flattered
the underdog by praising endurance, good cheer, and inventiveness; it offered

common people an opportunity to avenge themselves safely on their "betters" by poking fun at authority figures, snooty ladies, and effeminate gentlemen; and it made all this palatable with a thickly patriotic sauce concocted from the unshakable certainties of royalty and religion. As Raymond Williams has argued in *The Long Revolution* (1961), the music hall was never the last vestige of a living working-class culture that was finally destroyed by striptease shows, pop music, or television sitcoms. In constant transformation, the music hall in fact prepared the way for these contemporary forms of entertainment.[24] Politically speaking, however, the music hall was far too involved in the contradictions of lower-class life to have its reality summarized by the terms progressive or reactionary. "I may be an old poup," says Archie with some justification, "but I'm not a right-wing" (viii, 61).

Osborne, moreover, was not as naive as a superficial reading of the play may lead one to think. His view of the music hall was avowedly and blatantly mythical. He admitted that the music hall was often wrong, but "so was the nation itself. Patriotism was part of the rag-bag, and what a surrealistic (a later name) rag-bag it was, of patriotism, bisexuality, wives, being in love, Irish, queer, a toff, virginal or anything else."[25] Osborne in other words celebrated less the music hall than its penchant for grand sentiments and believed that his own theatre of excess was part of that same tradition: "Now, to react to people like this may seem sentimental," he said of his enthusiasm for the dying music hall. "But if it is, I can only say that I shall go on working towards a sentimental theatre for the rest of my life."

"A PURE, JUST NATURAL NOISE"

Sentiment is undoubtedly a powerful tool on the stage, and Osborne had already demonstrated his mastery at communicating strong emotions to a sometimes resistant or even hostile audience. With *The Entertainer* he succeeded in doing this again. Archie Rice may be less loud than Jimmy Porter, he is certainly not more pleasant and has none of Jimmy's youthful charm to compensate for it; but summoning all his stylistic mastery, Osborne managed to turn Archie, rather than the good and more commonsensical Jean, into the real hero of the play. He clearly wanted his audience not just to pity Archie but to admire and even in some respects emulate him.

Though he claims no longer to feel shame or pain, Archie is a true sentimentalist—one who does not channel his suffering into some kind of resolve or action, as Jean does, but who faces it head-on, day after day. Rooted into the very fiber of his being, pain can be sensed even in Archie's too insistent claims on detachment. On the music-hall stage, it lines his silly jokes and ill-executed soft shoe routines with a desperate edge—the kind that provokes the insensitive to mockery and instills in the sensitive the discomfiture of vicarious embarrassment. The last entertainers in the dying music hall, said Osborne, were people like Archie who knew they were fighting a lost battle but "had not given up. They were aware of their situation and, what is more, they were willing to talk about it. They were not afraid of being articulate. They became sad when they talked of the past, but they could laugh easily, and they did."

In other words, the vitality that Osborne admires is not to be confused with the gay and often empty clatter of the music hall itself. It is rather an emotional response to loss. So it is only as a doomed genre that the music hall gave rise to expressions of vitality, which, to Osborne, is an impotent emotion that expands inordinately, shamelessly, and noisily in the gap between the drab present and the fullness of the past. It expresses itself in the pure noise of lament or laughter, made by people who cannot or will not adjust to the demands of the present and the future. In that noise we should recognize the stubborn endurance of individuals whose suffering has annihilated their shame at being a nuisance to a world that impatiently wants to move on.

Osborne illustrates this at two crucial moments in the play. When Phoebe upbraids Billy for secretly eating from the cake she had bought in Mick's honor, Archie tries to call her to order and promises he will buy her another one. She turns on him, fiercely, calling his father a "bloody *greedy* old pig—that old pig, as if he hadn't had enough of everything already—he has to go and get his great fingers into it!" (vi, 57). She then bursts wildly into tears—despairing and consoling tears, because those irrevocable words have found their wrong target in the old man but in some deeper way have expressed the true nature of her pain. "And then," says Harold Hobson, describing the scene as it was delivered by Brenda de Banzie in the original production, "when you would think that an actress could do no more, she hides her face in her hands, and utters three separate cries, inarticulate, unbearable, that are like the sorrows of all the simple and unguarded beings there have ever been. George Relph, as the old man, stands in front of her, rebuked, perfectly still, perfectly understanding."[26]

This is a powerful scene of a sentiment so overwhelming as to swallow and therefore conceal its own mechanism. Like Billy, the audience may be "perfectly understanding" and yet remain unable to explain what has happened. The hysteria, however, can be traced back to its roots. Phoebe is not just talking about the cake; the incident releases all her feelings of resentment—a resentment of which Billy is just the unhappy but rather incidental object. Before that scene, a drunken Archie had been joking about making love with a "tart" on the kitchen table: "Have you ever had it on a kitchen table?" he asks son Frank. "Like a piece of meat on a slab. Slicing pieces of bacon" (vi, 56). Since Phoebe suspects him of bringing women home when she is in her bedroom, Archie's crude words cut to the quick. "Frank," she asks, "he's going to bring up one of those women, isn't he?" Her outburst at Billy for sneaking into the kitchen ("I don't want him in that kitchen. Tell him to keep out of it. It's not much, and it's not mine, but I mind very much" (vi, 57)) and for getting his fingers into the "tart" is a displacement of an anger that cannot be unleashed on a man who can no longer be shamed into respecting his wife, who no longer cares enough to hide his sordid behavior, and who is always ready to incriminate himself. "Old Archie could always kill anybody's punch line if he wanted" is his motto (vi, 55).

In other words, a whole conflict can disappear simply because it is so movingly and effectively summarized in one angry wail. A second sustained wail of anguish and longing is delivered by Archie, after a long drunken night during which he recalls a black woman singing a spiritual:

> If ever I saw any hope or strength in the human race, it was in the face of that old fat negress.... She was poor and lonely and oppressed like nobody you've ever known.... To see that old black whore singing her heart out to the whole world, you knew somehow in your heart that it didn't matter how much you kick people, the real people, how much you despise them, if they can stand up and make a pure, just natural noise like that, there's nothing wrong with them, only with everybody else. I've never heard anything like that since.... I wish to God I were that old bag. I'd stand up and shake my great bosom up and down, and lift up my head and make the most beautiful fuss in the world. (viii, 70–71)

As is well known, African-Americans, Jews, Irish, or any people who have seen their existence forcibly reduced to its bare essence are often envied for the "pure, just natural noise" of their lamentations. Roquentin, the protagonist of Jean-Paul Sartre's *La nausée* (1937), a man alienated from reality by obsessive conceptualization, attributes a similar wholeness of being to a black female singing the blues. Only the strength and purity of overpowering emotion can create such moments of authenticity. Archie does not think he can reach such purity or summon the necessary depth of feeling, but when Frank interrupts Archie's long and loving description with the news that Mick has been killed, Archie lifts his drunken head and sings his own blues. Reviewers were enraptured: "Mr. Osborne, concerned that we should feel," said Ronald Mavor, "punches and punches his hero until the feeling does come out with a great, terrible, song-like cry."[27] Archie's "wonderful, ashamed description," as Harold Hobson said, ends "literally with a song of despair which, in a high and beautiful pain, unites a sharp and savage irony with an almost unbearable pathos."[28]

With that lament however, Archie pulls the family's pain around him like a mantle and at least for a moment we tend to forget how that leaves the other characters in the cold. It takes a while before we realize that the story of how Archie, as a lonesome "half slewed" stranger marooned in a country that does not serve draught Bass, recognized his own plight in the pure noise made by "that old fat negress" is not as disinterested as it may appear. Archie is now more pitiable than the negress because the latter can at least give splendid voice to a pain in which the former is impotently trapped. Yet while recounting this moving event, Archie's mind has been occupied with something else. Once he is sure of having forged a bond of intimacy with his daughter, he suddenly veers around and shoots out the punch line: "Tell me, tell me something. I want you to tell me something. What would you say to a man of my age marrying a girl of—oh about your age? Don't be shocked. I told you—I don't feel a thing" (viii, 72). Jean is too intelligent to be taken in. She feels protective toward Phoebe for the way Archie is treating her and is understandably shocked and outraged at this bold confession. A few moments later, when the news of Mick's death breaks in on the family, it is not of Archie's betrayal the audience will be thinking but of the muddled feelings and misery that now find voice, as Archie, like the "fat negress," erupts in a song of lamentation.

Emotion liquefies reality, erases the distinctions that causal reasoning requires for making judgments. The whole play has been set up, both for stage-technical and thematic reasons, around a similar principle of conflation. Osborne's directives ask for the illusory world of the stage to be extended into the auditorium, the audience's territory. The invisible "fourth wall" must be torn down, the box set discarded, and the theatre turned into a music hall. The lighting should be "bang-on, bright and hard, or a simple follow-spot." As he further explains, "the scenes and interludes must, in fact, be lit as if they were simply turns on the bill." That illusion is also pursued off stage: "On both sides of the proscenium is a square in which numbers—the turn-numbers—appear" (12). Other stage directions pursuing a similar aim ask for an advertising board to be lowered during the intermission (11). Even the program notes lists scenes simply as numbers or turns.

The stage space itself is organized so that public and private nearly imperceptibly meld. Acting areas are differentiated through the simple means of swagging: curtains or flats are used to partition off the different locales where the action takes place. The way the stage is organized underlines the continuity between private and public self and also allows for interesting contrasts. When at home, private pain is staged—openly expressed, projected, dramatized. Archie uses his professional techniques to deal with domestic tensions, even to the extent of trying out his lame jokes on his family and cultivating the same sense of unassailability that is so characteristic of his music hall performance. Ironically, on the music-hall stage, when he faces his real audience, daring them with a show of invulnerability, we are more than ever aware of the nakedness of his private self, caught in the public spotlight.

Unlike *Look Back in Anger* that was blamed for having its dialogue built around the needs of one character, Jimmy, *The Entertainer* provides dialogue consisting often of quick one-liners that may pursue their own stubborn course but nevertheless blend in with the others in an excited din:

> FRANK: You know, you don't know what you're talking about.
> BILLY: I used to have digs in Claypit Lane—ten shillings a week all-in.
> PHOEBE: Frank, I thought you were going to sing.

> ARCHIE: If you can dodge all the clichés dropping like bats from the ceiling, you
>   might pick up something from me.
> FRANK: Well, plenty of others have picked it up from you.
> ARCHIE: Just you remember I'm your father.
> FRANK: When did you ever remember it?
> PHOEBE: Frank! Come on now, be a good boy. (viii, 62)

Here again, emotion is seen to bundle a variety of affects and to communicate itself as one totalizing gesture or *gestalt*. At times, moments of heated emotion may create the impression that the family is on the point of disbanding, and yet we come to realize that this mixture of pain, anger, and humor holds the family together in deep mutual involvement:

> PHOEBE: Be quiet, Dad. You've had too much to drink.
> BILLY: I could drink you lot under the table.
> ARCHIE: Oh dear, he's getting religious now.
> BILLY: I used to have half a bottle of three star brandy for breakfast—
> ARCHIE: And a pound of steak and a couple of chorus girls. He'll tell you the
>   whole story at the drop of a hat.
> BILLY: (*in rage*). I leave chorus girls to *you!*
> ARCHIE: Nothing like slicing yourself off a nice piece of bacon. (v, 37)

As everyone continues to drink and haul up old and new grievances, the emotional temperature at times nears boiling point. Yet, this is in many ways a close-knit and loving family, the kind Osborne cherishes. It is obviously at variance with the current notion that a family should consist of individuals collaborating in mutual respect toward a common goal. In its emphasis on efficiency and teamwork, the modern notion of community all too clearly betrays its subservience to the principles of the market. In Osborne's view, a living community consists of sharply divergent voices amalgamated by the strong passions that animate them. Here, for instance, he recalls a gathering of his own family on his mother's side:

> By dinner-time . . . the emotional temperature would be quite high. There
> would be baffling shrieks of laughter, yelling, ignoring, bawling, everyone
> trying to get his piece in. . . . The day would end up with someone . . . at the
> piano and everyone shouting songs at each other. They bawled and laughed
> and they moaned. . . . They 'talked about their troubles' in a way that would
> embarrass my middle-class observer. I've no doubt that they were often bor-
> ing, but life still had meaning for them. Even if they did get drunk and fight,
> they were responding; they were not defeated.[29]

This is the world Osborne tried to recreate in *The Entertainer*, and if the noise level is an indicator of its vitality, the Rices are far from being defeated.

The dialogue in *The Entertainer* includes still other examples of conflation or contraction, occurring for instance in Billy's speech. Billy has a way of switching topics, typical often of old people whose imaginative world closes around them and who may therefore forget that their listeners cannot follow such shifts without proper, logical transitions.

> BILLY: [. . . .] What have you been doing with yourself? Lots of these parties, eh?
> JEAN: No, not really.
> BILLY: Well, you've got to have a good time while you're young. You won't get it later on. I'll bet he won't be in till all hours tonight.
> JEAN: Dad?
> BILLY: I'm very pleased to see you, Jean. Are you all right? (i, 19)

At times these abrupt transitions in Billy's speech add an unintended comical effect: "You'll wait up all night if you wait for him," he says to Jean about her father Archie, in the same breath continuing his rant about a barmaid he disapproves of: "They wouldn't have employed someone like that in the old days. Like a common prostitute" (i, 22). That Archie too is a "common prostitute" is of course Billy's well-known opinion.

In this and other ways, Osborne proves to have a sensitivity for the various ways in which differences can be flooded by emotion, resulting in a more fluid sense of reality.

"WHAT'S THE USE OF DESPAIR?"

In one of his numbers, Archie wonders "what's the use of despair?" He is convinced that "if [people] see you're blue, they'll—look down on you." "Normal" people therefore do not care, except about "good old number one." Archie, of course, does not quite manage to be normal—that is, to remain untouched by events. Although he sings, "Why should I let it touch me! / Why shouldn't I, sit down and try / To let it pass over me?" he cannot prevent himself from pitying Phoebe and Billy and from loathing himself for betraying them (ii, 24–25). The more Archie denies his despair, the more genuine it becomes for the audience. When spectators are sufficiently moved by Archie's suffering, they might actually forget to wonder about Osborne's rather crafty "use of despair" in this play.

When we see the Rices assembled in mourning around Billy's coffin, draped in the Union Jack, it suddenly becomes clear to what extent Osborne, while ostensibly recounting the ordeals of one particular family, was consciously aiming at writing a play in which the nation would recognize its fate. Eight years before *The Entertainer,* Arthur Miller had grouped another family around a coffin—this time of a salesman, symbol of the American citizen's enterprising spirit. Billy's "they don't want real people any more" could well have been said by a tired Willy Loman, who, like Billy, in the end dies a victim of modern inhumanity and greed. What is buried in *Death of a Salesman* and *The Entertainer* is the past itself; what the family gains from mourning it is a desperate courage to march ahead into the uncertain future. Archie may be a cheat and loser, but as Linda Loman says of her husband, "I don't say he's a great man. . . . But he's a human being, and a terrible thing is happening to him. So attention must be paid." Like *Death of a Salesman, The Entertainer* consciously presents itself as a "contemporary tragedy," a term Olivier in fact used in his curtain speech.[30]

What distinguishes *The Entertainer* from its predecessor is that it betrays more clearly the blatant political uses of humanism. As Archie's song of lamentation shows, strong emotions have the power to erase potentially constraining or politically embarrassing differences, such as the ones between historical victors and victims of imperialism, even between those who betray and those who are betrayed. It is obvious from the way the play abandons itself to such grand emotions and from Osborne's protestations that he will "continue to work towards a sentimental theatre" that the audience is meant to see the beneficial effects of feeling. The heavily symbolic context of the dying music hall and the national humiliation in the Middle East suggest, moreover, that Osborne assigned to active grieving a role in the process of national healing. He claimed that what had sapped the country of its vitality, its innate strength, was the stiff upper lip attitude and the cult of cautious living. The market ideology of balanced accounts, promulgated by the welfare state, had created, as John Booth formulated it in a discussion of Osborne, "an outlook that strangles honesty and endeavor."[31] Deep down, Englishmen, said Osborne, are "tremendously passionate": "They are emotionally brutal. Perhaps brutal is too kind a word; they are vicious and barbed."[32] The English were once in contact with their feelings and could produce "a pure, just natural noise," Archie claims; "whispers of it" can still be heard "on a Saturday night somewhere" (viii, 71). The nation would have to rediscover that impulsiveness, and a "sentimental theatre" could help it to accomplish this.

Even though quite a few reviewers thought *The Entertainer* sneered at "patriotism, religion, idealism, and love,"[33] those who reacted warmly to the play's sentimentalism lost all sight of whatever more critical designs the play may have had. "Here is revealed the sum of his life," Raymond Marriott says grandly of Archie in the final scene, "and we know that when he goes off into the darkness . . . he will remain one of the children of God, no matter how lost and beyond redemption he may appear to be."[34] "John Osborne cries out that we must feel for [Archie]," Ronald Mavor reminds us, "and for his frightened wife, and for his neurotic son and for his mixed-up daughter, and for his passé, redundant father. Feel for them and weep for them as much as for the king of Thebes or the queen of Egypt." He concludes, "Oh, how good, how moving, how beautiful it all was. They are wrong who say that this is a depressing play. It is full of the understanding of the value of life. Its lesson is that we should love one another."[35]

It was only to be expected that Osborne's uncritical emphasis on sentiment would finally lead to simple sentimentality. What was worse, it allowed reviewers to read unabashed jingoism into the play. Reviewing *The Entertainer* in 1957, John Raymond called it "a grotesque cry of rage and pain at the bad hand history is dealing out to what was once the largest, most prosperous empire in the world." The fury at the Suez debacle, he thought, had not been directed at the operation itself but at its failure. "The general feeling was one of frustrated fury that the operation failed—that 'the Wogs didn't take a beating'." Osborne, in other words, had tapped into the "mood of national impotence."[36] The criticism in the play, as Frank's song about the "playing fields of Eton" demonstrates, may have focused on the injustice of the class system and the inadequacies of the Establishment, but foreigners nevertheless remained "wogs" for Frank, and pride in Britain survived intact despite the failures and hypocrisies of those who ruled the country.

Was it naiveté that led Osborne to believe in the subversive power of sentiment? In fact leading industrialists at the time concurred with him that what the country needed was more trust in its emotions. A contemporary study of Britain's economy between 1950 and 1958 blamed lagging economic growth with respect to the continent not on deficient material infrastructure but on a too rigid "state of mind."[37] Self-control, reticence, compromise, diplomacy, the ideals of a cautious bureaucracy managing a world empire, were quickly becoming barriers to increased productivity. What was needed to combat the "debilitating inertia and conformity" was more spontaneity and creativity—in short, more emotivity.[38] The Angry Young Men movement, without realizing it, was helping to create the ideology of a new age.

For the Royal Court Theatre, the most immediate effect of *The Entertainer's* reliance on sentiment was respectability and acceptance. After only one year and a string of commercial failures, the RCT had managed to get out of debt thanks to Osborne's successes. Originally, the English Stage Company at the RCT had taken nothing less than the modernization of British Theatre as its aim. It had done so most spectacularly by producing the plays of an unknown, unemployed actor that were lauded and abused for addressing contemporary themes in a contemporary idiom. Yet the RCT was also solidly backed by traditional and other establishment forces and was careful not to run too many political risks. Among the members of its council were the Earl of Harewood, cousin to the Queen; Sir Frederic Hooper, managing director of Schweppes, a company that soon joined other corporate sponsors of the Royal Court Theatre; and Neville Blond, the most successful textile exporter of the early postwar years, who was married to Elaine Marks of the chain-store company Marks and Spencer.

Mindful not to alienate the members of its council and its young but nevertheless middle-class audience, the RCT developed a strategy of taking from Osborne what it needed and distancing itself from him whenever his views became too radical. At the last minute Neville Blond, on instigation of the Earl of Harewood and the Earl of Bessborough, canceled a cocktail party that was going to take place on RCT premises to celebrate the publication of Tom Maschler's *Declaration.*[39] The reason, as George Devine was made to explain to the press, was Osborne's attack on the monarchy in that publication. "I congratulate the Earl of Harewood for his defense of the Queen," the *Daily Mail* said. " If she cannot answer back, her cousin has shown, in no uncertain manner, that he can—and jolly well will . . . ."[40] Osborne, who was in America at the time, showed surprisingly little emotion at the news of the Royal Court's repudiation of the "angry young man" movement it had helped to launch by staging his plays. In fact, as a reporter put it, Osborne "refused to be indignant." "These organisations inevitably consist of a large number of people, some of them a little blimpish and old-fashioned," Osborne explained. "But they have put on my plays, and that is all that concerns me."[41] There was little to be angry about. Canceling the party heightened Osborne's image as rebel, while it protected the RCT from its effects. Osborne was not naive. This was a very reasonable separation of business interests on both sides.

The Entertainer's financial success was assured when another great exporter, this time not of Britain's textiles but of its cultural capital, Sir Laurence Olivier, decided to lend a hand. "If Osborne ever says his prayers," a journalist said, "he may well include one on behalf of Sir Laurence, for without him, he may well have found himself in the same position as Colin Wilson."[42] One cannot possibly overestimate Olivier's stature at the time. Olivier, Osborne explained much later, "had a kind of heroic national view of himself as a bequest to the nation."[43] In fact, like the monarchy, he was the symbol of England itself.[44] This kind gesture of the famous actor toward the angry young playwright reinforced the play's message, as it was yet another sign of Britain's capacity to renew itself. Like the nation at Suez, Olivier, the great Shakespearean actor, went down, humiliated himself, but came out of that ordeal strengthened and triumphant. Few noticed that, once involved in the play, Olivier took firmly control of it, often to Osborne's dismay. When the play transferred to the West End, Olivier insisted that Frank's Brechtian mourning song, "those playing fields of Eton/ Have really got us beaten," be cut. Osborne had no choice but to comply since Olivier threatened to walk out of the play.[45]

Deprived of its few remaining barbs, *The Entertainer* could now become forever part of Olivier's repertoire and establish itself firmly as a play about triumphant nationhood. British integrity had been violated, and the Suez crisis symbolized most acutely its breach with the past. The death of the music hall, once symbol of the people's vitality, and the loss of British prestige abroad were still redeemable. What was necessary was to develop the whole emotional spectrum of mourning—something which an elegiac play, such as *The Entertainer,* successfully and beautifully achieved. The nation could now look forward to the future, confident that it would find there the values of the past.

CHAPTER 5

Luther (1961)
The Negative Way of Anger

RECEPTION

By 1961, Osborne had "arrived." He had also experienced his first failures. His documentary-style television play *A Subject of Scandal and Concern* (1960) had received few favorable notices, even though it featured Richard Burton in the role of George Holyoake, the last man to be imprisoned for blasphemy in 1842. Truly devastating had been the reaction to his first and only musical *The World of Paul Slickey* (1959): he had been booed at the stage door and pursued up Charing Cross Road by a jeering mob.[1] Though many all too clearly did not love him, few grudged him the respect due to the rare English playwright who had seen two of his plays produced simultaneously on Broadway—as had been the case with *Look Back in Anger* and *The Entertainer.* In barely four years, the unemployed actor had become the most highly paid, frequently interviewed, and most glamorous playwright alive. Divorced from Pamela Lane and married to the beautiful Mary Ure, the Alison of *Look Back in Anger,* Osborne was reported to travel with a personal tailor, a bodyguard, and a mistress.[2] In business terms, he had become Woodfall Productions, Ltd., for movies; Breakthrough Productions, Ltd., for plays; and John Osborne Productions Ltd., for income tax.[3] Yet, suddenly, the noise seemed to die away around him. Reporters found the playwright living tranquilly, if not monastically, in the Old Water Mill, a comfortable Sussex country house, fifty miles out of London. This is where Osborne now spoke about his religious experiences and his fascination with the historical figure of Luther.

This turn to religion came as a surprise to most people who, after *Look Back in Anger*'s angry tirades against religious stampedes and pealing church bells and *The World of Paul Slickey*'s unpleasant characterization of Father Evilgreen, had come to think of Osborne as an "anti-church militant."[4] Some were afraid that it might portend the end of Osborne's anger and the beginning of his recuperation by the Establishment,[5] but anger and devotion, politics and religion, Osborne knew, were not necessarily antithetical. In the historic figure of Luther, inward and outward turning forces of religion and anger had combined and changed the world forever. Osborne recognized himself in Luther's tortured spirit, theatrical temperament, and earthy but nevertheless poetically rich language.[6] It was, moreover, all too tempting to reduce Luther's philosophical position to his own. In *The Bondage of the Will,* a polemical reply to Erasmus, Luther, like Osborne, seemed to defend strong feeling and common sense against the weakening, feminizing effect of intellectual skepticism. "For not to delight in assertions," Luther said boldly, "is not the character of the Christian mind." He explained that by assertion he meant "a constant adhering, affirming, confessing, defending, and invincibly persevering." Erasmus, in contrast, seemed very much what Osborne would call a fence-sitter. Fearing the consequences of Luther's belligerent tone, Erasmus emphasized that statements were first of all opinions. This only irritated Luther further. "In a word, these declarations of yours amount to this," he answered, "that, with you, it matters not what is believed by anyone, anywhere, if the peace of the world be but undisturbed; and if everyone be but allowed . . . to look upon the Christian doctrines as nothing better than the opinions of philosophers and men."[7] For Osborne, it was too tempting not to see here a historical parallel of the struggles that had marked the late fifties—in politics, between those who called for visionary passion and those who preached caution and restraint; and in literature, between those who were mainly concerned with expressing honest feelings in plain language and those who cultivated modernist refinement.

Osborne steeped himself in study. An English translation of Heinrich Boehmer's well known *Martin Luther: Road to Reformation* (1946) had appeared in 1957 and must have featured among his study books.[8] A more obvious influence was Ronald H. Bainton's best-selling biography, *Here I Stand* (1955), which cast Luther in a romantically heroic, even theatrical light.[9] Both works offer compelling narratives about a humble man's rise to preeminence. Out of the cauldron of doubt, fear, and solitude, a personality is forged that with the courage of despair asserts itself against the opinions of its time. Finally, through a supreme act of will, it succeeds in creating a world in its own image. From there on, the narratives taper off. What else is there to be said once a sharply delineated personality sinks back into the variety of life itself? The Evangelical movement had become reality, and Luther's main concern was to keep it from falling apart by the same spirit of dissension that had called it into being. In other words, from then on, like most of us, Luther had to compromise and muddle along from day to day. He married, begot children, and died. This peaking of a narrative around a moment of unsustainable truth, insight, or certainty is a familiar pattern in drama. A tremendous intellectual and emotional expenditure forces the world to a standstill, compelling it to reveal its order. When next, the world spins on, the exhausted mind falls back, realizing it had merely mistaken its own frantic revolutions for the stillness of the universe.

Apart from these two biographies, Luther's own works, especially *The Bondage of the Will,* remained a constant source of reading pleasure for Osborne. In Luther's *Tischreden* (Table Talk), he found graphic evidence of a mind that all too readily rumbled with the noises of the belly: "I'm like a ripe stool in the world's straining anus, and at any moment we're about to let each other go" (II, ii, 65).[10] The advantage of seasoning the play with such pungent statements borrowed from the great man himself was that the Lord Chamberlain, who otherwise zealously pursued far less explicit formulations, felt less self-assured when it came to censoring Luther.[11] For the play itself, Luther's constant references to pigs, sweat, mud, and excrement provided a much needed gritty realism to counterbalance what otherwise would be a too lofty preoccupation with the soul. Psychoanalysis, moreover, made such a combination psychologically acceptable. *Young Man Luther: A Study in Psychoanalysis and History* (1958), by the American psychologist Erik H. Erikson, convincingly married the great mind to an unruly gut. Less a historical study than a psychological explanation of the post-adolescent masculinity crisis, Erikson's book had the advantage of being equally relevant to the historical Luther as to the Rebel Without a Cause or Angry Young Man phenomenon of the fifties. Osborne decided to follow Erikson closely, so as to cast Luther's life-long obsession with the mysteries of the bowel and his own engendering as a psychologically plausible form of painful struggle for self-expression and self-realization.

Impeccably directed by Tony Richardson, *Luther* premièred at the Theatre Royal in Nottingham on 26 June 1961. John Addison adapted suitable period music by Josquin de Pres and Jakob Obrecht. Stark, brown sets contrasting with heavy rich costumes were designed by Jocelyn Herbert, who would remain the Royal Court's only homegrown stage designer of importance. For the lead, Osborne had originally thought of Richard Burton, who was unavailable. The only other man who could fill the role, Osborne thought, was the young and upcoming actor Albert Finney. As the latter was then playing in Keith Waterhouse's *Billy Liar,* production of *Luther* was postponed to allow him to fill the role.

On 6 July 1961, the original cast presented the play at the Theatre Sarah Bernhardt in Paris for the International Theatre Festival. So when it finally received its London première at the Royal Court Theatre on 27 July 1961, the play had already gathered critical acclaim. The old guard among London reviewers was not too keen on the prospect of yet another Osborne success but felt a little intimidated by *Luther*'s enthusiastic reception by the French cultural and intellectual elite. The London reviews, however, were by no means wholly enthusiastic. The play's success was nevertheless assured, especially on the continent and in the U.S. After London's West End it moved to Broadway, where it won the Tony Award in 1964.

In England, critical reaction followed a by now familiar pattern: Osborne's plays were praised for their strong speeches and criticized for deficient structure. Unsure of what to make of Osborne's text, critics lavished attention on the performance of Albert Finney, already famous for playing Arthur Seaton in the successful Woodfall film production of Alan Sillitoe's *Saturday Night and Sunday Morning*. Finney was hailed as "the young wonder from Salford," the new Olivier in the make.[12] As could be expected, the papers were revolted by *Luther*'s scatological language and imagery. "But I counted at least 25 references to the bowels," Alan Brien remonstrated, blissfully unaware of the anal retentiveness revealed by such careful count taking. This obsession with excremental imagery, he added wittily, "not only seemed to betray the horrified delight of the playwright rather than of the character in the images but . . . also came near to arguing that the Reformation was invented to cure one man's constipation."[13] Then the press found in Brecht's *Galileo* (1943) a model to compare Osborne unfavorably with. When Brecht's Berliner Ensemble had visited London in 1956, it had met mainly with critical bafflement; but everyone was eager to show acquaintance with Brechtian staging techniques by detecting their influence on new English plays. Like Brechtian theatre, *Luther* was indeed expressionistic: it made use of a narrator to indicate time and place of each scene and it was episodic—that is, fragmentary—in structure, bold in its symbolism, and minimalist in its settings. Like *Galileo*, moreover, its story recounted a hero's public confrontation with authority figures and ended with his settling for domestic bliss.[14] Osborne's *Luther* could hardly be less Brechtian, however, in its insistence on regarding history and politics as a reflection of the troubles of one particular mind. For an ease with scenes bound together by the intensity of dialogue but otherwise shifting across space and time, Osborne could as well have gone back to Shakespeare. The same could be argued for the way *Luther* daringly unites the claustrophobic world of personal neurosis with the vast expanse of social caricature.[15] Critical comparisons with Brecht, however, continued to be made, if only because they were an easy way of arguing Osborne's "shortcomings."[16]

If for some reviewers, Osborne, since *The Entertainer*, had reached the stature of a failed Brecht, for others he simply remained a failed Rattigan. Despite clear evidence that drama had successfully moved toward alternative forms of coherence and plausibility, many reviewers clung with remarkable stubbornness to the principles of the well-made play. They clearly were unable to deal with what appeared to them as "disjointed and shapeless drama." *Luther* is a "snippety" play, they complained, "a series of disjointed revue sketches,"[17] a "collection of *tableaux vivants*,"[18] a "magnificent possibility" that Osborne had allowed to "dwindle[—] into a sketchy, narrow, and inconsequential tintype, neither fully written nor fully thought through."[19] They lamented lack of continuity and narrative climax,[20] insisted that the arguments ought to have been spelled out,[21] and that, in general, the play would have benefited from a more conventional form.[22] Many expressed their preference for two other historical plays then produced in the West End: Robert Bolt's *A Man for All Seasons* (1960) and the French playwright Jean Anouilh's *Becket* (1959). The play was most warmly received not in England but on the continent and, two years later, in the St. James Theatre on Broadway, where it ran for 211 performances.

Whereas an increasing number of reviewers cautiously embraced Osborne's experimentation, namely his willingness to abandon naturalistic staging, his "magnificent rhetoric,"[23] and his use of sermons as an effective mode of direct address,[24] critical responses continued to show a surprising level of fascinated bewilderment: "To read many of the criticisms," said Michael Foot, "is to be amazed and befuddled by the contradictory explanations of what Osborne is getting at. Can one play properly produce so many interpretations? And how is it possible that, at the same time, some of the critics have assailed *Luther* for its aridity and failure of imagination?"[25] If we take as criterion of the best in art an ability to suggest, with a few strong and well-chosen images, the presence of a virtually inexhaustibly complex, embedded argument, then *Luther* must be counted among the very best of Osborne's works.

Yet, *Look Back in Anger* is most readily identified with its author's method and personality, whereas *Luther* is often thought of as the less typical work—so much have we come to think of Osborne in terms of excess rather than of economy. *Luther,* however, is at the heart of Osborne's oeuvre. To overlook that amounts to a denial of the many possible aesthetic economies in drama and of Osborne's remarkable and quite unmatched ability to explore a great number of them. The economy of *Look Back in Anger* was that of the realist engaged in the portrayal of concretely lived, double-binding relationships whose major characteristic was the deceptive imbalance between verbosity and silence. The economy of *Luther* is a different one; it is that of the expressionist who with a few bold strokes summons up a whole world. These plays are alike in that they deal with issues that return with obsessive regularity in Osborne's work: the origins, paradoxes, possibilities and limitations of anger and the relationship between anger and the artistic voice.[26]

CONTINUITY AND CONTRAST

"For, although I am rude in speech," said Luther in *The Bondage of the Will,* "yet, by the grace of God, I am not rude in understanding."[27] Osborne could hardly have said it better. With *Luther,* the master of raw intensity proved he could also handle a subject of considerable conceptual complexity. Much later, in 1993, when presented with a handsome edition of Luther's *The Bondage of the Will,* Osborne reflected on his thirty-one year old self, assiduously reading in prepa-

ration of the play. Many years later, reflecting back on this time, he admitted he
was not truly prepared for such an enterprise. He lacked knowledge and experience. Sometimes, he added, youthful enthusiasm makes one attempt what
mature prudence would avoid.[28] His regrets must not be taken too seriously,
however. Like most of Osborne's admissions of failure, this one too can best be
read as an ironically stated assertion of the nature of art: the integrity of artistic vision depends on a certain lack of readiness and especially a lack of caution. To weigh each word before sending it off into the world is to risk being
crushed under that weight and to be reduced to silence. There is no art in the grocer's ledger, in the careful balancing of profit and expenditure. Art is more like
a forceful spit in the eye, especially in that of the critically gazing spectator.

Still, practical problems had to be solved, as twenty-four years of history
were to be condensed into three hours of drama. For his scene selection,
Osborne quite simply staked out twelve mileposts an audience could reasonably expect to encounter in the not unfamiliar trajectory of Luther's life. Young
Martin Luther enters the Augustinian order and is ordained in 1506, at the age
of twenty-three (I, i). A year later, he conducts his first Mass and is terrified at
the miracle of transubstantiation (I, ii–iii). This concludes Martin's prepara-
tory years, marked primarily by doubt and fear. A "decor note" signals that the
next act takes Martin from the cloister into the world, from darkness into light.
The irritant around which Martin's anger gradually hardens is the indulgence
racket, so unashamedly engaged in by Rome's prime commercial traveler, the
Dominican Inquisitor John Tetzel (II, i). Still, Martin does not immediately
act. He becomes a well-respected scholar and preacher, increasingly known
for his intransigent views (II, ii). At the age of thirty-four, he takes his first
political action by nailing his ninety-five theses against indulgences to the door
of Wittenberg's Castle Church (II, iii). A year later he is called in front of papal
legate Cajetan but refuses to cooperate (II, iv). In 1519, Luther's confrontation with Rome culminates in his excommunication by the worldly Pope Leo
X (II, v). Martin reacts defiantly with a book burning ceremony at Wittenberg
in 1520 (II, vi). In the play's final act, Martin has reached public recognition
and a wide following. A battle of wits at the Diet of Worms in 1521 pitches
him against Johan Von Eck. It ends with Martin's public refusal to recant,
expressed in the legendary words, "Here I stand; God help me; I can do no
more" (III, i). With these words, the breach between Martin and Rome is complete—and so, traditional historical accounts tell us, Modernity starts and the
Middle Ages end. In terms of self-development, Martin has not so much abandoned old doubts and fears as taken them in stride. The only counterweight
for the uncertainties of the universe is from now on an individual's strength of
faith, and one hears already the distant roar of bourgeois revolutions to come.
Yet the play does not end with Martin's self-assertion. Two scenes still follow,
putting that moment in perspective. Now that Rome has ceased to be the center, the once unified Christian world falls apart. Four years later, Martin calls

for the bloody suppression of the Peasants' Movement, a revolt that ironically has been inspired by his own rejection of established order (III, ii). We finally leave Luther at the age of forty-seven, married to an ex-nun, and dandling a little child on his knee (III, iii).

Such a vast historical panorama requires the tension of stark contrast to be effectively portrayed on the stage. Fortunately, the material lends itself perfectly to it, allowing Osborne to alternate scenes of dark and private intensity with vivid, public ones. For instance, the boisterous, carnivalesque atmosphere accompanying the market sale of indulgences in the opening scene of the second act dispels the gloom and oppressiveness that lingers after the first act. With the fling of a coin, Tetzel has solved Martin's problem. Doubt and fear do not have to be patiently borne or daily struggled with as long as Tetzel has indulgences to sell. The next scene, however, reintroduces doubt, exchanging the noise of the market for the quiet of a monastery's garden, where Martin seeks private counsel from a kind father figure, his older friend Staupitz, Vicar General of the Augustinian Order. Reflection ends when in the next scene Martin preaches among the crowd and dramatically nails his theses to the door. The audience's attention is always fully engaged as private scenes are swiftly followed by public ones, dark by light, silent by loud.

THE KNIFE AND THE BODY

Throughout, however, Osborne's focus remains on the growth of Martin Luther's resolve. Since he was less interested in action than in mind, Osborne's real difficulty lay in suggesting in twelve snapshots the living complexity of Martin's personality. Scribbles on loose pages torn from notebooks reveal Osborne's struggle with his subject. I must look into Marx, he reminds himself at one moment. He probably did not find time for it, as *Luther* never moves much beyond Freud, dealing with its hero's private life far more sensitively than with his public actions.[30] But psychoanalysis covers a vast domain through which Osborne had to clear his own path. Among the notes are fragments of insights, clearly gathered from textbooks on psychoanalysis. Taken together, they form a sort of psychological justification for Luther's neurotic symptoms and actions. Neurosis is an inability to come to terms with the present, says one note: the neurotic personality is locked in the past and distrustful of the future. Other short notes articulate his understanding of the infantile desires and fears that animate religion, which is rooted in an erotic awareness of one's helplessness and mortality. The insecurity of the male subject expresses itself most tellingly in castration anxiety. Osborne makes much of Luther's belief that rats may lurk in the toilet. Luther's fear that these will slash at his genitals while he tries to defecate is all too obviously sexual in origin. Castration fear leads to a longing for ultimate sovereignty: Luther cannot abide that he is of woman born; he wants to be his own creation. And is that not a universal desire, Osborne wonders?

Other short notes reveal his attempts at defining childhood, religion, and tragedy in psychoanalytic terms. Luther's acts of defiance against authority express, paradoxically, his longing for the innocence of childhood: it is his awareness of the insufferable difference between his actual condition as outsider and his idealized picture of two loving parents and a child that makes him rebellious. In other words, Luther is angry because he wants be loved not for what he does but for who he is. This would be all too common if it were not that Luther wants to be loved absolutely and unconditionally by a perfect authority figure. Yet, the businesslike, all too earthly Leo the Tenth certainly does not fit Luther's conception of absolute, divine power.

Other notes explore the essentially tragic vision of psychoanalysis. For the infant, the mother looms as an overwhelming presence so that what the child longs for most, namely the feeding breast, turns into a threat. The more the child desires, the more it fears others' desires. All our lives, we want to own the world, but the latter will finally own us. Awareness of such vulnerability finally leads to religion. The conclusion is evident, summed up in a last note: what have all great tragic figures—Oedipus, Hamlet, but also Luther—in common? Answer: they want too much; they are afflicted with an excess of desire.

Out of these insights, and especially out of a genuine fascination with the figure of Luther, grew what must be counted as one of Osborne's most strikingly effective and intellectually satisfying plays. A first concern was not to be buried under the wealth of material. Osborne once said about his method of composition that "I write in fountain pen, scribbling bits, not committing myself. I like to look at it sideways." [31] Now, more than ever, he had to practice a "sideways" vision so as not to be blinded by the aura of the gigantic historic figure that was to be the subject of his play. What he needed were a few bold and visually effective images around which a richly complex yet not fully articulated argument would coalesce. Symbols, he wrote in his notebook, are not just abstractions; they are actions. Was it not St. Augustine who said that a handshake is not just an expression but an act of friendship?

He put this now into practice, writing what was to remain his one and only visually stunning stage description: "A knife, like a butcher's, hanging aloft, the size of a garden fence. The cutting edge of the blade points upwards. Across it hangs the torso of a naked man, his head hanging down" (I, ii, 24).[32] This description follows on the opening scene in which Martin accepts holy orders, seeking the certainty promised in the ordination formula, "Now you must choose one of two ways: either to leave us now, or give up this world, and consecrate and devote yourself entirely to God and our Order" (I, i, 11). Still the choice that is to put an end to all choices does not end Martin's obsessive doubting. Does not the pettiness of life according to the rule belie the solemnity of the vow? Could exerting oneself at abject humility not be a perverse form of vanity? May meekness not serve as guise for a terrible rage? In Martin's case, the latter seems to express itself in sudden fits that are accompanied by violent ejaculations of vomit. Not surprisingly Martin soon complains to his superior that "all you teach me in this sacred place is how to doubt—" (I, ii, 29).

This is as much the audience knows before it is confronted with that striking image of a body hanging across a gigantic butcher's knife. As it introduces a scene in which the audience is informed of Martin's constant constipation, it is not difficult to recognize in the knife the symbol of Martin's suffering, the cutting pain in his bowels being its most immediate physical expression. In the course of the play, the image of the knife and the body resonate in different ways, recalling, for instance, how Abraham on God's command raised his knife against his son Isaac. Near the end of the play, an older Martin uses this image of Christian paradox to excuse the brutal slaughter of rioting peasants for which he had called. Martin had then assured the princes they were wielding the sword in God's name. Behind Abraham, knife raised above his son, stands God, knife raised above Abraham. In the final instance, "God is the butcher" (III, ii, 106). And, "if He butchers us, He makes us live."

Strife is the foundation of God's Kingdom. God not only sets fathers against sons, he also sets sons against fathers. Did Christ not say, "I have come to set a man against his father"? (III, iii, 125). Though a knife separates subject from object, wielder from victim, with deathly finality, the biblical story implies that it nevertheless strikes in both directions. Does a father not kill himself by killing the one through whom God "had promised him life"? (III, ii, 111). Does the son who sacrifices himself not also strike at the father? So at least thinks Hans who resents Martin's decision to enter the monastery. "I think a man murders himself in these places," he tells his son (I, iii, 49). This sacrifice is not an act of courageous self-abnegation but of spite. Martin may exclaim "I kill no one but myself," yet he knows that, by becoming a monk, he has killed the man who claims his only hope on immortality lay in the continuation of his blood (I, iii, 43, 49).

It is difficult not to consider the knife hanging above Martin as a sword of Damocles, an image of Martin's sense of pending doom that keeps him imprisoned in unbearable self-consciousness and gnawing doubt. One must trust the knife unconditionally in order not to be killed by it. Little Isaac, Martin tells, "struggle[d] not to flinch or blink his eyes" as he looked up at the knife in his father's hand, God's knife. What he had to trust, with perfect "obedience," was the eternal vigilance of God's unblinking eye: "if God had blinked, the boy would have died then, but the Angel intervened, and the boy was released, and Abraham took him up in his arms again. In the teeth of life we seem to die, but God says no—in the teeth of death we live" (III, ii, 111). Equally important, however, was that Isaac returned that unflinching stare. To keep the knife frozen in the air, Martin will have to meet God's unblinking gaze with Isaac's trusting resolve.

At the beginning of the play, however, Martin is far from having reached such confident acceptance of fate. In the scene so ominously presided over by the knife, Martin prepares to celebrate his first Mass in which he will call upon heaven for the miracle that will change wine and bread into the blood and body of Christ: "Receive, oh Holy Father, almighty and eternal God, this spotless host, which I, thine unworthy servant, offer unto thee for my own innumerable sins of commission and omission, and for all here present and all faithful Christians, living and dead, so that it may avail for their salvation and everlasting life" (I, iii, 45). With these words, the priest prepares Christ for a life-giving sacrifice. To the doubter, however, the words are like knives, striking in both directions. With the same force with which they pierce and change reality, they strike back at the speaker: "I lifted up my head at the host, and, as I was speaking the words, I heard them as if it were the first time, and suddenly— . . . they struck at my life" (I, iii, 48). Martin gets stuck in the words and has to be prompted by his counselor, Brother Weinand. If words can assume the force of reality, what if at that crucial moment a word spoken had been contradicted by a word unspoken? The historical Luther was said to have been obsessed with the idea that some priests, lifting the host, murmured to themselves, "Panis es, panis manebis; vinum es, vinum manebis."[33] At any instance, the holy can become the blasphemous: "Bread thou art and wine thou art / And always shall remain so" (I, iii, 47). Martin, seized by terror, "sweat[s] like a pig in a butcher's shop" (I, ii, 27). With every celebration of the Mass, it is Martin who dies under the knife. "And so," he concludes, "the praising ended—and the blasphemy began" (I, ii, 34).

THE CONE AND THE BAGPIPE

Being overdetermined, symbols summarize not only a number of interrelated thoughts but often their opposites as well. Their rich suggestiveness appeals particularly to the kind of artist that thinks an argument should be complex and yet engage the audience's emotions rather than its reason. "I don't think conceptually," Osborne once said. "If I see or hear an idea, I turn it into something concrete. I'm not a thinker in the accepted sense."[34] A playwright does not have to be. Coherence, plausibility, and closure are not the product of logical calculations; they are an inner conviction, the result of suggestion on the playwright's part and intuition on the spectator's. The audience does not insist on closing an argument, on being able to relate each detail to an overarching idea. The play simply has to give an *impression* of closure if only to validate the initial promise of sense and purpose that prompted the audience to become emotionally and intellectually involved.[35] The critic, however, shares the psychoanalyst's interest in the many untold stories subsumed under a few "intuitively correct" images, knowing all the while that even the most elaborate description cannot fully exhaust their meaning and, worse, that elegance can soon be lost under a profusion of argument.

As the stage description for the set representing Martin's unconscious continues, new symbols emerge. Below the giant knife and body is "an enormous round cone, like the inside of a vast barrel, surrounded by darkness. From the upstage entrance, seemingly far, far away, a dark figure appears against the blinding light inside, as it grows brighter. The figure approaches slowly along the floor of the vast cone, and stops as it reaches the downstage opening. It is MARTIN, haggard and streaming with sweat" (I, ii, 24). Shortly after, a procession of monks passes by his cell and disappears in an oddly looking structure upstage left, shaped like a "bagpipe of the period, fat, soft, foolish and obscene looking" (I, ii, 25). That the only phallic image is relegated to a marginal position in comparison to the "enormous round cone" and looks "fat, soft," and "foolish" is only fitting for an institution that channels masculine desire into feminine receptivity—where Martin, according to his father, has come to "look like a woman" (I, iii, 44). Together with the cone, the bagpipe alludes, and not too subtly, to another obsession of Martin, that with his own engendering. As Hans reminds his son: "You can't ever get away from your body because that's what you live in, and it's all you've got to die in, and you can't get away from the body of your father and your mother! We're bodies, Martin, and so are you, and we're bound together for always" (I, iii, 50).

If Martin turns away from the body, it is perhaps because he experienced most vividly his first failures and shortcomings there. He was a sensitive child, we learn, who craved love and acceptance, especially from his father, a figure of authority. Hans belongs to a fairly well- to-do class of semi–independent skilled laborers—the kind that invests in an enterprise and shares in its profit. Osborne defines him as "lower-middle class, on his way to become a small, primitive capitalist" (I, i, 12). He is a man of strong ambitions who, impatient with the constraints of life and class, wants to see his lot improved through his children. When the plague robs him of two sons, he puts all his hopes in the only remaining one, whom he treats with the impatience and resentment of a man who cannot bear the idea that his children consist of matter not entirely pliant to his will and need. "I loved you the best," Martin says to his father later. "It was *you* I always wanted. I wanted your love more than anyone's, and if anyone was to hold me, I wanted it to be you" (I, iii, 52). What he received instead were frequent beatings and incessant demands.

Hans is not just ambitious for his son; he wants to live through him. Martin has to become a prosperous lawyer and, of course, supply his father with grandchildren. All this Martin could have achieved for his father—being willing, studious, and intelligent as a boy. Still, his father's attitude would have remained the same. Proud of his son, he would at the same time be condescending toward him, counting his son's achievements as ultimately his. What Martin will later say of God applies equally well to his father: "He's like a glutton, the way he gorges me, he's a glutton. He gorges me, and then spits me out in lumps" (I, ii, 30). By entering the monastery, Martin seeks to retreat from a

father who expresses love only through cruelty, who demands obedience but
despises those who obey, and who, in general, thinks of his son as a man thinks
of a game leg, as an unwieldy extension of himself. "All you want is me to justify *you!*" Martin retorts angrily. "Well, I can't, and, what's more, I won't" (I,
iii, 50). Only by refusing to comply with his father's wishes can Martin force
Hans to take note of at least the negative force of his identity.

Nevertheless, twenty-four years later, Martin will have fulfilled Hans's
greatest wish by fathering a son. By then we no longer even hear of the mother,
who in the beginning of the play is conspicuous only by her absence at her
son's ordination. The historical Luther too lived in a nearly exclusively masculine world. "One comes to ask, over and over again, didn't the man have a
mother?" Erikson wonders in his psychoanalytical study.[36] Like Erikson,
Osborne attempts to make that absence meaningful. Unlike Erikson, however,
Osborne does so through poetic imagery, at once more economic and richly
suggestive than any explanation. "She made a gap," says Martin about his
mother, "which no one else could have filled, but all she could do was make it
bigger, bigger and more unbearable" (I, iii, 52). In other words, mother stands
for a longing and a pain that Martin carries through life. "Funnily enough,"
Martin says, "my mother disappointed me the most, and I loved her less, much
less" (I, iii, 52). Understandably so: the essential lack or incompleteness con-
noted by the concept "mother" is experienced more acutely whenever Martin
is struck by the glaring disjunction between the ideal and its particular embodiment in the woman he despisingly refers to as "my father's wife."

That Martin never forgave his mother for beating him for the theft of a nut
stands reported in history.[37] He does not hate his mother only because she beat
him harshly; so did his father. That the punishment she inflicted on him was
disproportionate to the crime is not an issue for Martin, who would not have
expected more measured justice from the irascible father whom he nevertheless continued to love. When the father beats his son, it is out of a fierce impatience with the limitations of the flesh. But the mother's heart is not in the
punishment, either because she does not love sufficiently or because she herself is merely an instrument of the father. Devoid of affect, her punishment is
obscene, instilling shame rather than revolt. Martin feels thrown back upon
himself, cut off from the universe, reduced to that unbearable body, "bent
between *my* knees and *my* chin" (I, iii, 53). The father's punishment hardens
the body, creating, as Martin says, "corns on my backside" that increase his
resistance, but the mother's punctures the inviolacy of the body, exposing its
inner weakness: "She beat me until the blood came, I was so surprised to see
it on my fingertips" (I, iii, 53). A backside covered with corns, the theft of a
nut, and fingers erupting into blood are images all too obviously sexually
charged. The mother's punishment apparently coincided with a moment of
secret pleasure for Martin, symbolized by the theft of a nut. From then on, Martin is trapped in a state of heightened vigilance between desire and fear, torn

between two contrary impulses—the impulse to abandon himself to the fluidity of the body in vomit, excrement, or sudden verbal ejaculations, and the impulse to retain the wholeness of the body through silence, constipation, and the containment of desire.

Female, death, excrement—these are the basic images that unite in Martin's fear of the dark hole. "I'm afraid of the darkness, and the hole in it," says Martin, having walked out of the dark recesses of the cone toward the dazzling light (I, ii, 24). The hole he is afraid of is not only the grave and the mother, but also the hole he huddles over, head between knees, in the *secretus locus monachorum*, "the monks' secret place," the latrine, where chronic constipation gives him ample opportunity to meditate concretely on the abjectness of his body. There, the dark hole, awaiting what he cannot or will not give, assumes the properties of a *vagina dentata*, as he, sick in the stench of his own failed being, imagines beneath him "a large rat, a heavy, wet, plague rat, slashing at my privates with its death's teeth" (II, iii, 76). The hole, in other words, represents both his desire for and fear of surrender. Trapped between the two, he can only sit and suffer.

THE CHILD IN THE CONE

All his life, Martin is hounded by an image that represents the opposite of isolation and entrapment, the image of "the lost body of a child, hanging on a mother's tit, and close to the warm, big body of a man" (I, ii, 24). This image of a family physically and lovingly united around an innocent child does not correspond with the reality of childhood. At the end of the play, an aging Martin carries a child once again—this time, his son Hans. It has been crying in its sleep; so even at that age a child is far from innocent and already racked by wordless anxieties. Martin longs for an innocence and unconditional love he knows he never had and thus never lost. The image rather represents the unattainable ideal of the holy family, a family holy even in the flesh; and the child corresponds to the "spotless host," offered for humanity's salvation.

Yet it is difficult for Martin to accept any form of mediation between the absolute sinfulness of the flesh and the absolute righteousness of God. He is too much aware of his own fundamental abjectness and vileness—a conviction he expresses through striking images: he is a worm that has to be crushed (I, i, 19), a sweating pig (I, ii, 27), a trough for the devil to feed from (I, ii, 31). The lost body of the child or the spotless host reminds Martin less of redemption and salvation than of the distance separating him from the state of innocence. When he reaches out to children in the street, they turn away from him (I, iii, 74). Even the birds that flock around his mentor, Father Staupitz, fly away at his approach (II, ii, 61). Father Staupitz, however, is not so easily persuaded that birds or children speak God's judgment on Martin's unworthiness. He rightfully suspects a degree of childish naiveté or innocence behind Martin's absolutism that, rather than being tempered by experience, hardens with each piece of fresh evidence of human weakness.

Martin conceives of divinity in the most absolute of terms—as a power beyond human scope and thus beyond negotiations or compromise. Yet his experience of divine power is also vividly concrete, enmeshed as it is with a child's memory of a never satisfied, stern father. The idea that one could flatter or cajole the godhead by being a good human being is absurd to him. Had he ever managed to impress even his own father through good behavior? How could "good works" or following prescripts then lead to God? As a monk he expressed derision for the monastic rule by paying it meticulous attention. "By your exaggerated attention to the Rule," Staupitz observes, "you make the authority ridiculous" (II, ii, 63). Worldly authority may be one of the masks of God, but should never be confused with God himself. For the same reason, he abhors indulgences because they humanize God, suggesting that one can "strike bargains" with him (II, ii, 70). He insists that God's demands cannot be met, that "there is no security at all, either in indulgences, holy busywork or anywhere in this world" (II, iii, 75).

The thought of God's absolute and implacable authority is existentially unbearable, threatening the individual with engulfment into the nameless. If we cannot become worthy of God's respect through actions or prayers, then we are doomed to live in failure, pushed forever into silence. Under certain conditions, however, abject humility may invert itself into bold self-affirmation. Once Luther accepted uncertainty as humanity's only certainty, he stood at the beginning of a new and powerful faith. In existentialist terms, self-engendering is the only adequate response to aleatory contingency. The image of Martin walking through the cone with a naked child in his arms now becomes blasphemous in another, rather unexpected way. The child is Christ but also Martin himself, the embodiment of his longing for an innocence given only to God. In search of certainty, Martin has attempted to give birth to God. The cone through which he approaches the light of certainty represents not woman or womb, but its blasphemous masculine correlative, the bowel and the anus.

The idea that Luther arrived at his most important spiritual insight, "justification through faith," while defecating is not Osborne's but Erikson's, based on a much contested but colorful testimony about Luther's "revelation in the tower." "Dise Kunst," Luther is reported to have said of his insight that faith is more important than good works, "hatt mir der Spiritus Sanctus auff diss Cl. eingeben." In Erikson's translation: "the holy spirit endowed me with this art on the Cl," in which Cl. would stand for "cloaca," the Latin term for latrine.[38] Whatever the historical truth of this may be, for Erikson as well as for Osborne, blocked bowels are Martin's neurotic symptom, the objective correlative for a feeling of "drying up" in the presence of the Absolute.

If nothing can bring him closer to God, Martin must allow himself to be penetrated by the Spirit. "You are a bride and you should hold yourself ready like a woman at conception" is Staupitz's advice to Luther (II, ii, 68). Martin indeed suddenly feels God's grace on him. Both spiritually and physically, faith leaves the absoluteness of God intact while allowing Martin a way out of oppressed silence. If he has faith, then God will be able to speak through him and release a living stream of words. "Breathe into me," Martin prays. "Give me life, oh Lord. Give me life" (II, vi, 98). "And I sat in my heap of pain until the words emerged and opened out," Martin recalls. "My pain vanished, my bowels flushed and I could get up. I could see the life I'd lost" (II, iii, 76). The release of his bowels is accompanied by a truly visceral understanding of the meaning of St. Paul's "the just shall live by faith." In other words, the physical correlative of Martin's sudden exhilarating conviction of certainty is the experience of abundant release that comes after a prolonged and painful bout of constipation. Martin, says Erikson, "changed from a highly restrained and retentive individual into an explosive person; he had found an unexpected release of self-expression, and with it, of the many-sided power of his personality."[39]

Martin has found a voice. The conviction of justification by faith endows him with irresistible charisma, whose Greek root *kairos* in fact means "divine favor." The release of his bowels now becomes associated with the act of creation, of giving birth to the "innocent child" of his ideal self. "You're like every man who was ever born in this world, Martin," says his father. "You'd like to pretend that you made yourself, that it was *you* who made you—and not the body of a woman and another man" (I, iii, 50). Many years later, Martin will affirm his father's understanding when he tells his son, "it's hard to accept you're anyone's son, and you're not the father of yourself" (III, iii, 125). From then on, when Martin unleashes his sermons on the people, he is giving birth to himself.

In contrast, when he is not guided by faith but crushed by feelings of unworthiness, his words dry up. He entered the monastery because he wanted to "speak to God directly," as an innocent child, "without any embarrassment." In such intensity of longing one hears all too clearly the voice of frustrated desire for love and acceptance. "When it came to it," Martin continues, "I dried up—as I always have" (I, iii, 45). Later when Martin is fast becoming a famous preacher, Staupitz reminds him how he, Martin, used to "fall up the steps [of the pulpit] with fright. Sheer fright!" (II, ii, 68). At such moments, far from being able to give birth to a living stream of words, Martin fails even to slip into the formulas he is expected to speak. The accompanying stabbing pains in his abdomen remind him then of how words, razor-sharp with intolerable significance, can strike cruelly at one's life. In this way, Martin's life oscillates between doubt and certainty, each in the acuteness of its sensation deepening the experience of the other.

GOD'S EYES AND THE DEVIL'S ORGAN

"God's Eyes!" is one of Hans's preferred swearwords in his peremptory dealings with Martin. One can imagine that, in the manner of swearwords, "eyes"
stands euphemistically for a less noble part of the anatomy. As it is, however,
the swearword calls up Martin's terror at the thought of the stern, unflinching
gaze of God—the gaze Abraham implicitly trusted, and Isaac confidently
returned. Originally, Martin had fled into the monastery to escape a too
demanding father, hoping to find acceptance in God's eyes and thus gain a
childish innocence; but, as he learned at his first celebration of the Mass, he is
unable to raise his eyes and meet God's gaze: "all I see of Christ is a flame and
raging on a rainbow. Pray to your Son, and ask Him to still His anger, for I
can't raise my eyes to look at Him" (I, ii, 33).

The opposite of "God's eyes," though not less terrifying, is the "devil's
organ." Where God is represented by a raging, petrifying flame, the devil is
associated with the hole, the dark, and the castrating plague rat—in other
words, with dissolution; the liquefication of the body; and the loss of boundaries in violence, desire, and death. "When I see chaos," Martin says, explaining why he called for the bloody repression of the Peasants' rebellion, "then I
see the devil's organ and then I'm afraid" (III, ii, 108). In a more general sense,
Martin detects chaos and the "devil's organ" in anything that threatens the sin-
gularity of the individual. "No man can die for another, or believe for another
or answer for another," he says. "The moment they try they become a mob"
(III, iii, 120–121).

Between the individual and the mob, there are apparently no intermedi-
ate stages—such as a community of mutually responsible citizens. Martin's
insistence that no one can "answer for another" recalls his angry rejoinder to
his father's accusation that Martin has failed him: "Just stop asking me what
have I accomplished, and what have I done for you," Martin says. "I've done
all for you I'll ever do, and that's live and wait to die" (I, iii, 50). No one can
justify anyone else; each has to live inexorably alone. His own failure to reconcile the requirements of selfhood with the demands of communal living has
led Martin to reject the notion that people may sometimes act for one another.
If they nevertheless seem to be doing so, then they must have lost all individuality and have become a mob; and then they create chaos where there was
once divinely ordained order. Only Christ can live and die for others; only
Christ can patiently submit and finally overcome the total annihilation of per-
sonhood that the Father requires. Any mob who claims to be doing the same
must therefore be acting "against Christ" (III, iii, 120).

Caught between the raging blaze of God's eyes and the dark hole that is
the devil's organ, Martin is thrown back upon himself, transfixed in his miserable existence, unable to speak, act, or create. Yet in the image of the "lost
body of a child" both extreme threats join to create a picture of warm, sensual

intimacy and supreme innocence. "Hanging on a mother's tit," the child derives nourishment from the dreaded liquefication of the body—a quality typified as feminine and elsewhere associated with dark, death, and devil. In the child's proximity, the "big body of a man"—which otherwise represents the petrifying threat of law, the rule of demand and punishment—provides protection and warmth (I, ii, 24). So feminine and masculine forces conjoin in maintaining the child's state of innocence.

The "body of a child" is a memory before all memories, before language and self-awareness. It is knowledge that drives the child out of its paradise and that disturbs the harmony of dark and light, feminine and masculine: "I lost the body of a child, a child's body, the eyes of a child; and at the first sound of my own childish voice" (I, ii, 24). The moment the child hears itself, it no longer simply "is" but "becomes for itself," distinct from those around it. The mother may want to feed as well as nurse and becomes a beckoning black hole. The father's "big body" stands between the child and its desires; his protection is now experienced as prohibition. With language comes anxiety, a state of simultaneous longing and dread, produced by the forbidden and intolerable knowledge that everything is at once itself and its opposite. What is that "body of a child" after all but a nameless parasitic creature called from darkness into light by nothing but blind, bodily desire. Even the most peaceful, innocent moments now reveal their "other" side. Martin lives in constant fear, "for instance of the noise the Prior's dog makes on a still evening when he rolls over on his side and licks his teeth" (I, ii, 24).

Still, Martin clings to the image of that holy family, that family holy in the flesh. It represents an unmoving and unmoved universe in which everything fully coincides with itself. In such a world, there is no difference, therefore no threat, anxiety, demand, doubt, and betrayal. The lost body of a child is the image of pure Being and pure Nothingness, before the Voice, before language and before difference. The body of the child is indeed "lost"; in fact, it was always already lost and necessarily so. Realization of this blessed state would result not just in the denial of everything that is, but in the denial of being altogether. As Martin, however, does not surrender the notion, the depth of his misery is as immeasurable as the distance that separates him from his ideal. This precisely is the measure of his singular existence: "there's no bottom to it, no bottom to my breath, and I can't reach it" (I, ii, 25).

Because of that utopia of peaceful and ideal transparency, being-in-the-world assumes an intolerable heaviness and therefore desperately seeks to empty itself into the steadily growing space between what is and what could be. What Martin first requires, however, is the assurance that the self-abandon which he associates with the "devil's organ" will ultimately lead to self-gain, that by losing oneself, one will gain oneself, that "in the teeth of death we live" (III, ii, 111). To accomplish that, Martin himself must become transparent to God; he must have "faith": like Isaac on the altar, he has to open his eyes and allow God's gaze to flood his being. When that happens, he is set free. Afterward, he can get up and take the measure of his existence; he can then literally see the life he has lost: "My pain vanished, my bowels flushed and I could get up. I could see the life I'd lost" (II, iii, 76). When he has faith, Martin, in other words, becomes both actor and spectator of God's Will.

Martin's is a tragic mind that, like Pascal's in Lucien Goldman's vision, struggles with the *deus absconditus,* a God that consists of internalized absolutes, a most forbidding super-ego, who sees without being seen, who never responds but always watches with disapproving eye—a struggle that nonetheless has to be fought out in the only arena available, this world:

> The tragic mind sees the world as nothing and as everything at one and the same time. The God of tragedy is a God who is always present and always absent. Thus, while his presence takes all value and reality from the world, his equally absolute and permanent absence makes the world into the only reality which man can confront, the only sphere in and against which he can and must apply his demand for substantial and absolute values.[40]

An audience assures Martin of the visibility of his struggle and of its supra-individual importance. In that sense, Martin loves his audience, as a sculptor loves the block of stone that gives body to his vision. It is true that he talks through them rather than at them, nevertheless, they help him to give shape to his ideas.

Ultimately however, Martin is his own best audience. When he cries out "I am alone. I am alone, and against myself" (I, i, 20), he is not just giving voice to the loneliness of a divided self; he is expressing fascination with his own abjectness. Even his loneliness is played out grandly, center-stage and against a cosmic backdrop. What better way of bearing one's misery than becoming a drama unto oneself—and to hope that God is watching too. What attracts him in suffering is the idea of suffering—an abstraction from experience that involves an element of spectatorship and theatricality: Martin imagines his suffering to be observed—by himself, by the universe, by God.[41] Proof of the spectacular quality of his suffering, of the importance of its imagined visibility, can be found in one of his more peculiar visions of torment. In that dream he sees many men and women lying in layers on top of each other, in a "pile . . . many people deep" (I, i, 21). The panic at the idea of suffocation and anonymity that accompanies that dream applies to his present condition; and yet, he realizes he lies on top, not at the bottom of the heap. He can apparently share the suffering of those at the bottom, but not their invisibility.

However, suffering, not joy, is his lot. God will not enter him because Martin is good or innocent; it is only by repudiating himself that Martin will gain himself, and it is only through excruciating solitude that he will learn to speak for all. Martin will have to fling away his life, will have to offer himself to

God's wrath, as Isaac offered himself to Abraham's knife. So Martin, even at the height of triumph, always sweats and suffers because the only way he can affirm life is in the act of denying it. Martin understands this intuitively. In fact, the answer may have come to him in an epileptic fit, when he uttered a wild, broken shout: "Not! Me! I am *not!*" (I, i, 23). Through form and content, the shout expresses his present condition and suggests a possible answer. The broken syntax in "Not! Me!" reflects his experience of fragmentation; the phrase "I am not" can be read as an expression of fear, an incomplete version of "I am not the one you are looking for." The curious emphasis on "not," however, opens up more interesting readings. "I am the one who is not or who fails to be" would confirm his self-hate and suggest the threat of impending annihilation through engulfment in the absolute. Its literal signification, "I am negation," may, however, be the most relevant: as God negates everything Martin is or does, Martin will henceforward identify with the act of negation itself.

"But where is your joy?" This is Hans's pertinent question upon visiting Martin in the gloomy monastery (I, iii, 51). The idea that adversity makes one stronger is one of the commonplaces of Christianity. Staupitz indicates as much when he says, "the moment someone disagrees or objects to what you're saying, *that* will be the moment when you'll suddenly recognize the strength of your belief!" (II, ii, 72). Martin indeed depends on opposition for the clarification of his ideas and the formation of his identity. He preaches like a man forging ahead into a stiff breeze. The result is a forceful, down-to-earth style, popular among his audience. His admirers, of course, do not realize that what their preacher loves and requires is the idea of their resistance and disapproval. What liberates and animates Martin's speech is the thought that "there are plenty who sit out there stiff with hatred." Anger is his source of inspiration—an anger sustained by the idea of being hated and of having to penetrate a wall of resistance and dislike (II, ii, 70).

For Martin more is at stake: only negation can give sense to an existence deprived of positive means of asserting itself. Moments which for him present incontrovertible proof of his separation from ideal innocence usually precede his strongest feats of self-affirmation. Right after a little boy gets up and walks away from his proffered hand, Martin delivers his ninety-five theses and his famous sermon on the importance of faith (II, iii, 74). Faith does not liberate Martin from his sense of unworthiness; it is rather that when he has Faith, he dares to flaunt his abjectness almost joyously. At the Diet of Worms, face to face with the wrath of the established powers, Martin's whole body seems to break out. The Knight serves as witness: "His scalp looked blotchy and itchy, and you felt sure, just looking at him, his body must be permanently sour and white all over, even whiter than his face and like millstone to touch. He'd sweated so much by the time he'd finished, I could smell every inch of him even from where I was" (III, i, 104). Years later, thinking back on that moment of personal and public exposure, when he triumphed but could as well have been utterly crushed, Luther says to the son he cradles in his arms, "I was almost like you that day, as if I'd learned to play again, to play, to play out in the world, like a naked child" (III, iii, 125).

THE NEGATIVE WAY OF ANGER

Commentators who have exerted themselves in clarifying the differences and similarities between Osborne's Martin Luther and the historical character on which he is based have remarked that Osborne's has none of the warmth and congeniality of the real Luther.[42] "Mr. Osborne has chosen to disregard the convivial and generous impulses of which there is ample evidence," said Evelyn Waugh, "and to make his hero sickly, rancorous, and foul-mouthed."[43] Luther did more than accuse and annihilate; he could at times be a patient, constructive thinker, a builder rather than a destroyer. In contrast, Osborne's *Luther* exalts negativity as the sole approach to God. Theologically, this would bring Osborne's Luther close to church fathers, like Dionysius the Pseudo-Areopagite, who, to safeguard the absoluteness of the Godhead, rejected any attempt to reach God actively or to define "Him" in positive terms. This came to be known as the via negativa, the negative way to God, or sometimes the "way of remotion."

The likeness is not altogether implausible. As Paul Tillich explains, Luther's God "is not a God who is a being beside others; it is a God whom we can have only through contrast. What is hidden before God is visible before the world, and what is hidden before the world is visible before God."[44] Yet Luther's negativity ultimately leads to its opposite, a bold asserting and affirming of the direct presence of the Godhead, an ardent faith that breaches all impediments to belief. For that reason, Luther rejected the via negativa as embracing a negativity beyond redemption that obscured the Godhead.[45] In moments of blessedness, when Luther feels the Spiritual Presence, he experiences "a feeling of fulfillment which cannot be disturbed by negativities in other dimensions." "In finite beings," Tillich continues, "this positive experience is always united with the awareness of its contrary, the state of unhappiness, despair, condemnation. This 'negation of the negative' gives blessedness its paradoxical character. . . . Without an element of negativity neither life nor blessedness can be imagined."[46]

Osborne's vision of Luther's negative approach to God is more relevant when we leave the issue of historical correctness behind and consider the play as an investigation into the neurotic origin of the kind of artistic voice Osborne was interested in and assumed to be his own. "If the play proves nothing about Luther," Charles Marowitz said, "it proves a great deal about John Osborne."[47] Other reviewers noted the same—in fact, some poked fun at the play for that very reason: "The play which recently opened in London is called *Luther.*

Mr. Osborne's name outside the theatre is in letters of the same size. A quick glance: John Osborne by Luther? Surely not."[48] Osborne clearly delighted in the confusion and contributed to it. Martin's interrogation by Cajetan consists of the kind of remarks often made about Osborne, the "angry young man" who made so much noise, little of which was original on closer investigation, and who incessantly criticized without ever contributing anything positive. Martin's heresy, says Cajetan likewise, is not original; it seeks to destroy everything but has nothing positive to offer in its place; it is the product of a frustrated rather than of a revolutionary mind (II, iv, 85, 89, 90). "So you're the one they call the excessive doctor," is Cajetan's greeting remark. "You don't look excessive to me. Do you feel very excessive?" To which Martin replies with the same irritation with which Osborne shrugged off people's attempts to label him angry: "It's one of those words which can be used like a harness on a man" (II, iv, 79–80). Osborne hated to be typecast, as much as Martin did, and distanced himself from any movement people associated him with. "Movement [is] a word he hates," said Stephen Watts after interviewing the playwright.[49] Journalists cast Osborne either as a farcical or tragic character. In the latter case, the resemblance with Osborne's Luther was striking: "He is alone," said Simon Kavanaugh, "utterly and irrevocably, in his agony: a part of no movement, and certainly not that of the Angry Young Men. But he is no ivory-towered idealist either. He participates strenuously . . . [but] refutes any suggestion that he has a solution to offer."[50]

Osborne has moreover identified his play *Luther* as the most obvious expression of a deeply ingrained puritanical element in his own personality.[51] "I have Puritan aspects to my character, and am morally intolerant in many ways. I believe in the eighteenth-century idea of moral virtue, in the Calvinistic, certainly pre-Freudian idea, that some people are better than others, are born better."[52] Osborne's life oscillated between exhilarating certainty and crushing doubt, a conviction of innate superiority and unbearable self-loathing.[53] He suffered prolonged bouts of severe depression, moments of "terrible gloom" and "speechless despair."[54] Friends (or former friends, since Osborne alienated so many of them) refer to him as a "lonely, self-destructive man who demanded total loyalty and couldn't accept friends on their own terms."[55]

Undoubtedly, in writing about Luther, Osborne sought to write about his own artistic struggle that centered around the problem of voice and audience. Depressed by the failure of his last play *Déjàvu*, Osborne admitted in 1992 to being plagued by a nagging doubt, dating back to the beginning of his career— a doubt shared by many writers during their lonely work: whom am I writing for? Is anyone listening? Why am I writing? Perhaps silence would be better.[56] How did Martin overcome such feelings of inadequacy, of being choked, of not being able to utter a word in the presence of overwhelming demands, indifference, or hostility? How was he finally able to open up and release a stream of words that would set other minds ablaze and change the aspect of the world? In the final instance, Martin's problem is an artistic one. "Martin, you're a poet," says the Knight when he sees Martin's fear at the bloody effect his words had in the Peasants' movement (III, ii, 109). If to imbue with general validity one's personal obsessions can serve as a definition of the artist's aim, then Martin's way out of his neurosis was the way of the artist. It manifests itself not as a peacefully coiling stream—as it was for Virginia Woolf in *A Room of One's Own*, for instance—but as a sudden jet, a powerful ejaculation of language. "I used to rage in an instant knocking out 900 words," said Osborne, but also admitted to being unable to put pen to paper for long periods of time.[57] Like that of the angry young man artist, Martin's vehemence is a measure not of his power but of his vulnerability: his faith has nothing to lean on, it has to stand solely by virtue of its own inner tension—hence, the suffering, the pain, the sweating. "I smell because of my own argument," cries Martin. "I smell because I never stop disputing with Him" (III, ii, 110).

In *Luther,* Osborne intimates that the artist's voice is often born out of anger, out of the conviction that it speaks alone, against the world. For that same reason, it also thinks to speak for the world, attempting to fill the vacuum between what is and what could be. It is always a futile act and therefore always in need of renewing itself from a source of limitless frustration. Nostalgia for lost origins is such a source—inexhaustible because it is both a necessary impossibility and an impossible necessity. The mode in which Osborne sought to work was that of anguish, a mixture of desire and fear. He explored it using pre-conceptual forms of knowledge such as intuition and imagery. He always balanced carefully between knowing and not knowing, afraid that otherwise his creation would evaporate. "Show him your backside and let him have it," says Martin to his son who is plagued by the devil (III, iii, 125). As in a bad dream, pursuer and pursued are one and the same. The moment they meet, the tension that separates them dissolves, and the dream is gone.

Part II

CHAPTER 6

At the Top, 1964–1971

In the mid-sixties to early seventies, Osborne was widely regarded as one of the most important British playwrights alive—a recognition no longer based on novelty or youthful charm but on proven technical, stylistic, and intellectual ability. *Inadmissible Evidence* (1964) and *A Patriot for Me* (1965) must be counted among his technically most accomplished works and will receive close attention in the following chapters. In 1965, Irving Wardle concluded that "the last decade has been the most fertile period in British drama since the Restoration and no one has contributed more to it than Osborne."[1] Many "angries" profited from the media attention Osborne's success had ensured for their work, but few survived the sixties and made an impact as lasting as Osborne.

Even so the years of recognition already carried the signs of Osborne's decline, caused not so much by his falling out of favor with the public as by his growing irrelevance in the world of innovative theatre. The drama of the late fifties and early sixties, formative years in Osborne's career, was shaped by the lingering reactionary attitudes it rebelled against. "The censor's first rule," Osborne said, "is Please Do Not Disturb. Do not offend, do not hurt anyone's feelings, *don't* get excited."[2] For a serious artist intent on affecting the audience, this meant almost by definition challenging the Lord Chamberlain's limited tolerance. Osborne therefore found himself in the vanguard of the battle against censorship and testified as being "utterly opposed to censorship in any form in any art" before a House of Lords Committee on 29 November 1966.[3]

Ironically, Osborne received the majority of his awards in the years of official censorship (Evening Standard awards in 1956, 1965, and 1968; the New York Drama Critics awards in 1958 and 1965; and an Oscar in 1963),[4] and his career started to decline almost immediately after censorship was abolished. As Lindsay Anderson put it, "in those days [of censorship] the Establishment seemed firmly entrenched and healthily reactionary. We had something to fight against.">[5] Without the "Do Not Disturb" sign of censorship, Osborne's anger lost its political significance and appeared self-indulgent.

The late sixties brought another dramatic renewal, one that left Osborne behind because it took place on the fringe of the traditional theatres in which Osborne had made his mark. Regarding theatrical institutions as emanations of a political and commercial establishment, the theatrical innovators of the late sixties looked for alternative venues: community theatres, factories, schools, cultural centers, marketplaces, and streets. The new names were Howard Brenton, David Hare, Snoo Wilson, Trevor Griffith, and David Edgar, all of whom had started out writing Agit-Prop, rapid intervention drama, sometimes written in collaboration, that responded to immediate political problems.

Censorship had made words dangerous. After its abolishment, drama was less interested in the subversive effect of "mere" words and shifted its attention to action—to performance. While the late fifties had been dominated by Brechtian performance techniques and the language experiments of Absurdism, the late sixties saw the emergence of techniques inspired by Antonin Artaud's "Theatre of Cruelty." Artaud's *Le théâtre et son double* (1938; *The Theatre and its Double*) presented a vision of a theatre gesturing toward the underlying terrible impossibility of existence. Not much of that complex, perhaps equally impossible vision survived in Peter Brook's 1964 production at the Aldwych of Peter Weiss's *Marat/Sade* . It was that production nevertheless that set the standards for the Theatre of Cruelty in Britain, mainly proving the commercial viability of theatre as a series of spectacular and violent assaults on bourgeois sensibilities.[6] In a similar way, playwrights such as Howard Brenton and Edward Bond would resort to visually violent scenes (what Bond called the "aggro-effect"), allegedly to shake the audience into political awareness.

Theatre of the late sixties and seventies was in constant upheaval, exploring its own limits and challenging what "bourgeois" theatre had taken all too much for granted. Experiments with audience participation deprived the audience of its inviolability; improvisation questioned text and author-dominated theatre, the theatre of the single vision; crudity and sexual explicitness challenged the last remnants of decorum. Unlike the theatre in which Osborne had worked, the new theatre was more closely allied to comic strips, newspapers, and political tracts than to traditional literature. What alarmed Osborne was that, in doing so, theatre became more interested in performance and less in language: "When millions of people seem unable to communicate with one another," Osborne said, "it's vitally important that words be made to work. It may be very old-fashioned, but they're the only things we have left. When I turn that electric light on, I don't know why it works, and I don't want to. It's a mystery I'm delighted to preserve. But the verbal breakdown is getting to the point where it's dangerous and nonsensical. I have a great allegiance to words."[7] What Osborne disapproved of most, however, and what certainly hampered reception of his work, was that the new developments implied a growing impatience with the myth of Art, so that inspiration and authenticity were rapidly becoming outmoded or politically suspect notions. True to its mission to remain a source of renewal, the Royal Court Theatre slowly adapted its image accordingly.

At the height of Osborne's career, George Devine, the man who had played such a crucial role in it, suffered a heart attack on a sweltering day in August 1965, after playing Baron von Epp in Osborne's *A Patriot for Me.* A month later, Devine retired as the ESC's artistic director. His death in January the following year brought to a close an era of fruitful cooperation between Osborne and the RCT. In Osborne's mind, none of the artistic directors that followed—William Gaskill, Lindsay Anderson, and Anthony Page—could fill Devine's shoes. For a time, Gaskill and Anderson honored the long-standing tradition of having Osborne's plays first performed at the RCT before having them move on to the West End; but according to Gaskill, *Time Present, Hotel in Amsterdam,* and *West of Suez,* all directed by Anthony Page, "failed to strike the same response in audiences as his earlier works. George Devine had died and some of Osborne's talent seemed to die with him."[8] Instead of Osborne, the RCT now championed new names, which included Christopher Hampton, Ted Whitehead, and David Storey.   In Osborne's opinion, Gaskill and Page were nothing but "titswingers," all too eager to follow trends that were making the RCT increasingly dependent on state subsidy. In 1969, the RCT converted one of its rehearsal rooms into the Theatre Upstairs, a smaller venue more amenable to experimental drama. From the early seventies, it opened its doors to Fringe groups—for instance, hiring David Hare, co-founder of the traveling Fringe group Portable Theatre, as resident dramatist from 1970 to 1971. "Whenever I think of going to see what they're doing," Osborne would later say of the RCT, "I find it's a play by someone called Les and directed by someone called Ron."[9] On another occasion, he complained that "the Court regime has really been taken over by *Time Out* magazine, which is awful. All sorts of pot and beer and Left agit-prop troglodytes."[10] With usual perversity, Osborne concluded, "the Royal Court, without George Devine, has become sentimental and old-fashioned."[11]

Osborne's image became increasingly that of a political conservative and, theatrically speaking, of a man out of touch with new developments in art. *Vogue* called Osborne a patriot and "chief spokesman for England"—dubious praise, though, in a decade marked by a rush toward increasing globalization.[12] In 1967, Harold Wilson's Labour government negotiated Britain's entry into the European Economic Community, the Common Market, with the argument that it would bring prosperity. "Such power and influence," cried Osborne, "has not been brought to bear upon a dull and torpid people since the Americans brought corn whisky to the defeated Indians."[13] Though the application was then vetoed by French president Charles de Gaulle, the move toward Europe

could not be halted for long and was completed under Edward Heath's conservative government in 1973.

In 1968, year of international political upheaval, Osborne's only form of
political protest was to write a letter to the *Times* defending himself against
allegations that his company, Woodfall films, had not ceased its distribution in
South Africa, though Osborne had favored a ban on cultural exchange with
that country.[14] For the rest, the turbulent political events of 1968 largely passed
him by. "I don't know whether my focus is getting smaller or my England is
getting smaller," he told Kenneth Tynan, "but if so I don't make any apologies.
I think it's more real, and more human." This sounded too much like an excuse
for political quietism at a time when political unrest took international forms.
Students were marching in Paris, occupying offices and paralyzing France, and
in the United States the National Guard was called in to contain student
protests contesting their country's war in Vietnam. Always eager to do the
opposite of what the trendy cultural elite considered proper form, Osborne
chose that very moment to call for reticence: "What was special about [the
fifties] was that we were all trying to raise the emotional temperature. One felt
one was living in an island of inertia. Well, one doesn't feel that any longer.
Nowadays my instinct is to lower the temperature rather than raise it, because
it seems to me that there's an unreal sort of medium hysteria going on in this
country. If anything, it needs a bromide."[15]

DEATH OF THE FATHERS

Time Present (1968), *The Hotel in Amsterdam* (1968), and *West of Suez* (1971)
signaled this shift in Osborne's political perception, though many remembered
having felt the trend already announcing itself in Bill Maitland's harsh disapproval of youth in *Inadmissible Evidence* (1964). All three plays featured in
major roles Osborne's fourth wife, the actress Jill Bennett. She had been a
friend of Penelope Gilliatt, Osborne's third wife, and had played Mrs. Daubeny
in *The Charge of the Light Brigade* (1968), for which Osborne had written the
script before it was taken over by Charles Wood. Osborne had also acted with
her in *It's Only Us,* by Peter Draper, a television play in ITV's Half Hour Story
series, broadcast on 26 June 1968. It is thanks to her that Osborne created a
number of interesting, while not quite flattering, roles for character actresses.

Both *Time Present* and *The Hotel in Amsterdam* bear as epigraph a quotation from Ecclesiastes: "A time to embrace and a time to refrain from
embracing. A time to get and a time to lose: a time to keep, and a time to cast
away." Accordingly, they feature people who resent the prevalent drift of time
with its inane cult of youth, its disdain for quality and style, and its relentless
pursuit of innovation. The critics were either perplexed or amused by
Osborne's apparently sudden conservatism: "Osborne began his career in fury
at a social structure that seemed to bar men like him from wealth, privilege and

social status. He now sounds like a Tory arriviste for whom all the champagne has proved to be flat."16

Pamela, the principal character in *Time Present,* presents herself indeed as High-Tory, though, as we suspect, mainly to vex Constance, the Labour M.P. whose apartment she shares (I, 207). Constance, as her name implies, is as constant in her friendship and admiration for Pamela as the latter is in her unsparing criticism of Constance and everything for which she in her female wisdom (her middle name is Sophia!) stands. She mocks Constance's campaign slogan, "striding into the Seventies with Labour!" protesting, "I haven't got used to hobbling about in the sixties yet" (I, 197). For Constance a politician's duty is to look forward and be prepared for the challenges of the future. "Time is in short supply in the present," she warns Pamela. For Pamela that is precisely why "we should keep [time] in its place. Whenever we can. Just because we can't win."

Yet if Pamela resists the pull of the future so desperately, it is mainly because she is held back by the weight of a past she has experienced vicariously through a father she loves and respects. Like the heroic-style actors Sir Henry Irving or Sir Donald Wolfit, Sir Gideon Orme is an actor of the old school who is now slowly dying in the sterile modernity of a hospital room. When the play opens, Pamela has just returned from her daily wake at his bedside. Other family members and friends will soon drift into Constance's apartment, delivering news of that powerful figure and sorting out their relationships on the background of his dying. Pamela's "bitchiness," her constant vituperation and her disparaging remarks directed at people who can hardly be called her enemies (several actor-friends, Constance, Constance's lover Murray, her eighteen-year-old half-sister Pauline, and her mother Edith) are a form of unacknowledged grieving for her father. Pamela is an actress herself, but through her father so much infected by a certain old-fashioned fastidiousness that she has difficulties finding suitable parts. The lucrative roles go to her friend Abigail, a Castro-loving film star, all too cruelly modeled on Vanessa Redgrave, whose myopic, bovine stare suggests a depth of being she wholly lacks.

Act I ends with the news of Orme's death. Several champagne-sloshed weeks later, Pamela, barely emerging from a long depression, decides to leave Constance. By then she is pregnant by Murray, Constance's lover, but is already efficiently planning an abortion. What drives her on is not the thought of Constance's anger, but of her forgiveness. She cannot abide the vulgarity of the reconciliation scene that Constance and Murray will surely have in store for her: "You're all bent on incest or some cosy hysteria," she tells Murray. "She's bound to blub. You're not above it, and we'll all end up on the floor embracing and comforting and rationalizing and rumpled and snorting and jammed together and performing autopsies and quite disgusting, all of it" (II, 230–231). If Pamela is so intent on fierce but lonely self-honesty, we realize, it is because she desperately wants to hold on to herself. She refuses to be "pronounced upon," as she puts it, and firmly declares, "I shall manage within my own, my own walls" (II, 224).

Time Present premiered at the Royal Court on 23 May 1968 and, though not scoring the success that people had by now come to expect from Osborne, did well enough to warrant a transfer to the West End. For playing "one of the longest parts ever written for a woman,"[17] Jill Bennett won the *Plays and Players* Award for Best Performance of the year.

In *Time Present,* Osborne brought together a number of characters whose only action consists of their endless talking, not always amusingly or coherently—in fact, quite often without apparent rhyme or reason. At its best, the dialogue attains a poetic beauty or intensity not unlike that of Chekhov, but unlike the latter's drama, Osborne's is not held together by thematic and symbolic unity. Instead, Osborne's dialogue maddeningly revolves around a powerful but absent figure that is supposed to function as a font of mysterious significance. The same nearly plot-less structure that characterized *Time Present* returned in Osborne's next play, *The Hotel in Amsterdam.* This did not meet with everyone's approval, and at a gala preview attended by various dignitaries including Princess Margaret and Lord Snowdon, half a dozen people walked out noisily before the end of the second act.[18] Quite probably, many others remained out of respect for the leading actor Paul Scofield, who, after his tremendous success as Sir Thomas More in Robert Bolt's *A Man for All Seasons* (1960) was widely considered the greatest actor of the post-Olivier/Gielgud generation. When the play opened at the Royal Court on 3 July 1968, it met with very mixed reviews.

Three couples active in various capacities in show biz and art have come to an expensive hotel in Amsterdam to escape their boss, a hard-driving film producer whom they refer to as K.L., and describe as "the biggest, most poisonous, voracious, Machiavellian dinosaur in movies" (I, 20). "He takes nothing out of the air around *his* head," scriptwriter Laurie complains. "Only us. Insinuates his grit into all the available oysters. And if ever any tiny pearls should appear from these tight, invaded creatures, he whips off with them, appropriates them and strings them together for his own necklace" (I, 76–77).[19] Now, without the ever-plotting K.L. to set them against each other, they are ready to enjoy each other's good company. However, they cannot restrain themselves from constantly wondering what K.L. is doing at that very moment, whether he has discovered that they have escaped from him, and what he will say upon their return.

Two evenings later, happy and relaxed, they allow themselves to fantasize about prolonging this experience, of building a small and mutually supportive community for themselves. Yet the fragility of their happiness becomes clear upon the arrival of Margaret's sister, Gillian, a young woman with an uncanny talent for inducing in others paralyzing self-awareness and guilt. As Laurie says, upon the news of her imminent arrival: "Oh, she'll be sick or pushing her food away or leaving it and pretending she's enjoying it and filling us up with guilt and damned responsibility. Damn her, we've just got together again, she's an odd man out" (II, 111). His opinion of her is confirmed when they learn that Gillian has already betrayed them to K.L. Laurie, who has been drinking steadily since breakfast, now makes use of his friend's absence to declare his love to the latter's wife. She reciprocates his love, but "the magic spell has been broken." A phone call reveals that K.L. has killed himself. Sobered, they ready themselves for the voyage back. "I wonder—if we'll ever come again?" one of them asks. "I shouldn't think so," Laurie replies, adding lamely, "but I expect we might go somewhere else. . ." (II, 135). With the disappearance of that hated figure, it has become impossible not to see the hole at the heart of their existence.

Osborne introduced yet another fragile community in his next play, *West of Suez,* first performed at the Royal Court Theatre, on 17 August 1971. The setting is an island in the Mediterranean, once part of the Empire but now a tax-haven for American and British citizens. Wyatt Gillman, played by yet another star-actor, Ralph Richardson, is a seventy-year old second-rate writer whose present fame is built on a carefully staged mediagenic eccentricity. Surrounded by his four daughters, their husbands and friends, he whiles away the time, savoring the island's comfortless comforts of sun, water, sand, drinks, boredom, obnoxious tourists, and sullen servants.

In the words of one reviewer, *West of Suez* is "a bleak and cheerless play,"[20] but at its best also a moving study in incoherence. It asks us to eavesdrop on people who not only fail to understand each other, but often fail to understand themselves, as is evidenced in the following dialogue between Frederica and Edward, a couple locked into the boredom and despair of marriage:

FRED: [. . . .] Why do you get cross when I ask questions?
ED: I don't. Only when you expect answers.
FRED: Friends? [She puts out her hand to him]
ED: Friends.
FRED: I did put out my hand.
ED: Yes. I know. First.
FRED: Don't say anything . . . I try to be detached.
ED: Why not? If it makes you feel more real?
FRED: Real? What's that, for God's sake?
ED: You can produce effects in real people. Including me, even. As if you were them. Or me.
FRED: I'm afraid I don't understand that. And I shouldn't think you can.
ED: No. Sometimes I don't feel I can understand a word of anything anyone says to me. As if they were as unclear as I am . . .
FRED: Too abstract for me. (I,19)

The repressed viciousness of this dialogue is almost tangible: Frederica's claiming to be detached is her way of implying what Edward refuses to believe, that she is capable of feeling pain. And he resists Frederica's gesture of being friends, considering it an attempt to force him into some sort of compliance. The cruelty is reciprocal, an almost offhand marital routine, that, though neither will care to admit it, still strikes at the marrow of their being. Their mutual distaste speaks in every word and action, as when Ed at first apparently ignores Frederica's sudden desire to sip from his drink, but then with deliberate rudeness calls for the waiter to bring him another one. Such grim gestures form the texture of their relationship, binding them to each other in a perverse intimacy.

A welter of dialogue among a great number of characters festers around the central figure of Wyatt, a public speaker adept at hiding himself even from himself. He appears hidden in a cloud of words, self-consciously dramatizing himself, putting himself on show: "I *have* had a time. Spoke to such a nice lot of people. Charming lot in the shops, and I went to that smashing little market. Got a splendid new hat" (I, 31). Wyatt loves to play the "holy innocent" but is in fact a crafty old fox who dons the naiveté of a child in order to be cruel or charming at whim. It is, so we sense, out of sheer boredom that during an interview with the island's local journalist, he permits himself to say what he knows will cause offense. "All the good things I've seen of the island seem to be legacies of the British, the Spanish, and the Dutch," he tells her. "As for the people, they seem to be a very unappealing mixture of hysteria and lethargy, brutality and sentimentality" (II, 62). He tells her "women only really love bullies" and claims to be "very fond" of the British class system. He has reached a stage in life where he believes, as he says, that only grief matters. The only real sin, in his opinion, is "the incapacity for proper despair" (II, 64). He refers to himself most humbly as merely a "clown" (II, 66).

The verdict on this shabby lot is spoken by an American beatnik, who unleashes a torrent of abuse on Wyatt's despised world. "There's only one word left," he shouts, "and you know what that is. It's fuck, man. Fuck . . . That's the last of the English for you babies. Or maybe shit. Because that's what we're going to do on you. Shit" (II, 69). When Wyatt tries to walk away, he is shot by rebelling natives, eliciting from Edward the closing remark: "My God— they've shot the fox . . ." (II, 70). Only a self-righteous generation could commit the fundamental sin of shooting the fox and thus destroying the purpose, the pleasure, and the grace of the hunt. What is there left now for the characters but to contemplate the hollowness of their lives and to confront, unaided, the prospects of a most cynical age.

MINOR WORK

Osborne's other work of that period comprises two adaptations (*A Bond Honoured* (1966, after Lope de Vega)and *Hedda Gabler* (1970, after Henrik Ibsen)) and three television plays (*The Right Prospectus* (1970), *Very Like a Whale* (1971), and *The Gift of Friendship* (1972)).

A Bond Honoured is Osborne's adaptation of *La fianza satisfecha,* a 16th century play attributed to Lope de Vega. Directed by John Dexter, then associate director of the National Theatre, and featuring Robert Stephens and Maggie Smith in the principal roles, it was staged by the National Theatre Company at the Old Vic on 6 June 1966, and linked, rather improbably, in a double bill with Peter Shaffer's successful farce *Black Comedy.* The play can be read as Osborne's answer to the Theatre of Cruelty, as the performance incorporated techniques first seen in Peter Brook's production of Peter Weiss's *Marat/Sade.* Entrances and exits were dispensed with and all actors were seated on stage in a circle, emphasizing the ritual aspect of the proceedings. "The acting style," Osborne explains in a stage direction, "must be extremely violent, pent-up, toppling on and over the edge of animal howlings and primitive rage. At the same time, it should have an easy, modern naturalness, even in the most extravagant or absurd moments" (I, i, 15). Physical violence was stylized, and wounds were symbolically indicated by the actors tying red bands around the wounded limb. The language, likewise, was "earthy, idiomatic, physical and yet somehow stylized, intractable, almost operatic."[21]

La fianza satisfecha tells the story of Leonido, a monster in human shape, who rapes his mother and, as he boasts, thirty virgins (among whom his sister Marcella, who could well be his own daughter). In the Spanish original, Leonido's cruel and un-Christian deeds (he also blinds his old father and becomes a Muslim to blaspheme against the Christian faith) are recounted in order to demonstrate Christ's limitless love. In the end, Leonido indeed experiences God's grace and redeems himself by dying Christ-like on the cross.

It was Kenneth Tynan, the critic who had helped Osborne in his career, who suggested the play to Osborne, perhaps in the belief that Leonido was a sort of angry young man of his time. Osborne, who worked from a literal translation, did indeed attempt to foreground the play's contemporary relevance. When Gerardo, Leonido's father, complains about his son, he might as well be speaking of England's Angry Young Men generation. Leonido's aimless rebelliousness, he says, is the behavior of a pampered and ungrateful youth: "— time it was all war and uncertainty. Now everything is easy come by and you and those like you hang about sniffing blood ungratefully and harrying everyone and everything in your rancorousness" (I, 3, 26).

Scholars examining Osborne's work as an adapter praised his judicious editing of what in the original is an all too flowery, baroque composition. "Where Osborne translates," Daniel Rogers concluded, "he does so with invigorating ruthlessness and a firm grasp of essentials," but, he warned, the "'Christian framework has been buckled if not wrenched apart."[22] Most reviewers agreed that Osborne obscured the religious implications of the play and to some extent turned Leonido into an existentialist hero whose desperate energy expresses nothing but repugnance at the tedium and hypocrisy of life. All too many men, Leonido believes, are "born dotards" (I, i, 19). He himself, and one hears Jimmy Porter speaking, is "awake to life itself." So much so, in fact, that he is incapable of a moment of rest. "Why is it," he tells his sleepy servant Tizon, "that of what they call the five Hindu hindrances you have only one: sloth? I have all the other four, craving, ill will, perplexity and restless brooding?" (I, i, 19). In Osborne's adaptation, Leonido rapes his sister, not, as in the original, to force God into acknowledging his existence, but because he cannot and does not want to withstand desire. As he says, "I always worked for passion rather than for profit" (I, iii, 29).

One could almost say that Osborne's Leonido is a man consistent and honest to a fault. Believing that civilized manners conceal the brutality that rules life, he refuses to dissemble. If others, like his father, force themselves upon their wives in the name of marriage, he will simply live up to reality and commit rape. So, in a sense, when he rapes his mother, he acts consistently in the brutal but true spirit of his own engendering. Later he follows the same logic in raping the offspring of that forced union, the beautiful Marcela, whose supposed chastity is the object of lengthy negotiations between his father, Geraldo, and his sister's suitor, Dionisio. In contrast with such mercantile disposing of the fruit of one's loins, rape is the pure enactment of desire.

Osborne treats Leonido sympathetically though not uncritically, emphasizing both his tremendous energy and desperate daring, but also the suffering to self and others that his nihilism entails. Osborne's Leonido attempts the impossible feat of a pure and sovereign self-creation through evil. He rejects Christ the "divine lawyer" who demands his fee and instead insists on "a harsh tribunal and the full exercise of justice" (II, ii, 55). He is in fact intent on besting Christ himself: "I have the best bond," he says. "Let the Good Lord pay pound for pound. I'll settle later" (III, vi, 40). Overdrawing his heavenly account, the accumulated capital of Christ's passion, he finally must die on the cross in order to redeem himself (II, ii, 54). [23] When his servant Tizon stabs and kills him, his father Gerardo regains his sight. The play ends with Tizon pointing out the dismal moral of the story: "Well, King, he played a good tune on vituperation. It may not be a bond honoured, but it's a tune of sorts to end with" (II, ii, 62).

Osborne's *A Bond Honoured* is the story of a splendid impossibility, namely that of extreme and uncompromising truthfulness. Having engaged in an existential experiment of unparalleled ruthlessness, Leonido has ended up as a disinterested aesthetic product, his very own artistic creation. That Osborne entertained high expectations with this play became clear when he publicly raged at the mixed reviews with which it was met.[24] With the memory of his critical defeat with *Paul Slickey* fresh in mind, Osborne sent out a series of hysterically worded, angry telegrams to the papers, some of them four pages long, declaring war on the critics:

The gentleman's agreement to ignore puny theatre critics as bourgeois conventions that keep you pinned in your soft seats is a thing that I fall in with no longer. After ten years it is now war. Not a campaign of considerable complaints in private letters but open and frontal war that will be as public as I and other men of earned reputation have the considerable power to make it.[25]

Such hysteria was only bound to provoke merriment. In others, like Benedict Nightingale, it confirmed their dislike of a playwright who could not abide anything but adulation and who was increasingly suspected of having mistaken his former success with the media as proof of the intrinsic and lasting merit of his work:

Every time Osborne opens his mouth, whether in *The Observer* or on television, there emerges the most extraordinary combination of intelligent aperçu, dreary blimpishness and inconsequential drivel—and arrogance, above all arrogance. Maybe it is the defensive arrogance of a vulnerable man (I wouldn't know), but that doesn't make it any less embarrassing. Osborne still seems to me to be the victim of our latter-day romanticism, our tendency to regard the creative writer as a sort of prophet, someone who has the right to expect a respectful hearing whatever subject he chooses to spout about. He is the very antithesis of Pinter, who disclaims all mantles and remains opaque to a fault. Osborne seems to expect his opinions to command attention simply because they are his.[26]

ANGRY WOMAN

"I have been fascinated for a long time by *Hedda Gabler,*" Osborne said. She is an angry young woman "born bored" but, like Jimmy Porter, endowed with "the gift of energy" (7,8). Unlike Jimmy who loved sex and food, Hedda however remains "petty, puny, frigid" (7). Together with Christopher Hampton, who also adapted the play in 1972, Osborne is one of the many in an army of modern translators and adapters (Eva Le Gallienne, Henry Beissel, Otto Reinert, Charles Marowitz, and others) who have marched in the footsteps of William Archer and Edmund Gosse, the first to introduce to the English public Henrik Ibsen's vision of Hedda Gabler's complex and tortured personality.

At first sight, not much distinguishes Osborne's translation from that of Archer and Gosse. He has simply trimmed Ibsen's overlong stage directions and left out all exclusively Norwegian references. Osborne's Tesman, for instance, no longer begs Hedda to address his aunt with "du," the Norwegian equivalent of "thou." Osborne has made the play more modern and more English, eliminating the many moments of stilted awkwardness that characterize the original translation. "And be sure to call in the afternoon," becomes the snappy "until later" (35). If Archer/Gosse's Tesman was still complaining about "perspiring" too much, in Osborne he is quite plainly "sweating" (41).

"I wish we had gone a little more economically to work" becomes "I think you could have splashed about on the house a little less" (33), and so on.

Osborne rightly emphasizes that *Hedda Gabler* is not just a one-charac-ter play—as, of course, had been said of his own *Look Back in Anger.* "The important point about the adaptation and production of the play," he says, "is very simple: the complexity of the character of Hedda Gabler is richer only if the other characters in the play are also seen to be made as rich as they are" (8). Perhaps for that reason he made Tesman less farcical than he appears in the Archer/Gosse translation by cutting down on his all too typical interjec-tions such as "eh" and "fancy that!" or "Just think!" and reducing them to an occasional "Um?" or "what about that?" In other instances, Osborne's mod-ernization has resulted in the elimination of some important time and class bound references, such as Judge Brack's imposing eye-glass—which in fact also symbolizes the voyeuristic delight he takes in Hedda.

Any adapter has the option to explain what Osborne calls Hedda's frigid-ity in the light of her uneasy relationship with her womanhood. Hedda's tragedy is that as a woman she can only live vicariously the kind of heroic life she dreams of and associates with her deceased father, general Gabler. By necessity, then, she becomes an artist, and her materials are men such as Eil-ert Lovborg. Osborne's short introduction to the play, however, bears no indi-cation that he saw Hedda's problem in such gendered terms. "Like many frigid people," he says, "[Hedda's] only true feelings are expressed in jealousy, pos-sessiveness and acquisitive yearnings" (7,8). The result is that Hedda becomes a harsher and therefore less interesting character. Where Archer/Gosse's Hedda looks "searchingly" at her husband when she asks whether Lovborg's manu-script could be rewritten if it were lost, Osborne's Hedda does so "coolly inquiringly" (65), clearly already having made up her mind to destroy the fruit of Eilert and Thea's loving labor.

Osborne's adaptation of Hedda Gabler premièred at the Royal Court on 28 June 1972, starring Jill Bennett in the role of Hedda. In 1980, he adapted the play for Yorkshire Television. Directed by David Cunliffe and with Diana Rigg as Hedda, Denis Lill as Tesman and Philip Bond as Lovborg, it was broadcast on 3 March 1981.

WORK FOR TELEVISION

Osborne's deteriorating relationship with the RCT forced him to seek recourse to writing for television, a genre he did not hold in high esteem. *The Right Prospectus* was transmitted by BBC1 on 22 October 1970. The idea, Osborne said, came to him in a dream: "I very often find ideas in dreams. This one is a very common experience—the adult who dreams he is back at school."[27] As the blurb on the published edition informs the reader, *The Right Prospectus* is "an agreeably outrageous entertainment."

Mr. and Mrs. Newbold, a young to middle-aged couple, are visiting a minor public school, not, as we at first assumed, as concerned parents but as prospective students. They have no children as yet and, in fact, dread the very idea: "They don't want *you*. Why should you want *them?*" (14). They will instead create their own youth experience. Mrs. Newbold is well prepared for it, coming from a solidly middle-class family and familiar with public schools and university. Mr. Newbold, in contrast, is an upstart who, through hard work, managed a successful public career. Having not savored the benefits of public school, he now seeks for what he was never given when young, time "to grow" and "think about love," to feel that "the Past is still with you, it's not all gone forever," that the "present is now and the future, the future's no more than the ball thudding into the nets. And sleep afterwards. Sleep like we've not known for years . . ." (16).

But Newbold's dream to recapture an illusory past becomes a nightmare. The Newbolds enroll in a minor public boarding school for boys and enter a system so regimented and shortsighted as to remain oblivious to the couple's age and Mrs. Newbold's sex. Husband and wife join different and competing houses so that Newbold, the husband, is left to long for Mellor, his wife, with a lonely and miserable intensity. Where he stumbles through the semester, increasingly and hopelessly behind in academics and sports, she fits in most cozily, happily unaware of her husband's longing. When at the end of the term, the couple returns home for holidays, Mellor, now highly pregnant, is more self-contained than ever. Newbold feels more inadequate and more alienated from his wife than ever before.

Newbold's inability to regain the past ends *The Right Prospectus* on an unsettling note which Osborne took up again and developed further in a second television play. "Do you see yonder cloud that's almost in shape of a camel?" Hamlet asks of Polonius, looking at the night sky. In the course of a short dialogue, Polonius has agreed that the cloud looks indeed like a camel, like a weasel, even, and in fact, finally, "very like a whale." At which Hamlet in an aside replies, "They fool me to the top of my bent." *Very Like a Whale* is quite aptly the title of a television play by Osborne, published in 1971 but not broadcast by ATV until 13 February 1980, with Alan Bates in the main role.

For Sir Jock Mellors it is the present that proves to be "very like a whale." A leading industrialist, Mellors is one of those responsible for having created a world that eagerly looks toward the future in order not to see the shabbiness of the present. Now at the height of his success and recently honored by the Queen, the past and the present are catching up with him. Like Everyman, Mellors goes from wife, to daughter, to friend, ex-wife and son, father and dog before realizing that he is utterly alone in a world of his own miserable and heartless creation. "Everything will be *new,* constructive, forward-looking," he tells a reporter. "There will be, there will be—no today. Only tomorrow. *I* know. I *made* it. We will live in a vast village that is always just about to exist because the present is pretty—*quite* unthinkable. . . ." That present, in fact, is, as he stammers, "Very Like. Like a Whale." Having been indeed fooled to the top of his bent, he collapses and dies after this interview. His death goes unnoticed even by his own father.

Published in 1972 and directed by Mike Newell in a Yorkshire Television production starring Sir Alec Guiness, *The Gift of Friendship* returns once again to the subject of time. Jocelyn Broome, a respected aging writer, takes advantage of his wife's planned absence to invite a former schoolmate Bill Wakely to dinner. Wakely, a fashionable writer, is surprised at the invitation, clearly not expecting Broome to approve of his work. He is, however, curious enough to answer the summons, though he does not hold Broome in high esteem. "He's made a morality out of eccentricity," he tells his wife, who is offended that she has not been invited by a man she despises and refers to as a "snob and a prig."

The meeting is a cold one, defined by mutual distrust. In the end, Wakely discovers that Broome has appointed him his literary executor ("rather like being a guard on an obsolete railway train") in order to protect his work from "professors in over-endowed American universities." As a gift of friendship, Broome offers Wakely a first edition of one of his books, *Intensive Care.* The next morning, Wakely has already spilled ash on the book and burned a hole in the flyleaf on which Broome has inscribed his dedication: "Not so much one of the seven as the eighth. Although the seventh led to it—clearly."

After Broome's death, Wakely learns from Broome's diaries how much the latter hated him: "What a shabby little creature Wakeley is. Fawning on everyone because he is so scared." He discovers Broome's life was marked by deepening depression, a dislike of the present, a fear of the future, and an impotent longing for the past. Most importantly, Wakely learns the meaning of Broome's enigmatic inscription on his gift of friendship. On his desk are seven books, each marked on the flyleaf with one of the seven deadly sins. For *Intensive Care,* the sin is that of ambition, which, in Broome's view, is born from sloth rather than from talent. Whether this is Broome's verdict on Wakely or on himself is left unclear.

Even these minor works present the principal themes of Osborne's oeuvre: the trial and the verdict, the irretrievable loss of an illusory past, and failed ambition. This is nowhere more evident than in *Inadmissible Evidence,* a play in which a lawyer stands on trial, and to which the next chapter is consequently dedicated.

CHAPTER 7

Inadmissible Evidence (1964)
The Birthing of the Self

RECEPTION

Inadmissible Evidence is a tour de force for writer, leading actor, and audience. It depicts two days in the life of William Henry Maitland, during which the thirty-nine year old solicitor loses his grip on reality, until he finds himself deserted by friends and lovers, his professional and personal life ruined. A notoriously long play, most of its three-and-a-half hours consists of emotionally wrenching speeches. For Osborne, it was hard writing, made tolerable only by the constant, pleasurable fizz of "shampoo."[1] No such comfort accompanies the leading actor on his meandering journey through Bill Maitland's interminable set speeches. What one reviewer called a "one-man marathon in a hall of distorting mirrors"[2] requires tremendous stamina and sensitivity from the lead, who has to hold the stage virtually without interruption throughout the entire evening. For the audience, the play's unrelenting focus on one character's psychological disintegration is not just harrowing but finally exhausting. "Why everybody deserts him is clear," said one reviewer. "I would have given a lot to desert him myself during the interval."[3]

In many ways, *Inadmissible Evidence* is a bad play, "a dramatic experience that doesn't quite come off," as Anthony Burgess remarked, noting "the lack of dialectic synthetising a crisis, of movement, of character interest outside the great solipsist pool of the central figure."[4] Many do give up on the play, leaving it during the interval, convinced they have long understood its point. Others endure it stubbornly, as they undoubtedly do with other punishing plays, such as Eugene O'Neill's *The Iceman Cometh* (1948), amid an increasing number of nodding heads and empty seats. Repelled by the hero's self-indulgence, bored by his endless pleas for attention, irritated by the play's repetitiveness and apparent shapelessness, they are in the final instance mesmerized mainly by their own inability to abandon something that gives them so little pleasure. "I hate this play," John Peter said with some passion. "I hated it when I first saw it nearly 29 years ago and I hate it now. And yet it nags and troubles my mind: there has not been a day since I saw it that I have not thought about it, in some way, however briefly."[5]

It is tempting to use the term "organic" to describe an apparently shapeless play that elicits the complexity of response associated with a total experience and that allegedly was written in a half-drunken state. Yet it is carefully and shrewdly constructed; Osborne referred, rather unusually, to the play's intricate technicalities. He especially mentioned its language, which he claimed was subtly innovative but in a way bound to escape people's attention.[6] Even more interesting is his declaration that he wrote *A Patriot For Me*, the play that was to come next in the line of production, alongside the more arduous *Inadmissible Evidence*. Straightening out the latter's technical problems was exhausting work so that in the evening he turned with relief to the less hauntingly intense world of *A Patriot For Me*. Technically, the plays are opposites. While scenes in *Patriot* move quickly due to a deceptively loose filmic structure, *Inadmissible* is a sprawling play, intolerably slow and repetitive if not carried by a highly talented character actor. There was something sad and inexorable about *Inadmissible*, Osborne summarized, whereas *Patriot* possessed some of the consoling beauty and grandness associated with the Austro-Hungarian Empire.[7]

Both plays depict an often rehearsed theme in the history of drama, human passion clashing with the customs and laws of its time, and both must be situated in the context of the increasing liberalization characteristic of the sixties. Shortly after *Inadmissible*'s first production in 1964, thirteen years of Conservative reign came to an end. Having campaigned under the banner of science and youth, Labour, led by Harold Wilson, won the elections with a small majority of five. Important liberal reforms were soon to take place: capital punishment was abolished in 1965, homosexual relations between consenting adults were legalized through the Sexual Offences Act of 1967, and divorce was simplified through the Divorce Reform Act of 1969. A new era had begun. When the play reached the stage, the Beatles had sold a then incredible 110 million records of "A Hard Day's Night" and the James Bond movies (*From Russia with Love* (1963) and *Goldfinger* (1964)) were making a furore. Female fashion became naughtier and mores looser. Following the 1960 trial, exculpating Penguin Books for publishing an unexpurgated version of *Lady Chatterley's Lover,* other daringly uncensored prose publications, such as the Marquis de Sade's *Justine* (1791) and John Cleland's *Fanny Hill* (1749), saw the light. Both *Patriot* and *Inadmissible* were mileposts in the ongoing battle with theatre censorship in which Osborne played a leading role. Nearly every line from *Inadmissible* had to be defended. Though many concessions inevitably had to be made, the play that finally reached the stage was for its time remarkably frank about sexuality and courageous in its attacks on outmoded laws regarding divorce and homosexuality.

Its outspoken views on sexuality notwithstanding, the play is mainly remembered for signaling "John Osborne's demise as an Angry Young Man and his emergence as the Voice of the Mid-Life Crisis, the male menopause."[8] Osborne was thirty-five, and the distrust of modernity typical of all his heroes was no longer attributable to youthful discontent. *Inadmissible*'s hero Bill Maitland was, some complained, "a failure luxuriating indulgently in failure"[9] who not only harangued against the drabness and smallness of welfare state consumerism but also spewed his bile upon those two prime objects of modern adulation, technology and youth.[10] The latter was particularly ironic since Osborne's *Look Back in Anger* was often held responsible for having introduced the youth phenomenon to Britain. With *Inadmissible,* Osborne, said Graham Samuel, had shown himself to be "a compulsive Blimp of the Left."[11]

The first production of *Inadmissible Evidence,* directed by Anthony Page, took place at the Royal Court Theatre on 7 September 1964, and was altogether respectfully rather than enthusiastically received. The *Evening News* hailed Osborne as "a rare talent in the theatre"[12] and Milton Shulman, long an Osborne skeptic, praised Osborne's writing for its "supple virility and thrusting drive."[13] He even went so far as to commend the play for its "greater professional tautness"—an opinion few reviewers shared—and considered it for that reason a "more satisfactory work than either *Look Back in Anger* or *The Entertainer.*"[14] Most critics continued to express their unease with structure, complaining the play was "too long, too repetitive, and too self-indulgent."[15] Some claimed it lacked theatricality, that it was simply "an incredibly wordy sermon on sex." "This is the finest example of a non-play I have ever seen," said Brigid Chapman. "There is no plot, no action, no interesting situations, no climaxes and no comedy—there is not even a clever set to look at."[16] What remained was a character study of "a gigantic figure of compulsive self-destruction"[17] who expresses himself in a "steady flow of splendidly articulate disgust."[18] In general, critics were awed rather than convinced or charmed by the play, but since Osborne had shown that he was a force to be reckoned with, fewer critics had the temerity to reject what they could not understand. For the *Times* reviewer, Osborne had once again proven that he was able "to break all the rules and get away with it."[19]

The critical strategy of focusing on leading actor rather than on playwright, used with biting effect for *The Entertainer* and *Luther,* once again was a convenient way of evading difficulties of text and structure. For the main part, Osborne had been looking for someone who, like Olivier, looked at the world from some hidden depth or perhaps from a great internal emptiness: cool and controlled on the outside, tortured within. Every good actor that auditioned proved a disaster, until director Anthony Page introduced Nicol Williamson, a young and upcoming actor.[20] At twenty-seven, Williamson was too young to play the role of the thirty-year old Maitland, but, as Osborne noted in his diary, the man's vision of himself and of the world was prematurely old. Those angelic looks, he thought, were deceptive. The eyes told all: they had seen everything.[21] Williamson slid into the role as if it had been written expressly for his own turbulent nature. "The seeds of Maitland are in me," he proclaimed to reviewers, who duly noted Maitland's churlishness and petulancy in this Scottish actor whose "smile looks like a sneer."[22]

Williamson was said to animate the part from within, lending subtlety of affect to speeches that fill five to seven pages in the printed play text. "Mr. Williamson criticises his role as he plays," said Alan Brien, "reacting now with stony gargoyle gloom, now with glowing sexual conceit, his face twitching with nervous energy and then collapsing like sinking soufflé, as he listens to his own voice."[23] He even added something indefinable to the role; as Ronald Bryden said, "he fills every cranny of Maitland's portrait with knowledge: the nervous sweating, the lurching jocularity, the sick waves, tangible as nausea, of self-disgust. He makes Maitland a glass man, each shift and terror transparent, while amassing the twitching motives and counter-motives into a semblance of individual solidity. He gives failure a face crystalline enough to reflect our own."[24] What everyone agreed was a superb performance earned Williamson the Best Actor of 1964 award.

After the play's run in the Royal Court Theatre's repertoire, it was transferred to the West End and Broadway. Williamson played Maitland twice more in New York and in the 1968 Woodfall film version of the play. When Osborne directed a revival for the Royal Court Theatre in 1978, Williamson again filled the role that had now become closely associated with him. In 1993, when the play was revived with another lead actor, it appeared that Williamson, much like Maitland, had ruined a once promising career through unprofessional conduct and general self-destructive behavior; but for *Inadmissible*, the same defiance and self-loathing that would prove detrimental to his career assured he was to be a perfectly plausible Maitland. To an interviewer he said that he "acted best when he was contemplating death. 'Not the character's but my own.'"[25]

In playing Maitland, Williamson in fact seemed to die on the stage every night and was not averse to berating the audience when it proved unworthy of such a sacrifice. Once he stopped the performance of *Inadmissible*, starting again only when fidgety spectators had been cowed into silence.[26] In another instance, he staggered off stage with chest pains, and the curtain lowered, until, sixteen minutes later, his understudy took over. After the interval, Williamson returned to complete the play and in a curtain speech offered the audience their money back, explaining the role was "terribly, terribly difficult" and, since he had been suspected of sustaining a heart attack, quite literally "killing."[27] All this lent a realism to the play that later performances with different actors could hardly be expected to match.

An attempt was subsequently made to turn *Inadmissible* into a classic, but an ill-fated revival at the Lyttelton (Royal National Theatre), premièring on 17 June 1993, showed it had not survived the test of time very well.[28] That the play's content was dated was easily dealt with by presenting the play as period piece, accompanied by a program offering a wide array of historical and cultural notes on the sixties. The program presented Osborne as an innovator and rebel whose work had inspired many of the liberal reforms that were now taken for granted. Feelings and attitudes, however, carry the stamp of time as well and are harder to account for or modernize. The play demands that an audience sympathize not with Maitland's motives and arguments—which are inadequate, willfully perverse, and blatantly unjust—but with the honest impulse behind them. In 1993, there was no longer any language in which to couch such an irrational sympathy. The phrases of the past—authentic, raw, virile—seemed naive and were suspected of harboring prejudices. Moreover, by presenting a villain as a victim, the play committed the worst sin possible in the new Liberal orthodoxy. "Maitland's invective, his capacity to abuse becomes a redeeming feature," Nicolas de Jongh noted disapprovingly before dismissing the play as a "sob for a cad."[29] More than one critic wondered "if [the play] has anything to say to a modern audience."[30] 1964 reviews had hailed *Inadmissible* as a "modern version of *Everyman*,"[31] but no one believed any longer in the universality of its emotions. This was all too clearly a man's play.

Perhaps to counter the charge of promoting the work of a notorious misogynist, the National Theatre had hired feminist director Di Trevis for this revival. The ironies of having a feminist director revive an Osborne play were not lost on the *Daily Express:* "[Osborne] has created a body of work that is a Jurassic Theme Park for the male chauvinist dinosaur who threshes around unhappily on his journey to doom and destruction [. . . .] How satisfying that a curmudgeonly old misogynist like Osborne should have his 1964 drama so impeccably revived by a woman."[32] Paul Taylor ascribed the tittering to which this unusual pairing of director and playwright had given rise in the press to the misconception that "putting a feminist in charge of an Osborne play is roughly the equivalent of hiring a Nazi to revive *The Sound of Music*."[33]

As it happened, the pairing was not a felicitous one. Di Trevis approached the play historically, explaining its tensions not as generated by an inherent tragic sense but as resulting from specific social conditions. Though interesting in some respects, the resulting production was rather too cool and distant. The attitude of Di Trevis, as interviews show, was one of inquisitiveness rather than sympathy. The play, she explained, showed a man's obsession with women, and her production was to "take misogyny apart."[34] "Let's expose it and show how it works."[35] The key to the play, she thought, was Maitland's relationship with his daughter Jane, who enters the play once and then only to listen silently to her father's abuse. Whereas Osborne's final scene leaves the hero sitting abandoned at his desk, daring the spectator to judge his failings, Di Trevis had it recall the opening scene with "a closing tableau in which most of the cast are seen sitting in a jury-box and staring accusingly at the protagonist."[36] Among Maitland's accusers are his daughter and other women in his life. This added a sense of closure and judgment to the play that Osborne had wisely avoided.

Osborne's major objection, however, was not the director but the leading actor. Without an actor's tortured personality, Maitland risked becoming simply a self-absorbed bore. Though Trevor Eve had had a respectable career as stage actor, he was best known for his role as detective Eddie Shoestring in a successful television series of the late Seventies. Shrewd and hard-faced, forceful and technically superb, Trevor lacked Williamson's tragic charisma.[37] "Nicol Williamson, great actor that he is, always had the lineaments of an extraordinary human being," said Michael Billington. "Mr. Eve is more like your next door neighbour falling apart before your very eyes."[38] Unlike Williamson, Eve was not too keen on being confused with his role, and, like the director, he understood the character's woes to result from his "*misconception* of women, sex and love."[39] This was bound to sound self-righteous to Osborne's ears. Theatre practitioners or critics that sit in judgment of characters, thinking of them mainly in terms of their need for enlightenment or therapy, Osborne thought to belong to what he derisively called the "adjustment school." That school contains the kind of person who feels like "packing off . . . Hedda Gabler to the Marriage Guidance Clinic."[40] So when he briefly attended a rehearsal, a clash was inevitable.

The actors were just improvising their way through a difficult scene, when Osborne interrupted to remark with perfect affability that "you see, this scene is really about two people being in love."[41] This suggestion of reciprocity where others saw more one-sided relationships proved unwelcome. Trevor, who sensed Osborne's disapproval with his interpretation of Maitland, was so upset that he had to be persuaded to stay in the production.[42] Osborne was promptly escorted out of the theatre with the invitation to come back at a later point in the rehearsals. He never returned and afterward expressed his grievance in a letter to fellow playwright Arnold Wesker:

> The 'production' of *Inadmissible* has been the most bitter, ignominious experience of my life. Director (nice woman, but . . .) feeble. No authority and full of fashionable 'expressionist' shit. Leading actor a TV star of monumental ego and *minuscule* talent—a familiar combination. I was *banned* from the theatre and never spoken to—not by *anyone*.... It's accepted that writers are treated like shit.[43]

The event strengthened Osborne's well-known dislike of "Colditz-on-Thames," as he called the gray concrete building of the National Theatre.

Apart from the American critic Clive Barnes, who insisted that the play was indeed a classic and that Di Trevis' production was the best of revivals,[44] reviewers gave a nearly unanimously negative, not to say downright condemning, verdict:

> Di Trevis's leaden, lumpen and sprawling production muffles all the hurt, suffocates most of the pain, so that the entire enterprise takes on the arid intellectual flavour of a Brechtian exercise in audience alienation. Not that this has ever been a work to bring a tear to the eye. But it has always held a snakelike fascination, a hypnotic fury which defies indifference. That is gone. Instead of the snake, we see merely the shed skin.[45]

The few who liked the play, often did so for the wrong reasons. Inevitably, at a time when the Men's Movement was gaining publicity, the very same quality that caused offense to some, namely Maitland's misogyny, provoked an equally shortsighted adulatory response in others. Steve Grant from *Time Out* could barely hide his admiration for what he called this "sexist porker," and Martin Spence opined that "in our liberated world, Osborne's misogyny seems refreshingly macho, almost revolutionary,"[46] but all in all the play was received as little more than a "dusty period piece."[47] Without Williamson to give body to the lines, spectators became more than ever impatient with the play's "swollen proportions and tundra-like stretches."[48] Robert Butler summarized it well: "This indecent account of a man's life needs to gain a Williamson or lose an hour."[49]

THE TRIAL

The play begins with a Kafkaesque nightmare scene. Bill Maitland stands arraigned in his office, which has transformed itself into a court of law. Two of his employees have turned judge and prosecutor; his family and friends watch as he takes the stand. The charge: publication of pornographic material. It soon becomes clear, however, that the indictment stands for the broader charge of indecency and that it is Maitland's habit of spilling the contents of his troubled soul that is found to be particularly indecent.

Maitland always expected this trial; yet, now that it has arrived, he finds it difficult to defend himself. Although the law is his profession and the trial takes place on his own territory, he is disoriented and has trouble understanding the judge. The world in which he felt at home has been reduced to the "bones and dead objects" of his old office, and the larger world that judges him functions according to assumptions he does not comprehend. Anxious to please the judge and, in the same gesture, to expose the inanity of the conventions by which he will be judged, he affirms his belief in progress and technology. His litany of ill-assorted clichés is soon exhausted, and finally he can only convince the court of what it already knows, his personal inadequacy and insufficiency.

We will think back on this nightmare when, at the end of the play, Maitland sits alone in his office, abandoned by everyone, convinced that he has been denounced to the Law Society and that arrest is imminent. By then we have witnessed, for more than three hours, the damage self-loathing can inflict upon others as well as self, and we now understand the correctness of Maitland's self-incriminating defense in the nightmare trial: "I never hoped or wished for anything more than to have the good fortune of friendship and the excitement and comfort of love. . . . With the first with friendship, I hardly succeeded at all. [. . .] With the second, with love, I succeeded . . . in inflicting . . . more pain than pleasure. I am not equal to any of it" (I, 16).

How do we pass so quickly from the premonition of failure to its realization, barely two days later? It all starts innocently enough. One morning

Maitland finds that he cannot get a taxi and that the caretaker does not acknowledge his greeting. Such minor incidents unsettle him, making an already difficult man downright impossible. In Act II, a sore thumb plays a similarly destabilizing role, increasing his obsession with loss of control. He becomes the helpless observer of his own decay: "A fat little tumour," he says of his thumb. "On the end of another" (II, 88). It is one more rip in the texture of his reality, another place where the seams are coming apart.

The rest, like a self-fulfilling prophecy, takes care of itself. His growing insecurity increases his dependency on others; alarmed by his excessive demands for attention and care, people slip away one by one despite his tightening grip. While he fully realizes what is happening, he finds himself saying what he should not say and not saying what people expect him to say. To his young clerk Jones, whom he distrusts, he wonders aloud who is going to betray him to the Law Society; to his office telephonist Joy, whom he desires, he is unable to speak the few reassuring words that will enable her to continue their relationship. What had in the past impressed others, his energy and quick mind, he now turns against himself. He becomes the prime agent of his own destruction, dismissing people or forcing them to abandon him. In the end, the world moves on and Maitland is left behind.

But the audience cannot as easily move on and leave Maitland behind. We have entered his private nightmare and have witnessed his daily misery, and this knowledge finally erodes our position of judgment—something that cannot happen to a court of law. Aware that too much knowledge impedes judgment, a court circumscribes the cases it has to judge. Daily misery has no legal status; as evidence it is inadmissible because it clogs up the judicial machinery. But the audience does not enjoy the protection of such judiciary protocol. Even if it concentrates on what is reprehensible in Maitland, it cannot follow any thread without getting hopelessly entangled in it.

THE CRIME

Something that a modern audience will find most objectionable in Maitland is his attitude to women. Any new office girl quickly learns the routine of endlessly fetching glasses of water for Mr. Maitland, while smiling at his well-intentioned yet nonetheless patronizing and intrusive comments. It is not difficult to guess at the emotional insecurity that lies at the root of such behavior: by constantly laying claim on its time, attention, or affection, Maitland assures himself of the world's continuing willingness to cater to his needs. Whatever the motive may be, it is the source of his most abusive behavior. By offering little or nothing in return, he cruelly disappoints those who love him. His mistress Liz is supposed to be at his beck and call any time, night or day, but can never be sure if or when he will pay her a visit. His secretary and lover Shirley is the first to reach the end of her generosity, but others will follow. One by one the women in Maitland's life abandon him when they realize how little he is aware of their existence and their needs—when they understand that what is important to Maitland is not so much their being, as their being-for-him.

The audience to some extent is made to share Maitland's lack of awareness. The play depicts these women only in so far as they relate to the protagonist. The three most important women in his life—his wife, his mistress, and his daughter—are kept safely away from the spectators' independent judgment. We are never allowed to see Maitland's long-suffering wife Anna, but must reconstruct her unhappy existence from her sobs at the telephone and reports about sleepless nights. His mistress Liz is another voice we can only imagine at the other end of the line during some of Maitland's interminable phone conversations; she shows up only at the end of the play and then merely to announce that she will leave him. His much-discussed daughter Jane has one long appearance during which she listens in silence to her father's recriminations before he dismisses her from his life. There are of course the many other women whose names and oddities form the texture of his memories: his ex-wife Sheila with her "white, flaky skin," Maureen with her "hand-knitted suits," and Audrey Jane "who took elocution and dancing and wore patent shoes" (II, 63, 67). We never actually see these women, the lost loves of Maitland's past. They only briefly flicker into existence when names of clients remind Maitland of theirs. It is Maitland's guilty conscience that paints their picture; the audience never regards them in their own right but only in relation to him.

Their absence, however, is surprisingly effective as we image them to be so many lost figures crowding Maitland's imagination and conscience. We now understand the other side of Maitland's one-sided dependence on these women. It not only makes him cruel; it also renders him vulnerable. It is precisely this dependence on the generosity of others, this complete lack of emotional mercantilism, that leaves him an easy target for wounding accusations. "What have you ever done for me," Shirley asks him pointedly. "Nothing. I suppose," is Maitland's honest answer (I, 39). It is clearly guilt that fuels his insistence on the honesty of their failed relationship: "I don't think I let you think it was an enduring love affair," he replies to her angry tears, "—in the sense of well of endless, wheedling obligations and summonses and things. But, if you think back on it, detail by detail, I don't think you can say it was fraudulent. Can you?" His language uncharacteristically devolves into legal jargon, betraying an uneasy conscience. Then he adds, in what seems very much like an attempt to move the burden of guilt back onto her shoulders: "You can't disown it. If you do that, you are helping, you are conspiring to kill me" (I, 40). There is true urgency behind this final plea to stand by him, whatever the cost to herself—a plea which Shirley dismisses, decisively and radically, but not without suffering pain herself. She is in tears when she breaks her professional and personal bonds with him.

Remarkable, of course, is Shirley's evident pain in abandoning a man who often treated her callously. For his benefit, she sums up what the affair amounted to, "detail by detail": "One weekend in Leicester on client's business. Two weekends in Southend on client's business. Moss Mansions—remember them? Four days in Hamburg on client's business. One crummy client's crummy flat in Chiswick. And three times on this floor" (I, 40). She even knows he promised her to his clients when he had no time for her, being too occupied with wife or mistress. Maitland invariably abuses his lovers' trust and affection, cheating on his wife with his mistress and on his mistress with casual lovers.

A chain of cruelty ties the women together in pain and yet keeps them apart in enmity. Maitland's mistress Liz knows about his other lovers, and his wife Anna knows about Liz. Indeed, he makes sure they know. He deliberately returns from Liz to the marital bed, at three or four in the morning, to lie side by side with his sleepless, unhappy wife: "We both just lie there. And if I'm lucky or drunk enough and I do go to sleep, she lies there choking in silence unable to sleep again till she wakes me in the morning" (II, 91). In a pattern of petty cruelty that crushes himself as much as the women, Maitland uses his mistress to punish his wife, his new lover to punish his mistress, and his wife and mistress to punish his lover. Then, in abeyance of the day of reckoning, he drinks, pops pills, jokes, insults, and turns from one abused woman to another in search of consolation.

Shirley's tears and bitterness in recalling the bare bones of their relationship take Maitland aback, even though he has already lined up a replacement for her in the figure of his telephonist Joy. By the end of the next day, Joy will have left him in turn, but with words that are harsher and less marked by pain than Shirley's. "I'm still surprised to hear you say it though," he responds to her when she tells him she now understands why people dislike him so much. "I always am. And I shouldn't be. . . . Why does it shock me? Why?" (II, 87). It is not her view of him that shocks Maitland, who has no illusions about his own behavior. What shocks is the recognition that one has finally reached one's secret goal. A pattern already manifests itself: Maitland obsessively pursues what he most fears, namely his own abandonment and isolation.

Perversely, it is his greedy dependence on the sympathy and generosity of others that humanizes Maitland—that is, if we take it as the cause of his suffering, of his growing guilt and constant expectation of punishment. It has also a more tangible and immediately recognizable effect. The effort to suppress the memory of what makes him feel guilty renders concentration impossible. It is making his memory unreliable, which directly affects his professional efficiency. "Do you know I can't remember one detail of what she looks like," he says of his wife, "not since I left this morning and we'd had the row about the weekend." Throughout the play he complains that he can no longer "retain very much of anything"—a serious admission for a man whose success in the business of law depends (on his own saying) not on talent but on a quick mind (I, 42). Now that mind is going: "I sat down to read the Charterhouse of Parma.

It took ten days and I gave up round about the middle somewhere. I can't tell you what it's about. I can't grasp anything." He realizes that his growing inability to concentrate will finally ruin his career: "I used to be good at my job because I had what they called an instinct and a quick brain. Quick! I can't get through the Law reports" (II, 91). So his desperate, hopeless attempts to ignore the actuality of other people's suffering has intensified his own.

DECEPTIVE SYMMETRIES

All this is perhaps psychologically interesting, but would remain unremarkable if not for Osborne's complex representation of characters' identity. The play is organized so as to exploit and frustrate expectations evoked by its predominant naturalism. For instance, the nightmare scene should logically conclude the play, as the nadir of a life that has been folding in on itself; but its placement at the beginning sets a tone of desperation that we can never quite forget. When the next scene shows us an apparently confident and assertive Maitland, we search for the insecurity at the center of his customary bluster; when he later rants at his daughter, we strain to hear the victim in the victimizer. As the action develops we learn that Maitland is indeed a loser: his world gradually contracts so that we end where we began, with an isolated self, shrunk around private anxieties, having forfeited its right to expand at the expense of others.

In this way, the play starts and ends with a solitary being, signaling the predominance of the private over the public—an ironic situation for a man whose profession entails public service and whose every professional action is necessarily situated within the public constraints of the law. After the nightmare scene has alerted us to Maitland's private obsessions, we are not surprised to find that other characters are important only in so far as they relate to his crumbling world. Apart from a brief dialogue between two of his office clerks at the beginning of the play, each act, beat after beat, shows us the world from Maitland's point of view as he converses with colleagues, lovers, clients, or family. In the way it foreshadows the play's closure, the nightmare scene is an example of an obvious structural symmetry that shapes our receptivity and sets our expectations. When, at the end of the play, Maitland hangs up the phone on his wife and sits waiting in his office, we realize he is expecting a daytime analogue of the nightmare trial.

Other symmetries are more complex, first announcing themselves as differences. We may find it strange, for instance, that with the exception of Mrs. Garnsey, the clients who appear in Act II do not correspond to those that Maitland and Hudson discussed in Act I. The other legal cases brought to our attention in Act I—those of Mr. Simley, Mr. Bennett, Mrs. Rose, and Mr. Zubuki—may then seem excessive: they do not seem to play a role because the clients who ultimately show up in Maitland's office are Mrs. Tonks, Mrs. Anderson, and Mr. Maples. Of those, Mrs. Tonks and Mrs. Anderson represent, like Mrs. Garnsey, women who want to divorce the men they love because they can no longer bear their demands for assurance, affection, or sexual fulfillment. As their stories unfold, the absent husbands appear as lost and miserable as the wives who try to divorce them. Having all these clients played by the Mrs. Garnsey actress reinforces the impression that particularity, and hence difference, is of no importance. Although each of these cases is distinct, its theme remains the same: each concerns personal failure in the face of excessive demands. The difference, in other words, is deceptive, as it is finally a symmetry.

The only male client to appear in Maitland's office is Mr. Maples, whose case also represents that of Mr. Bennett and Mr. Simley, discussed at the beginning of the play. So this is yet another instance of difference fulfilling the role of symmetry. We do not need to see Mr. Bennett, accused of indecent assault, or Mr. Simley, "the bank manager who's a flasher"—both men with whom Maitland instinctively sympathizes. As a young husband, father, and successful business man who has risked everything to alleviate an illicit desire, Mr. Maples stands not only for himself but also for men such as Bennett and Simley. This game of deceptive differences is not practiced for its own sake; it is thematically and psychologically relevant. Each difference conceals a similarity, and each similarity a difference: this is the logic ruling Maitland's world so that, no longer certain of the distinction between the particular and the general, he indeed has to rub his eyes on more than one occasion. Establishing distinctions is important: to lose one's sense of the other is in the final instance to lose one's sense of self. In Maitland's world, everyone seems to resemble everyone else, though with an essential difference, the badge of a particularity that Maitland should recognize if only to guarantee his own identity.

But how difficult it is to determine the specificity of identity. Take Mr. Maples, for instance, a character created by a double and complex mirror effect. In at least one respect he is made to resemble Maitland's female clients: a stage direction tells us that "when Maples replies, his delivery adopts roughly the same style as in the Mrs. Garnsey—Anderson—Tonks dialogue" (II, 75). Like the women, Maples no longer feels in control of his fate; he helplessly witnesses his own passions and serves as a mirror in which Maitland discovers his own condition. If Maitland responds differently to Maples than to the women it is because, whereas the women fight men whose suffering resembles theirs and Maitland's, Maples faces the impersonal enmity of the State. He has been set up by the police into revealing his secret homosexuality and is now facing humiliation in his professional and personal life. While examining this case, Maitland for an instant recovers his militant self, which has made him an effective if not always honest solicitor. In contrast, when Maitland dealt with the women's request for divorce, his attention was so much absorbed by ruminations about the process of desertion and the emotional toll it takes on both partners that he, without actually intending to do so, practically dissuaded the women from filing divorce. In this case, he refuses to let Maples plead guilty and assures him he will not hesitate to fabricate evidence, if that is needed to prove that his client has been forced into drawing up a false statement. The law, he had said to Hudson at the beginning of the play, is "there to be exploited. Just as it exploits us" (I, 20). It is for such unprofessional conduct—the practice of matching one unfairness with another—that Maitland is ready to brave sanctions.

A similarity in the style of delivery makes Maples a less conspicuous presence among women clients; Maitland's response to his plight introduces a distinction. That difference is immediately diminished and yet simultaneously highlighted by a second and more intriguing mirror effect. Although Maples and Jones share nothing except age and a certain physical unattractiveness, they are played by the same actor. This doubling to some extent deprives Maples of his particularity: like Maitland's women clients, who are all played by the same actress, Maples becomes less himself and thus more generic. Yet there also is an important difference: Mrs. Garnsey can represent all Maitland's women clients because she is a client herself and because her case, though legally different, involves an existential anguish shared by all. The doubling of Maples by Jones, however, at first sight raises more questions than answers when we recall that Jones is not a client but Maitland's despised and mistrusted clerk.

Having two dissimilar characters played by the same actor can help to define both. The doubling may then illustrate how much Jones and Maples differ from each other. This is indeed confirmed by a stage direction:

> JONES-MAPLES has some of JONES's unattractiveness but with other elements. In place of his puny arrogance and closed mind, there is a quick-witted, improvising nature, not without courage. His flashes of fear are like bursts of creative energy, in contrast to JONES's whining fixity and confidence. (II, 73–74)

In their attitude toward passion no two characters could be more dissimilar. Maples pays lipservice to common values by working hard, marrying, and raising a daughter, but his noncomformist desires drive him into situations where he risks losing all he gained. Jones, on the other hand, has made those values so successfully his own that there is no place for aberrant desires. He is perfectly satisfied with his mini car and mini dreams. Like Jones, Maples represents a modern young man, yet one upon whom a difference has been forced through his particular sexual orientation. That difference is important to Maitland because it prevents Maples from living the good life as mindlessly and stolidly as Jones does. By being unlike Jones, Maples becomes more like the women. His case, like that of the women, reminds Maitland of the rift between potentiality and actuality, between the world we desire and the world that is—a rift, as we will further see, filled with suffering and a sense of the tragic, a rift that characterizes Maitland and of which Jones, Hudson, Jane, and others remain unaware.

Still, the doubling of Maples by Jones evokes similarity as much as difference. If Maitland recognizes his own condition in Maples' sense of defeat and isolation (as well as in that of the women with whom his case is associated) that mirror effect is distorted and diffused by Maples' doubling with Jones. The conflation of such dissimilar figures—one the subject of Maitland's sympathy, the other of his loathing—suggests that Maples is a potential Jones, just as Jones is a potential Maples, so that the division between Maitland's sympathy and loathing is not as clear as it seems. Jones's repelling difference distorts the mirror effect and prevents Maitland from fully discovering himself in Maples; but Jones's blending into Maples also diffuses our sense of Jones's personality, which Maitland's loathing too clearly defined.

In the same way that Maitland is bound to Maples by his sympathy, Jones's identity is held fixed and distant by Maitland's contempt. Yet Maples' doubling by Jones binds Maitland to the man he despises. It is the dramatic equivalent of an impossible transitive property: if $a = b$ and $b = c$, then $a = c$, yet it is given that a and c are opposite values. Figures are at once incompatible and interchangeable, as we see in Maitland's respective attraction and repulsion for men who are mirror images, doubles despite their distinctive traits.[50]

To complicate matters further, Osborne compounds this mirror effect with yet another. In the nightmare trial, Jones is Maitland's defense counsel who turns prosecutor when Maitland decides to take up his own defense. This could suggest that Jones is simply the kind of man who misuses someone's trust, (at the end of the play Maitland indeed suspects that his clerk will betray him to the Law Society) but the dream also complicates Jones's character: most distinguished by his lack of enthusiasm or loyalty, Jones is a perfect Janus-figure who could equally well defend or attack Maitland. His presence generates an unarticulated ambiguity that qualifies the certainties conveyed by the play's strident, often hectoring tone. Maples' doubling by Jones implies that Maitland's relationship with his clerk is more complex than he conceded when he calls him "a tent peg. Made in England. To be knocked into the ground" (I, 21). This is important because apart from his strange reluctance to dismiss a man of whom he so strongly disapproves, Maitland offers him not the least degree of sympathy.

The ambiguity of Maitland's attitude is still deepened by yet another partial symmetry. Jones, we are told, in some respects also resembles Maitland's daughter Jane. This is surprising, given the difference in age and attitude between the two, but to Maitland, both are children of the future. Jones is a "child of the jet age, a new age of fulfilment with streamlined institutions, a sense of purpose and looking forward to the new frontiers of knowledge." What disturbs Maitland about him is his imperviousness. Maitland's sarcasms fail to shock him. There is no struggle in Jones, no expenditure, and hence no sense of loss, only perhaps a deep-seated, unacknowledged cynicism masked by a dull mediocrity: He goes through life convinced that nothing is "really worth the candle" and that "it's all much the same when you come down to it" (I, 21; II, 60).

Jane seems very different from the complacent Jones. Unlike Jones, she is politically active, although, as Maitland suggests, in a naive sort of way: "Jane's sure to marry an emergent African. That is, if she hasn't already sent her virginity to OXFAM . . ." (II, 53). Nonetheless, with Jones she shares a comforting sense of purpose and fulfillment: "She won't get into any mess like us," Maitland says. "Or, if she does, it won't matter, it won't overwhelm her or get the better of her" (II, 50). As if to emphasize how similar these dissimilar figures really are, he uses Jones's philosophy of complacency to describe Jane's attitude. "You'll know it wasn't worth any candle that ever burned. You will have to be blown out, snuffed, decently, and not be watched spluttering and spilling and hardening" (II, 86).

Both Jane and Jones serve as foil to Maitland. He is what they are not: "You are unselfconscious, which I am not. You are without guilt, which I am not" (II, 85). Neither Jane nor Jones, he thinks, knows what it means to be constantly nibbled at by a "fibbing, mumping, pinched little worm of energy." If they are everything he is not and therefore despises, then they are also what he secretly would like to be. Jones is perfectly adapted to the world in which he lives. "He's got all the makings of a good, happy, democratic underdog" (I, 22). Jane is pretty, free, self-satisfied, not tortured by doubts and insecurities. Maitland is convinced that they are not plagued by impossible yearnings and therefore remain free from suffering.

The one whose candle we see "spluttering and spilling and hardening" is Maitland. Unlike Jones and Jane, he feels ill at ease in the world. "There isn't any place for me, not like you" (II, 83). He constantly must take his bearings and compel others to affirm his identity. How can he even be sure that he exists? Nothing tortures him more than the idea of his invisibility: he suffers when his father refuses to believe his account of "all sorts of things we'd done together. [. . .] When I bent down and kissed him, he didn't look up." His wife's parents avoid speaking to him and never refer to him in their letters. "Look at me," he says to his daughter. "Why you can't have looked at me and seen anything, what, not for years" (II, 82).

To hurt is to be seen. The girl is reduced to silence as she finds herself trapped between the immensity of her father's expectations and the finality of his rejection, between his expressions of longing admiration ("I've leapt at the very idea of you, before you were ever born" (II, 86)) and his utter revulsion ("Nothing, certainly not your swinging distaste can match what I feel for you" (II, 84)).[51] Nothing less than the romantic attachment of lovers would have satisfied him. He had dreamt of taking her out to dinner. They would "hang on to each other," exchange secret "signals," "lean forward and look at each other with such, such oh, pleasure—we'd hardly be able to eat our dinner" (II, 83). What he received instead is the cool indifference of one generation for the other.

BIRTHING THE SELF

In a world in which one's essence is nothing but the sum of apparent distortions in endless mirror effects, Maitland longs to be known purely and for himself. To his enormous, unquenchable need, women respond maternally as well as erotically. The result is that, at the time of parting, they hardly know whether they are cruelly deserting or simply leaving him. Significant exceptions to this pattern of angry frustration and guilt are the more self-sufficient women who do not consider themselves primarily as potential or actual mothers. His mistress Liz, as far as we know, is childless and can say of herself that she "always managed to avoid guilt" (II, 89). It may not be quite true, but she at least manages to summon up enough courage or cowardice to leave him without hurting herself too much. Others too are able to sever ties without great regret or guilt. "What do you want me to do?" replies his new lover Joy when he begs her to stay. "Press myself in a book for you?" She then adds with no apparent hardship to herself: "You know what? I think they're all right. I don't like you either" (II, 87). It is a harsh, self-protective response, delivered without the tears that qualify the anger of his former lover Shirley and his wife Anna—significantly, the one a woman pregnant with her first child, the other a mother of two. So the degree to which the women feel constrained by a sense of maternal responsibility may well explain how much or how little they will suffer.

If Maitland consciously or unconsciously appeals to a woman's maternal feelings, one may suspect that he does so like a child to its mother; but that calls to mind a type of relationship too personal and direct to define the one Maitland entertains with the women in his life. The reality of a woman's life—of anyone's life—only fills him with futility and guilt. If she presents herself to him as an absent presence, that is both familiarly close and safely distant, he can confide himself through her rather than to her—as a believer does to the priest who sits veiled in the darkness of the confessional. In other words, neither Anna nor Liz are important to Maitland but the idea of their distant, listening presence. For that reason he begs them to stay home and to wait for his calls, and whenever anything goes wrong in his life, he does not visit them but reaches for the phone.

Since his reality disintegrates in these final two days, Maitland is forced to reach out all the time. Much of the play, therefore, consists of long monologues directed by Maitland at an invisible woman at the other end of the phone. Significantly, these monologues are most confiding, personal, and searching when contact is bad or dubious—that is, when Maitland could in fact be talking to himself. A stage direction tells us that "the presence of the person on the other end should be made very real indeed, but, sometimes it should trail off into a feeling of doubt as to whether there is anyone to speak to at all" (II, 48). During such moments "more than ever the ambiguity of reality is marked, of whether the phone is dead, of whether the person at the other end exists" (II, 51). The phone is "stalked, abused, taken for granted, feared," another stage direction informs.

The phone cord is quite literally Maitland's lifeline: he is afraid "of being cut off, of no sound from *either* end" (II, 51; my emphasis). When on the morning of the second and last day, Maitland wakes up alone in his office and finds himself unable to make sense of the switchboard when the phone rings, we sense his panic at not being able to interpret the signals coming from the outside world. The phone assumes some of the qualities of an umbilical cord, turning Maitland figuratively into a fetus, a creature parasitically ensconced in a suffering female body to which it is at once intimately bound and yet only impersonally related. "Sometimes I think you're my only grip left, if you let me go, I'll disappear," he tells his sobbing wife at the other end of the line. "I'll be made to disappear, nothing will work, I'll be like something in a capsule in space, weightless, unable to touch anything or do anything, like a groping baby in a removed, putrefying womb"(II, 52).

This uterine imagery gives sense to the play's otherwise apparently irregular dramatic structure. The play, we now understand, enacts the violent, painful, and in fact impossible, birthing of a self. *Inadmissible* starts with a nightmare of rejection and continues with the process of ejection. Mostly self-induced, the process starts with the protagonist noting signs of his impending dismissal: the world, it seems, is no longer going to cater to his needs. No sooner than has he noticed this, he triggers the process of ejection, ironically by increasing the pressure of his desperate hold on a world that is slipping away. As the process accelerates, we see him actively participating in cutting the last remaining bonds, rejecting his daughter and declining his wife's invitation to come home to her.

In the end, he is truly alone—or, at least, appears to be so. Finally, we do not know whether Hudson truly refused the offer of a partnership, whether Jones has truly denounced him to the Law Society, whether his clients will truly never return for his services, whether his daughter or mistress is really irrevocably lost to him. So when Maitland finds himself free from all sentimental and professional attachments it is rather an ideal moment of imagined abandonment and indictment, the necessary condition for the public trial fantasy with which the play started. What Maitland is anxiously but also ecstatically expecting is nothing less than the realization of the dream, an ideal dramatic moment in which his self will be on show, watched by an audience receding in darkness. Like an actor peering through a curtain of surrounding light, Maitland will struggle to distinguish familiar faces. Groping for unfamiliar lines, his first peroration will flounder in a jumble of phrases, but then his stammering expression of confusion, of doubt, of fear, will become a growing wave of forceful self-expression. When failure will stand in the limelight, meeting the smugness of the Law, what will be born will be the essence of his very being.

"HIMSELF PURELY"

A similar moment is described in Arthur Miller's *A View from the Bridge* (1956). Eddie, the main character in that play, undergoes the horrifying experience of standing outside his society—the society from which he used to derive his identity. In a final confrontation scene, he faces the man who has "stolen his [good] name" and addresses himself not so much to him as to the people who stand by and watch. It is that bold moment of naked exposure to the judging scrutiny of others that attracts the play's narrator Alfieri. As the latter says at the end of that play, "something perversely true calls to me from his memory—not purely good, but himself purely, for he allowed himself to be wholly known and for that I think I will love him more than all my sensible clients" (II, 86). Like Eddie, Maitland is neither sensible nor purely good, but it is his total exposure that fascinates us and that endows him with a certain greatness.

This required the gradual stripping away of all external attachments to the world, of everything that constitutes one's ordinary personality, until what is left is in fact an impossible and therefore aesthetic product, a pure self. What has happened in that process of ejection is a process of inversion. Like a glove that is turned inside out, Maitland's relationship to the world has been reversed. Once an embryo floating a world that catered to his needs, he has assimilated that world into himself and now, ejected from it, speaks for it as the only true human being, the last representative of a lost universe.

The process described is that of art itself, the transformation of the personal into the anagogical voice—a transformation that takes place in the absence of others and yet evokes for the others the yearning for an essence they believe to have lost. Art is inadmissible, suspending all judgment. Even while dealing with moral issues, with questions of justice or injustice, goodness or badness, art is attuned not to these categories but to fate, experienced whenever one's quest for certainty clashes with the fundamental impossibility of things. It is because everything contains its opposite—because of the injustice in justice, the goodness in badness—that such a quest is doomed to fail and that one is robbed of one's ability to pronounce judgment.

When identification takes place, which will also depend on the actor's ability to endow the lines with believable emotion, spectators will ascribe to Maitland a complexity of motivation and behavior that they usually reserve for themselves alone. They will then read that character perversely and interpret his actions as indicative of emotions contrary to those commonly accepted. Impatience with others will then no longer reveal a superficial nature but will instead add to psychological depth and complexity. Bluster and arrogance will become measures of evident self-loathing and suffering; abuse, proof of total commitment to the world; and prejudices, sign of high expectations. Like Maitland in the nightmare trial, *Inadmissible Evidence* is in that sense the "wicked, bawdy and scandalous object" that seeks to "vitiate and corrupt . . . debauch and poison" our minds. Osborne dares us to judge, but at our own peril.

CHAPTER 8

A Patriot for Me (1965)
Society and the Hidden Self

A Patriot for Me is one of the small number of historical plays Osborne wrote that includes *A Subject of Scandal and Concern* (about the last man convicted for blasphemy), *Luther,* and *God Rot Tunbridge Wells* (about Handel). Typically—but in a way that is no less typical for Shakespeare's history plays, for instance—all these plays, although set in the past, really deal with the present and are in fact state of the nation plays.[1] Inspired by Robert Asprey's *The Panther's Feast* (1959)[2], *A Patriot for Me* takes place during the last quarter-century of the Habsburg Monarchy of the Austro-Hungarian Empire, from 1890 until 1913. That this was the period of cold war between the Empire and Russia for control of the Balkans that resulted in WWI was of course not insignificant for Osborne's audience: 1965, the year *A Patriot For Me* premièred, was only four years after the construction of the Berlin Wall, four years also after the anti-nuclear Trafalgar square sit-down at which Osborne and a great many other protesters were arrested, three years after the Cuban missile crisis, and only shortly after the Gulf of Tonkin incident caused the escalation of the war in Vietnam. The story was not without topical relevance. Just before the onset of WWI, the war that put an end to the Empire, it appeared that one highly placed military officer who had headed the Empire's Intelligence Service had betrayed his country. To uphold appearances, the army had instructed the officer to take the honorable way out by committing suicide. There were rumors that as a secret Jew and a homosexual the man had been especially vulnerable to blackmail by the Russian enemy. Osborne's audience could think back on the 1956 spy scandal centering on Guy Burgess and Donald Maclean, who had betrayed their country spying for the Soviet Union.[3] Incidentally, Guy Burgess, who died in 1963, was known to be a homosexual.

One can immediately see what attracted Osborne to the story, not necessarily the theme of homosexuality on which the critics would focus, but an idea that had also been present in *Inadmissible Evidence,* namely that one man can be utterly isolated in the midst of success and finally publicly denounced and ruined.[4] Of course, the story also resembled that of Luther who turned against the very organization that had so carefully nurtured him. As always, at the basis lay the outsider motive, so important in a postwar England marked by the promise of social mobility: a hero suffers from a sense of psychological or social alienation, which in this case takes the form of sexual deviation. His suffering leads not only to fierce self-loathing; it convinces him of his uniqueness, of the fact that common strictures perhaps may not apply to him. The play was indeed, to quote Peter Gill who directed it in 1995, not so much about history nor about homosexuality but "very much about England, class and exclusion."[5]

PRODUCTION

A Patriot for Me occupies a very special place in Osborne's work on different accounts. Though it is one of Osborne's most ambitious, most complex, and best executed plays and though it was generally praised and appreciated by the public, it was the first to be produced at considerable financial loss to the Royal Court Theatre and to Osborne himself. The Lord Chamberlain had insisted on cuts so extensive that, had Osborne agreed to them, the play would simply not have made sense. Apart from many more or less sexually explicit lines (e.g. "You were born with a silver sabre up your whatnot" (III, ii)), three scenes, crucial to the play's message, were expected to be cut out in their entirety (I, x; II, i; III, v). Osborne simply had no choice but to refuse the Lord Chamberlain's wishes. The Royal Court Theatre then made the courageous decision to produce the play privately, in club, open only to members of the Royal Court Theatre.[6] Osborne and the RCT management still hoped that the censor would eventually relent, but though notices were favorable and many important figures, including Sir Laurence Olivier, interceded on Osborne's behalf, the Lord Chamberlain maintained his position. In fact, he would have prosecuted the Royal Court Theatre for circumventing his veto had the Labour government not refused to act on his advice. However, sufficient damage was done. Because the Royal Court played in repertory, revenues from *A Patriot for Me* ceased after barely seven weeks. The only way of recouping the costs of what was indeed a very expensive production (thirty-seven actors and several musicians, all in period costume) would have been to transfer the play to the West End at a percentage for the Royal Court and Osborne. But that required a license for public performance, which would not be forthcoming. Osborne, who had invested a substantial amount of his own money in the production, lost out likewise.[7]

Ultimately, the theatre would win—at least a couple of years later, with the passing of the Theatre Act of 1968 that abolished censorship altogether. By boycotting *A Patriot for Me*, theatrical censorship had once again proved to be wholly out of touch with modern views. Times clearly were changing. The first unexpurgated version of D.H. Lawrence's *Lady Chatterley's Lover* had been published in 1960. The early sixties had seen daring theatrical productions both in England and abroad, for instance, plays by the homosexual French playwright Jean Genet (Peter Brook's production of *The Balcony* was staged in 1960; *Les Paravents* had its world première in West Berlin in 1961). The Lord Chamberlain's action against *A Patriot for Me* was widely deplored. Harold Hobson wrote in the *Sunday Times,* "If I did not know it to be utterly untrue, I would think that the Lord Chamberlain had gone out of his mind."

Ostensibly, the reason for the Lord Chamberlain's action was that the play dealt explicitly with sexual situations of a kind that would remain criminal until the Sexual Offences Act of 1967. Nevertheless, the Lord Chamberlain's decision was remarkable at a time of increasing tolerance. The repeal of the law against homosexuality was being actively discussed in the House of Lords even at the time of the play's production. Several publications had brought the issue of homosexuality into the open. The Wolfenden Report, drawn up by leading figures from church, state, and medical science, had recommended decriminalization of homosexuality as early as 1957, and its findings were widely available in print. Wayland Young's investigation into the narrative of sexuality *Eros Denied* (1964) had received widespread attention not long before *A Patriot for Me* was performed. The censorship laws were no longer applied as strictly as before. Quite a few sexually explicit plays and movies escaped censorship. Comedies especially could count on tolerance. This was the case with Joe Orton's *Entertaining Mr. Sloane* (1964), a play heavy in references to all kinds of sexual situations; Frank Marcus's comedy about lesbianism, *The Killing of Sister George* (1965)*;* Marc Camoletti's highly successful sex farce *Boeing-Boeing* (1966)*;* and Charles Dyer's comedy about an aging gay couple, *Staircase* (1966). Even some serious movies and plays with sexual content had been passed—as had been the case, for instance, with the dramatic adaptation of Alan Sillitoe's *Saturday Night and Sunday Morning,* J.B. Priestley and Irish Murdoch's theatre adaptation of her novel *A Severed Head,* and Harold Pinter's play *The Homecoming.*[8] None of these movies and plays, however, had shown, as *A Patriot for Me* did, two men in one bed or men dressed up as women at a drag ball—and all without the express aim of inviting sniggers.

If *A Patriot for Me* came under such heavy scrutiny at a time of increasing tolerance, it was perhaps because the thirty-six year old Osborne still personified the impatient arrogance of the modern generation. Though he was now sometimes heralded as "the best living writer in English for the stage,"[9] he still remained, and always would, too bitter a pill to be easily swallowed by the cultural or political establishment and thus to earn protection. His letter of hate to his Fellow Countrymen, written four years earlier was not yet forgotten. Neither was his double bill *Plays for England* (1962), with its satire on

Royalty worship (*The Blood of the Bambergs*) and its loving portrayal of sexual perversions (*Under Plain Cover*). The Lord Chamberlain had a special reason to remember him: his office's thick file of correspondence with Osborne dated back as far as 1955, when Osborne had staged a play co-written with Anthony Creighton called *Personal Enemy* that had also dealt with homosexuality. It had been produced at the Opera House in Harrogate, but only after a battle with the Lord Chamberlain that had left the play so lopsided that it had made little sense to its audience.[10] Not only did Osborne have a long history of wrangles with censorship, he was a forefront fighter in the struggle for its abolishment.[11] He publicly called it "ridiculous and infamous" and "a betrayal of liberty."[12] Lord Cobbold, the then Lord Chamberlain, must have seen no reason to facilitate such a career.

That the play dealt with homosexuality of course did not help. So far homosexuality had lurked beneath the surface of nearly every Osborne play. In *Look Back in Anger,* there were the references to Webster, Alison's homosexual friend. There was also a hint that Alison's mother may have had detectives investigate her future son-in-law, not just because of his long hair but because she suspected him of harboring perversions.[13] In the light of Jimmy's constant, campy bantering with live-in friend Cliff, that suspicion was understandable and shared by many a critic and reviewer. *A Patriot for Me* did not stop at allusions, however. Act two opens with a drag ball scene which, in the words of R. Hill, assistant secretary to the Lord Chamberlain, "present[s] homosexuals in their most attractive guise, dressed as pretty women" and thus "will to some degree cause the congregation of homosexuals and provide the means whereby the vice may be acquired."[14] As Charles Heriot, the Lord Chamberlain's Official Reader put it, the play "would certainly attract all the perverts in London."[15]

What it certainly did not attract was a drove of good actors. To play the major roles, Osborne's plays had usually been able to count on young dashing talent or established star performers: Richard Burton in the movie version of *Look Back in Anger* and the television play *A Subject of Scandal and Concern,* Laurence Olivier in The *Entertainer,* Nicol Williamson in *Inadmissible Evidence,* and Albert Finney in *Luther.* Now for *A Patriot for Me*, director Anthony Page approached Marlon Brando and Peter O'Toole to play Redl, the first important homosexual role in theatrical history. They declined. John Gielgud and Noel Coward, both homosexuals, refused offers to play the role of the magnificent drag queen, Baron von Epp. Finally, a famous but foreign actor, Maximilian Schell, agreed to play Redl. Half Austrian, half Swiss, Schell had the advantage of lending a modicum of authenticity to the portrayal of the military character. The director of the English Stage Company, George Devine himself, volunteered to play Baron von Epp and, as it turned out, with pleasure and much success.[16]

RECEPTION

When *A Patriot for Me* was finally produced in club on 30 June 1965, the problems with the Lord Chamberlain gave it a false but commercially beneficial notoriety, but the scandal about the play's theme of homosexuality determined people's expectations. What did it have to say for or against homosexuality? That was the question everyone asked. "Never before have such explicit details of the conversation and attitudes of homosexuals been seen on the English stage," said Milton Shulman of the *Evening Standard*.[17] Most attention went, as was to be expected, to the notorious drag ball scene. The reviewer of the *Daily Telegraph* clearly disapproved of it: "There was a certain amount of tee-heeing when the curtain rose on a stage-full of men dressed as women, but this died away. The scene ended in dead, and I think shamed, silence."[18] Most agreed—and perhaps with a measure of disappointment—that the play was not really scandalous: "It is an entirely proper and unsuggestive work," said the reviewer of the *Daily Mail*, "with nothing in it that any but the immeasurably dirty-minded or illiterate could take exception to."[19] Though George Devine, afraid of provoking the Lord Chamberlain into taking more drastic measures against the play's production, had begged journalists not to poke fun at the magistrate's decision, many could not resist the temptation to heckle "His Serene Noodleship, the Lord Chamberlain."[20]

The issue of homosexuality was and would remain central to any discussion of the play and distorted its reception from the onset. An early reviewer lamented that Redl was not a more positive character: "In view of public prejudice, I could have wished that the first play to raise the veil so completely could have had a hero more deserving of analysis and sympathy."[21] Others went one step further, claiming that the play far from defending homosexuality was in fact denigrating it: "This play can only be viewed as an utter condemnation of homosexuality," said the reviewer of the *Evening News*, adding, "this can be hardly what so liberal and intelligent a writer had in mind."[22] Harold Hobson, always a staunch defender of Osborne, said something similar: "It contains also a denunciation of homosexuality more searing than anything I have seen or read elsewhere."[23] The reference was in particular to Redl's aggressiveness toward some of the participants at the drag ball—a reaction that we will account for later on. Countess Delyanoff's mockery of what would now be termed "gay pride"—her way of retorting to Redl's taunt that she will never know the body of her lover as he knows it—provoked Harold Hobson's remark that he had "never heard a speech that so searingly and contemptuously dismisses homosexuality."[24] Lord Annan during a debate at the House of Lords in 1968 said, "I cannot conceive of any play less sentimental toward homosexuality, more cold-eyed and ruthless in its exposure of the horror of life of a particular kind of homosexuality and less likely to induce anyone to get into this practice."[25]

So the pattern of any discussion was set and would be faithfully adhered to in the future. When the Royal Shakespeare Company revived the play on 13 October 1995, less than one year after Osborne's death, with Peter Gill as director and James Wilby in the role of Redl, the issue of homosexuality was again in the forefront—in fact, more so than ever. The program included an insert by Angela Mason from Stonewall, the gay-lesbian freedom organization, entitled "A Special Case," wholly devoted to the issue of homosexuality. Reviewers for gay magazines pondered questions such as whether James Wilby, who as the eponymous hero in the movie version of E.M. Forster's *Maurice* (Merchant- Ivory Productions 1987) had played homosexual love scenes, could as a heterosexual man really play homosexual roles convincingly. Then some claimed, predictably, that the sensitivity with which some of Redl's declarations of love were written "could only come from a gay man, covert or otherwise." Trixabelle del Mar therefore crowned Osborne his "honorary Queen" and suggested that the disparaging remarks about homosexuality were symptomatic of the self-loathing of a secretly homosexual playwright.[26]

The critics had now indeed a new stick to beat the dead horse with: Earlier that year, Osborne had been "outed" as a closet homosexual in a revelatory interview given to the *Evening Standard* by Anthony Creighton who claimed that he and Osborne had been lovers in the 1950s. Their friendship had ended when Creighton had dared to disapprove of Osborne's representation of homosexuality in *A Patriot for Me.* "I think people should be able to appreciate," Creighton now said to the press, "that *A Patriot for Me,* which stigmatizes homosexuality, is a portrait of his own self-hatred."[27]

Perhaps, and then again perhaps not, but the nature and timing of these revelations were certainly unsavory. Since the seventies, Osborne's reputation as innovator and rebel had started to wane; in the nineties he was generally considered an old blimp who once in a while still wrote an outmoded, rancorous play. In 1965 *A Patriot for Me* had been a daring transgression of all theatrical rules of decorum, a courageous gesture on the part of a playwright who used his previous financial successes to stage a play in which he believed and of which he feared society would disapprove, and now there was quite a bit of glee in pricking that balloon too.

STRUCTURE

In an astute article on *A Patriot for Me,* George Bas claims that the issue of homosexuality in the play is the proverbial tree that hides the forest.[28] I believe this to be right and propose to investigate first the general layout of the forest before descending to that all too notorious tree. It is always dangerous to approach any work of art by isolating an issue and generalizing on the basis of it. Social issues do seep into a work of art, but once there they play a role quite different from that in reality. The disparate elements constituting art are like the figures in a dance and should be studied first as part of a complex movement. So *A Patriot for Me* is best approached, at least initially, not through a discussion of its representation of homosexuality, but through an analysis of its internal economy, which, as will soon become clear, turns quite naturally into a discussion of major themes, of which homosexuality is only one.

Structurally *A Patriot for Me* is Osborne's most complex play, despite frequent allegations by reviewers and critics that it is "ramshackle"[29] or that it has a "loose, filmic structure."[30] Of course, the task was daunting. The action spread over twenty-three years and over several different geographical locales: Lemburg, Warsaw, Vienna, Dresden, and Prague. It is a play of truly epic proportions, its twenty-three scenes lasting three and a half hours and involving some ninety different characters. To hold it all together, Osborne chose a method based on indirection, suggestion, and association; director Peter Gill was right to call it a "fascinating and dense piece," "both elusive and allusive."[31] To those who think of the Osbornian style as one of directness, not to say bluntness, that method may seem untypical. Yet in truth nearly every Osborne play is a strange mixture of excess and economy, and the key to its understanding often lies in a stray phrase lost in apparent verbiage. One gleans it intuitively, afterward sensing the play's rightness without always being able to justify it in analysis. This I believe explains (at least in some cases) the discrepancy between the often disgruntled notices that the plays receive and their success with audiences. As Helen Dawson, Osborne's widow, put it, his plays work on stage,[32] and for a theatre person, that may often be enough—for a critic, of course, it may not.

The play is constructed as a series of associations, parallels, and inversions which knits all scenes closely together in a complex woof, colored by a few dominant metaphors, of which the duel, the gaze, and the "dual body functioning" are the most important. On the microlevel, a continuous associative flow from scene to scene creates a sense of continuation within the vast shifts in time and setting. This technique establishes an impression of repleteness of significance which is well-known to those familiar with fractal images: What looks like a minor detail suddenly opens up, revealing an unexpected new vista. Here too Osborne continuously pulls to the foreground in one scene what seemed a detail in the preceding one. If among the gossip at the drag ball (II, i) we hear a joking reference to a Jewish Dr. Schoepfer who crusades with suspicious zeal against homosexuality, then typically the next scene will show Dr. Schoepfer at a lecture (II, ii). If we hear in one scene, in passing, that one of Redl's lovers, Mischa, is going insane (III, ii), then we will see Redl visiting him in the hospital in the next scene (III, iii). If there is a minor reference to the boater hat of the British ambassador's handsome son that hangs above

Redl's bed as a token of his conquest, then that hat will return in a scene shortly after where Redl receives it back from his Russian spy masters as visible proof of their victory over him (II, I; II, iii).

Details also prove significant in the long run, and often in unexpected ways. For instance, the brief excerpt from Dr. Schoepfer's lecture ends by defining homosexuality as a "flight from incest" (II, ii, 92). It seems a throw-away phrase, a simple reference to a rather fanciful psychoanalytic theory of the day, added for the sake of historical veracity. We might expect it to slip from memory as soon as we hear it, and yet it reverberates uncomfortably. If we could look at the text, we would discover that, in explaining to Taussig his failed relationship with the Countess Delyanoff, Redl had admitted that they were too "awkward" together. "It was like talking to my sister," he said, adding, perhaps a little too casually, that his sister had just died: "can't say I thought about it more than ten minutes" (I, ix, 66).

There are many more examples that show how the text hangs together in similarly minute and unexpected ways. When in the opening scene we meet a solitary Redl waiting in an empty gymnasium early one morning, we may already sense he is a man doomed to a lonely death. That image of Redl as a forlorn presence in a room will stay with us until the end when we wait outside his hotel for the shot that puts an end to his life. It is, structurally speaking, a brilliant move on Osborne's part to end the play not with that suicide but with a reference to that minor character, the enigmatic Dr. Schoepfer, whose file is being investigated by Russian Intelligence officers, suggesting that here too is an unhappy soul whose sexual misery has made him vulnerable to blackmail. Such a structure may indeed be filmic, but it is certainly not loose. On the contrary, the constant flow in the meandering stream of action creates an impression of dreadful inevitability which casts over the whole play a sense of tragedy.

THE DUEL

The tightly interwoven action also moves with broader, wider sweeps. On the macrolevel, the whole action is subsumed under a few interrelated dominant metaphors. The play starts with a duel between two young officers, Siczynski and Kupfer, in which Redl functions as Siczynski's second. That image of internal dissension, enacted within the temple of a masculine society, the gymnasium, reverberates throughout the play.[33] Kupfer had insulted Siczysnki by calling him "Fraulein Rothschild," referring mockingly not just to his Jewishness, which Siczysnki would have tolerated, but more importantly to his effeminacy or possible homosexuality, which is unacceptable. Later we learn that Kupfer himself is a homosexual. Siczysnki will have to die to disprove that he is not what he is; Kupfer will have to kill him to prove to the world that he himself is not what he accuses the other man of being. That is a well-known pattern; what is more unusual is the part Redl plays in it. Redl, unlike the aristocratic Kupfer, is of lowly birth. For an otherwise hardworking and cautious man, his support of Siczysnki seems dangerous and suspicious both to his superiors and to Kupfer. For Redl, this instinctive loyalty to a man he hardly knows is an uncharacteristic, excessive gesture that, as we will see later, warrants closer attention.

The idea of the duel, of battle, of internal dissension, often unacknowledged by the participating characters, provides the overall metaphoric *gestalt* that lends relevance and significance to disparate moments in the play's action. Set up in the first scene, it can be said to continue until the very end when Redl takes revenge on Kupfer. Once he has surpassed Kupfer in rank through sheer hard work and determination and has become head of the Empire's counterespionage, Redl delivers Kupfer to the Russians. Not much later, Redl puts an end to his own life in grand military fashion after his role as double agent has been revealed. Even his suicide resembles the duel, as it takes the equally paradoxical form of a rule-bound impulsivity. Redl is not only ordered to shoot himself, he is given a manual on how to use the pistol. The play ends as in *Hamlet* with all major players dead. Even the army is not victorious: its attempt to conceal the scandal is defeated when a revelatory article appears in the *Times*, and corpses will soon heap up in grotesque numbers with the outbreak of WWI.

Though some claim that in betraying his country Redl has chosen to live according to his own convictions, the play goes out of its way to show that by killing himself Redl is not asserting his free will and independence. The image of Redl studying a manual before shooting himself with the Browning pistol is one of those apparently needless, excessive details typical of Osborne ("REDL *pours another glass of champagne and settles down to read the manual*" (III, vii, 123)), but it shows that Redl until the very end follows instructions. If the whole play is a battle, it certainly is not one that liberates, that creates or confirms an independent identity. What we do sense, though—and what is so admirably captured in the metaphor of the duel—is the tension between the yearning for self-assertion on the one hand and the conventions that shape that very yearning on the other. The play does not offer any way out; on every level it is marked by a profound and uneasy ambiguity.

Within that general tenor of significance established by the dominant metaphor of the duel, key scenes are made to echo or clash with one another, drawing attention to similarities and contrasts. This is most clearly the case with the ballroom scene at the Hofburg Palace in Vienna, i.e. the emperor's court, which is contrasted later with a secret drag ball organized annually by Baron von Epp. On both occasions, the military establishment, surrounded by its satellites, is present, though playing vastly different parts. It is the atmosphere that is different; at the drag ball, it is "generally relaxed and informal, in contrast to the somewhat stiff atmosphere at the ball in Act I" (II, i, 72). Both societies, however, are constituted more or less by the same powerful figures and pride themselves on their ability to create a sense of brotherhood and equality. The army, we hear from Hötzendorf and Möhl, is a place where all differences melt and merge: "It goes beyond religion. It serves everyone and everyone serves it, even Hungarians and Jews"; "it's the same experience as friendship or loving a woman, speaking the same tongue, that is a *proper* bond, it's *human*, you can see it and experience it, more than 'all men are brothers' or some such nonsense" (I, vi, 48, 51). At the drag ball, Baron von Epp speaks of homosexuality as a true counter culture: "Don't you think we should all form an Empire of our own? . . . Instead of all joining together, you know, one Empire of sixty million Germans, like they're always going on about. What about an Empire of *us*. Ex million queens" (II, i, 83).

In both cases, such fantasies of a utopian brotherhood are followed by exclusions and exceptions, which usually are expressed in the form of snide anti-Semitic comments. Enlarging on his army ideology in a later scene, Hötzendorf characterizes Jews as "outsiders, they feel outsiders, so their whole creed of life must be based on duplicity—by necessity" and for that reason they are quite unable to serve the Empire (III, ii, 107). In a similar way, Baron von Epp excludes Jews from his homosexual utopia: "They're the least queer in my opinion. Their mothers won't let them" (II, i, 83).

The contrast between the Hofburg reception and the drag ball is striking, yet even more striking are the similarities. They immediately give the lie to Baron von Epp's ideology that gatherings such as the drag ball celebrate the right to difference: "This . . . is the celebration of the individual against the rest, the us's and the them's, the free and the constricted, the gay and the dreary, the lonely and the mob, the little Tsarina there and the Emperor Francis Joseph" (II, i, 77). Clearly, this is not a case of "us vs. them"; the us's and the them's are virtually interchangeable. Duplicity is the establishment's strength, not its weakness. It is not by chance that the symbol of the dual monarchy of the Austro-Hungarian Empire is a double-headed eagle. Kunz, the most adept at swimming in both waters, personifies that quality best. He is a convinced Machiavellian, without illusions and unheeding about those of others. During the reception at the Emperor's palace, he shocks Hötzendorf with his blunt declaration that "We all play parts, *are* doing so now, *will* continue to do so" (I, vi, 49). At the drag ball, where he is equally at home, he defines that gathering not as a jubilant affirmation of identity but, again, as a masquerade, a temporary reversal of the reigning order, a "carnival" (II, i, 86).

The Empire relies on people like Kunz, discreet, efficient, though for many a little too cynical. Such a man, says Hötzendorf, is "like a razor. When you've used him, put him back in his case" (I, vi, 46). Kunz dons any mask required of him, whereas Redl is oppressed by a sense of intrinsic difference beyond his homosexuality. He is sufficiently cautious to praise his general's army ideology but in fact only agrees with one part of it, that "the army creates an elite"

(I, vi, 48). With Colonel von Möhl's all too idyllic fantasy of a common brotherhood, of differences melting away in the hot-burning flame of common pursuit and loyalty to the Emperor, he has to take exception: "I don't agree that
all men are brothers, like Colonel Möhl. We are clearly not. Nor should be, or
ever want to be. [. . . .] We're meant to clash. And often and violently" (I, vi,
51). It is therefore typical that Redl comes to the drag ball in full uniform, as
if signaling his reluctance or unwillingness to merge with the others. Yet for a
moment, swept up by the general gaiety of the occasion, he forgets his isolation. Exchanging pleasantries with Ferdy, a youngish male prostitute in drag,
Redl relaxes and even giggles like a schoolboy; but when Kupfer appears and
insolently refers to the Siczysnki episode, Redl is reminded that even here
among apparent equals differences persist. The silly capers of the young man
with whom he had such fun a moment ago suddenly become unbearable and
he lashes out, slapping him violently.

The slap reestablishes the difference, both social and existential, that was
always there. In an extensive stage direction to the drag ball scene, followed
by a page of notes, Osborne indeed emphasizes the fact that the trained eye
can immediately detect subtle distinctions in the dress and appearance of men
in drag—distinctions which often have to do with money, class, and position
in "normal" life. There are the "paid bum boys" who have invested time and
resources in this party because it opens possibilities for lucrative employment
later. There are also the "discreet drag queens," "the more self-conscious rich
queens," the "rich, discreet queens," and the queens who use drag to express
not their admiration but their dislike of women. Osborne relentlessly reminds
us of how class imposes its discriminating power. At one moment the Tsarina
and Ferdy are chatting together and Redl, Stefan, and the Baron move away
from them. A stage direction reads: "Some class division here too" (II, i, 78).
The male whore now clearly receives the swipe that was meant for the aristocratic Kupfer. Ferdy, being one of the paid bum boys is for Redl an easy and
safe victim on whom to vent an anger that was in fact provoked by disgust with
"Kupfer, drunkenness and himself" (II, i, 86). Ferdy also gets slapped not
because his campy behavior is intrinsically revolting to Redl (as some reviewers have suggested) but because it implies a freewheeling equality and insou-
ciance that are deeply false.

The message is that communities prey upon themselves, and the homosexual and Jewish communities are no exceptions. Siczynski was exploited by
Jewish moneylenders and so is Redl whose biggest debts we hear are to "Mik-
las and Fink," a firm named after a Hungarian and a Jew (I, v, 41). When Redl
has his first homosexual affair he is robbed and beaten (I, x). In a later scene
with another casual lover, we see that Redl has come to expect the robbing;
apparently it is the price one has to pay for illicit pleasure (III, i). By accepting it, he is able to control to some extent its effect upon himself. He tells the
thief what to take and what to leave. Again and again scenes are juxtaposed to

show internal dissension within a community of apparent equals or the deceptiveness of apparent difference. The latter, for instance, is shown in the juxtaposition of the scene in which Dr. Schoepfer defines homosexuality as a threat to civilization and the scene in which his dossier is being examined by the Russian secret police (II, ii; III, x). "Us" and "them" in the final instance always prove to be interchangeable.

After Redl has broken up with the Countess, who becomes his greatest enemy by stealing his lover from him, he taunts her with her Jewishness, calling her even a "little Jewish spy"—as if the term did not equally apply to himself (III, i, 101). Similarities persist beyond the divide of man and woman, homosexual and heterosexual. To prove that differences are often deceptive, scenes are organized to reflect each other as inversions of the same situation. At the beginning of their relationship, the Countess reminds Redl of the loneliness that awaits him if he resists her love:

> COUNTESS: If you leave me, you'll be alone.
> REDL: That's what I want, to be left alone.
> COUNTESS: You'll always be alone.
> REDL: Good. Splendid. (I, vii, 60)

Redl can't stand the way in which she tries to see through his defenses. Later, however, tables are turned, and we see what it means for Redl to be in love. Now he is the one who observes the beloved who has deserted him to marry the Countess: "You've not looked at him, you never will," he tells her (III, i, 101). In a still later scene with a different lover, Redl is the one who begs his lover to stay, summoning a picture of a dreadful and lonely old age: "You little painted toy, you puppet, you poor duffer, you'll be, with your disease and paunch and silliness and curlers and dyed wispy hair and long legs and varicose veins like bunches of grapes and prostate and thick waist and rolling thighs and big bottom, that's where we all go" (III, v, 119). So scenes are organized to show not only difference within apparent similarity but also similarity within apparent difference.

This belief in the simultaneity of sameness and difference also informs the play's concept of love. "What, what does one, do you suppose, well, look for in anyone, anyone else, I mean [. . . .] I mean: That isn't clearly, really, clearly already in oneself?" Redl answers this question asked by Siczynski with a doubting negative: "nothing I suppose" (I, i, 19). Siczynski's question is important in light of the third dominant metaphor, that of the "dual body functioning," but the doubt contained in Redl's answer is important too because why bother to look for something we already have? Does the search, the reaching out, and the willingness to take risks while doing so, not indicate that one does not coincide with oneself, is not sufficient unto oneself?

It is this yearning, this looking for the self in others that distinguishes some characters in the play. The prostitute Hilde, Redl, and the Countess Delyanoff each express such a yearning to find themselves realized not just in themselves but in and by the other. Each takes the risk that such a self-exposure entails—the risk of being rejected, hurt, betrayed. It is this vulnerability that makes them lovable to the audience, that redeems the prostitute and the spy, that makes them more authentic in their humanity than other, better adapted characters.

THE GAZE

With the simultaneity of sameness and difference, we have entered the realm of impossibility, which, as we will see, is another name for the tragic. That impossibility is best expressed by the play's second dominant metaphor, that of the unreciprocated gaze. After all, this is a play about spying, about watching without being seen. Is that not also the definition of unrequited love? It is not by accident that the man who has spent his life desiring, almost always without being desired in return, finally becomes a master spy. "One would like to be loved, if it's possible," Hilde says. Redl replies, "Love's hardly ever possible" (I, iv, 37). A television play by Osborne, *The End of Me Old Cigar* shows that love can suddenly bloom in the most extraordinary places, such as in a brothel, but what is required is mutual trust, a willingness to reveal the nakedness of one's very being—and that, for Redl, who finds himself in bed with a prostitute, is impossible. He fails to see his own plight in Hilde, who nevertheless recognizes her own solitude in his:[34]

> HILDE: May I put my head on your arm?
> REDL: If you wish . . .
> HILDE: No, I'll finish my champagne. (I, iv, 37)

The prostitute Hilde longs for love and senses some of her own yearning in Redl; she therefore is able to "see" him. In fact, she has such an acute awareness of his being that she guesses the origin of his suffering. She knows he is more interested in what happens in the next room than in her company, so she allows him to spy through a hole in the wall on the lovemaking of the handsome waiter Albrecht (I, iv, 38). What Hilde says of Siczynski also applies to Redl: "I used to look at his eyes," she says, "but he never looked at me" (I, iv, 36). It is a pattern repeated later. Countess Delyanoff too sees Redl, but Redl does not return her gaze. Yet when he is truly in love, Redl too can see as he proves in a speech both passionately driven and excessively detailed. When the Countess takes revenge on him by seducing his lover Viktor, he taunts her by saying that she will never look at that man in the way he has done:

> I tell you this: you'll never know that body like I know it. The lines beneath his eyes. Do you know how many there are, do you know one has less than the other? And the scar behind his ear, and the hairs in his nostrils, which has the most, what colour they are in what light? The mole on where? Where, Sophia? I know the place here, between the eyes, the dark patches like slate—like blue when he's tired, really tired, the place for a blow or a kiss or a bullet. You'll never know like I know, you can't. The backs of his knees, the pattern on the soles of his feet. Which trouble him, and so I used to wash them and bathe them for hours. His thick waist, and how long are his thighs, compared to his calves, you've not looked at him, you never will. (III, i, 101)

The gaze not returned suggests the loneliness of the gazer. When we first meet Redl, his acquiescence to loneliness is striking. He seems to have decided early on that life as others lead it is not for him. For Taussig and Kupfer, being sent to War College in Vienna provides new possibilities of an active social life; to Redl it means only the promise of advancement through hard work. "That'll be enough for me," he says grimly (I, iii, 31). This is an attitude typical of the lower-class boy who knows he will not receive help on his way up. But it also goes beyond that. These are the words of a man who knows that he will not find what he needs, however hard he tries, but who also realizes he will never cease to long for it. Though he tries to learn not to want, he cannot control his eyes. He spends most of his free time sitting in cafés looking at people, at "the Passing Show" (I, viii, 64). Watching without participating becomes the emblem of his utter loneliness.

To be truly seen by those for whom one yearns and has observed so well is the fulfillment of all one's hopes for love. Redl might be said to send out delicate signals in the hope that the right kind of person will see him. His habit of sucking on peppermints, the carefully selected and tastefully displayed expensive smoking paraphernalia, such as the cigar cases, are acceptable touches of delicacy in the military world as long as they are accompanied by manly behavior and the smell of horse and leather. Those subtle signals of his difference are presented to be appreciated by those who share his sensitivities. In fact, the world seems to be divided between those who dislike Redl's peppermint breath and those who appreciate it. Siczysnki likes it; Taussig dislikes it. Hilde, who liked Siczysnki, also likes Redl's peppermint smell. To those who like it, the smell indicates a delicacy, perhaps a secret but charming self-doubt that stands in sharp contrast to the arrogant self-assertiveness of the aristocratic Kupfer who blows his stinking breath in people's faces (I, i, 18).

To see as well as to be seen, that is what Redl hopes for when he is in love. When he makes love to a man for the first time, he regrets that his lover refuses to leave the lights on (I, x, 69). To conceal one's eyes is to harbor a secret. We soon learn that Redl's first lover is afraid lest his eyes betray his bad faith: After the lovemaking, he robs Redl while the latter is beaten by his lover's accomplices.

All too often, the eyes of others, seen or unseen, prove dangerous to Redl. To be truly seen involves a risk he cannot afford. Closer scrutiny might detect disgust or desire, feelings he so carefully tries to hide, and that might render him vulnerable to prying questions or, worse, to blackmail. He refuses to make love to Countess Delyanoff with the lights on and is uncomfortably, even angrily, aware of her examining eyes: "Damn your eyes," he shouts at one point (I, vii, 60). A young man in a café who interprets his glances all too correctly might be a male prostitute or a blackmailer, or possibly both. In any case, his insolent "I know what *you're* looking for," provokes Redl into immediate raging fury (I, ix, 67).

So Redl is always on his guard, trying to prevent his eyes from betraying his desires and to guess what other people's eyes reveal about their intentions toward him. "I can't relax or be at ease," says Redl to the Countess, who asks him why he is always so watchful: "You always seem to be at the ready in some way, listening for something . . . some stray chance thing" (I, vii, 59). The words recall Siczysnki's admission to Redl that he has "always expected to *be* challenged a hundred times" (I, i, 16). In a conversation with Taussig, Redl tells him he is never sure whether he is being hunted or not. Attending official parties is particularly exhausting: "They're like beautiful, schooled performing dogs. Scrutinizing and listening for an unsteady foot. It's like hunting without the pig. Everyone sweats and whoops and rides together, and, at any time, at any moment, the pig may turn out to be *you*. Stick!" (I, ix, 66). At the drag ball, he lets his guard down, but just for a moment, as if prompted by Kunz's explanation to Redl's lover Stefan that "this is a place for people to come together. People who are very often in their everyday lives, rather lonely and even miserable and feel hunted" (II, i, 85). "He looks flushed and suddenly relaxed"; "he is drinking freely now, and is excited and enjoying himself"; he "is being captivated by Ferdy, and start[s] to get recurring fits of giggles" (II, i, 76, 81, 82). When Kupfer appears, he is soon back on guard: He adjusts his monocle, "sobers up and stiffens," "stands more erect than ever," and soon looks "like a frozen ox" (II, i, 86, 87, 90).

When he is aware of being studied, his face becomes "stony" (I, vii, 56). "I can't breathe," he complains to the Countess, indicating that her scrutiny is oppressive (I, vii, 59). The fear of being finally publicly revealed for what he truly is haunts him. The ultimate fear is that the body itself will betray him— for instance, that the dreaded broadening of the backside will make him a homosexual for all to see. Painting the horror of advancing age and lost beauty to his unfaithful Viktor, he ends by saying, "In the bottom, that's where we all go and you can't mistake it. *Everyone'll see it!*" (III, v, 119).[35] Redl's fear of prying eyes of course proves to be justified. It is particularly mortifying for the master spy to be told that Russian Intelligence officers have been watching him for the last ten years, that they know every detail of his life and have photographs of his intimacies with his lovers to prove it (II, iii, 96).

"THE DUAL BODY FUNCTIONING"

Seeing without being seen is the fate of the lonely voyeur, the unrequited lover, and the spy. To have his gaze returned is what the lonely watcher wants and yet fears most. This fear of and longing for the other as an emanation of the self is expressed in a third dominant metaphor, that of the "dual body functioning."

The term first appears when Redl visits his unfaithful lover Mischa, who has betrayed him first with Kupfer and then with a young woman he plans to marry. As a result of this identity struggle, Mischa is now hospitalized with a nervous breakdown. Redl claims that he no longer cares; he has already organized Kupfer's transfer and has a replacement for Mischa lined up. After his lover Stefan's marriage to Countess Delyanoff, Redl has given up all hope that his lovers will be faithful to him: "Since Stefan I've let them go their own ways" (III, ii, 105). Mischa, despite his unfaithfulness, feels a deep bond with Redl. He tells Redl that he is "on a star . . . Just like you. I expect you were sent to Vienna too, sir, because you are the same kind of element as me. The same dual body functioning" (III, ii, 111).

Mischa's words recall Siczysnki's question whether we ever search for anything but ourselves in the other. The opening scene in which Siczysnki asks Redl that question ends with the duel and Siczysnki's death, but not before a few swift strokes have established an unspoken deep intimacy between the two men. They have hardly ever spoken to each other before, but Redl admits that he has often observed Siczynski practicing his fencing, "more times than I can think of," and Siczysnki that he never doubted Redl would accept to be his second notwithstanding the risk involved for Redl's career (I, i, 16, 17). Redl and Siczysnki have a lot in common: They are both Galician Jews, though Redl won't admit to it; both are loners, though Redl is better at camouflaging it. Later we learn that both spend long hours in cafés, sitting by themselves, looking at people but hardly ever taking part in their lives. Though they hardly know each other, and could in fact have been living on separate stars, to use Mischa's words, they were, it seems, always aware of each other—as if they were indeed two instances of the same element. Now that their paths have converged, death has become inevitable.

The dream that Redl tells Siczynski pushes the theme of a never fully acknowledged mutual identification further toward the *doppelgänger* motif. In his dream, Redl visits an "upright, frank, respected" friend, "someone I liked," who has been court martialed and is now detained in gaol. Redl knows that a visit involves great danger to himself, and not just because of the circumstances: "It wasn't just because I knew I would be arrested myself as soon as I got in there. It wasn't for that." Apparently then what is at stake is a more fundamental fear. As he had expected, he is immediately arrested. The price for following one's desires, for being as frank as the man on the other side of the wire netting, is loss of liberty, perhaps of life (I, i, 20). The worry and fear, he claims, have nothing to do with the near certainty of arrest. At the moment of arrest, "I couldn't tell whether he was pleased or not. Pleased that I'd come to see him or that they'd got me too. They touched me on the shoulder and told me to stand up, which I did. And by that time he'd gone" (I, i, 20). The man disappears at the moment Redl moves to the other side of the netting; it is then as if Redl has taken his place, as if the man in fact were the real Redl. To coincide with oneself is quite literally to be caught.

The disappearance of the accused in the dream foreshadows Siczynski's death; and the visitor's arrest, the trouble Redl anticipates for revealing his sympathy for Siczysnki. The dream indicates that Redl both longs to be and fears being Siczysnki. Siczysnki, one could say, is the person behind Redl's persona. To be like Siczynski is to be himself but that means being unpopular, without a chance of making a career. Despite his great personal beauty, Siczysnki is isolated, tracked down, finally killed. By identifying with the prisoner in the dream or with Siczynski in reality, that is, by accepting a self that he has repressed, Redl knows he is embracing their fate, disappearance or death. Even before the end of the scene, when Redl cradles Siczysnki's dead body in his arms and wipes the blood from his mouth, Redl's identification with Siczysnki is complete. He will never admit to being Kupfer's enemy but will find it hard to conceal his resentment and finally will act upon it. Kupfer is not just the man who killed Siczysnki; he is the man who forces Redl further away from what he considers his hidden self. In the next scene, we see how Redl distances himself from Siczysnki, how he speaks disparagingly of him during an official interview with Möhl:

> MÖHL: Was Siczynski a friend of yours?
> REDL: No, sir.
> MÖHL: What was your opinion of him?
> REDL: I hardly knew him, sir. (*Realises quickly he needs to provide more than this.*)
> He struck me as being hyper-critical, over-sceptical about things. (I, ii, 26)

The memory of Siczynski will keep haunting Redl who had prophesied about Kupfer that "someone'll chalk him up . . . sometime." Redl will be that someone. By taking Siczysnki's place in the protracted but never acknowledged duel with Kupfer, Redl also foreshadows his own death.

SOCIETY AND THE HIDDEN SELF

The flight from incest into homosexual attachments is doomed to failure because homoeroticism appears to be a front for the incestuous quest for the self in the other, for the dual body functioning, for the gaze that will be fully returned. It is a quest both irresistible and fatal. Clearly, the issue of homosexuality is not pursued as a sociopolitical reality; rather homosexuality represents with unparalleled acuteness of experience what Osborne conceives of as an existential reality from which many of us suffer. Asked why homosexuality plays such an important role in his plays, Osborne said that he was interested in it for its "ambiguity."[36] In other words, he is interested in homosexuality only to the extent that it can serve as a useful figure in a tragic vision based on an awareness of a fundamental impossibility: in Osborne's drama, people do not become their true selves; indeed, it is doubtful whether for Osborne there is such a thing as a true self. But they never cease to long for such a literal self-realization even though they suffer daily the impossibility of coinciding with themselves. The gap between their persona and what they think of as their person, that terrible and unbearable vacuum, they either fill with fantastic and bold dramatizations of the self, as Jimmy Porter does, or with a quiet heroism, as in Redl's case.

Having no clear resolution, no moment when the misery of one person assumes a supra-individual and therefore redeeming importance, *A Patriot for Me* is not a tragedy in the traditional sense. Yet Redl is nevertheless a tragic figure. Kunz, who serves as a foil to Redl, accepts the necessity of donning masks and playing roles. Redl too is convinced of the necessity of play acting. To Siczynski he says, "I'm quite plausible and not half a bad actor, for one . . . reason and another" (I, i, 16). He proves it by being such a successful careerist. But until the very end, Redl, unlike Kunz, sweats and suffers under his mask. When it threatens to slip off, as when he weeps and cries out at night in his sleep in the presence of the Countess, he gets up and leaves so as not to give himself away (I, vii). At times, the sense of derealization pushes him to the brink of a nervous breakdown. Mischa, who has already fallen into that abyss, summarizes it when he says, "we're absorbed into the air at night" (III, iii, 110). Redl too feels he literally loses himself, evaporates: "I feel myself, almost as if I were falling away and disappearing" (I, vii, 59). In a letter to the Countess, he says, "I seem to . . . speak out of nowhere" (I, viii, 62).

Redl turns his ability to live the unlivable into an act of heroism; it is proof that he is part of an elite, that at least in spirit he might be aristocratic.[37] For that reason, he also cherishes his difference. When he tells the Countess—who, with the duplicity of a spy, offers to help him—that loneliness is what he wants, that it is splendid, she replies, "No it isn't. You know it isn't. That's why you're so frightened. You'll fall alone" (I, vii, 60). She is right, of course. In search of self-realization, Redl continuously falls in love and is continuously betrayed. In the end, when he stands revealed as a double agent, he is truly alone. For five hours officers wait outside his hotel for the shot that puts an end to his life. István Szabó in *Oberst Redl* (1985), a film inspired by Osborne's play which he had seen in a successful revival starring Alan Bates, portrays those last hours: at ever greater speed, retching from misery and fear, an agitated Klaus

Maria Brandauer as Colonel Redl paces his room before shooting himself in the head. But in *A Patriot for Me,* Redl's isolation is such that it is not even described or shown. In his last hours, Redl has truly become invisible.

What the play ultimately questions is hinted at in its ironic title, *A Patriot for Me.* Originally, it was Emperor Francis II's shrewd question when a man was introduced to him as a "true patriot": "Ah! But is he a patriot for me?" In a double monarchy racked by nationalist tensions of every ilk, loyalty to the person of the emperor was paramount. As the title of a play about a homosexual man's doomed quest for self-realization, however, the phrase calls the very idea of a community in question. We think of Archie Rice in *The Entertainer,* dancing on a background of a grotesque, nude Britannia, and singing with typical ambiguity that he only believes in "good old number one." Yet Archie Rice, we know, is a man who, when given the opportunity to flee abroad, prefers to be jailed for tax evasion in his own country. He is aware that his fate is linked with that of his country, shabby as it may be. That the patriot for me is paradoxically the only true patriot we also learn from Redl's ultimate fate. Apparently it is his deep-seated duplicity and egoism, his continual search for self-realization behind a mask of conformity, that has led him to betray his country. And yet until the very end, it is his ability to suffer the pangs of self-alienation that protects the army ideology of brotherhood. In a program note for the 1964 production, probably written by John Osborne himself, the Royal and Imperial Army is represented as a democratic, in fact meritocratic, institution: all private, racial, national and class differences are transcended into the common cause of service to the emperor. Indeed Redl, of lowly birth, is allowed to ascend the career ladder nearly all the way to the top, leaving behind others, like Kupfer, who are of noble birth. He manages to do so only because he suppresses his differences: he claims he is a Catholic and hides his Jewish origins; he suppresses his homosexuality, trying to lead a "normal" heterosexual sex life at great cost to himself; he hides his poverty by incurring immense debts and by inventing a rich uncle. It is to hide his difference—his homosexuality, his poverty, his Jewishness—that he becomes a spy and betrays his country. In this way, his fate is completely bound up with that of the army. The public scandal he avoids by killing himself is in fact also that of the army: Möhl knows all too well that people would enjoy to see "the *élite* caught out! Right at the centre of the Empire" (III, vi, 121). Society and the individual relate to one another in an uneasy, predatory way. For the individual, society is hateful because it prevents him from being what he thinks he is, without always realizing that in the final instance the idea of a "true self" is the very product of that hate.

Part III

CHAPTER 9

The Long Descent, 1972–1994

Though he had known tremendous success and had amply savored its financial rewards, Osborne had always been and would remain fascinated by failure. Written even before Osborne became famous, *Epitaph for George Dillon* (produced in 1957) is a story of a man who fails at the moment he becomes successful; *Inadmissible Evidence* (1964), written at the height of his success, shows us a lawyer who suddenly loses his confidence and with it his control over his life; *The Right Prospectus* (1970) and *Very Like a Whale* (1971), written while he was battling with deepening depression, are stories of a successful man's gradual isolation. One can only assume that in the seventies and eighties Osborne must have observed with some fascination the same process happening to himself.

From the mid-seventies on, he became a voice not of the present but of the past, a playwright who had found his legitimate place in the annals of theatrical history and was to be encountered more often in university entrance exams than on the stage. The seventies and eighties marked new developments in the theatre that made Osborne increasingly irrelevant. In its quest for new experiences, drama turned toward alternative voices—those of women, homosexuals, and immigrants. In 1972, the RCT produced Caryl Churchill's first full-length play *Owners*. Shortly after, she joined the fringe group Monstrous Regiment, a company founded in protest against male dominated theatre, whether traditional or radical, with the express aim of creating a theatre by women for women. Their first successful work, written in collaboration with Churchill, was *Vinegar Tom,* a play contesting traditional views of witchcraft. Other important women playwrights of the time were Michelene Wandor (*Care and Control* (1977)), Liz Lochhead (*The Grimm Sisters* (1981)), Pam Gems (*Queen Christina* (1982)), Sarah Daniels (*Masterpieces* (1984)), and Timberlake Wertenbaker (*Our Country's Good* (1988)), all of whom eventually had plays staged at the Royal Court.

1975 saw the emergence of Gay Sweatshop, a fringe group specializing in works about homosexuality. After a short period of experimentation, during which the company staged a wider variety of works, it decided to focus exclusively on plays written by gay playwrights, supposedly the only ones who could truthfully depict the homosexual experience. Later, following the same logic, the company split into two groups, one for gay men and another for gay women. Group-written plays included *Mister X* (1976) and Martin Sherman's *Bent,* which, with Ian McKellen in the lead, broke box office records at the RCT in 1979. Work by homosexual women gained recognition as well, as happened with Jill Posener's *Any Woman Can* (1976). The seventies also saw work, later to be called "postcolonial," by playwrights of color, for instance, Tunde Ikoli, Wole Soyinka, and Mustapha Matura, whose plays were promoted by the fringe group Foco Novo.

Osborne was not in tune with such developments. In 1986 he moved from his estate in Kent, still in the proximity of London, to an estate in Shropshire. There, from a magnificent old mansion amid thirty acres of green, he vituperated, like some latter-day Evelyn Waugh, against the world at large. Once in a while, he still returned to London where he stayed at the luxurious Cadogan hotel. In 1988, he tartly remarked that the only plays worth going to were a burlesque musical called *Sugar Babies* and a farce *One for the Pot.* "I just sort of lost interest in the theatre," he admitted to a reporter:

> It's all so different from when I started out. I got bored with it and I think
> they got bored with me. It's such a definable pattern. I emerged at 26 or 27,
> was apparently successful, two plays on Broadway, that sort of thing. Then
> people get tired of you. The same thing happened to Coward and Rattigan.
> You have got to be 70 or have a terminal disease before they start being nice
> to you again. There's nothing you can do about it.[1]

Too many people indeed got bored with Osborne. "I was sitting on a panel the other day discussing the future of the British theatre," Michael Billington reported in 1973, "when the name of John Osborne came up. An eminent former critic described his recent work as 'absolute shit.' [. . . .] I was astonished by the liverish intensity of the attack."[2] When a decade later, Billington proposed a BBC Radio Osborne retrospective, he "got a polite call back from a young producer thanking me for my ideas but clearly stating that Osborne was a bit, you know unfashionable."[3] More recently, playwright Mark Ravenhill, after his success with *Shopping and Fucking,* resented being compared with the angry man Osborne, the more so since the latter was known for his homophobic comments.[4]

There were also other reasons for Osborne's gradual disaffection with the world of theatre. He enjoyed the pleasures of the countryside and played an active role in it. He became a regular churchgoer, making appearances at local charities and even opening his gardens to the public in support of a new roof or new parish bells for the local Anglican Church. In a 1979 interview, he even declared, "I'd rather go to church than a theatre any evening."[5] His personal life had improved after he divorced Jill Bennett in 1977 and married Helen Dawson in 1978. The latter abandoned her fourteen-year old career as journalist and drama critic for the *Observer* to devote herself to her husband. She organized his interviews, typed his work, sometimes even finished his articles when illness confined him to bed, and on several occasions saved his life when he fell into a diabetic coma.

Clearly, what had not improved was his health, both mental and physical. His unhappy marriages with novelist and critic Penelope Gilliatt (1963–1968) and Jill Bennett (1968–1977) had thrown him into deep and lasting depression, characterized by constant, heavy drinking and harrowing writer's block.[6] Champagne and cigarettes were to remain part of his life, as well as severe depression and ill health. In January 1982, he sent a long, typed letter to his sixteen-year old daughter Nolan (from his marriage with Penelope Gilliatt), accusing her in bitter terms of Cordelia's sin: "How sharper than a serpent's tooth it is to have a thankless child." The ungrateful child was no longer welcome in his home and was to be withdrawn from her expensive private school. The irony of the reference to *King Lear*, a play Osborne was convinced Nolan would never read on her own, seems to have escaped him. Had he lost his mind? Were his accusations cruel and unjust? Angry letters from Nolan's defenders reminded Osborne of the difficulties encountered by the young girl who had grown up in America and Britain, torn between the irrational demands of an alcoholic mother and an overindulgent father in constant need of recognition. But Osborne refused to change his mind. Even Nolan's later marriage and motherhood could not alter his convictions, and he was to die without acknowledging daughter or grandchild.[7] This too created an uncanny parallel between work and life, in this case endowing Bill Maitland's rejection of his daughter in *Inadmissible Evidence* (1964) with prophetic significance. Osborne later told reporters that "there was something so, I don't know, insolently smug about her, and *devotedly* suburban. Oh, absolutely! [. . . .] she became determinedly lower middle class—everything I detest—and we've just got nothing in common at all." Needless to say, such a stance did not endear him to the general public—which may well be why he took it so defiantly, even adding that he had transferred his paternal affections to his godson Ben Walden.[8]

In any case, these troubles did not make him a happy man either. In 1982, he suffered from constant pains behind the eyeballs and under the jaw, cardiac murmur (from rheumatic fever in childhood), numb feet, and was diagnosed with diabetes and hematuria and urged to abstain from tobacco and alcohol.[9] He obeyed the doctor's injunctions only for short spells and in 1987 nearly died from a liver crisis. For days on end, he would sink into despair.[10] In 1989, on the eve of his 60th birthday, he fell into such a deep depression that a party for 84 guests had to be canceled the very last minute. In 1994, he suffered a diabetes-related ulceration of the foot. Amputation was considered, but the foot slowly healed. Just when it seemed he would recover, he fell ill again—a sickness that eventually ended in slow, harrowing death.

The years leading up to this final sickness were marked by public recognition of his contribution to the arts but also, and often simultaneously, by humiliations. In 1977, he attended a Playwrights' Conference in Australia but was badly treated in the Australian press.[11] In 1992, Osborne was offered a lifetime achievement award at the annual Writers' Guild of Great Britain Awards. Asked to give a short speech, he stumbled drunkenly onto the podium and mumbled: "This is a horrible profession which has never been held in such contempt—it is awful." The rest was drowned in catcalls and booing, and he had to be rescued by some friends, among whom was actor Alan Rickman. Later that week, appearing on Start of the Week, a BBC Radio 4 broadcast, Osborne apologized, denying that he had been drunk and claiming that his teeth were falling out during his speech: "I was trying to hold my teeth in and speak at the same time."[12] The event eerily reflected a scene he had described in one of his television plays, *Very Like a Whale,* written in 1971: at a New York Conference to which he is invited as the celebrated speaker, Jack Mellors, leading industrialist recently honored by the Queen for his services to the country, is unable to say what is expected of him and is publicly humiliated for it.

If Osborne was held in some contempt by the cultural elite, it was mainly because so many regarded him as a renegade. The man who had once been hailed as a voice of the future now appeared to be a traditionalist. In 1971, Osborne had become patron of the Common Market Safeguards Campaign, whose other members included socialist Michael Foot and the playwright J.B. Priestley. In 1974, he lent his support to the Get Britain OUT Campaign and signed a letter circulated by Edward Bond urging the government to maintain its cultural boycott of South Africa. In the same year, he wrote to Charles Berman from United Artists, London, offering his support in defense of Bernardo Bertolucci's *Last Tango in Paris,* which was then being prosecuted under the Obscene Publications Act. In the eighties, however, his articles proclaimed him, willy-nilly, as a spokesman for traditionalist and nationalist sentiment, and he increasingly appealed to right-wing sympathizers. In 1982, he wrote in defense of the monarchy, praising ceremony as an antidote to bland corporate life style. Trooping the Colour, he said, is a "magnificent theatrical expression of our turn for mystery, tradition and, unequalled gift above all, for nation invention." "Minorities," he claimed patronizingly, "must have their rights but their duties also, one of which is that they are here to learn, not teach democracy."[13] Another target of his displeasure was "the love that, nowadays, dares to screech its name": "Wilde, and indeed Coward, would have winced at this margarine motley masquerading as butter." It was all too easy to misread such statements as a collection of hateful remarks targeting easy victims. As always, Osborne's enemy was not the immigrant or the homosexual but the bourgeois prig whose sanctimony fueled his rage. Reviewing a program about homosexuality, for instance, he pointed out the doublethink that characterizes much of the liberal championing of trendy causes:

> Nodding cheerfully at the assumption that homosexual liaisons are more unstable than 'straight' ones, the liberal apologists ignored the gays' sneers at married conformity in spite of their own evident, limp conformity of ambition. The 16-year old wanted little more than to bend over a hot ironing board all day until his man came home from the disco.[14]

Another more obvious reason for having fallen in disfavor was his incessant unpleasantness to a great many people important in the Arts. In 1974, Osborne asserted in a letter to a friend that he never paid any attention to the critics. They were a parasitic breed, he said, annoying rather than dangerous— ignorant hacks who exerted little real influence on the art scene.[15] This was nothing but wishful thinking, however. The reality, of course, was different. Far from being indifferent to reviews, Osborne carefully collected them and was all too often incensed by the negative ones. He had declared war on the critics after the debacle of *Paul Slickey* (1959), once more after receiving mixed reviews for *A Bond Honoured* (1966), and would do so again in 1977 after the debacle of *Watch It Come Down*. It was then that the following curious announcement appeared in the *Times:*

> British Playwrights Mafia:
> Recruiting commences 17th
> October 12.00 hours for newly
> formed fighting unit. Enquiries to
> Col. Wood. C.G. C. sqn. Nth.
> Ox. L. BPM (Yeomanry) 91
> Regent Street, London W.1 of
> Lt.-Col John Osborne, c./o The
> Loyal BPM (Yeo.), Edenbridge,
> Kent.

Col. Wood in the announcement is playwright Charles Wood, Osborne's friend, a one-time professional soldier who had worked on the script for *The Charge of the Light Brigade* and whose play *Meals on Wheels* Osborne had directed in 1965. Osborne sent letters to all major British playwrights, requesting their help in amassing a body of evidence to prove critical malpractice. He then gathered their replies into a humorous, biting playlet published in the *Sunday Times,* "Turning the Tables: Kicking Against the Pricks." Osborne also sent threatening and abusive postcards to the London critics Wardle, Levin, and Nightingale.

Wood and Osborne soon remained the only two members of the British Playwrights Mafia, exchanging with one another rather puerile messages about designing a club tie (crossed pen and sword and the words "fuck 'em" underneath) and visiting an imaginary prison where obnoxious critics were languishing in chains.[16] Yet there was a serious even desperate undercurrent to this prank. Osborne was becoming invisible and feared it as much as Bill Maitland had done in *Inadmissible Evidence*. He had to draw attention to himself somehow. His fear and rage increased when in 1978, he started to receive alarming and pitiful letters from playwright David Mercer who after a period of success with plays such as *Belcher's Luck* (1966), *Flint* (1970), and *After Haggerty* (1970), had fallen into discredit and was now convinced that a conspiracy among leading London critics was keeping audiences from seeing his latest plays. When Mercer died of a heart attack during a visit to Israel in 1980, at the age of 52, Osborne was convinced the critics who had made Mercer's later life so unbearable were to be held responsible.

ADAPTATIONS

Much of Osborne's work in that period is marked by openly stated disdain for critics and even for the audience, as will be seen from the chapters on *A Sense of Detachment* (1972), *Watch It Come Down* (1976), and *Déjàvu* (1992). The figure of the lonely, abused, or humiliated artist is central also in minor work of the period, such as *You're Not Watching Me, Mummy* (1978), *God Rot Tunbridge Wells!* (1985), and even in his adaptation *A Place Calling Itself Rome* (1972), whose warrior-hero Coriolanus could be regarded as a despised vituperative artist of sorts. Other works deal with the battle of the sexes, possibly reflecting Osborne's growing unease with the prominent role of women in theatre and society: an adaptation of Strindberg's *The Father* (1989), a short stage play *The End of Me Old Cigar* (1975), and a television plays *Jill and Jack* (1974) seem to prove that point. His other works of the period are born from a more general apprehension of modernity and what he must have thought of as the gathering forces of evil: this, at least, is what appears from his adaptation of Oscar Wilde's *The Picture of Dorian Gray* (1973) and his stage play *Try a Little Tenderness* (1978).

Osborne always chose carefully the plays he wished to adapt. Their vision, in one way or another, had to coincide with his own. It comes as no surprise that he was attracted to Shakespeare's *Coriolanus,* the story of a churlish hero whose quick temper collides with the ungratefulness and fickleness of the people. Having saved Rome from invaders, Coriolanus is first lauded, and then almost at once, in an astonishing reversal, banned from Rome as traitor to its political institutions. Coriolanus returns in league with the barbarians, threatens to sack Rome and to exact vengeance. The tears and rebukes of his mother undermine his resolve, however, and for that he is punished by the barbarians with death.

How could Osborne resist identifying himself with a hero of which Menenius Agrippa, friend to Coriolanus, says, "His heart's his mouth;/ What his breast forges, that his tongue must vent, / And, being angry, does forget that ever / He heard the name of death" (III, i, ll. 256–259). Originally he had planned to set the play's action in an African republic but abandoned that idea for an adaptation more amenable to serve as podium for his well-known complaints about contemporary society. Osborne's *Coriolanus* is set in a Rome made sufficiently timeless and universal to represent the only place and time Osborne is interested in, contemporary England.

The play was never staged, perhaps partly because it embraces an unpopular point of view. The people of Rome receive no easy shrift in Shakespeare's *Coriolanus*. They are all too easily misled in their ignorance; taken individually, however, as, Shakespeare does, each is not without kindness and generosity. In contrast, Osborne has much less faith in the people and used the play to demonstrate the pitfalls of democracy. He moreover turned the more unpleasant of the two tribunes, Sicinius Velutus, into the only black character in the play—and a woman to boot.

Another reason for not staging the play is that Osborne's most celebrated talent, his energetic language, does not particularly shine in this adaptation. It is of course hard to improve upon Shakespeare's language, as is all too clear from the following comparison:

> CORIOLANUS: You common cry of curs, whose breath I hate
> As reek a' th' rotten fens, whose loves I prize
> As the dead carcasses of unburied men
> That do corrupt my air—I banish you!
> And here remain with your uncertainty!
> Let every feeble rumor shake your hearts!
> Your enemies, with nodding of their plumes,
> Fan you into despair! Have the power still
> To banish your defenders, till at length
> Your ignorance (which finds not till it feels,
> Making but reservation of yourselves,
> Still your own foes) deliver you as most
> Abated captives to some nation
> That won you without blows! Despising,
> For you, the city, thus I turn my back;
> There is a world elsewhere. (III, iii, ll. 120–135)

The same speech, shortened and larded by Osborne with the clichés of the twentieth-century, falls curiously flat:

> CORIOLANUS: You common cry of curs. You take up my air. Banish me? *I* banish *you!* Stay here in your slum. And strike. Communicate. Get shaken with rumours; fads; modishness; greed; fashion; your clannishness; your lives in depth. May you, but you won't, one minute of that depth, know desolation. May your enemies barter and exchange you coolly in their own better market-places . . . I have seen the *future* . . . here . . . and it doesn't work! *I* turn my back. There is a world *elsewhere!* (I, xv, 57–58)

Osborne's Coriolanus then stomps off, singing, "The Working Class/ Can Kiss My Arse," in parody of "The Red Flag." One can only wonder why the greatest critic of the Alternative Service Book would impose a similar adulteration upon another hallowed text that in its natural vigor all too brilliantly exceeds his own powers of vituperation.

Osborne succeeded rather better with his next adaptation, Oscar Wilde's *The Picture of Dorian Gray* (1890), which was published in 1973, first performed at the Greenwich Theatre on 13 February 1975, and televised for BBC in 1976, with John Gielgud in the role of Lord Henry Wotton, Peter Firth as Dorian Gray, and Jeremy Brett as Basil Hallward. The novel, with its endless self-indulgent descriptions, which Wilde for the most part copied out of art catalogues, begs for the editor's scissors, and Osborne wielded them most deftly, leaving in what is most important, namely the deterioration of Dorian's character. Michael Billington, for that reason, thought that "Osborne's play is actually much better than Wilde's novel."[17]

What drew Osborne to the subject in the first place? Osborne subtitles the play, "A Moral Entertainment," and in a rambling, maddeningly unclear introduction relates evil to the contemporary cult of youth. The Victorians, he claims, still saw the sinfulness of clinging to youth. For them it was blasphemous, a pact with the devil. We, however, have lost that feeling, and with it the sense of sin. Yet, once in a while, as with the Manson killings in 1969 to which he refers, we again realize the depth of evil that may hide behind youthful innocence.

Youth was not Osborne's only target; another was women. In 1988, Osborne returned to the National Theatre, twelve years after the disastrous staging of *Watch It Come Down* (1976) and two years after a public quarrel with the theatre's director Sir Peter Hall, or Dr. Fu Manchu in Osborne's lingo, over the casting of Joan Plowright in a (for that reason) aborted revival of *The Entertainer* that would have starred Alan Bates as Archie Rice. This time, he offered not his own work but that of a playwright with whom he closely identified, August Strindberg (1849–1912). "There are curious parallels in both our professional and personal lives," he told a reporter helpfully. "He became a terminally unfashionable playwright, vilified most of his life after making a very good start at quite an early age."

Not surprisingly, he chose *The Father* (1887), commonly regarded as one of the Swedish playwright's most misogynist plays. Osborne thought the play's revival came most timely. "My God, we all know we have had it as far as women are concerned. They rule our lives," Osborne said, gleefully shoveling coal on the fire of liberal indignation, before adding innocently, "I don't want the misogyny to get in the way of people seeing what a stunning play it is."[18] Some members of the press immediately obliged by being predictably dismissive or indignant. "One misogynist meets another," Janet Gorman announced, and Carl Miller deplored that the NT had joined "the feminist backlash with a reverential revival of this silly play about a man agonised by thoughts of his wife's infidelity."[19]

In his introduction, Osborne presents *The Father* as a part for a great actress and in passing mocks the feminist playwrights of the past twenty years for not having added to the list of star vehicles for actresses written by so-called misogynist men. In fact Strindberg, unlike Ibsen, did not write the kind of grand parts for women Osborne seems to have in mind. Neither Laura in *The Father* nor Julie in *Miss Julie* assumes the stature of a Hedda Gabler. To put it quite plainly, the latter may be a "bitch," but she is a most splendid one. Hedda, after all, is an artist who uses men as her material. Laura and Miss Julie never reach Hedda's dramatic heights. They are creatures driven by their desires rather than "femmes fatales." Laura may, like Hedda Gabler, strive for power, but it is a power devoid of demonic beauty. She remains mean and small throughout her battle, using every strategy fair or foul to get her way.

In his introduction, Osborne also presents Strindberg as a great humanist, but if humanism is meant to stand for the belief in the irreducible complexity of the human mind—as Osborne clearly intends it—then Strindberg's plays are not the product of a particularly broad humanistic imagination, since they reduce human complexity to a concise set of principles. From *Miss Julie,* for instance, it is all too clear that, though Strindberg takes pride in having created complex "souls," as he preferred to call his characters, his idea of complexity amounts to adding a few more variables into the character formula. Conforming to the strictest rules of fatalistic naturalism, Strindberg's characters are helpless embodiments of natural (biological) principles, formed and constrained by social circumstances. Almost mathematical abstractions, they could quite feasibly be presented by marionettes. This is not meant as a criticism. In fact, the major beauty of even the most naturalistic Strindberg play is that it invariably demands a quietly solemn, almost ritualistic performance, even during the most harrowing moments.

Working from a modern literal translation by Jonas Gustafson together with the 1907 Edgar Bjökman and N. Erichsen English version of the play, Osborne produced an adaptation that is both modern in its language and yet pleasantly formal in its rhythms. The result is that the expressionistic thrust of the work shines through its naturalism at precisely the right moments. At the height of their mutual hostility, man and wife become mouthpieces of ancient cosmic principles:

> CAPTAIN: [. . . .] And when I thought you despised my meager manhood, I wanted to force you as a woman . . . being taken by a man.
> LAURA: Yes, and that was your mistake. The mother was your friend. But the woman was your enemy. Love between the sexes is a battle. And don't imagine for a minute that I ever gave myself up to you. I gave away nothing. I just took—and only what I wanted. (II, 34)

Directed by David Leveaux, with Susan Fleetwood as Laura and Alun Armstrong as the Captain, *The Father* opened in the NT's Cottesloe Theatre on 26 October 1988. Osborne's work as an adapter was generally praised; Osborne himself was disappointed with the production, which featured some surprising expressionistic sound and light effects and was indeed less enthusiastically received than he wished.

TELEVISION PLAYS

It cannot be denied that Women's Lib made Osborne uncomfortable. In the fifties he had pronounced himself rather foolishly on issues of gender, lamenting that modern women had exchanged charmingly elusive femininity for a stridency that would look ugly even in men. In the seventies, he wrote a series of minor comedies about gender whose humor barely hides discomfort and ill will.

Jill and Jack, directed by Mike Newell, was first transmitted by Yorkshire Television on 11 September 1974, starring Jill Bennett as Jill. It is quite simply a theatrical romp, exposing male and female behavior through the well-worn device of role-reversal. It takes a few moments before we realize that Jill, the hard working, wealthy woman in show business, displays stereotypical male attitudes while her friend Jack, an aspiring actor, is, in the way women supposedly are, concerned only with his appearance. Once acquainted with the mechanism behind this joke, the spectator will be hard pressed not to regard it as a front for Osborne's customary misogynist views of grasping, narcissistic women imposing themselves on their patient, ill-used men.

Offering four important roles for women, *The End of Me Old Cigar* is yet another and perhaps more forceful stab at the same subject, the battle of the sexes. It is a passably funny comedy of manners, a sort of *Lysistrata* in reverse in which women, instead of withholding sex from powerful men, offer them their sexual services in order to discredit them afterwards.[20] A caricature of feminist hysteria, Lady Regine Frimley intends to lead a revolution for womanhood. For that purpose, she has converted her country house into a brothel and has recruited women friends as high-class prostitutes. Intent on toppling the male by exposing his pitiful sexual antics, she has equipped her rooms with two-way mirrors and cameras. "We're the girls' Jesuits," Regine cries passionately. "Give us a girl for the rest of her grooming, her indoctrination, and I'll make her first a whore and then her whole self, her *self* for life. The prick is just where it is. The cunt is where the heart lies" (I, 22). Yet in the midst of such crudities (a parody, in fact, of radical feminist writing), Isobel Sands, a lonely housewife locked in a loveless marriage, and Leonard Grimthorpe, a disarmingly incompetent and quasi-impotent man, fall in love. What brings them together is not only a passion for old music hall songs but a willingness to expose their insecurities and uncertainties to one another.

As its title (a well-known bawdy music hall number) indicates, the play is about the phallus, which at more than one moment, is subjected to Regine's mocking tirades. But while vulnerable and scorned, the phallus nevertheless reigns supreme since Lady Regine in the end finds herself betrayed by one of her male employees and thwarted in her designs. Before then, however, Len and Isobel have confronted the wonder of gender difference:

> LEN: [. . . .] You can never be a man, you know.
> ISOBEL: *You* can never be a woman. Isn't it sublime?

Len then explains what that difference consists of:

> You—women—*are* the secret of life. *We* are uncertain, undefined, perhaps unnecessary, as you say. . . . We have to be more: flamboyant, spurious, enduring, tender, frightened, oversensitive and protected, more reckless, indiscreet. You've been taught that you're a woman of sorts. I that I'm a man. [. . . .] Girls learn to *be,* boys to *act.* You are a woman. You are a girl child. You were a virgin. You became a mother. You *are.* Yet, like me, us, you are still full of divine discontent. (II, 44)

Only a moment of intimacy can produce such foolishness. Between Isobel and Len, the phallus blossoms most tenderly, serenaded by Len in a poem of Lawrentian sentiment: "What I have," says Len, "this thing so despised or ignored—is yours. It sounds strange. We may never? Or never meet again. But it *would* be yours, not just *my* object. Yours too. *Ours . . .*" (II, 44). They consequently reach a happiness unknown to those whose true impotence lies in their inability to turn the phallus into a gift of love.

Directed by Max Stafford Clark, *The End of Me Old Cigar* premièred at the Greenwich Theatre on 16 January 1975, starring Rachel Roberts as Regine and Jill Bennett as Isobel. Osborne later reworked the love scenes between Isobel and Leonard into a television play *Almost a Vision* (Yorkshire and Trident television 1976). Osborne called it "a modern comedy of modern manners," a play he had written to while away the time when he could not continue work on a more important but unnamed project, probably *Watch It Come Down.* His attitude toward *The End of Me Old Cigar* betrays a degree of commendable uneasiness—though also a rather sad defensiveness:

> Anyway, it makes me laugh, although from past experience what makes me laugh very often makes audiences sit fuming or so often walk out. I have always found it astonishing how personally people react among audiences. If somebody doesn't walk out, I always think I must be losing my touch.[21]

This is the self-assessment of a writer convinced that after a body of important work he has earned the right to levity of this sort.

Irving Wardle may not have walked out on the play since he had to review it for the *Times,* but he was clearly one of those who sat fuming throughout the play's many absurdities of exposition, character, and plot. Robert Cushman in the *Observer* deplored what he called "the frigid raillery—spinsterish even when scabrous—which dominates this author's worst plays, and disfigures even his best."[22] All in all, the play was not well received.

His next work for television, *You're Not Watching Me, Mummy* (Yorkshire Television, 30 July 1979), depicting the loneliness of a successful actress, did not fare much better with the critics. After her show, Jemina, who longs desperately for her ovaltine and bed, is surrounded by the usual parasites of the art world. This, of course, is Osborne's excuse for presenting some of his well-worn and only mildly humorous caricatures: a homosexual dresser jealously fussing around his actress; a ridiculously vain theatre critic whose withered arm symbolizes his impotence; a frigid, Marxist lesbian playwright in love with her own work; an obnoxious, gum-chewing American drama student in black leather jacket, and so on. Outside the dressing room, London is prostituting its past glories to Japanese tourists who, in Osborne's book, are always as "uncomprehending" as lesbians are "frigid," critics "impotent," and Americans "dumb." Reviews were not unjustifiably damning, the more so since the production was of a lamentable quality.

Its companion piece in the same 1978 Faber and Faber publication, *Try a Little Tenderness*, was never broadcast. Ted Shilling is a middle-aged writer of working-class background who has retired to the countryside. There he soon finds himself beleaguered by his son's young friends, who are taking over the house, and scorned by his wife's upper-class family. Ted, is, in his own words, not a patient man, simply someone who knows to abide his time (55). That time comes when an army of beatniks led by Larry Best, a modern show biz mogul, invades the town. Ted's revenge is swift and encompassing. Exploiting the hate of the old establishment, represented by Lady Arkley, and rich burghers, such as Mrs. Stringer, who resent having their peace disturbed, he organizes an all out attack on the pop festival, involving marauding peasants, tractors, cows, sheep, hunters on horse back, hounds, and even gliders from the local aeronautical sports club. In the meantime, he has planted drugs in his own house and invited the police to crack down on the youthful squatters there. What starts as a comedy soon turns into a full-scale war, an ugly battle in which both sides are hurt. Amid all the violence, Ted, accompanied by Slim, his son's lover, remains a peaceful onlooker, enjoying his bloody creation. Is he satisfied? "No, but I never expected to be" (93).

God Rot Tunbridge Wells! (1985) together with *England, My England!* (produced posthumously) are products of Osborne's passion for music. The first deals with the German-born English composer George Frederick Handel (1685–1759), the second with Henry Purcell (1658–1695), two composers known for writing splendid music of state and whose fame is consequently thoroughly enmeshed with the glory of old England. Both television plays were directed by Tony Palmer, known for operas and bio-documentaries, who was also to direct Osborne's last stage play, *Déjàvu* (1992).

Old man Handel, disgusted with life, with an ungrateful audience, and lamentable performances of his work, crawls into bed, willing or at least longing to die, and takes his leave of the world with a last curse: "May God rot Tunbridge Wells"—the place where his Messiah is being massacred in performance (66). What this scene develops into is not docu-drama, however—no attempt to capture what the historic Handel might have been like, but, once more, a portrait of the loneliness of the artist—and that artist, in the final instance, is always Osborne himself. "As for my worth," we hear Osborne saying through his hero Handel, "I have always been cognizant of it, in the teeth of mercenaries and carpers." He readily admits, he has also "been blessed by great magnanimity of others. I must not complain too idly" (66).

Televised magnificently by Tony Palmer, *God Rot Tunbridge Wells!* is a feast of beautiful images, beautiful music above all, adorned with generous captions by Osborne's hand and heart. At times, it is all too clearly a sort of raucous coffee table book, a work of art more for director and prop master than for playwright. Where the language swells and dominates, it turns into an Osbornian testament rather than the brief and chronicle of an interesting composer's life: "They said I was imperious and quick to anger. It's true I did not easily brook opposition but I was fair and would always admit my error— when, but when it was demonstrated to me. Even in chiding and finding fault I tried to amuse rather than hurt" (71). When Handel thinks back on the singers whose careers he served with the fruits of his imagination, it is Osborne we hear speak of the many star actors whose lives he has enriched: "Writing their parts has too often been like serving a puffed-up actor, bedding a plain woman out of kindliness rather than lust or lending money to the ingrate of heart" (70). When Handel says, "I work swiftly and have always. *Messiah* in twenty-one days," we cannot help but be reminded of Osborne's boast he finished *Look Back in Anger* in three weeks. If you have delivered good work, Osborne says through Handel, it will only inspire envy in those arid souls, the critics, who will "rush off searching for something to displease them" (73).

In *England, My England*, his very last and posthumously televised play, Osborne used a similar method, emphasizing the splendor and energy of Purcell's Restoration England in order to contrast it with the dreary present:

> What Charles wanted, and what Purcell wrote about so gloriously, was a country of tolerance, irony, kindliness. Not like today, where the modesty of heroes is despatched with derision; despatched by malignant opinion-formers who bamboozle the tabloid conscience of a sullen democracy, and have thus thrown up a generation for whom 'Honour' is a meaningless currency. May God rot the tyrannies of equality, streamlining, classlessness and, most of all, absurd, irrelevant 'correctness.'[23]

AUTOBIOGRAPHIES

Osborne's television play on the subject of Henry Purcell was the last work he completed before his death on Christmas Eve 1994. On his table were several unfinished projects, one of them the third volume of his autobiography.

The first volume, *A Better Class of Person*, published in 1981, was greeted with general acclaim and established him in many reviewers' minds as "the best stylist of our age."[24] Osborne deftly played on its success, turning it into a teledrama that was broadcast under the same title by Thames Television in June 1985, featuring Eileen Atkins as his mother Nellie Beatrice. The *TLS* called the autobiographies a "suburban rake's progress."[25] Written at a time of increasing exclusion from the current theatrical scene, they represent Osborne's attempt at forging a public image that would create interest in and shape the desired receptivity for his theatrical work. The voice that speaks from these volumes is honest to a fault—the kind of blistering honesty we find in Jean Jacques Rousseau's *Confessions* (1781) where it equally serves as the perfect excuse for inexcusable behavior.

The first volume deals with the years of childhood and adolescence, leading up to his first success with *Look Back in Anger*; the second part, *Almost a Gentleman*, published in 1991, continues his career, tracing the years of success with *The Entertainer, Luther, Inadmissible Evidence,* and *A Patriot for Me*, and ends in 1966, announcing years of bleak depression following on the death of George Devine. As he nears these painful years, the dash and energy that made *A Better Class of Person* such a joy to read abandon him. Language itself falls apart as he resorts almost exclusively to fragmentary quotations from notebooks, painting a bleak picture of a life lived in fear of isolation, sickness and death.

It was Cardinal Newman who said "it is almost a definition of a gentleman to say he is one who never inflicts pain." The important word is almost, and Osborne is almost a gentleman, as it appeared when he rushed to include a chapter vilifying the memory of his fourth wife Jill Bennett, upon hearing of her suicide in 1990, that is shortly before publication of the volume was due.[26] When the book was published, these gratuitously cruel gestures, together with casual insults addressed at former friends and spouses, were widely deplored. They did help to sell the book, but they reflected sadly on a career that since *A Sense of Detachment* had begun its slow descent.

CHAPTER 10

A Sense of Detachment (1972)
The Limits of Authenticity

RECEPTION

Six actors come onto the stage, cast a dismissive look at the audience, and then peevishly wonder what the play will be about and when they are going to get paid. They sit down to study the program only to find it lacking in every respect: too much about the author and director, too many trivial details about the actors. After lots of bickering and interventions from the audience (all duly scripted and performed by two actors planted in box and stalls), one of the actors, referred to as "chairman," proposes some plan of action and roughly assigns some roles. The topic is love in all its manifestations, its poverty and richness. A "chap" enumerates all the girls and women with whom he fell in love, madly, often pathetically. A "father" plays the piano and sings songs from the good old days. A "grandfather" stands up and sings hymns. An "older lady" reads out loud from a catalogue of pornographic stories. The others, each in turn, step forward and recite love poetry, old and new. A "girl" is bitchy, deflating, and sarcastic only in the end to join the chap in a paean to love, to feelings undervalued in modern times. Sheridan Morley sums it up well: *A Sense of Detachment* is "a mixture . . . of poetry, piety and porn over which Osborne bellows his final message to the 1970s 'God rot you'."[1]

To the few who had good things to say about the play, among them the usual staunch Osborne supporters Michael Billington and Harold Hobson, *A Sense of Detachment* was a breakthrough in Osborne's technique.[2] Osborne had finally ventured into the more turbulent waters of radical experiment—though as one reviewer tartly remarked, a little late and a little irrelevantly, that is "after 15 years of John Cage and Samuel Beckett."[3] The *Sunday Times* stood virtually alone in its unconditional support of the play: "If you want to know a play that can now be seen in London of which one day the English theatre and English literature will be proud, this is it."[4] Most critics were appalled at being offered what they saw as an exercise in self-indulgence. "Don't waste your time," concludes the review in the *Spectator* laconically.[5] Benedict Nightingale sums up why:

> If you imagine some demented somnambulist blundering about the house and pouring out his doubts and irritations to the wallpaper, or an endless encounter group involving tired, disgruntled holiday-makers who have been booked into a non-existent hotel, or the Ancient Mariner hazily free-associating for a couple of hours on his psychoanalyst's couch, you may get some inkling of what *A Sense of Detachment* is like. It shows the triumph of vague feeling over hard thought, impression over fact, notions over ideas, paranoia over anger, prejudice over conviction, and perhaps clutter over art. It is bad, and also sad . . .[6]

So bad it was, apparently, that the *Financial Times* called it Osborne's "farewell to the theatre."[7] With the musical *The World of Paul Slickey* (1959), *A Sense of Detachment* (1972) shares the dubious distinction of being one of Osborne's most reviled plays. Close runner up in that curious list of finalists would be *Watch It Come Down* (1975), while fourth place would go to *Déjàvu* (1992). Yet *A Sense of Detachment* occupies a special place in Osborne's oeuvre, and the playwright even confesses to having "some affection" for it. [8] The first volume of his autobiography, which traces the years leading up to his great success with *Look Back in Anger,* ends with a look forward in fondness to *A Sense of Detachment,* the play that ironically heralds the downturn in his career. As I will argue here, *A Sense of Detachment* is the Osborne play *par excellence*; more than any others, it forces us to confront critical problems peculiar to Osborne's work and its destructive and tragic conception of theatre.

THE RUSE OF ANTI-THEATRE

As a drama that refuses to be dramatic in the accepted meaning of the term, *A Sense of Detachment* immediately inscribes itself into a tradition of anti-theatre, of plays that take as their subject the theatre itself while refusing to obey well-accepted theatrical conventions. One cannot possibly read it without thinking of two better known continental plays to which it consciously (and self-consciously) refers, Luigi Pirandello's *Sei personaggi in cerca d'autore* (*Six Characters in Search of an Author*; 1922) and Peter Handke's *Publikumsbeschimpfung* (*Offending the Audience*; 1966). Osborne, of course, rarely acknowledges sources, especially if they are not Anglo-American ones. Neither *The Entertainer* nor *Luther,* he claimed, was influenced by Brecht, as many critics contended. Both could not be more genuinely English, the one going back to the music hall, the other adopting the episodic structure of Shakespearean plays. *A Sense of Detachment* cleverly anticipates the critique that it has all been done before and better on the continent. One character remarks of a scene that it is a "bit of your old Pirandello, like" (I, 14). Handke is never mentioned by name. He is absent from Osborne's interviews and auto-biographies as well. One can imagine that Osborne disapproves of him, finding him arcane and humorless—in other words, too thoroughly Teutonic. Yet two characters in *A Sense of Detachment* refer to the "theatre of antagonism" and the "device of insult," terms commonly associated with Handke (I, 13). Undeterred by this parody of critical reductionism, several reviewers pointed out the presence of Handke's *Offending the Audience* in Osborne's play.[9] Since *Six Characters* and *Offending the Audience* cast such a considerable shadow over *A Sense of Detachment,* we have to map out major similarities and differences before determining whether Osborne's play occupies its own place under the sun.

As the title indicates, the six characters in Pirandello's play interrupt a rehearsal with the request that the director stage their drama, a play so full of pathos that the author has refused to put it to paper. Intrigued by their story and bored with the Pirandello play on which he is currently working, the director agrees. The scenes that the "characters" enact in front of the director and the actors lead to disputations about the nature of theatre and the superiority of illusion over reality. The director is a technician rather than an artist and scoffs at such ideas. Yet in the end illusion powerfully asserts itself. In front of the surprised eyes of the director and actors, a gripping tragedy unfolds whose enactment is the sole *raison d'être* of these characters.

In this and in a number of other plays about theatrical illusion, Pirandello is like a prestidigitator who shows us his bare hands and turns his jacket inside out. Nothing up the sleeves, he says, and then to everyone's amazement conjures a rabbit from his hat. After having been tricked into believing that it was looking behind the scenes, that it was introduced to the mechanics of theatre itself, no holds barred, the audience is taken unawares by the "real" drowning of the little girl and the "real" suicide of her young brother. Told straight, the same story would have struck us merely with the banality of its passions. Pirandello's deceitful honesty, however, has made us unmindful of conventions, and we succumb once more to the tragedy. There is more to it, as we will see, but on this level the play is about a story whose impact was preserved because the author refused to tell it out straight.

Handke's *Offending the Audience* takes Pirandello's experiment with a theatre that acknowledges and exposes its own theatricality one step further. There is apparently no sleight of hand, no magic in this and a number of similar *Sprechstücke* ("speaking plays") Handke wrote about the same time; the actors have no tricks up their sleeves since they present themselves in all their nakedness, not as characters but as mere speakers. "We could do a play within the play for you," they tell the audience, in a clear reference to Pirandello. "By representing what is happening, we could make you imagine these happenings. . . . We could become full of pathos" (26–27).[10] Instead, they do everything in their power to alienate the audience from everything it finds natural— going to the theatre, for instance, listening to stories, watching actions being represented on the stage and taking them for real. The speakers refuse to be characters and insist that they are not playing, that there is no magic circle in which actual time is suspended and the illusion comes into being. *Offending the Audience* takes the form of a negative, of a refusal: "Here you don't receive your due. Your curiosity is not satisfied. No spark will leap across from us to you. You will not be electrified" (9).

What is the purpose of such a non-drama? Since no action is represented on stage, the audience cannot project its emotions onto characters and empathize with them. This effectively disrupts the keyhole convention of bour-geois theatre where, as Brecht and Artaud contend, the spectator-voyeur hud-dles in darkness and watches the actors-exhibitionists at work. The speakers instead force the audience to watch the drama of its own emotions. In other words, the real subject of the play is the audience—its frustrated expectations, its anger or disappointment: "You are an event. You are *the* event. . . . You inflame us. Our words catch fire on you. From you a spark leaps across to us" (12). On a most immediate level, then, Handke's drama is that of a theatre reversed, with the audience becoming the actors ("*the* event") and the actors the audience (the ones who will become "inflamed").

The situation is of course more complex since the speakers can be said to "write" their audience, controlling them with language that allegedly creates no fiction but hypnotizes, enrages, or lulls to sleep. A relentless stream of words tells spectators who they are, what they do, how they will behave. In another *Sprechstück, Kaspar* (1967), Handke refers to a similar use of words as "speech torture." The eponymous hero of that play is a masked character, constructed and then deconstructed by prompters who subject it to a veritable torrent of words and disruptive sounds. In *Offending the Audience,* the spectators have become the Kaspars who are being tortured with words: "We will offend you because offending you is also one way of speaking to you. . . . The distance between us will no longer be infinite. Due to the fact that we're offending you, your motionlessness and your rigidity will finally become overt" (29). The spectators are "butchers," "buggers," "bullshitters"—and the list goes on for several pages (31). When the stream of insults runs dry, the speakers face their audience in silence while "roaring applause and wild whistling is piped in through the loudspeakers" (32). By having both audience and actors applauded under these circumstances, Handke does more than reversing conventions. The silent, impassive mutual confrontation of speaker and audience on a back-ground of taped applause not only mocks convention; it makes the audience uncomfortably aware of the chill, inhuman reality beyond the symbolic.

Sprechstücke, says Handke, "do not want to revolutionize, but to make aware" ("Note on *Offending the Audience* and *Self-Accusation*"). What they make us most aware of is our entrapment in language. Usually the whole machinery of theatre conspires to keep us from that awareness. It allows us to think of words the way we commonly do, as magic mirrors: though words reflect our reality, we nevertheless believe that we can step through them into the timeless realm of ideas. This belief that we can step out of the here and now and enter into the timelessness of illusion—a belief that is central to the art of theatre itself—requires the separation of words from ideas, the former being the material conveyors of the latter. Handke, following Wittgenstein, claims that words are not the vessels of the real but its building blocks. Instead of carrying meaning, language makes meaning. We cannot transcend reality by moving into the realm of ideas—indeed, the very belief that we can do so is the product of language.

But it cannot be said that Handke breaks out of the theatrical mold altogether. By presenting our linguistic entrapment in a setting that is meant to deny it, he deftly exploits a number of paradoxes. The most important one, perhaps, is the denial of the representational quality of language:

> We cannot represent the gasping for breath that is happening now and now, or the tumbling and falling now, or the death throes, or the grinding of teeth now, or the last words, or the last sigh now, that is statistically happening now this very second, or the last exhalation, or the last ejaculation that is happening now, or the breathlessness that is statistically commencing now, and now, and now, and now, and so on, or the motionless now, or the statistically ascertainable rigor mortis, or the lying absolutely quiet now. We cannot represent it. We only speak of it. We are speaking of it *now.* (26–27)

The effect of these words is at once tantalizingly logical and illogical—not unlike that of René Magritte's "Ceci n'est pas une pipe." Actuality escapes representation, yet it is precisely this very acknowledgment of the limits of representation that summons up the ungraspable terror of dying. The latter, we suddenly understand, is not the cessation of time; it is the irrevocable falling into time, the headlong tumble from the symbolic into the actual. "We cannot represent it. ... We are speaking of it *now,*" the speakers say, associating the act of speaking with the act of dying. Their refusal to transcend reality into representation is the most effective way of bringing home to us the reduction to nowness that comes with death.

Handke, in other words, relies on paradox to be the best way to unsettle his audience. The illusion of non-illusion is the first paradox, one that exploits the audience's set expectations upon entering the theatre. The drama they will witness represents the impossibility of representation. It starts with a non-start and works itself steadily, though with little sense of development, toward a non-concluding conclusion. Other paradoxes follow. Language expresses nothing, the play tells us. The "litanies in the Catholic churches" or the voices of "simultaneous interpreters at the United Nations" produce a sound not intrinsically different from "the gradually increasing noise a concrete mixer makes

after the motor has been started" ("Rules for the Actors" 3). Having thus
defined language as a sound without beyond, Handke puts it to good theatrical use by making it evoke what such a language can best evoke, namely that
moment when the symbolic folds back into the real, the moment of death. He
then proceeds to use that language to insult the audience. "We will contradict
ourselves with our offenses," the speakers tell the audience:

> We will only create an acoustic pattern. You won't have to feel offended. You
> were warned in advance, so you can feel quite unoffended while we're
> offending you. Since you are probably thoroughly offended already, we will
> waste no more time before thoroughly offending you, you chuckleheads. (29)

In brief, actors who act that they do not act offend the audience with insults
that are meaningless only if the audience is willing to accept the actors' definition of language. Unable to reach conclusive meaning in a context that traditionally presupposes it, the audience is left to watch the drama of its own
discomfort.

So despite appearances to the contrary, Handke's is a profoundly theatrical art because it preserves what is most central to it, namely conflict, which
it achieves by means of paradox, which in turn heavily relies on established
conventions and set expectations. Theatre is the best place to stage such a conflict since drama presupposes the very conventions that are challenged in
Handke's play. Handke cleverly uses the theatrical apparatus to draw attention
to the material production of meaning. Ultimately the problem Handke poses
is a philosophic one that can find no resolution either on or off stage, and he
poses it most eloquently by skirting it: if language does not indeed provide a
gateway to a non-material, conceptual realm, as we tend to assume, why do
we continue to tell stories? Why is it that plays that refuse to tell stories can
only survive parasitically on the narrative conventions they reject? Why is it
that positing the intrinsic meaninglessness of language requires the presupposition of meaning because it is the latter that sends us on our hopeless quest to
resolve paradoxes? Now looking back at Pirandello's play, we can see that it
ponders a similar question. At its center is not really the pathetic conflict of the
story that the characters seek to tell but the conflict between the untold and the
told. It is this tendency to locate the conflict not in the story itself but in the
impulse toward storytelling that Handke and Pirandello have in common. It
also happens to be, at least in Pirandello's eyes, the mark of the true artist.

In his 1925 preface to *Six Characters,* Pirandello distinguishes between
those writers whose sole purpose is to imitate the elements of life and those
who aim at capturing ways of being.[11] The first, the historical writer, he says,
delights in telling stories and describing events, people, or things. The second,
the philosophical writer, shares that pleasure too, but uses the descriptions to
create a particular sense of life. That kind of writer considers form the neces-

sary yet always necessarily deficient expression of something that precedes and exceeds it. Conjuring up that mysterious "something" is the real object of the philosophical writer's creative work. Arthur Schopenhauer called it *Will;* Henri Bergson, *élan vital*; Freud, in a related sense, the libido.[12] So whatever the philosophical writer represents will be a mask for something else. This is an important insight.[13] It suggests that for the philosophical writer, the point of representation can never be found in *what* is being represented; the purpose of representation rather is to demonstrate its own necessary failure. A work of art should make us experience *loss,* should make us sense the pressing force of the unexpressed; it should make us realize that appearance and essence (what Kant called *das Ding an sich* (the thing in itself)) never coincide. What creates the *sense of life* in art is neither the mask (the appearance) nor the essence (which can never be truly expressed) but rather that *tragic* movement of difference whereby the one unceasingly, but always fruitlessly, seeks the other. This is what constitutes the aesthetic experience, which, according to Arthur Schopenhauer, is the closest we will ever come to the world of Will.

There can be no doubt as to what kind of writer Pirandello finds superior. The philosophical writer, he says, writes to fulfill a "spiritual need" (364–65). The real topic of *Six Characters* is not *what* the characters represent but rather what forces them to seek such desperate fulfillment through representation. As Pirandello puts it, *Six Characters* is about the "inherent conflict between life (which is always moving and changing) and form (which fixes it, immutable)" (367). *Six Characters* is a comedy suffused with tragic sense not because of the dark story it finally tells but because it shows how characters, who are masked so as to show the emptiness of form, are propelled by a blind life force to endlessly reenact the terrible deeds that are the sole excuse for their existence.

THEATRE EXORCISM

The philosophical writer's work presents itself either as synthesis (Pirandello) or as antithesis (Handke) of past conventions and derives meaning as much from what it fails as from what it succeeds in representing. What is then that philosophy such a writer subscribes to? Since it is the pressure of the as yet unexpressed that thrusts the writer into creating and the inevitable failure to do justice to what seeks expression that guarantees the continuation of that impulse, one could call it a tragic Hegelianism. The quasi-religious importance such a vision ascribes to the writer as mediator between language and its beyond explains why Pirandello can indeed speak of writing as fulfilling a spiritual need. Handke may seem very different, but he holds on to two central features of a romanticism which he, like Pirandello, otherwise rejects, namely the privileged position of the artist and the inviolability of text.

Osborne clearly belongs to the same tradition, especially in the way he fiercely clings to the prerogatives of the playwright-*auteur* whose art is the repository of a most pressing vision. Of almost transcendental importance, that vision does not necessarily require the approval of actors, audience, or critics. In fact, a measure of incomprehension is best proof of the transgressive and transcending nature of the work of art. *A Sense of Detachment* reflects that attitude. It is a strange, moody anti-play play, born from an obsession with the speed with which the once authentic turns into stale aesthetic convention. In its pursuit of authenticity, of what Pirandello called "a sense of life," it presents itself as the ultimate laughing synthesis of every possible convention, including the conventions Pirandello and Handke's anti-theatre have called to life. Echoes of *Six Characters* and *Offending the Audience* can indeed be heard in Osborne's play, but they reverberate with the ironic sound of parody.

Pirandello and Handke are present in the play, not as inspiration or as models to be emulated, but as reference. As such they do not occupy a special position but are rather presented as part of the whole contemporary theatre industry which Osborne treats in a spirit of mild parody. There are gently mocking references to Arnold Wesker, David Storey, Edward Albee, Charles Wood, "Charlie" Farnsbarns, Christopher Hampton, "Sammy" Beckett, and Edna O'Brien. At the time of writing, many of these had managed to stake out their own territory in the world of theatre or literature and had acquired a degree of name recognition. Harold Pinter is singled out for a special, teasing reference. In the early seventies he was fast becoming a name brand for definite stylistic conventions (the famous Pinter pause, the Pinteresque atmosphere, the "menace"). Osborne knew what it felt like to be daily stretched on the rack of his own conventions. To be successful you had to become a name; but once you became a name you were expected to remain faithful to that name—to that of angry young man or absurdist, for instance.

Is the play then all mockery and disdain? What does it try to achieve? As is usual with Osborne, it is far easier to say what the play does *not* do. Like Pirandello, Osborne presents us with six characters in search of a story, but whereas genuine urgency pressures Pirandello's characters into their quest, Osborne's do not even bother to hide the fact that even this search has been scripted for them ("*You* try learning the bloody stuff. I've forgotten half of it already," says the "girl" acridly (I, 14)). Apparently then, authenticity is not to be found in the search for form. Is it perhaps the genuineness of vituperative excess for which the play strives? Like Handke, Osborne wants his audience to know they are not held in high esteem. He has his actors refer to them as "*that* lot" (I, 16). He has even armed them with a small collection of mud-slinging rejoinders in case the audience thinks of reacting back in kind: "Go and fuck yourself if you can get it up, which I doubt from the look of you," "If you're Irish, get out of the parlour"; "Get back off to the shires, you married pouve" (I, 15). These insults are neither subtle nor particularly witty and are flung at the audience without much power of conviction, in a sort of offhand way. The acknowledged master of vituperation clearly has not put his heart in

them. Neither do they confront the audience with any kind of Handkian paradox, which would be another way of creating a genuine moment of bewilderment. The edge has been taken off them; they have a quoted quality; they too
have become parodic.

Of course Osborne does not rely on any of the usual narrative conventions
to create moments of intensity. In fact, like Handke, he gleefully thumbs his
nose at them. Referring to the audience's need for a story, the chairman says,
"We'll stick in some safe bit for the audiences, so that they can delude themselves that there is some intention and continuity" (I, 24). A planted interrupter
sums up what many audience members indeed expect from a dramatic story:
"I like something entertaining, but that leaves you with something to think
about afterwards" (II, 29). Unlike the "speakers" in Handke's play, the actors-
characters in *A Sense of Detachment* are as much at a loss as their audience.
They do not find the idea of committing themselves to a play without the safety
net of conventions appealing. Like Pirandello's director, they are trained to see
theatre in terms of technique and try to find out what is expected from them by
defining everything that happens in terms of "devices." They do not necessarily associate concepts with names, as I will do here, but it is obvious that to
them an empty stage cannot be just an empty stage; it has to be Peter Brook's
conception of the empty stage. A projection screen ("Oh, not one of *those*," the
chap mutters (I, 11)) may indicate that the play will adopt some of the techniques associated with Erwin Piscator. When there is no straight story to tell
but just a group of actors trying to figure out the author's intention, the play
may be Pirandellian. When someone uses strong language the play must be of
the kind that uses such language ("oh . . . is it going to be that sort of language?"
(I, 12)). An actor who talks disparagingly about the audience must be using the
device of "offending the audience"—which, of course, makes us think of
Handke. When someone in the audience addresses the actors it must be an
instance of audience participation ("Oh, I think he's *participating,* or something" (I, 12)). *A Sense of Detachment,* of course, uses all of these devices and
often quite deftly and with good effect. It does present an empty stage; it does
use slide projection; it does have six characters in search of a play; it does use
obscenity and audience participation. Unlike Pirandello and Handke, however,
it does not ascribe to these newer techniques superiority over the older ones.
On the contrary, it defines them as yet more tiresome theatrical clichés. As one
interrupter puts it, "Joan Littlewood did this years ago" (I, 28). Osborne suggests what I believe Pirandello and Handke in their own way also knew, namely
that the essence of the theatrical experience must be located elsewhere.

The entire whole first act is meant to exorcise "obvious over-familiar theatrical device[s]," ghosts of previous plays and previous productions that prevent us from experiencing drama anew. Theatre, Osborne suggests, will not be
saved by this restless search for innovative techniques. Spectators who have
stayed on for the second act should be willing to leave their preconceptions

behind and travel with Osborne to what he thinks of as the beating heart of theatre. Theatre, he tells us, cannot be saved by better stories, better techniques, or subtler psychology. All these are useful tricks, yet fundamentally irrelevant; most of the time they are mere adornments that hide what theatre is really about. True, they do play a function. They are pegs on which to drape our emotions which in all actuality were stirred by something far more difficult to describe. Osborne suggests that if you want to know what theatre is really about, you have to remember those moments you were moved for no obvious reason at all. In fact, everything seemed to conspire to make that moment of emotional surrender impossible. The story was gushingly sentimental, the actors were mediocre, the audience was bored, and yet you sat in your chair and wept—or perhaps you laughed until the tears stood in your eyes. Nothing prepared you for this experience and afterward you cannot explain it to yourself. Perhaps the misery you had so carefully kept in check all these years suddenly got the better of you while you watched a play being lost on actors and audience alike. Perhaps you responded not to the indeed embarrassingly sentimental speech but to its underlying impulse. Beneath all that banality you may have detected a note of genuine yearning for communion—a yearning that sprouted from a loneliness that you know to be also yours. Perhaps you sensed the despair in that brazen actor who hurls his lines like daggers at a despising or indifferent audience. You will carry this experience with you forever; and yet you cannot discuss the play with your friends. The play is an embarrassment because it fails to provide you with a valid excuse for emotional involvement. *A Sense of Detachment* is meant to be that kind of play—a search, so to speak, for the roots of theatre.

THE ROOTS OF THEATRE

Those roots, however, are invisible; only the narrated, represented parts of theatre—character, plot, theme, and structure—are open to examination. Osborne has chosen no "speakers," as Handke did, but instead actors who play at being actors. As in Pirandello's play, these rather unusual *dramatis personae* bear generic names, "chap," "girl," "older lady," "grandfather," and "father." The sixth character, the "chairman," is the one most ostensibly concerned with the actors' responsibility toward the audience. The word chairman, though, conveys none of the artistic intentions we usually ascribe to a director. This chairman has no vision of the play and does not want to make anything; he just tries to impose some sense of order and in the end admits that he has failed. The difficulties he is faced with are indeed evident. Why do we need a girl, an older lady, a father, a chap, and an older man when in the absence of a conflict, or even of a Pirandellian untold narrative, nothing determines the choice of these types? The play is nevertheless replete with details about these characters' lives, which, in the absence of a story, are all equally redundant. We are therefore left to suppose that choice of characters and biographical details derives meaning from an untold autobiographical and historical context. The father who was born with the century and died in 1940 is very much like Osborne's own father, for instance. The hymn singing grandfather can also be traced back to Osborne's autobiographies. We can go to the same source for the chap's experiences with love, which are all too reminiscent of Osborne's. That the chap's mother is absent is understandable to all who know Osborne's dislike of his mother, Nellie Beatrice. The presence of the older lady and the girl is more difficult to explain. We learn that the girl is Scots, like Osborne's second wife Mary Ure, though it is unclear why she has to be, except in order to represent the kind of robust common sense Osborne ascribed to Ure. In the absence of a story, none of these details is necessary. Extrinsic rather than intrinsic reasons therefore determine their relative value.

It is of course not by chance that the characters represent both sexes in a cross section of ages, with three generations of men and two of women. In this way Osborne contrasts older and newer conceptions of life, though not always in the way we anticipate. The older people appear to be more enthusiastic about the future than the younger ones. If there is a theme or rather a central preoccupation behind the rambling events presented to us, it is life in what Labour Prime Minister Harold Wilson (1964–1970) with bright-eyed optimism used to call "the twentieth century." It is a term that fills Osborne with dread rather than anticipation. If the play has to be about someone, it certainly could be said to be about the chap; his memories of childhood, his first loves, and his affection for his piano playing father assume central importance in the play. To preempt what Osborne expects will be the general critical verdict, the latter is identified as "another exercise in nostalgia." As he died in 1940, he was spared the kind of modernity which Wilson had in mind when he referred to the twentieth century. None of the characters is truly at home in that kind of modernity. The two old people of course do not want to be left behind and so show their eagerness to march ahead. The older lady is most enthusiastic about the new ways, especially about the liberalization of sexuality. But as she reads through pornographic accounts of a dispiriting number of sexual variations, each equally appalling in their dreary silliness, we see her growing weary and rather disappointed. She never quite loses faith in militant progress though and in the end mounts the pulpit in defense of the reality of women's lives.

The fact that the play, despite its apparent randomness, is divided in two acts invites us to look for a sense of progression that might determine structure; but the structural principle is marked not so much by a sense of progression as of exhaustion. One after another, devices and styles are tried out and then kept on until they are drained of any pretense to meaning. Act I serves to exorcise conventions that people apply to a play in order to comprehend and be done with it. Act II exhausts forms of entertainment through song and dance of every style and genre, then it exhausts all critical clichés that will be used in discussing what, for most critics, was indeed an embarrassing production. Finally the chap starts on what was promised to be the story of the play, namely a history of his infatuations with women. If we expect it to lead anywhere, we are wrong. Instead of a story, we get a list of names and events:

> CHAP: I can't go through the *whole* list.
> GIRL: We're not asking you to. Next.
> CHAP: Then there was Shirley and her sister.
> GIRL: What about them?
> CHAP: I just wonder what happened to them, that's all.
> GIRL: Well, we all wonder that sort of thing.
> CHAP: Shut up, you lousy bitch. I wouldn't tell you anyway.
> GIRL: And then?
> CHAP: Well, believe it or not, there was Fanny. (I, 36–37)

It seems as if the "chap" has taken Yeats's advice to heart, that it is "our part/ To murmur name upon name"—lines from "Easter 1916," a poem indeed quoted in the play (II, 51). Each of these women is remembered for the sound of a name or, at the most, for a singular quality or occurrence: Aunty Viv, for instance, was called the "Gypsy Queen" and had "a funny way with handling the children" (II, 35); Audrey was a girl in school, "a frightful bully" who "had a gang of boys mostly and used to sit on your head and try to suffocate you" (II, 36)—and the list of names, recognizable only to those who know Osborne's autobiographies, continues, without much sense, without any particular narrative logic. Later the chap will make a point about the difference between the immensity of our emotional investment and the puniness of our later recollections: "Who *were* they? All I remember most is their names, what they wore, sometimes what they looked like. Not very much" (II, 58). For the audience, however, it is a test of endurance because none of these names turns into a dramatic character so that the interrupter quite reasonably shouts, "We don't know who any of these people *are*. What they are *doing*. Where it's taking *place*. Or anything!" (II, 37). Even the chairman loses track and has to ask, "does anyone remember where we were?" (II, 31).

In the meantime the older lady has started on her recitation of pornographic plots from a catalogue of hardcore movies:

> A picture story of hard rape! Six men drinking in a small bar in Germany decide to grab the pretty little blond barmaid and have a giggle with her but, as many things do, it went wrong. She resisted! They ganged up on her and tore her clothes off of her and proceeded to violate her in every way that they could. Each one had a go at fucking her, some in her bum, some in her mouth. They held her on the table and screwed until she finally passed out from the spunk forced down her throat. I have seen some rape scenes while I have been in this business, but *WOW*. (II, 42–43)

As the reviewer of the *Sunday Times* reports, the older lady starts reading these extracts with "eager curiosity" which, nearing the end, turns into "sad, discouraged weariness." The chairman then takes over, reading the last synopsis, and in the words of the same reviewer, "delivers its terrible conclusion with a miraculous amazement, recoiling from a vision of evil that makes his face unforgettably appalled."[14] The pornography is alternated with lyrics about love, England, solitude—all brimming with sentiment and delivered with what the same reviewer describes as "exquisite diction":

> My true love hath my heart and I have his,
> By just exchange one for the other giv'n;
> I hold his dear, and mine he cannot miss,
> There never was a better bargain driv'n. (II, 43)

All cast members take turns on the poetry. When that too comes to an end, the chap and the girl switch gears, mount a pulpit, and deliver Brendan Behan-like speeches about the Irish question. All that time, images are projected onto the screen, delivering a sort of ongoing humorous, ironic, or deflating commentary. Music is used in a similar way too, to highlight, distract, or parody.

Each section is punctuated by exasperated groans or vigorous protests from the planted interrupters: "Is this ever going to end" (II, 47)—a sentiment probably shared by the audience. Quite understandably, they demand their money's worth. The football supporter in the stage box wants entertainment; the middle class gentleman in the stalls wants serious art. No one cares about the audience. The actors respond with dismissive or insulting remarks. The stage crew too makes several appearances to prove that the whole theatrical enterprise is marked by this general indifference and despise. During the interval the crew makes use of the audience's absence to throw a party on the stage. When spectators come back in, the partying stage crew slowly and with ill grace return to their various tasks. The playwright has no illusion as to what effect all this will have on his audience, as we learn from his grim stage directions: "as the audience returns, if indeed it does return," "when what is left of the house has got back in" (II, 27), "if there is still any [audience] left" (II, 32). It's hard to know with whom his sympathies lie, with those who stubbornly stay (perhaps because, like the interrupters, they want to get their money's worth) or with those who leave in anger or disappointment. In this way the play meanders slowly and painfully down to its final topic.

The last topic starts with the middle-class interrupter commenting rather smugly on the male-biased, not to say misogynist, views of women that were expressed throughout the evening. Such views are currently and with good reason contested, he says, eagerly associating himself with the kind of bushy-tailed, clean-souled liberalism that Osborne so heartily detested (II, 54). This understandably leads to some more speechifying, this time about the "woman question." The older lady mounts the pulpit in spirited defense of the reality of women's lives. That reality, she says, is denied or mystified by men who persistently view women as objects of desire to be used for their pleasure or as "Eternal Woman" to be venerated. But the chap gets the final say on this matter, and it is in this last speech that the various strands—poetry, porn, politics, and piety, to paraphrase Sheridan Morley freely—come together.

After an evening marked by exaggerated or ironic sentiment, nobody will find it strange to hear the chap speak with an emotion so lofty that it borders on parody. It is hard to know how seriously we have to take this speech; isn't everything after all a device? All its exaggeration notwithstanding, the speech does propose a fairly coherent argument, and when compounded with Osborne's public pronouncements on similar matters, becomes something amounting to an Osbornian credo. The danger of paraphrase, however, is that an emotive jumble of elliptic statements then turns into dogma—which was exactly what the whole exhausting prelude to the speech tried to prevent. It is in fact a statement of faith against all odds, a sort of exasperated but magnificent gesture that is meant to triumph perversely by admitting to its own insignificance and irrelevance.

The chap's argument, if we can call it that, runs somewhat as follows: yes, I can see how silly and misguided my obsession with women is. That is what women nevertheless will always be for me, figments of the imagination. Do you realize, however, that it is precisely because they are men's inventions that women exert such powerful influence over them? I know such ideas run against the grain of modernity, yet I will cling to them. I will defend what I know is a groundless belief against the reasonable arguments of liberals and feminists, "those long-shore bullies with bale hooks in bras and trousers seamed with slogans and demands," that new class of narrow-minded individuals whose so-called social conscience masks a desire to bully others into conformity (II, 57). I realize that such people are the wave of the future. They will present themselves as a group of people oppressed by the dominant ideology, cornered and forced into the offensive with every means at their disposal, fair or unfair. Do not be fooled by that attitude. Whereas I am tortured by nostalgia for a time that perhaps never was, that was only conjured up in images and songs; whereas I am daily racked by a desire for women who I know only exist in my mind, and am therefore eternally ill at ease, eternally an outsider, eternally disappointed, they fit snugly into the present. Heralds of a joyless future these people are. This future is taking shape today, now that everyone in Britain eagerly looks forward to entering the European market, a faceless, streamlined, rationalized system where people will no longer interact but exchange (II, 58). Something as silly and wasteful as love—and tonight we've portrayed love to you in all its manifestations—will have to be rationalized out of existence: "Economic Unions do not fall in love. They amalgamate" (II, 58). Love runs counter to progress, "it involves waste, exploitation of resources, sacrifice, unplanned expenditure, both sides sitting down together in unequal desolation" (II, 56).

But you can take my word for it—and what follows is implied rather than stated—that with it will also disappear the essence of theatre, because art, as we have seen tonight, is not the sum total of its devices. It is a lost impulse, a useless feeling, a hopelessly utopian, irrational and wasteful energy, a spark that briefly lights up the darkness that separates the world from our boldest dreams, plunging us afterward into ever deeper solitude. This does not happen because of the devices it employs but very often in spite of them. A new group of playwrights, however, will appear who will write pieces about issues. Everyone will group around them, nod, discuss, and praise themselves for being so sensitive and enlightened. Plays of the past will be rejected because they do not speak in the right kind of way about the right kinds of things, dealing in socially misguided ways about irrelevancies such as unhappiness, joy, or despair.

All this is said and more is implied in a typical Osbornian lingo, either through under- or overstatement, though anyone who is familiar with Osborne's views can puzzle it out easily enough. More recent history of the theatre, with its surprising return to tragedy and despair, shows that Osborne's dire view of the future of drama was not justified. It is also a typically romantic vision of art, of woman, of woman as art and art as woman—a vision so hackneyed and yet so sincere that the author could not possibly have said it without bedding it in an interminably long, ironic, and self-deflating preamble. By the time we have attained the vision, we have waded through layers of tedium and vexation and should finally have reached the necessary "sense of detachment" without which we would never accept the embarrassing cliché for the undeniable sincerity of its engendering impulse.

Emotions, we know by then, will be exaggerated, and yet delivered with a conviction instantly undercut through some joke, some image, some interruption. The same, we feel, must count for the vision—and yet we should sense a difference, if only because the chap's vision entails a degree of synthesis lacking elsewhere in the play. The chap tells all this with deliberate campiness, in a kind of offhand rapture, as if he upholds the vision while simultaneously exposing it to ridicule. He looks boldly toward the future, embracing the girl and with it the twentieth-century: "So century, century as is and will be—APPROCHE MOI! *Approche moi.* To me . . ." (II, 58). The girl kisses him, and the credo turns into a love declaration in which the lofty lyricism of love poetry combines with the explicitness of pornography—so that on this level too the play comes together. "Oh, heart, dearest heart," the chap begins, and then, exhausting every resource of language in an attempt to express his feelings, marvels at how words both express and separate us from the reality they represent:

What does *that* mean! Rhetoric. I do, I have, I've wanted you, want you, will, *may* not and so on. I love you, yes. I shall. Shan't. Heart . . . And I want, yes— here we go—want to fuck you . . . Not cum-uppance or any of that . . . Heart: I want you. Legs high. High. Open. Prone: if you like. We can both laugh. And enjoy. Enjoy me if you can. I *do* enjoy you. I *do*. I want you, thighs enveloping my head. Mist. I shall want to breathe . . . Give me *you*. I'll do what I can with me. I hate to use the words between us—but—I want what I know, have known, we know has taken, done, enjoyed, laughed over; cherished. Between us. Girl. Chap. We are lost without . . . You *know*. Don't you?

GIRL: Yes. I really think—perhaps—I do.
CHAP: Do. Don't. Will. Won't. Can. Can't. I wish I were *inside* you.
    Now. At this moment . . . However.
GIRL: So do I. *However* . . . (II, 58–59)

The language pants and strains into meaning or rather into demonstrating that love does not follow the principle of equal exchange but of surplus meaning, of waste, that it spans past, present, and future, affirms and negates—and all simultaneously.

Capping off the speech in the same style, a synthesis of the obscene and the romantic, the chairman sings a naughty variation on a romantic love lyric: "My balls are like a red, red rose" (II, 59). Then he throws the towel in, admitting that he's "not a good chairman at all." As at the end of Act I, the cast, holding hands, sing Widdicombe Fair, imposing a sense of structure and closure on the play. This time they do not use the song to parody modern playwrights. That obsession with the names of modern drama, each of which has come to represent a theatrical cliché, has apparently been successfully exorcised. They can now deliver the song in its original version and as if in a gesture of goodwill each produces a word creating a banner with the traditional wish, "The very best of British luck." They do not try to gain the audience's sympathy, as is clear from the chairman's "may the Good Lord bless you and keep you. Or Got rot you." The cast leaves and shortly returns to face the audience, in case anyone might think they left in shame. As in Handke's *Offending the Audience*, they do not take a bow; they allow themselves however to be booed by the interrupter in the stalls and applauded by the box man.

THE AUTHOR DETACHED

This take it or leave it attitude should not fool us into believing that Osborne does not care about his audience's reaction, and yet it does leave him in a particularly vulnerable position. As Handke does in *Offending the Audience*, Osborne seeks to prompt the audience into reacting in less predictable ways. "All we want [the audience] to do is to react truly and sincerely to what they see on stage. We don't want them to make exhibitions of themselves for that would be only another theatrical cliché," director Frank Dunlop stated in a pre-performance interview.[15] The conventional, predictable responses were indeed already provided by the play itself through its two planted interrupters and by having itself booed and applauded simultaneously. It was now up to the audience to invent something more original. If the performance could be said to have some aim, it is probably this, to trigger some genuine reactions from the audience: "it would be a pity if there were not," a stage direction admits (I, 14). Still, audience participation and improvisation are two dreaded words in Osborne's vocabulary. They are exercises in bad faith, attempts at renewal which ultimately are always self-defeating since audience and actors all too easily succumb to each other's expectations, try all too desperately to play the game correctly, so that they escape from one theatrical cliché only to fall victim to some other. In fact, when a journalist asked if actors would improvise, Frank Dunlop hastened to reassure him: "Not at all, everything that happens is very carefully scripted. But, if necessary, the actors are ready for variations."[16] The closest Osborne comes to the dreaded word improvisation is when he instructs the chairman, chap, and girl to be "inventive or spontaneous" (I, 15).

That inventiveness was often put to the test because the actors, not the playwright, had to bear the brunt of genuine interruptions the play generated. There were malicious attempts to sabotage the performance by persistent heckling; there was aggression and abuse borne from genuine frustration and disappointment. Denise Coffey as girl was most adept at improvising responses to real and often very disturbing interruptions—responses that were far subtler than the list of insults Osborne provided with the play. In one case she wittily identified a particularly irritating heckler as "Sammy" Beckett in a vengeful mood. Lady Redgrave, the famous actress Rachel Kempson, whose unenviable task it was as older lady to read the pornography extracts, had to endure damning criticism and real abuse. One woman threw her boots on the stage, shouting "Aren't you ashamed, Lady Redgrave." The use of her titled name, that of her husband Michael Redgrave, was meant to cruelly remind her that she had more than her own reputation to uphold. Once, driven to distraction by two particularly noisy hecklers, Kempson jumped off the stage and slapped her offenders.[17] They left but were followed by some of Kempson's fans and beaten up in the street.[18] So Osborne's hope for genuine interruptions, for a theatre that would break through its frame, was fulfilled—and broken teeth and a black eye were visual measures of authenticity.

Though as an actor he was on many occasions generous with fellow actors and full of sympathy for those who nightly braved the public's boredom or resentment, Osborne was quite ready to denounce actors who were unwilling to go down on the playwright's fast sinking ship. When there were signs of mutiny from actors who balked at the coarseness of the script, Osborne publicly disparaged the whole acting profession: "I gather that some actors have complained about the script. Indeed some of them chose not to appear in the play after reading it. It's not really surprising. Actors are very conservative people. They live in places like Beckenham and do the *Daily Telegraph* cross-word puzzle. As a race they are terribly disapproving."[19]

So the play not only targeted its audience but its actors as well.

Critics were the third group that Osborne sought to challenge. "I know what the reviews will say," he told journalists. "I could almost write them now, especially the one which starts 'Mr. Osborne has given us another exercise in nostalgia.'"[20] The play itself lists more predictable objections: "Is it all going to be as formless as this?" (I, 14); "I suppose we needn't ask if there's a *plot* or not" (I, 24); "usual obligatory cracks about critics" (II, 33), etc. In this con-test with critics, Osborne shows that he is as familiar with the clichés of their profession as they are with his. Chap, chairman, and girl throw them about happily in a parody of a "lively intellectual confrontation": "but he really has got a bit too predictable now, hasn't he?"; "it struck me there was a certain amount of strident waffle", and, deadliest of all responses, "What did you think of the devices" (II, 33–34). Critics did not take this preempting of their reac-tions kindly. Alan Brien said Osborne was "like the provocative drunk in the bar who jeers at you and insults you and then wants you to hit him, for some-thing that's going to satisfy him, but has very little meaning for you."[21] Bene-dict Nightingale compared him to a "narcissistic and rather cowardly boxer, at once pugnacious and defensive, who creates the illusion of having been in a genuine argument by giving himself a few painless jabs on the nose."[22]

CONCLUSION: THEATRE ARENA

Like Handke and Pirandello's plays, *A Sense of Detachment* takes the process of theatre as its ultimate subject, questioning everything about it except the correctness and prerogative of the author's vision. As far as the latter is con-cerned, *A Sense of Detachment* certainly goes to tremendous lengths and in the process risks alienating actors, audience, and critics; but the few who follow Osborne all the way through disdain and mockery to the other side, where a hard-earned detachment starts, should be rewarded with some important insights.

A Sense of Detachment shows to what degree the principle of excess, of wastefulness is central to the Osbornian universe, uniting his views on art, love, and politics. It is easy to see the quandary in which such an aesthetics of excess and wastefulness put Osborne, though the degree to which he allowed it to hold sway over every aspect of his life certainly should win him the distinction of most consistent playwright of his times. Applied to the realm of politics, such aesthetics made him vulnerable to the charge that he was nothing but an old blimp infatuated with Britain's lost glories. Glory to him, however, was never beautiful without loss—something the more politically partisan among his crit-ics usually fail to see. If he prefers the past over the present it is a preference always conditioned on present knowledge of its superfluity. The Kantian notion that the beautiful is that which serves no purpose to Osborne implies that something first has to lose its purpose before it can become artistically interesting. We see this principle at work in most of his plays. In *Look Back in Anger,* Colonel Redfern's imperial troops are beautiful only when they wait fully arrayed and in splendid formation to be shipped back home. There, stripped of all purpose, the pompousness of its officers becomes quaint, embarrassing, and therefore ultimately fascinating. *West of Suez* is not a play written in defense of the British empire; Wyatt's imperial grandeur is magnificent only in so far as it is no longer justified by an empire. Homosexuality, as *A Patriot for Me* shows, has artistic potential only in so far as it represents a feeling in excess of what is socially possible and acceptable. As his later plays prove, the socially integrated homosexual or the militant homosexual urging for integration is for Osborne only a source of irritation or a subject for mockery. The music hall, as *The Entertainer* proves, only became beautiful when it ceased to reflect society's tastes and needs. The same applies to patriotism or the monarchy, which became attractive to Osborne only when people ceased to believe in their usefulness. The late fifties and early sixties were so congenial to Osborne because it was a period of transition when old structures were fast becoming useless while new ideas were not yet solidified into stifling conventions. It was a time when excess in all its forms stood out sharply on a background of general dreariness and actual poverty. Osborne's career declined when Britain modernized, caught up with the rest of the world, and was in many ways more confident and at peace with itself.

It is never noon in Osborne's aesthetic universe. The sun is always setting or rising; things must always be on their way out or in their way in. Whatever *is* rather than *was* or *will be*, whatever does not throw a shadow of longing or of loss, is not only artistically uninteresting but a valid target for his anger. To be constantly out of focus was his aim, to provoke others to wonderment and vexation. Not to be summed up by a cliché he had to outrun all clichés—as he attempted to do in what can only be described as his most exhausting cliché marathon, *A Sense of Detachment.* This aesthetic view forced Osborne to cast his own life in a tragic light. He was increasingly presenting himself as a dinosaur, striding among the sleek creatures of the present, embarrassing them with the weight and awkwardness of his views, seducing them with the exuberance of his wit. That the press for the most part accepted the self-image he proffered them is proof of how successfully he bridged the gap between his art and his life.

A Sense of Detachment is the logical consequence of such a conception of art, but it also, I believe, alerts us to its dangers and, in fact, its actual impossibility. Undoubtedly the play has its moments of beauty, when—as some fan letters and the few positive reviews seem to indicate—the audience was charmed by the songs and poetry. It was certainly not to the avant-garde, to the theatre of Pirandello and Handke, that the play paid homage, but to the only theatre that Osborne truly admired: popular English entertainment, the sing-alongs in pubs and the music hall. Some of that atmosphere, which indeed includes bitchy exchanges between performer and spectator, he surely communicated successfully to the audience with this play. But the only success Osborne could accept was one closely tied to failure. Not even trusting the world to play its role, he wrote into the play a necessary vision of a gradually emptying house, a vision that guaranteed the authentic thrust of his artistry. The play comes complete with recalcitrant actors, disapproving audience, and snooty critics. We see the play literally gaining in emotional intensity as Osborne imagines the room slowly being vacated, leaving the lone actors facing a handful of baffled audience members. It was a dangerous road to walk, especially since failure was of course never intended to become absolute; it always had to remain tied in with success. To preserve its meaning, failure had to be experienced as loss, as a promise of brilliance not fulfilled, as genius wasted, as an "expense of spirit in a waste of shame."

In a peevish letter to an insistent critic, Osborne declared that *A Sense of Detachment* had to be read as a musical score, a series of affective annotations awaiting the performers' animating magic.[23] Perhaps for that reason, because the whole superstructure is allowed to dissolve in this play, leaving only the roots of theatre, it is a play that appealed mainly to playwrights. Edward Albee, Terence Rattigan, and even the much detested Arnold Wesker wrote letters full of support and genuine admiration. [24] Without that superstructure, however, what remains is a frighteningly self-enclosed and self-obsessive world, an example of an artist's growing detachment from reality itself. It was not the play itself but the image of an isolated shadowboxing Osborne that provided dramatic conflict, of a man at war with the world and himself, writing plays that spoke of a self-preoccupation that unhappily had become increasingly irrelevant to others.

CHAPTER 11

Watch It Come Down (1976)
A Most Necessary Failure

The story of Osborne's later career, from the mid-seventies onward, tells of growing artistic isolation and, what is worse, of growing irrelevance. His private obsessions, once validated with the stamp of public recognition, now shriveled around an increasingly isolated and often rather nasty self. Osborne, it seems, was more and more writing about himself for himself. Despite constant criticism that his work was thematically and structurally undisciplined, his plays continued to become more muddled in intention and execution. The curious mixture of excess and economy that had always typified Osborne's work now became more pronounced and sometimes truly baffling. He seemed to be saying at once too much and too little: too many references to a reality extrinsic to the play remained undeveloped or were inadequately pulled back into the narrative, so that the work seemed not sufficiently rounded, not completely finished.

It would be easy to attribute the unevenness of Osborne's work to mere shoddiness, the impatient gesture of a playwright who has given up on his audience. Yet, Osborne clearly still expected something from his audience since he continued to write for the stage, where the impact of public recognition or opprobrium is most directly experienced. Though he no longer had the charisma of the young, capricious would-be revolutionary, he (and his heroes) apparently still demanded the same, to be a lost cause and to be loved for it. Together with *A Sense of Detachment, Watch It Come Down* best expresses Osborne's ambiguous relationship with his audience. It is one of Osborne's most excessive and strangely inaccessible plays that, as I will argue, shows the limitations of a vision that takes failure and excess as the font of authenticity.

RECEPTION

Published in 1975, before its production, *Watch It Come Down* is now merely one among many of Osborne's neglected plays—little known, little discussed,

and certainly rarely performed. Chronicling the destruction of the well-to-do
Prosser household, the play premiered at the Old Vic on 24 February 1976,
and after a short run transferred to the National Theatre's new location on the
South Bank.

1976, like 1956, was a watershed year in Osborne's life: whereas *Look
Back in Anger* had then launched him on his career, *Watch It Come Down,* in
an equally spectacular way, announced the beginning of its end. The production of *Watch It Come Down* was planned as a celebration of the reopening of
the NT and the twentieth anniversary of Osborne's first great success, but
Osborne and that new pearl of the British welfare state proved to be a mis-
match of profound symbolic significance. The National Theatre epitomized
what had been taking shape over the last twenty years, a new pact between
state and culture of which Osborne heartily disapproved.

He had only offered his play to the National Theatre because of special
circumstances, not the least among which was his breach with the Royal Court
Theatre. In 1956, *Look Back in Anger* had served as the manifesto of the Royal
Court Theatre's new art policy, bringing it national, even international, fame.
After the death of its founder and first manager/director George Devine in
1965, estrangement had set in between Osborne and the institution he had
called his home. Public recognition for the Royal Court's work had paid off in
the form of relatively heavy state subsidies, and this increase of revenue in turn
changed the Royal Court's policy. Plays could now be chosen for production
not because they were dramatically inventive or theatrically viable, but because
their message served a politically expedient purpose. This led to a smugness
Osborne found intolerable: playwrights could now build up their careers biting the hand that fed them, pursuing a radicalism that depended almost completely on state subsidies since their plays hardly ever played to capacity.[1]
Endorsed by an institution Osborne had helped to build, they offered their "revolutionary" message to a new generation of broad-minded spectators, who paid
for their entrance into the society of the radical chic with ritual demonstration
of stolid tolerance.

When the Royal Court showed no interest in Osborne's new reactionary
plays, the breach was complete, and having *Look Back in Anger*'s anniversary
play produced at another theatre was Osborne's way of making that breach
public. It is hard to imagine that anything but mere expediency could have
motivated the NT to choose Osborne's latest play for its reopening performance. The result was disastrous, and *Watch It Come Down* met only with
scornful reviews.

Still the play deserves attention because it stands out from the rest of
Osborne's oeuvre by an extremism of subject matter and, more interestingly, by an ambiguity of genre and style. While almost indecently excessive in word and action, *Watch It Come Down* is at times cryptically
economical, fragmentary, or elliptical. Osborne shows little concern for his

audience, shows even less desire to play up to them—which he could easily have done, as we will see, by giving more ingenuity or eloquence to the lovers' quarrel at the heart of this play. The many references to a world preceding the action or lying outside its scope—references left vague and undeveloped—impress upon the audience a nagging feeling that the play is not sufficiently self-contained. Not every element in the many possible conflicts can be settled within the confines of the play, and the playwright does not tell us all or does not care to explain it better. Of course, it is always possible to attribute some meaning to fragmentary references, to pull them back into the play in one way or other, yet the point is that we, the audience, are given so little consideration. It is as if the playwright does not care whether we get it or not—as if he had already decided that where we have not yet been ourselves, he cannot or will not lead us.

More importantly, and the crux of the present interpretation, it is as if the play foresees its own failure. This is an old obsession of Osborne's. Not only does failure appear as subject in early plays such as *Luther* (1961) or *Inadmissible Evidence* (1964), it runs as a theme through Osborne's autobiographical writings as well. He never portrayed it quite as grimly, though, as in *Watch It Come Down,* a play that was little appreciated by the critics and certainly did not prevent the further "coming down" of his own career.

THE PROBLEM OF GENRE

It is not difficult to see why *Watch It Come Down* was angrily dismissed. Even a play as excessive as *Look Back in Anger* still paid lip service to the well-made play. By the seventies, Osborne was less and less willing to concede to that conventional model; nor was he much interested in adopting the developing alternative methods of breaking through narrative constraints—methods that relied less on text and more on performance aspects such as improvisation. He continued his quest for authenticity in writing by experimenting with excesses of language. The resulting vigor, however, was often that of a tangle, which many critics agreed was in dire need of pruning.

The feeling that something speaks with the force of genuine emotion is often not more than a fleeting sensation. In the long run, a play's resistance to a spectator's attempts to analyze it may prove damaging to a playwright's reputation. When critics are not able to evaluate a play on its own, intrinsic principles, they assess it by what it is *not* rather than by what it is: they hold it up against an already existing model and consider it flawed if nothing very meaningful can be said about the differences they perceive.

It is particularly tantalizing to reject *Watch It Come Down* for not fulfilling the promises of the many genres to which it seems to be alluding. The play's opacity is the more remarkable as it covers ground well trodden in the history of drama. Its protagonists, Ben and Sally, are the kind of people that like to stage their marital disputes among friends. Since the savage games of married couples have been part of the comic repertoire from Plautus through Molière to Albee, Osborne could have found himself in good company. Even if comedy is clearly not what Osborne is aiming at with this play, a number of interesting conflicts could possibly emerge from such a set-up.

With Ben and Sally Prosser live two family members (Sally's sister, Shirley, and Ben's mother, who remains unseen in a room upstairs) and three friends (Raymond, Jo, and the dying Glen). One could expect that the news that this community, comfortably housed in a converted country railway station, will soon have to disband because of Ben and Sally's separation should be unsettling for the guests. After ordering Raymond to break the news to the others, Sally waits to see their reaction: "Should be interesting. Their concern, I mean," she says (I, i, 12). The guests have until then been quite conveniently lodged in these surroundings, but now they will have to sort out allegiances and make provisions for the future. Here is material for a conflict whose development could structure further action. Yet very little is done in the way of exploring the guests' reactions to the news. Ben's mother, whose role in the play is never elucidated, apparently never receives the news. Raymond, who serves as Sally's message bearer, reports that Shirley is upset and offers to mediate. At one moment, Shirley consoles Ben with a kiss and intimates that more could be in the offing, but the audience can expect no more from this sketchily drawn character.

The other characters do not offer a dramatically interesting reaction either. Glen, who is sick and dying, should be most inconvenienced by the news of his friends' separation. Yet he only seems slightly miffed at Raymond for informing him. Ever expansive Jo, always so generous with her affections, and now suffering under the stress of seeing her dear friend Glen dying, vows to continue her friendship with both Ben and Sally, whatever the outcome of their marital crisis. She even makes it clear that she would not object to becoming the lover of either Ben or Sally— or both of them, if needed. In brief, no real conflict emerges from Raymond's revelation. What should be a volatile catalyst produces little or no effect.

Even if the reactions of the guests remain uninteresting in dramatic terms, the couple's marital warfare could still have been the play's focus. Indeed *Watch It Come Down* resembles, in some respects, a play like Edward Albee's *Who's Afraid of Virginia Woolf* (1964) that turns quarreling into art. Like George and Martha, Sally and Ben stage their quarrels before a captive audience of guests. And like that couple, Ben and Sally are professionally expressive, he being a film director and she a novelist: as they put it themselves, they like to "exaggerate" or be "rhetorical." Moreover, *Watch It Come Down* features the same kind of deeply paradoxical relationship, unhappy yet durable— the type we find in *Who's Afraid of Virginia Woolf* or Osborne's own *Look Back in Anger.* Endlessly pending separation is an integral part of such a relationship, crisis a powerful homeostatic mechanism. Offers of reconciliation are immediately (and often with good reason) suspected, deepening mutual resentment and leading up to the next round of compulsive bloodletting.

This could produce good drama, and *Watch It Come Down* to some extent does follow a similarly involved interactional pattern. "The more pain I FEEL, the more resentment comes out of *her,*" complains Ben about his wife Sally to Marion, his "ex" (II, 53). Such a perversely distorted dynamic could trigger some dramatically interesting marital clashes. Accounting for it on the basis of evidence given in the play is not so easy. Sally may resent pain of which she is not the cause, and drawing blood, even at great emotional cost to herself, can be her way of relating to Ben, but this possible psychological scenario never appears in the play.

The play does not even examine the source of Ben's pain, yet again an answer suggests itself if we follow the vectors of Ben and Sally's desire—or, sometimes, of the lack of it. Ben's relationship with Sally has reached an intensity of sexual disaffection and estrangement all too common to couples on the point of divorce. Marion remembers the last stages of her marriage to Ben all too clearly: "We've become islands at the edges of the bed. You're on your own. I'm on *my* own. [. . . .] We never did things at the same time of day. We couldn't. I followed you like a dog when I knew you wanted to be left alone. You wanted to sleep in front of the television" (II, 53). Sally indeed refers to herself bitterly as a "married nun" and claims that their "sex pitch has been washed out for years" (I, i, 11). This is confirmed by Ben who taunts her with having the "curse" for "twenty-eight days a month" (I, ii, 29).

This is not to say that desire is absent in this play; passions do leap up and quite spectacularly and confusingly so, though not between Sally and Ben. After a particularly bitter and violent fight with Ben, Sally wants to leave with Jo. Attraction is mutual, and both women express their desire for one another. Ben, likewise, compensates for the sterility of his marriage by lusting after Shirley, his ex-wife Marion, Jo, and even Glen. His physical closeness to Glen makes it tempting to suggest that the women are substitutes or channels for an otherwise impossible homosexual love. This seems confirmed by the initial configuration of characters in the opening scene: the set, a converted railway station, is divided into two separate spaces, and at the rising of the curtain each reveals a tableau of asexual intimacy between a woman and a man who, we later discover, is homosexual: Raymond attends to Sally who sprawls on a rug in what was once the waiting room and now Ben and Sally's living room; Jo attends to Glen who is propped up in bed in what once was the parcel office and now a guest room. It would then not be too farfetched to suggest that problems associated with a similarly deceptive heterosexuality constitute a major theme in the play.

This, however, cannot be the case since there is no psychological or social need for such a disguise, and the play does not avoid other expressions of homosexuality. Glen, who is upper class, may be somewhat embarrassed by his need for boys but nevertheless continues to bribe young guardsmen into having sex with him, often at the risk of suffering a severe beating. Neither does Ben try to evade the reality of his sexual feelings. He loves Glen, is not averse to kissing him on the mouth in the presence of others, realizing in any case that the others believe him to be an "old pouf." It is not Glen's desire he requires in response but rather the man's unwavering belief in his work. Together they form a sort of mutual support group, with each surrounded by a private world of friends and dependents.

Apart from this, not much more understanding can be gained from an examination of the characters' passions. Sexual and affective allegiances in the play are so intense and varied as to become almost absurdly confusing. We learn, for instance, that Sally's father did not return Ben's sympathy for him, thus repeating the pattern of unequal affections that tied Ben to his own father (I, i, 16). Beyond this, little can be made of the other relationships, though Osborne insists on spelling them all out, carefully distinguishing between degrees of affection, between loving, liking, admiring, and fancying: Ben does not like Raymond but trusts him to take care of his wife. Sally likes and even loves Raymond, claiming still to love but not to like Ben. Ben likes Glen and Jo, but does not like Shirley very much although he would like to go to bed with her because he fantasizes that she is the "enigmatic tally" of her sister. Sally suggests that Ben's daughter prefers talking to her rather than to Ben. Glen likes neither Ben's mother nor Sally's sister Shirley (I, ii, 24). He does not fancy Raymond but likes him "well enough." Raymond says that Sally does not like Glen very much (II, 50), but Glen admires Sally for making "far more than there was of herself" (II, 50). Ben claims that Glen "loved and was loved" whereas he himself is "neither loved nor loving" (II, 52). Marion says that Glen loved Ben. Ben doubts it, although he himself loves Glen so much that people believe him to be gay (II, 52), and of course the "Major," a shady character who tyrannizes the countryside, does not like any of the "nuts" in the railway house and promises money to any of his men who would shoot one of the Prosser's dogs. "You, you're not popular," in fact is the phrase Doctor Ashton uses in reaction to the demolition of the Prosser's home (II, 56). In other words, a disorderly bundle of affections and desires of every kind sends vibrant energies through the play, wounding and gratifying alternately or simultaneously. Any clear pattern, however, is lost in this confusing skein of liking, loving, lusting, and their opposites.

Perhaps we ought to read the play as a succession of powerfully described moments of being. If these are successfully drawn, they may create the illusion we are encountering a fullness of being that is aesthetically quite as effective as narrative coherence. While the exact sources of Sally's resentment and Ben's pain remain obscured by a disorderly heap of affective and sexual tensions, the battle to which each leads certainly derives much of its momentum from such energies.

If *Watch It Come Down* were such a play, it would seek to demonstrate interactional patterns rather than explain psychological motivation. Many plays about battling couples sacrifice no dramatic effectiveness for the absence of a convincing psychological argument about the origin of the dispute. As Ben puts it, perhaps too bluntly: "There's always a public for vulgarity and cruelty if it's put over well" (I, i, 14). But is it "put over well" enough to allow an audience to derive some pleasure from the onslaught? We wince at George and Martha's punches below the belt in Edward Albee's *Who's Afraid of Virginia Woolf,* yet we are also awed by their brilliant inventiveness and their perfect sense of timing. The couple's quarrel reaches such heights of verbal ingenuity that our admiration matches or overcomes our discomfort. What masterful teamwork, we think, and laugh, but it is a laughter never devoid of compassion for a couple whose relationship is secured by so much suffering. It is the quarrel's perfection, though, that gives us the permission to laugh and admire what otherwise would make us uncomfortable. In contrast to Martha and George who admire each other's gambits, the Prossers derive little joy from the quarrel. They resort to crudeness and physical violence rather than to eloquence or witticism:

> SALLY: "Oh, shut up, bitch-face." (I, i, 14)
> BEN: Will you, you, will you, for one minute, just stop that fucking pile of shit spewing out of your fucking mouth! [. . . .] Or you'll get my fist right in the fucking middle of it. From my puny fist even if it breaks my arm. . . . (I, i, 19)
> SALLY: You've begun to smell . . . [. . . .] Physically. I can smell you in bed. And now in here . . . .(I, ii, 31)
> SALLY: If you had any balls, I'd have kicked them into the siding. (II, 47–48)
> BEN: And you shut up, fat-mouth. A friend's dying in there. (II, 48)
> BEN: Oh, shut up, pig-mouth. He's *dying* in there. (II, 54)

Here is no poetry. Violence and vulgarity remain base, not elevated by the purity of profanity.

The violence is not restricted to words alone. At one point Sally and Ben battle physically, crashing through the staircase banister. Far worse, however, is the violence coming from the apparently peaceful countryside we see through the window. At the end of Act I, Sally and Raymond bring the wet, dead body of Ben's dog into the house. The animal has been abused and killed by neighbors, and Sally ensures that we are not spared any of the details: "They tied, yes tied her to a tree and set all the male dogs on her. And then they shot her . . . In front of us" (I, ii, 41–42). At the end of the play, invisible assailants, referred to generically as "yobbos," take the house under a barrage of gun fire until it literally comes down on its inhabitants. During this conflagration, Ben is shot to death. In the meantime, Glen has already succumbed to his mysterious illness, and Jo has committed suicide by jumping under a train. In short, the play cannot be read as an interesting psychological exploration of motive and character, nor can it be enjoyed as a sort of poetry of violent interaction. It is all too excessive and directionless.

RHETORIC AND AUTHENTICITY

A kind of poetry is nevertheless what these characters are striving for when they express their love and failure. "We all, *the few of us,* need one another," cries Sally to the dying Ben, a husband she has battled to the very end (II, 57). This is not the only time a character resorts to a melodrama, at once distasteful and oddly absorbing in its exaggerations. It occurs again when Ben recalls a dinner with his daughter—an awkwardly tall girl of eleven with, as her stepmother Sally unkindly puts it, a "face like a bun" (I, i, 18):

> She tackled her spaghetti, her steak, her ice cream. Her coke. We said less and less. I wanted her to go. *She* wanted to go. To be with her friends, her mother, I don't know who. I drank an extra half litre of wine. I ordered the wine. Got the bill in a hurry. I looked at her, and, well, yes the awful, the thing is I cried all over the tablecloth. In front of her. She watched my jowls move. I looked away. But I couldn't. Through the marble and columns and the rest of the silencing restaurant and waiters scrupulously *not* watching. I couldn't even get out 'Let's go'. Then, suddenly, she leapt off her too low chair and put her arms round me. And *she* cried. Like a 'B' movie. She took my hand and we walked out past all the rows of tables. I left her at home and we neither of us said a word; just held hands. (I, ii, 38)

Such a happy reconciliation is indeed reserved for 'B' movies; we discover from a later telephone conversation that the story did not end quite so happily. After Ben broke down in the restaurant, his daughter had to find her way home by herself. Again and again, the feelings of the moment exceed reality, and so does Jo's language when, strained to incoherence in an effort to voice her drunken love for Ben and Glen, it gives off sparks of poetic truthfulness:

> I think and welcome you within all I know up to this now, this moment, with my heart full and my brain clear and empty. Forgive me for what I am not. But I am—I am a loving creature . . . I'm frail and I break but bear with me . . . It's hard to love, isn't it? It's like religion without pain, I mean it's not religion *without* pain. It's not flowers and light and fellowship. It's cruel and we inhabit each other's dark places. Let's drink to that. (I, ii, 39)

This speech initiates one of the warmest and also most uncomfortable scenes of mutually confirming communality in Osborne's plays—a scene which in its warmth and awkwardness is not even to be rivaled by the "painful whimsey" of Jimmy and Alison's bear-squirrel ritual in *Look Back in Anger.* Ben, Glen, and Jo abandon themselves to their feelings, hugging and kissing one another and declaring their fears and affections, fully aware of the possible ridiculousness of their self-dramatization and the insufficiency of their rhetoric. Jo's self-invented grace, leading up to it, represents in the only possible manner, namely in that of high camp, the validating myth of Osborne's dramatic world, that the apparent falsity of a scene does not necessarily belie its honesty.

It seems impossible to reconcile fullness of being with the hollowness of such artifice; yet this is what Osborne insists on doing. As the play progresses, we recognize artifice not only in emotions but in the whole set-up of the play. What started as realism ends as farce. When the faceless yobbos outside take the house under fire, it collapses on its inhabitants, like the cardboard structure it in fact is. The cruel events which lead up to that point could make the play either mawkish or wearisome, and yet *Watch It Come Down* can nearly be blamed for not taking violence seriously enough. Confronted with a scene of general carnage, Doctor Ashton delivers from the heights of his disapproving *sang-froid* a ludicrously commonsensical verdict: "Well, you do lead odd sorts of lives, don't you" (II, 57). They certainly do and also die odd deaths: Glen, a bookish man, has on the brink of death the presence of mind to quote a variation of Lytton Strachey's famous exit lines: "Well, if this is terminal care I can't say I think much of it" (II, 50). This is quite apt too, because his loyal Jo, the Carrington to his Strachey, is in the meantime preparing her own suicide, having left him in the presence of little loved fellow queer Raymond. After the vicious struggles over minor matters, Ben's death too is oddly anticlimactic. With the converted railway station under heavy artillery attack, he rushes out onto the platform. Then shot and dying, he calls for the ever available Raymond and manages to leave this world with a departing quip at the man whose friendship with his wife he always resented: "Look after her, Raymond. I know I can rely on you . . . even when I'm *bleeding* to death" (II, 57).

Still, this artifice does not detract from the play's sense of tragic loss. We are asked not to doubt the reality of the longing and suffering of these characters, self-indulgent or self-inflicted as these feelings may be—and not *despite* but *because* of their exaggeration and opacity. Not in the precision of self-expression but in the impossibility of establishing a perfect fit between feelings and words does Osborne locate honesty. For this reason high camp is particularly effective because it is the art of the misfit, of the person who does not find a niche in society or who experiences an emotion so in excess of language that it can only be expressed as blatant artifice.

Finally we are asked to believe in these characters *because* they are failures: Glen's last book has failed to capture the wisdom for which it was striving; Ben's films, once hailed as revolutionary, "are not much"; Shirley's political demonstrations "are a terribly real joke on us all"; and Jo's self-professed, all-embracing love is "no good" (I, ii, 40). Ben and Sally did not manage to live together peaceably, but neither did they manage to separate. The same can be said of Marion and Ben who never found marital happiness but never truly separated either. Glen and Ben, some would argue, have failed to establish a love relationship and instead continue to rely on a go-between like Jo. The latter has failed to define her life in her own terms and therefore commits suicide when Glen dies. Ben could never separate from his mother who lives in his house, but he never could deal with her either and leaves her in the care of Raymond and the others. Surrounded by her cats, the old woman watches television all day in her room upstairs. If she remains unseen in the play, it is to illustrate to what extent she has been reduced to an inescapable nagging voice that reminds Ben of yet another failure—this time the failure to live up fully to his obligations as a loving son.

A PECULIAR ECONOMY

In a more general sense, the Prossers, as the name suggests, prosper yet suffer from a realization of incompleteness. It is this suffering that makes them in dramatic terms real. If failure is their shared lot, that which unites them against the world outside, it is also the condition of their genuineness. Apparently, genuineness is what fills the space opened up by lack, and the failure to articulate that lack adequately guarantees its authenticity. Indeed, the play has been accused of not being sufficiently articulate: Alan Brien in *Plays and Players* (April 1976) described its language as "clotted cryptic shorthand, characteristic of middle period Osborne, somewhere between an epigram and a telegram."[2] There is indeed a hermetic, self-conscious quality to many of the characters' pronouncements—evident, for instance, in Sally's tongue-twisting description of the new inhabitants of the British country side as "Mindless millionaires wading in the jungle warfare of the new-style trout stream—" (I, i, 17).

Good playwriting requires that such self-conscious rhetoric—like the excessive, affected emotionality—be cut. So why did Osborne not do so? The answer can be found in a rather obscure and yet essential passage—the navel of the play, so to speak—in which the dying Glen, before "reced[ing] from consciousness," recounts the scene that gives the play its title:

> GLEN: [. . . .] I saw two signs on the road coming down. One was a little triangle of green with a hedge and a bench. And a sign read: 'This is a temporary open space'. . .
> RAYMOND: Oh yes?
> GLEN: And the other was a site of rubble near the Crystal Palace I think, perched high up over London, where the bank managers and cashiers fled at the beginning of our—our—of our century. It said 'Blenkinsop—Demolitionists. We *do* it. You *watch* it. *Come down.*' (III, 50)

The passage is another typical example of the play's peculiar economy: Obviously important since the play derives its title from it, it is never returned to nor explained. Probably, the "temporary open space," once the site of now demolished historic houses, will soon be filled with modern buildings designed for ease and usefulness.

The destruction of historic London in the name of progress was always a sore point for Osborne. In 1964, he wrote a number of angry letters to the *Daily Telegraph,* ridiculing that paper's hypocrisy in lamenting the destruction of Mayfair for office and showroom buildings:

> I am appalled every time I pass by Clarges Street. Lady Hamilton's house going. Charles Fox's, and so on. Soon, no doubt, Shepherd Market will disappear, and Curzon Street after it. But that is precisely the price you Tories have always been willing to pay for a society run by moneymakers. Do you expect human values to dominate the aims of businessmen and boards of directors? But don't complain of it. It's the system *you* promote. You can't have your free-for-all enterprise, your shareholders and chairmen of money-grubbers and decency, taste, comfort and honour as well. So please, no more nostalgic drawings of condemned beauties. You don't want beauty. You never have, you never will. Not if it costs you anything. You just want the loot. So take it and shut up. That authentic voice of yours becomes more disgusting than ever.[3]

The voice of false authenticity, Osborne claims, preaches values only to mask its own ruthless greediness. The *Daily Telegraph* retorted that these splendid houses were the most perfect expression of the very attitude Osborne deplored. These houses, Osborne conceded, were built by the rich and privileged: "Whigs, I suppose. But at a time when the aristocratic and classical virtues it celebrated had not yet been betrayed by the *Daily Telegraph* (and *Morning Post*) readers of the Industrial Revolution. [. . . .] The inescapable remains: supporters of your sort of newspaper will always sell out even traditional Tory values like loyalty, taste, the enjoyment of beauty and craftsmanship (even though it be necessarily the craftsmanship of others), even tradition itself—for a good old fast, easy buck."[4] The new ideology, in other words, cannot stand anything that is useless, superfluous, excessive. The philistine dreams of a perfect economy of balanced accounts; Osborne, on the other hand, locates *true* passion, authenticity, genuineness in its opposite, in disbalance, excess, anomaly.

The calculating philistine rules the present and makes the future. His philosophy governs even the most private aspects of life. Couples are now expected to be partners and work on their relationship: "Marriage has been carefully constructed into the pattern of success, and has become a secondary profession for many of us, and there are now great holes where there was once passion and identity."[5] It can of course be expected that something useful and effective will be erected in these "temporary open spaces" of relationships. In

Watch It Come Down, Ben may ask of his own particularly uneconomic marriage bond, "why has it got all so bad, so brutish, so devilish, so sneering," but he knows that mutual destructiveness is the price of genuineness. As Jo says, "It's hard to love." Far from being comforting and consoling, love requires a good deal of suffering—or, as Jimmy Porter tells Alison in *Look Back in Anger,* it takes "muscle and gut." As Glen formulates it: "Men and women are often very unsafe indeed together" (I, ii, 24) .

The same distaste for perfect economy, the ideal of the present and the future, leads Osborne to sin quite consciously against some of the rules of good playwriting. The philistine presides over the theatre in the guise of the critic whose notions of good playwriting are still based on the perfect economy of the well-made play, and who regards each sentence as a hologram of the whole play. Osborne calls it "the Keep 'Em Bareminded and Pregnant School of Drama. Or . . . 'The Theatre of Sucking Up'. 'Cut that line, they don't know what you're talking about. . . . They start to get restless round about here, can't you slip in a joke about nationalized railways?' "[6] Before 1968, when the Lord Chamberlain still held sway over the theatre, Osborne's stubborn resistance to cuts made his fame; after 1968, the same refusal to delete lines or scenes which others thought useless or distracting created a less welcome notoriety. Where efficiency rules, the first thing to go overboard is something as useless, excessive, and anomalous as the integrity of the artist.[7] The high camp of emotions, the artificiality of certain expressions, the farcical excesses of certain scenes— all serve to express Osborne's vision of the relationship between failure, excess, and authenticity.

That personal integrity was at stake cannot be doubted. The play's resistance to a number of conventional interpretations, its obsession with unpopularity and extreme violence, culminating in the physical destruction of the Prosser residence and some of its inhabitants, confirm what is already intimated by an all too clearly symbolical setting, namely that the play's realism is a front for a nightmarish private reality—Osborne's haunting realization of his inevitable decline in the midst of blind societal aggression. It is not merely accidental that the world of the Prossers is very much that of Osborne and his third wife Penelope Gilliatt with whom he had devastatingly cruel quarrels. One senses the playwright's personal involvement in the fact that the couple's quarreling is too grim to be comical. Some of Sally's most forceful attacks on Ben resonate with what must have been for many spectators recognizably autobiographical effectiveness. Her constant references to her husband's physical decay came at a time when Osborne's own health was rapidly declining. Such self-reflexivity is a common feature of Osborne's art, as is his habit of delivering his plays equipped with the critical ammunition that will invariably be employed in their destruction. We hear that Ben's films, very much like Osborne's plays, were once hailed as revolutionary but never escaped the criticism of being undisciplined: "Largesse requires needle control," is Sally's tartly tease. Even Osborne's own failed relationship with his daughter and his enduring fantasy of living in a converted railway station have been assimilated into this play.[8]

THE DECLINE OF IMAGINATION

Artistic vision and integrity also imply an awareness of the larger significance of such personal concerns. Unlike the younger generation of playwrights who considered themselves researchers first and artists second, Osborne never gave up on the grander belief in the artist's anagogical voice, his ability to tap into the spirit of his age even while talking about private matters. Such a larger dimension is also present in the play, although embryonic and barely developed. This is not just a story of failure that reflects the playwright's own failing; the downfall of the Prossers symbolizes the decline of the twentieth-century. Glen, who has found refuge in the Prosser's home, "write[s] about the twentieth century and the people who lived it" (I, 41). He did even more than that, says Ben; he "made his own life out of the twentieth century" (I, 52). That means "he didn't trim, he didn't deceive himself, he preened his perverse English personality and grinned at everyone, and made them feel better, things more likely to happen but not matter anyway" (I, 52). It was an age marked by certain absurdities, resulting from the humanistic belief in the centrality and limitations of man and the conviction that impatience with human frailty or imperfection is dictatorial. This century is being torn down like a useless, anomalous Edwardian section of London to make way for the callously indifferent world of the twenty-first century.

The twenty-first century "despises imagination" (I, 40). The contrast between the new and the old is reflected in the differences between Shirley and Jo. Jo is a hopeless romantic who has no counsel to offer the separating couple, only her unconditional love, even her sexual availability. Shirley, who is much occupied with political demonstrations, already belongs to the new era of cold certainties, of "bullies who tell you what to do and think" (I, 41)—an era that resents the inherent instability and soul tearing which Ben and Sally's world daily demonstrates. Even so, despite the emotional suffering he experiences in that world, Ben maintains that "there will never be more perfection than there is now" and that the inhabitants of the new world will be "worse off. More frightened, more huddling for comfort. They do it now. Thin and careless like none of us had ever been" (I, 40). That old world, bad as it was, had reached an unparalleled degree of perfection because it conceived of human nature as self-contradictory and yet had the courage to live and love these contradictions. Those that follow them will want to smooth out imperfections and regulate even the most intimate aspects of human behavior, or, as it is put in the play, it will be a "world that despises imagination and only gives instruction in orgasms" (I, 40). Imperfect loving and liking, the play shows us, are preconditions of living. The shrinking of that world of affective interdependence is what the characters in this play fear most. The effects are all too visible in the cruelly indifferent violence that rages in the apparently peaceful countryside and finally invades and destroys the Prosser household.

A NECESSARY FAILURE

If at the end of the play the Prossers' universe comes down under a rain of bullets, this is not to be attributed to the power of the bullets, but rather to the feebleness and artificiality of the Prossers' world. The place clearly has never become a true home; it has preserved its sense of temporariness, of being a waiting room for an assortment of idealistic failures who are playing their vicious, pathetic games while awaiting inevitable destruction. In the meantime, we witness on every level the perversity and cruelty of that household. The romantic humanism of their world is at no point presented as a viable alternative to the new ideals.

In other words, Osborne does not locate authenticity in the past, in unhappy marriages, or bad playwriting. As authenticity, to him, is neither an expression nor a thing but an impulse or energy, it requires the tension of difference. Authenticity is produced not by the past, but by the vestiges of a useless past in the present; not by unhappy marriages, but by passionately unreasonable relationships in an age worshipping efficiency; not by a badly written play, but by elements in a play that stand out stubbornly and indecently, hurting a critic's too narrow conceptions of aesthetic balance. We are not obliged to praise this play perversely for failing either: whatever Osborne's intention may have been, it was certainly not to make bad theatre. In fact this play—which is relatively short and written, so to speak, in the margin of a major, better known play, *West of Suez* (1971)—expresses its message quite successfully according to an economy all of its own, and it does so effectively on three different levels: on the level of content, it tells the story of a failure; on the level of drama, it turns that story into an allegory of the battle in the present between the forces of the past and those of the future; on the level of theatre, it presents the spectacle of a failing playwright who invites yobbos to "watch it come down."

That last level is the most complex as it directly reflects Osborne's techniques and beliefs. Many critics have noted the elegiac quality of Osborne's later works.[9] Jeering and sneering notwithstanding, his last play *Déjàvu* is morbidly concerned with its own failure and with the way the critics will formulate its rejection. Ironically, a writer so often accused of lack of discipline has in fact consistently adhered to his own beliefs, even when they proved no longer viable and became self-destructive. *Watch It Come Down* is significant as it most logically expresses the impossibility of Osborne's theatre of honesty: Authenticity, Osborne believes, cannot be articulated since it is the impulse behind the excessive and blatant artifice by which the speaker attempts to fill an incompleteness, an existential vacuum. That excess establishes the speaker's authenticity; hence, the speaker ironically comes to depend on the lack or emptiness he so abhors for his sense of genuineness. Analogously, the "temporary open spaces" in the cityscape of London are necessary for the creation of the true Londoner, as they quickly fill with the latter's righteous and often self-righteous indignation. In the theatre, Osborne has to assume that his audience will lack understanding: it is their supposed priggishness that allows him to experience the thrill of art as indecent exposure.

In this respect, the irony of staging *Watch It Come Down* to celebrate the opening of the NT cannot have been lost on Osborne. That building to him symbolized the triumph of the twenty-first century:

> Now, like one of those wartime pillboxes glimpsed from a train, the monstrous concrete piety of the National Theatre broods, a monument to prevailing madness fixed on a fantasy future in which present chaos will give way to a world of orderly richness for everyone's children and, worse, grandchildren. One doesn't have to be childless to be repelled by the spectacle of such fanatics hurling themselves Into Europe as if it were as tangible as the River Jordan. Carry me over into sceptical, camp ground rather than that benighted certainty called the Twenty-First Century. I must say, I'd like to be around to pick up the pieces when somebody breaks the kiddies' hearts.[10]

The Prossers stand for a way of life that conflicts with the ideals symbolized by that modern building. The audience had their role already scripted for them. They were the yobbos, a faceless nameless lot incapable of generosity, intent on destroying what they could not understand, and perhaps also intent on witnessing Osborne's own failure: "We *do* it. You *watch* it. *Come down.*" Ultimately, Osborne finds himself in a bind: as an artist speaking for others, he must hope his audience will understand him, yet, only its lack of understanding can generate the anger and excess necessary to his work. If the play had been a success, its vision would have been proven false. *Watch It Come Down* may not be a *good* play, but it is nevertheless Osborne's most necessary failure.

CHAPTER 12

Déjàvu (1992)
Elegy for Lost Origins

Déjàvu may be considered a *Look Back II,* says Osborne in an Author's Note, winking at the popular interest in sequels and the academic one in re-appropriating, rewriting, transliterating works. The play is still set in the Midlands, but now urban dreariness has made way for the peace and comfort of country living. Whereas Jimmy's attic room in a Victorian building heavily symbolized the ascent and simultaneous marginalization of a new class, a large, cozy kitchen in a tastefully renovated farm house signals the country comforts of a leisured class living off its accumulated wealth. Thirty-six years later, the ex-angry young man, known to his friends rather flashily as J.P., has been twice married and twice divorced, and is now left with a son Jim and a daughter Alison from his second marriage. Living off capital bequeathed to him by ex-father-in-law, Colonel Redfern, he has changed his habits drastically. Instead of tea, he quaffs expensive wines; instead of beer and cheese, he sups on succulent little quails. Friend Cliff, too, is better off. He has married, has two sons, and works in an executive position at the BBC.

Of the two furry creatures, the bear and the squirrel that in *Look Back* danced so congenially in celebration of Alison and Jimmy's (apparently short-lived) reconciliation, only "Teddy" has remained, but merely to serve as the butt of Cliff and J.P.'s jokes. Teddy, they claim, has left them behind to move into the twenty-first century. He has become what J.P. has always avoided becoming, namely "a member of the public" (I, 9). For purposes of abuse and mockery, Jimmy and Cliff turn Teddy, the "creeping little cuddly conformist" (II, ii, 63), into any modern social stereotype: immigrant, worker, yuppie, adolescent, gay activist, concerned citizen—all united, in Osborne's mind, by a narcissistic devotion to their own little needs:

CLIFF: He's very vulnerable.
J.P.: Aren't we all? Thin-skinned, I think you mean. Like all dissemblers, he
    shrinks from hard words. Thinks he's cuddlesome, I suppose.

213

CLIFF: He is.
J.P.: So are lioncubs. But they like raw meat.
CLIFF: Teddy's aware that to survive he must become increasingly competitive.
J.P.: So he should. (I, 23)

J.P. is as abusive as ever, but his allegiances have changed with his habits. While church bells once drove him crazy ("Wrap it up, will you? Stop ringing those bells! There's somebody going crazy in here! I don't want to hear them" (I, 25)), now he opens the window to let the sound in ("I like to *hear* them (I, 21)). He no longer longs for a "little ordinary human enthusiasm" either (I, 15); in an age marked by relentless self-expression, J.P. wants "a little warm, inhuman reticence" (I, 27). He is still troubled, though, by questions of allegiance ("Either you're with me or against me," cried the Jimmy of *Look Back*), suspecting his children of visiting him only to scrounge off and report on him to his ex-wife. What he finds in his daughter's diary, however, is only the news of her unplanned pregnancy.

As in *Look Back,* the play starts and ends with a woman ironing, while the men are reading the papers. Also as in *Look Back,* the woman thus occupied changes from Alison in the first act, to her friend Helena in the last. The pregnant Alison, in *Déjàvu* as well as in *Look Back*, leaves the house. Unlike the Alison in *Look Back,* however, her namesake in *Déjàvu* does not return in the end, nor does Helena have any qualms about leaving J.P. Summarized like this, the play seems rather poor in conception and facile in execution—an aging playwright's attempt to cash in on a previous success. In fact, nothing could be further from the truth. In *Déjàvu* , Osborne is playing a deceptive, teasing game on his audience, while simultaneously expounding, in what is for him a rather atypical way, the gist of his aesthetic philosophy.

RECEPTION

The play was published in 1991—uncharacteristically, a year before production, an interval painfully spent bickering and negotiating. To be properly symbolic, *Look Back II* had to be staged at Osborne's alma mater, the Royal Court Theatre where *Look Back in Anger* had premièred in 1956, but since George Devine's death in 1966, Osborne's relationship with the Royal Court had rapidly deteriorated. Now the institution whose survival had once depended on Osborne's box office appeal refused to stage his play. Osborne then sent *Déjàvu* to that other institution with which he had entertained a most problematic relationship, the Royal National Theatre. In 1975, the National had opened its first season in its new building across the Thames with Osborne's *Watch It Come Down,* generally considered to have been a flop. Now offered the chance to direct Osborne's first original stage play in seventeen years, director Richard Eyre declined. Bitter words followed, with Osborne claiming that both theatres had become strongholds of mediocrity.

Eventually a new venue was found, the Liverpool Playhouse, as was a director, Tony Palmer, the latter an unusual choice. Specializing in opera and music documentaries for television, Palmer had little experience with textual theatre. He had, however, directed Osborne's 1985 television film about Handel, *God Rot Tunbridge Wells!*, and, since Osborne considered his dialogues to be music, a series of arias, the choice seemed appropriate. Palmer suggested Peter O'Toole for the older Jimmy Porter, an appropriately symbolic choice. Only three years younger than Osborne, O'Toole was Jimmy Porter's contemporary. He had been involved in the early years of the Royal Court, playing Jimmy Porter in a 1957 production of *Look Back in Anger*, and had worked with Osborne and Tony Richardson in their 1968 Woodfall film production of *The Charge of the Light Brigade*. With this aging actor in the principal role, *Déjàvu* would not only be bankable but also reflect on its own past.

For O'Toole, acting in *Déjàvu* would not be without possible glory. He would be joining a tradition of star actors showcasing their skill and endurance in Osborne plays: Richard Burton in *A Subject of Scandal and Concern* and the film version of *Look Back in Anger*, Laurence Olivier in *The Entertainer*, Albert Finney in *Luther*, Nicol Williamson in *Inadmissible Evidence*, Maximilian Schell in *A Patriot for Me*, Ralph Richardson in *West of Suez*, Jill Bennett in *Time Present*, Paul Scofield in *Watch It Come Down*, and Alec Guinness in *The Gift of Friendship*. Osborne believed that his plays required "a special style of actor and special style of acting," not to make up for the deficiencies of the writing, as some evil tongues claimed, but because the lines were technically difficult to deliver:

> [My work] requires very proficient actors. That is why they are very difficult to cast. They require a great deal of pure acting skill of a special kind, I think. . . . [The actors] must have an extraordinary technique as far as using the dense text, because it always is very dense. Also, they must have a wide intellectual grasp and tremendous pure verbal facility and a great ear and stamina and a lot of power and feeling.

In his heyday, O'Toole was just such a proficient actor, with a fine technique and arresting personality. It seemed then that actor and playwright would both benefit from each other's talents.

It would have been especially reassuring for Osborne to prove with *Déjàvu* that his plays could still attract actors of O'Toole's stature, but when rehearsals were well underway, O'Toole balked at the lengthy and difficult monologues (the play was said to be four hours long) and walked out on Osborne two weeks before the opening date. Angry denunciations followed, with Osborne insisting that Peter O'Toole, or "Gloria O'Swanson," as he called the aging film actor, had neither the memory nor the stamina to learn his lines. It was a most discouraging setback. It did, however, allow for Tony Palmer to return to the play, since O'Toole had preferred not to be directed by him. Finally Peter Egan was chosen for the taxing role of J.P. A technically proficient actor, Egan lacked

O'Toole's natural perversity and audience appeal. Although with a grizzly, peevish beard, he did look rather like the elderly Osborne—which suited a play featuring a protagonist who all too clearly expounded the playwright's ideas.

With the imminent production of a play expecting to celebrate Osborne's "come-back," articles appeared documenting the playwright's life as a country squire on his new large estate in Shropshire, surrounded by his beloved dogs. Photographs showed him perusing the papers in a spacious country kitchen, against the background of an Aga—a large, hand-assembled, and fearfully expensive cast iron stove. This was all too reminiscent of the hero of *Déjàvu*—including the offhand remark, "I always thought I was better than most people. . . . And I still think I am, I really do,"[1] clearly meant to effect a snort of disbelief or outrage from the "prigs."

All in all, it was an inauspicious start, but, at least, the well-publicized quarrels with three sizable and eminent national institutions, the Royal Court, the National, and Peter O'Toole, had put the spotlight back on Osborne. The play previewed at the Thorndike Theatre in Leatherhead in May 1992 and premièred at the Comedy Theatre on 10 June 1992. It was Osborne's eighteenth and, as it happened, last West End production, the sad finale of forty-three years of working in the theatre. Various dignitaries in the world of arts and entertainment attended the first night, several (as happened to Joan Plowright) to find they were to be named and mocked in the play.

The reviews were less than enthusiastic, though the majority of them were surprisingly respectful as if, indeed, the aging playwright had become part of the national heritage. Faced with a text whose density and apparent whimsy almost defied attempts at interpretation, many sought refuge in a well-worn, frustrating line of Osborne criticism: this was not a good play, they said, but, nevertheless, "a fascinating phenomenon."[2] How low Osborne had fallen in most opinions was evident from the dubious praise some bestowed on *Déjàvu*, that it was "much better than anyone could have expected."[3] Others made a half-hearted effort to champion Osborne as a hero of straight talk—in Lynn Barber's words, "one of the last few precious bulwarks against the creeping Californian blandness of the age."[4] They thought the play was "agreeably splenetic"[5] and that "there is something exhilarating about the reactionary old whinger's rabid political incorrectness."[6]

Most were clearly puzzled by the play and uncertain about Osborne's intentions. "I never . . . used to be sure when he was being serious, or when he wasn't," Helena said of Jimmy in *Look Back* (III, i, 78). "People found it hard to know when they were being confided in or insulted," Cliff reminds the Alison of *Déjàvu*. "It was the tone of voice," J.P. explains. "But no one got it" (II, ii, 69). In what J.P. refers to as "joke abuse," it was harder than ever to trace the dividing line between humor and downright nastiness (II, ii, 62). Many failed to see the comedy in what sounded all too much like simple narrowmindedness. Others did laugh, but rather too loudly and too easily, oblivious of J.P.'s tragic side—what Osborne, in an Author's Note to the play, called his "inescapable melancholy" (vii). To them, J.P. was just another Alf Garnett, a character (rather like the American sitcom hero Archie Bunker) whose hilariously reactionary opinions aired in a hugely popular television comedy.[7]

Critics also found it difficult to evaluate what sometimes seemed Osborne's attempt to feed off his previous plays. Quite naturally, *Déjàvu* returns to *Look Back,* but anyone familiar with Osborne's work will also hear echoes from *The Entertainer, Inadmissible Evidence,* and *A Sense of Detachment*—to name just the most obvious ones. Starting with J.P.'s call to Cliff, "What ho, Bernardo!" *Déjàvu* also borrows generously from all major Shakespeare plays, most importantly *Hamlet, Macbeth, The Tempest, King Lear, Twelfth Night,* and *Henry IV.* Neither was there much new and unexpected in J.P.'s abuse of modern society: Osborne had too clearly culled it from his weekly columns for the *Spectator* and other published articles and letters. The dialogue was also teasingly specked through with mocking references to the critical reception of Osborne's plays and sometimes to their production history—arcane facts of Osbornian trivia, known only to the occasional scholar. Who, in the audience, for instance, could be expected to know that J.P.'s mention of "some cunning French play" entitled *La paix du dimanche* refers to *Look Back's* French title (I, 3).

Director Tony Palmer presented "the multiplicity of references to other literature" as the play's strongest point, adding he would "be distressed if such an amazing piece of writing totally escapes [the critics'] cloth ears."[8] Some reviewers took the self-reflexivity and metafictionality bravely in stride. Michael Billington praised the play's postmodern aspect, its self-parodic wit, and called it "a piece of discursive armchair theatre." Malcolm Rutherford, who liked the play and easily picked up on most references, nevertheless thought, "you have to be steeped in theatre fully to appreciate it." Implying that so many insider jokes intimidated or bored a typical West End spectator, he stated that Osborne's style and method in *Déjàvu* required "a regular theatre-going audience which may no longer exist."[9]

Other critics were less cautious or polite, rejecting the play for its excessive length,[10] the "scatter-gun, overlong nonsense,"[11] the "tedious string of one-liners,"[12] its "terrible tendency to rant."[13] Peter Kemp reviewing *Déjàvu* for the *TLS* was the most damning, calling it "a dull flop" and a "coarse fiasco," remarkable only for its "retarded adolescent eagerness to shock." "The relentless stream of reactionary bile becomes wearingly predictable," said Emma Lilly.[14] "The bigot returns," Di Parker started her review, before shrugging off *Déjàvu's* heroes, Cliff and J.P., with a dismissive, "this pair of 'carping dodos' did nothing for me."[15] In 1956, *Look Back's* reception had been bolstered by Kenneth Tynan's famous recommendation that he doubted if he could love anyone who did not wish to see the play. Several reviewers now repeated that phrase, but with an ironic and sometimes malicious twist. "Thirty-six years on," said Charles Spencer, "I couldn't love anyone who wholeheartedly approved of *Déjàvu*."[16] Ian Shuttleworth could not love "anyone who believed their time would more profitably be spent watching *Déjàvu* than lying in a darkened room masturbating."[17]

Déjàvu did not become the focus of a passionate debate between those who loved and those who hated the play, as had been the case with *Look Back*. Those who felt offended by the play did not rise to the bait, unwilling to grant Osborne even the consolation of his possible relevance. *Déjàvu* played to half-empty houses and fizzled out after a short run. "I don't mind the attacks," Osborne had confided to an interviewer in 1968, "but there is a special English kind of withdrawal that is particularly irksome, when they yawn. They are very good at that here."[18]

THATCHERISM

More than a comment on the quality of Osborne's work, *Déjàvu*'s production difficulties and lukewarm reception illustrated the extent to which Osborne had become a marginal figure in the theatre. It had been a long and dizzying fall, from an early media-driven success and notoriety to virtual public neglect and ridicule. Yet Osborne had not been silent during the seventeen years since *Watch It Come Down*. In 1989, the National had produced his adaptation of Strindberg's *The Father,* and Osborne had written three television plays (*You're Not Watching Me, Mummy* and *Try a Little Tenderness* in 1978; *God Rot Tunbridge Wells!* in 1985). Disappointed with current developments in the theatre, he had increasingly shifted his talents to prose writing, which proved a better medium for that density of language so natural to him. The first part of his autobiography, *A Better Class of Person* (1981) was considered a masterwork in its genre and reached a wide audience after Osborne dramatized it for television in 1985. A second, less accomplished volume, *Almost A Gentleman*, appeared in 1992, the year *Déjàvu* was produced.

He had also been busily writing minor work, having been made responsible for a weekly "Diary" column for the *Spectator,* in which he, often in an amusing way, gave vent to his ever-growing list of prejudices. In the eighties, he wrote some insightful book reviews for the *New York Review of Books* as well as a column "Looking Back on the Week's TV" for *Mail on Sunday.* The latter quickly turned into a barely disguised podium for his own, increasingly reactionary, views on every possible current issue. He had also dashed off a series of angry letters to the press, taking on everyone who infringed upon his peace and comfort: "unfairly" sued by two of his former servants, he expressed outrage at the intolerable arrogance of the modern working class ("Up the workers"[19]); fearing that an EEC regulation was going to deprive him of his beloved untipped Turkish cigarettes, he protested the insolence of Brussels; and angry at low-flying airplanes over his magnificent country estate in Kent, he complained about other people's materialism.

Snoo Wilson claimed that these articles and letters to the press did not serve Osborne well. He had become "politically unacceptable—he disqualifies himself so consistently." Their actual effect may have been more complex. Few took Osborne seriously. At his best, the gabbling old dodo could still be clever and amusing, but, to many, his outspoken views on homosexuals, immigrants, workers, and women resonated most uneasily in the political climate of the 80s and early 90s. In 1991, when the play was published, eleven years of Thatcherism (1979–1990) had just come to an end—years associated with an impatient individualism and defiance, best expressed in Thatcher's leadership style. "She doesn't have discussions, she states her opinion," one member of her cabinet said. "She is almost totally impervious to how much she offends other people."[20] What had apparently disappeared was the idea of the "just society"—in fact, perhaps of society itself. As Thatcher said in an interview for *Woman's Own* (31 October 1987), "there is no such thing as society: there are individual men and women, and there are families."

Consistent with that view, Thatcher's government abolished welfare state collectivism, selling publicly owned properties and industries often at windfall profits for the purchasers. The ideal of equalizing incomes through taxation was abandoned, public services and subsidies for education and the arts, restricted. As the welfare state was rolled back, a substantial underclass came into being, many of whom were seen roaming London's streets. Osborne may never have been a Thatcherite, as he claimed, yet eleven years of Thatcherism had promoted the kind of reactionary individualism that Osborne and his new hero J.P. seemed to embody. By 1991, Jimmy's curt reply in *Look Back*, "try washing your socks" to Cliff's complaint that his feet hurt, had lost its innocence, yet Osborne chose it as one of two epigraphs to his new play. He now wanted his audience to remember that Jimmy had always been an individualist, impatient with the whining and griping of the lower-middle class, whose philosophy, he was convinced, had been codified in the welfare state. While the Jimmy of *Look Back* had found his enemies mainly among the upper-middle class, the likes of his wife Alison and brother-in-law Nigel, the J.P. of *Déjàvu* now drastically realigns allegiances:

> No, it was the people I'd thought of as being oppressed or ignored by Nigel or Alison, Nigel and Alison, who were unteachable. They were avid and malign. Like those Ministry of Food women who used to preside over their trestle tables in provincial town halls, allocating ration books, if they felt like it, puffed up with power and illiteracy. They felt so secure behind their trestle barricades and ministerial stamps. 'You'll have to fill in Form NF72. Why haven't you got one?' They were the post-war sappers for all the rolling army of fanatics that have followed them ever since. (I, 31)

The world that Thatcher sought to erect on the ruins of the welfare state was hardly more appealing to Osborne. In 1982 Britain went to war against Argentina over the Falkland Islands, 10,000 mi. from its home shores. The

British victory, a feat of logistics as much as heroics, was by many regarded as redress for the humiliating 1956 Suez debacle. For having so dashingly put an end to self-doubt and uncertainty, Thatcher was rewarded by a landslide electoral victory in 1983. In *Déjàvu*, Suez, therefore, has become an event the young no longer care to remember. "It's mere history," J.P. says sarcastically, though for him, as for Osborne, it all too clearly is not (II, ii, 59). Osborne's career had blossomed in an impoverished England that, after the loss of its empire and its mismanagement of the Suez crisis, had anxiously turned inward. In *Déjàvu*, J.P. prays for strength to endure "the noise and clamour of those who would impose their certainties upon us. God rot their certainties. . . . Endow us with the courage of uncertainty" (III, ii, 101).

The ruling sensitivity was clearly no longer in tune with the tragic thrust of Osborne's plays. For one section of the population, Thatcher's policies brought unheard of benefits. New wealth was streaming into the country, but of a short-lived, risky kind that did little to alleviate the soaring unemployment rate. North Sea oil drilling, an answer to the OPEC oil crisis of 1974, turned Britain into a major oil producer. Most importantly, a more adventurous, sometimes reckless, finance capitalism created a new affluent class of young upwardly mobile professionals, "yuppies." England, for these people, was not much more than a temporarily advantageous position in the global flow of capital. These were, incidentally, the people whose attendance ensured a long and successful West End run for Caryl Churchill's *Easy Money* (1987), either not noticing or not caring that the play was in fact an indictment of their lifestyle.[21]

Osborne resented the internationalism of the day. For his second epigraph to *Déjàvu,* he chose a John Henry Newman verse: "Keep thou my feet; I do not ask to see / The distant scene; one step enough for me." He believed that in art attempts at reaching out toward a global audience would invariably lead to international dreariness. In an interview with Lewis Funke, he emphasized the importance of the immediate space around the artist, "rather than some rather ill-defined international space that really most of us don't take a great part in. We observe it, but we don't have much control over it." Politically, he was similarly averse to the idea of a global community. His own Euro-skepticism, in fact, far exceeded that of Thatcher, and he disapproved most heartily of her naive admiration for all things American.

Shortly after the Falklands, Thatcher turned against what she termed, "the enemy within," the unions, pitching her newly nationalized police force first against Arthur Scargill's mineworkers strike. Desperately violent rather than valiant, the mineworkers' struggle made many, including Osborne, lose sympathy for a union leader who surpassed Thatcher in ruthlessness and arrogance. Having defeated the mineworkers, Thatcher responded with similar intransigence to the 1986 printers' strike against modernization schemes enforced by media tycoon Rupert Murdoch. Her successes effectively broke the power of the unions and put an end to the corporatist spirit of the seventies that, according to some, had made the country ungovernable.

The downside of Thatcherism became glaringly evident, especially during the recession years that ended her reign. A string of financial scandals, including Robert Maxwell's appropriation of his employees' pension fund, drew attention to the unparalleled greed that had run and ruined Thatcherian economy. The extended and fortified police force was accused of brutality and unfairness, especially against the new immigrants from India, Pakistan, and Bangladesh. Educated, hardy, and experienced in business, many of these second wave immigrants prospered in Thatcher's competitive England. Their success, combined with the visibility of their cultural and religious difference, caused resentment among the increasing number of indigent British natives. While recognizing and exploiting this resentment, Thatcher's government did little to alleviate the plight of these immigrants, caught between their home culture's mistrust of their modern ways and their guest culture's suspicion of their traditions. In a most unexpected and spectacular manner, attention was drawn to their situation when Salman Rushdie, Indian-born British author of Muslim background, had to go into hiding after the 1988 publication of *Satanic Verses*.

Typically, Osborne was most unpleasantly struck, not by the brutality and hypocrisy of Thatcherism, but by the zeal with which the liberal elite rushed to the defense of Thatcher's victims. "All the most loathsome and degraded elements in society," he remarked, were "allowed to take a moral stand when their own world is as despicable as could be imagined."[22] In *Déjàvu*, J.P. teases his daughter for supporting the colliers' wives "when they were flipping concrete blocks like tiddly-winks on the heads of passing cab-drivers, scabbing lackeys of the greedy classes" (I, 29). He also resented the way the Iranian death sentence propelled Rushdie to sudden, and perhaps not quite deserved, fame, allowing him to pontificate with prophetic and often pompous assurance. In *Déjàvu*, J.P. and Cliff's quest for new and powerful swearwords tellingly settles on a vigorous "Sushdie!" "Yes. That sounds quite rude. Salman Rushdie. Sushdie. Quite filthy really" (II, ii, 69).

NEWSPEAK

Osborne's belief that liberal sensitivity, rather than dictatorial prohibition or censure, constitutes the main source of today's deep-seated conservatism became apparent in his virulent dislike of political correctness, a form of self-censorship advocated to attune speech to the varied reality of modern society.[23] As political correctness became an object of public debate around 1987, curiously coinciding with Gorbachev's policy of "glasnost " (openness) and "perestroika" (reconstruction), and thus with the end of communist threat and the Cold War, some suggested it was an attempt on the part of the political right to find a new way to discredit the ideal of the tolerant and caring society, born in the political turmoil of the late sixties. Many on the political left were as suspicious of those who denounced PC as of those who championed it, associating sanitized speech with the cautious blandness of American corporations.

Already in the late fifties, industrial psychologists had discovered that protests about working conditions could be defused by the simple strategy of renaming them. By reformulating and personalizing problems as soon as they emerged, what could have led to a serious labour dispute could be quickly contained and settled as an issue of a single worker's maladjustment.[24]

The next step was to insist workers adapt their speech to the requirements of the workplace. Speech codes served the needs of control systems based no longer on a conflict-prone hierarchical-coercive model but on the more efficient, insidious one of people management. Among a diverse and multicultural work force, the benefits were obvious: deflating race, gender, and class-based tensions created a "harassment free environment" that benefited productivity and thus the owners as well. American education, long a bastion of behaviorism, sought to benefit in similar ways from self-censorship, in the belief that changing language would change thought patterns and thus behavior. Press and politics had a more avowedly perverse attitude toward language control. Cautiously inoffensive speech ensured a cost-effective way of broadening the target audience and opened up new vistas in hypocrisy. One could now be most liberal or "correct" in speech while most conservative in action. There was, in other words, no good reason for associating self-censorship and obsessive language control exclusively with the left. In fact, many leftists saw in "political correctness" a sorry attempt to evade political problems by displacing them onto the level of language—in Terry Eagleton's words, "a self-righteous fetishism of language which is no more than a symptom of political frustration."[25]

In 1960, Osborne had thought "the greatest enemies of the English language and character, as well as its artists, are rich men, Government agencies and working intellectuals."[26] Now, he believed damage was being done to language from every side. At times it seemed, for instance, that only a small cultural elite was willing to make a last stand to safeguard the nation's language from being unduly infected by foreign barbarisms. More dangerous for the art of vituperation were the concerted attempts by "decent," "concerned" citizens to deprive the English idiom of its barbs and to make it pleasing and inoffensive. Osborne had been in the vanguard of the battle against censorship, often fighting for every word in his plays. Unofficial censorship, however, waged in the name of common sense, tolerance, even, ironically, of radicalism, proved harder to combat and its effects harder to assess. Osborne's major objection to political correctness was that it eliminated all sign of tension and conflict in discourse and thus threatened to rid language of history itself.

"When Oldspeak had been once and for all superseded, the last link with the past would have been severed."[27] Osborne saw everywhere evidence that Orwell's dire prediction was coming true. In 1980, he bristled when in the Anglican Church the Alternative Service book came to supplement or supplant Cranmer's Book of Common Prayer:

Someone once wrote of the French historian Michelet that he wrote history in a language in which it was impossible to tell the truth. Just so, the language of the Alternative Services is written in a style in which it is impossible to be religious. It blasphemes against language itself in its banality and fawning to please. As for its claims to lucidity, these are the appeals of empty men who have lost their nerve and trust in most ordinary understanding. This understanding cannot explain 'Through a glass darkly', but can be illuminated by it. [. . . .] Is it to be unchallenged that the language of liturgy should go the way of politics and become that of the grocer?[28]

In *Déjàvu,* Cranmer is J.P.'s daily bread, an offense to an ungodly age that has found a niche among the cookbooks in the kitchen. Cliff, leafing through it, reads aloud passages J.P. has marked—excerpts from The Order for the Burial of the Dead that all too ironically reflect on Cranmer's own fate:

I said I will take heed to my ways, that I offend not in my tongue. I will cup my mouth as it were a bridle. [. . . .] While the ungodly is in my sight. I held my tongue and spake nothing. I kept silent, yea, even from good words. [. . . .] But it was pain and grief to me. (II, i, 48)

The prevalence of sanitized speech led many to appreciate anew the true beauty of words. Suddenly Shakespeare, the King James version of the Bible, and the Book of Common Prayer appeared in an almost revolutionary light: "For the immediate present," Osborne concluded in an article, "the Prayer Book 1662, until it is banished from the shelves along with *Robinson Crusoe* and *Little Black Sambo,* remains the most politically incorrect Christmas gift for 1992."[29]

The moral brigade, Osborne feared, had returned, and this time with a vengeance. People who in the past were shrugged off as cultural philistines now spoke with newly acquired assertiveness. Their objective was not to investigate and experience, to go under and suffer the burden of ambiguity, but to be seen standing on the right side of every issue. This cult of smugness, Osborne feared, was receiving official sanction in college courses aimed at offering what modern society values even more than clean water and fresh air, namely a spotless conscience. Mediocrity and deep-seated conservatism now proudly marched under the banner of a radicalism that exerted itself mainly in policing other people's language. As cultural literacy decreased, people's apprehension of words increased. "Don't you think it piquant," J.P. remarks, "that a most devoutly illiterate generation should be so maidenly about the form of words?" (I, 11).

J.P.'s own language, in contrast, has become so willfully complex and dense that the audience is often left grappling for meaning. More than ever, Osborne indulges freely in games of compulsive alliteration and other verbal acrobatics: "the put-upon pit wives' excursion" (I, 6), "may the Good Lord in his everlasting chapel cheerfulness bless and keep her for taking this principality front-parlour mouse off my hands for so long" (I, 7), "a hint of hiraeth, pit-pony Porter, masquerading as a nature's thoroughbred" (I, 7). J.P. calls this display of verbal prowess "wordmanship" (I, 30). Replete with references to local figures and situations recognizable only to the pure-bred Englishman, J.P.'s language functions as a shibboleth, a smokescreen to throw off the throng of Americans, Australians, and world citizens who, he hopes, will experience the poverty of their un-English English. J.P. himself constantly draws attention to his own ability to parody every possible immigrant idiom, from West-Indian to Australian English, and for good measure, even throws in a line or two of Welsh—only of course to mock its inability to function as a complete and modern language:

> J.P.: Well, I know the Welsh for 'May I please have a packet of Daz?'
> ALISON: What is it, then?
> J.P.: (Precisely) Am cwn amwrn dai llangollen barra kowse—packet of Daz!—
> There! (I, 7)

Humor alleviates the possible meanness and smallness of such parodies. In a similar way, offensiveness always hints at a larger purpose. It is meant, we are asked to believe, to combat functionalism, the efficiency model of a one-dimensional humanity whose language is too firmly tied to the requirements of the present. The gatling gun of J.P.'s abuse, however, excels at force rather than at precision. Among his pet peeves (a trendy word of which he would disapprove) are postal codes; the Alternative Service Book; the caring industry; "pushy professors in soft jobs" (I, 16); new college courses such as Black Studies and something he refers to as "Gay Engineering" (II, ii, 60–61); "black feminist dikes" and man-haters (II, ii, 72); homosexuals who draw attention to themselves ("strutting sodomites" (I, 32), people who "wear [their] heart on [their] cock" (I, 11)); "gay-lesbian thé dansants" (I, 10); miners who are on strike but no longer look as skinny and abused as those in D.H. Lawrence; trendy bishops; nonsmoking signs; people who speak English with a different accent (Australians are the worst); people who are obsessed with the dangers of buttered toast and incest ("expert[s] on anal dilation in abused children" (I, 9)); people who turn pleasure into a problem; people who worry, especially about people they do not know; people called Kevin, Wayne, Debbie, or Trish; people whose conversations are specked through with fashionable words such as "communication skills," "challenge," "safe sex" ("like meatless steaks" (I, 12)), "senior citizen," "concern" ("Concern? The busybody's gin" (II, ii, 79)); people calling themselves "chairs" or "spokespersons"; people who feel "oppressed" ("Someone has to oppress [them] otherwise [they] wouldn't exist" (II, ii, 74)); people who speak with downward inflexions; people who believe in Europe; people who say they live in the UK ("Sounds like belonging to the Co-op" (II, ii, 57)).

We are asked to consider this offensiveness a knee-jerk response to the irritant of a complacent consensus. An Author's Note informs us that J.P. is "a man of gentle susceptibilities, constantly goaded by a brutal and coercive world" (vii). To what he believes to be the dominant melody, J.P. responds by producing the much needed counterpoint. To smoke out every possible form of priggism, targets have to be wide-ranging. Cliff calls J.P.'s glib pronouncements "grandiloquent small talk" (I, 21). Such talk is always produced in a spirit of willful but also playful contrariety, and its intention is humorous, if only because to be thus humorous doubles the offense. Osborne insists on a "*mild* delivery": "In other words, it is not necessary or advisable to express bitterness bitterly or anger angrily. Things should be delicately plucked out of the air not hurled like a protester's stones at the enemy" (vii–viii). J.P. must not be seen to be too deeply involved in his abuse and mockery. Cliff and J.P. are putting on an act, J.P. referring to Cliff as Mildred, Whittaker, or dreamboat; Cliff to J.P. as El Cheapo, Lord Sandy, daddy blue-eyes, Gaylord, whitey, Cornet, and colonel. This reinforces the irony of their exchange since, in the way of actors, they are at once playful and serious.

Yet at crucial moments, J.P.'s irony is allowed to dissolve; the two trains of thought, held together in dialectical tension, then unravel and are distributed, and most unequally so, between J.P and another character, usually Alison. This happens, for instance, after J.P. has learned, by reading Alison's diary, that Alison is going to become a "one-parent family" (I, 49):

> J.P.: You ask for hope that is in no one's gift. Certainly not mine. You wouldn't come to me.
> ALISON: You're joking.
> J.P.: Yes. Hope does not feign feeling it cannot have.
> ALISON: Don't patronize me, *Dad.*
> J.P.: It doesn't dissemble or explain what is unknowable.
> ALISON: Don't bother.
> J.P.: It is deaf to comfort and counselling.
> ALISON: You *are* deaf.
> J.P.: To those who believe their heart strings are not in place to be struck and broken . . .
> ALISON: You're broken, broken and washed up. (II, i, 50)

Here, as in other instances, the negative or deflating part of J.P.'s opinions has been projected onto Alison in order to allow J.P. a moment of seriousness. A stage direction explains that "CLIFF and ALISON may repeatedly undercut J.P.'s more lyrical flights without diminishing him, still allowing him to remain intact" (II, I, 49). The result, however, is that Alison, whose brutal comments stand in sharp contrast to the gentle poetry of her father's words, now appears to us a shallow mocker and detractor of a man who deserves our protection—all this, perversely, in the moment of her own greatest distress.

Osborne, in this and other ways, constantly builds up his hero by pulling him down. J.P. all too readily admits to being wrong, even to being a failure: "It's taken me almost, well, indeed, a lifetime to realize that I am wrong about—well, everything" (I, 25). He has no high opinion of himself; he all too readily agrees with whatever anyone accuses him of. He is "still, ultimately and finally a futile gesture," he says, believing only in, what he calls, "honest indecision" (III, i, 83). My "one and only paltry function," J.P. claims, is to "provid[e] prigs with holy unction" (III, i, 93). The reason for such humility is not difficult to surmise. J.P. is anxious to avoid having his own epithets hurled back at him, and having his abusive and judgmental language be called strident, self-righteous, shallow, or power-hungry in turn. In a laudatory foreword to a collection of Jeffrey Bernard's "Low Life" essays from the *Spectator*, Osborne pointed out that the celebrated vituperators of English literature may be impish but are nonetheless gentle spirits, in love with the spirited crack of the whip but certainly not with its bloody effects:

> Jeffrey Bernard has always been that fine figure and bane of prigs, schoolmasters and pushy careerists, a Bad Influence. What such people always overlook is that the renegades they abhor so are the least likely to want to exert influence, of all things, whether by persuasion or example. Bad influences might be envied their irresponsible freedoms but not their forfeiture of approved opinion; the country is presently stuffed with every invented machinery imaginable, committees, boards and councils, all devoted to the folly of good influences.[30]

This may be true. At the same time, there is something perverse in J.P.'s humility, which is rather that of a man who, under the guise of self-professed futility, proceeds to tell people exactly what he thinks of them. By admitting defeat even before a battle has been waged, he makes it impossible for his adversary to retort without appearing shallow, mean, and ruthless.

The end of the play corroborates this view. It seems, at one moment, that Alison, like the Alison of *Look Back,* will be returning home. When Cliff looks through the window and sees her arriving at the house, J.P. quickly improvises a welcome celebration with champagne and some of Alison's favorite music, which he detests. Not to seem too eager to receive his daughter back, he then, has to light his infernal pipe which Alison abhors; but Cliff returns with the news that Alison has again departed, having returned only to collect her things. The play ends with Cliff asleep under a newspaper, and J.P. directing himself to Teddy in an admission of defeat: "You're a lucky fellow. Mediocrity is a great comforter, my furry little ursine friend. And very democratic. It's all yours. Oh, *lucky* bears!" (III, ii, 101). This then is yet another cruel blow to the "man of gentle susceptibilities" (vii). But he will take it all bravely in stride. Before leaving the stage, J.P., armed with the superior cultural attributes of a past civilization, is allowed a pathetic moment of self-assertion, clearly aimed at making the audience uncomfortable:

> J.P. turns on the tape recorder. Champagne Aria. This time perhaps to a gen-
> uine recording. Eberhard Wechter. Or maybe just the orchestra. Whichever
> works best. Anyway, J.P. mimes to it, in his most ebullient fashion. At the end
> of it, he exits with a grand operatic flourish, the most upward theatrical inflex-
> ion he can muster. CLIFF *lies asleep beneath the newspaper.* (III, ii,
> 101–102)

J.P. clearly expects no sympathy from the "lucky bears" in the audience. He
seems in fact to believe they will not react at all, perhaps having followed
Cliff's example and fallen asleep. Nevertheless this very defeat and even failure with the audience is presented as a triumph in a sad age. J.P., the great misanthrope, is in Osborne's opinion, the only true human being left in an
inhuman world. A parenthetical remark, added to the final stage direction,
reveals Osborne thumbing his nose at an audience who is not even expected
to understand:

> (In the unlikely event of audience dissent at the end of the performance, the
> loud playing of martial music can be effective. 'Molonello' played by the
> Grenadier Guards, the quick march 'St. Patrick's Day' or, to be more 'Euro-
> pean,' the 'Radetzky'.)

LOST ORIGINS

There is something desperately assertive in having an unsuccessful play and
an only partially successful career conclude with military music. A little more
than two years before Osborne's death, Matt Wolf, reviewing *Déjàvu*, declared,
in what turned out to be an unexpected prophecy, that it amounted to "a staged
obituary." Osborne left several projects unfinished at his death, and *Déjàvu*
was indeed to remain his last major work.[31] It was as if, with this final return
to *Look Back,* Osborne had rolled up his career and walked it not only off the
stage but into the grave. Quotations from the Burial of the Dead and Tennyson's *In Memoriam* ("Ring in the larger heart . . . the kindlier hand . . . Ring
out the darkness of the land" (I, 21)) endow *Déjàvu* with an unmistakably elegiac quality.

Death was, of course, already tangibly present in *Look Back.* Haunted by
the memory of his dying father at whose deathbed he, as a ten year old, learned
about "love . . . betrayal . . . and death," the adult Jimmy felt called upon to
comfort the dying Mrs. Tanner, the woman who had set him up in a sweetstall
and whom he loved as much as he hated his own mother. In *Déjàvu,* J.P. is still
similarly compassionate, but now about his old dying dog—only to be mocked
for it by his daughter ("Go on. Talk to your bloody dog. She can't answer back"
(I, 36)). Finally, the line of deaths connecting *Déjàvu* to *Look Back* tightens
when Jimmy receives a phone call with the news that his friend Hugh, Mrs.
Tanner's son, has died in the United States from a "mysterious" illness—AIDS

to anyone who associates Hugh with Osborne's one-time friend, director and film maker Tony Richardson.

Finally, the deaths, inevitable betrayals, and departures in *Déjàvu* and in *Look Back* are offset by *chosen* acts of loyalty and love. Jimmy rejected his mother whom he believed to be heartless but bestowed his filial devotion unstintingly upon his friend's mother. Though he hated his mother-in-law with a passion, he did feel sympathy for her rather lost and bewildered husband, retired army officer Colonel Redfern, who, we learn from *Déjàvu,* returned this sympathy with a legal bequest to J.P. In a gesture reminiscent but exceeding that of Maitland in *Inadmissible Evidence,* J.P. rejects his daughter Alison as well as his son Jim. Again, this act is counterbalanced by a chosen act of loyalty to his godson, Hugh's son Ned, who "doesn't throw up at the sight of a little mess of muddled enthusiasm" (III, i, 94).

What speaks out of this medley of bonds ruptured and forged is a deep distress at the thought of being bound securely within the flow of history or determined by one's biologically given, factual origins. Tolerable and indeed desirable are only the largely mythical ones (an intense, but after all only partial memory of a dying father, for instance). Osborne's heroes prefer to choose their own parents or sons or, even better, to locate them safely in the mist of memory. In the latter case, the child becomes to some extent the offspring of his own illusion. Some of the mythical quality of the imagined father then rubs off on the son who, quite aptly, sees himself writ larger than life—at once more real than anyone else and yet more dramatically grand. It is this view of himself that makes Jimmy shout, "I may write a book about us all. It's all here. *(Slapping his forehead.)* Written in flames a mile high. And it won't be recollected in tranquillity either, picking daffodils with Auntie Wordsworth. It'll be recollected in fire, and blood. My blood" (II, i, 54). Quite fittingly, Alison reaches a similar dramatically enhanced self-image only by losing her child: "It doesn't matter! I was wrong, I was wrong! I don't want to be neutral, I don't want to be a saint. I want to be a lost cause. I want to be corrupt and futile!" (III, ii, 95). This voluptuous surrender to drama is likewise built on a sense of irreparable loss.

That *Déjàvu* is more than just a sequel to *Look Back* becomes evident in the importance it assigns to J.P.'s relationship with young Jimmy, the son whose absence is imposed by the play's structural parallels with *Look Back.* As a modern day rebel, young Jimmy is the opposite of the Jimmy Porter from *Look Back.* Rather than being mired in impotently raging anger, he roams the countryside, setting fire to relics of Britain's imperial past. When young Jimmy vandalizes an ancient country church, he smashes a memorial to Cornet Shanks, a common soldier who died in 1857 from wounds incurred during an Indian mutiny, when he heroically led the troops into battle after his captain had been wounded (II, i, 47). Such sparkle and panache spent on a losing battle is very much in line with the "knight in shiny armour" image, introduced in *Look Back* to explain Alison's otherwise unlikely infatuation with Jimmy, though was not the only valiant knight in that play. Much like Cornet Shanks, Jimmy's father had died of wounds incurred in a lost battle—admittedly, against rather than in service of an oppressor, namely on the Republican side in the Spanish Civil War. In his turn, Jimmy followed his father's example by fighting—without results but with great expense of energy—a world deprived of the "good, brave causes" of the past. In *Déjàvu,* Osborne ensured that the spectator would equate Shanks with the trumpet playing J.P. by having Cliff refer to the latter as "Cornet" (III, ii, 101). With one sledgehammer blow, young Jimmy has killed off three knights, Cornet Shanks, J.P., and J.P.'s father.

This blow establishes a clear-cut difference between the two generations. The first Jimmy mourned the loss of a father he had never truly known; the second symbolically kills a father he believes he knows all too well. The rebellion of the first Jimmy was inspired by a tragic awareness of the necessary insufficiency of the present measured against the immensity of an impossible longing. Out of this emerged drama—or at least an artistically enhanced self-image. Rather than seeking to relieve himself in destruction, Jimmy desired nothing but to pitch against the resulting smallness and tedium of reality his own unparalleled acuteness of feeling. In doing so, he hoped to achieve nothing, except perhaps to instill in others a similar visionary striving to regain in the future what was lost in the past—namely a fullness of being, the illusory nature he is all too ironically aware of. In contrast, the second Jimmy's rebellion is neither tragic nor comic, lacking the intensity of feeling typical of the first and the irony necessary for the latter. Drawing attention to nothing but itself, it is criminal rather than artistic, an attempt to arrive at certainty and self-sufficiency through patricide, destruction of patrimony, refutation of lineage, refusal of tradition—and, what is more important, through erasure of the *myth* of origin. Young Jim is not sensitive to soldier Shanks' tragic or chivalrous aura, thinking of him quite simply as a servant of the oppressing and imperialistic class.

Youth seeks to "erase the past"; according to J.P. their motto is "don't miss what you've never had. Or thought you never had" (III, i, 83). "Unconnected to the past," (which, for J.P., means the *dream* of the past), they are also "hopeless about the future" (II, ii, 64–65), though they may have learned to mask their cynicism with a PC-lingo of care and concern. Like Maitland in *Inadmissible Evidence,* one of the many Osborne plays to which *Déjàvu* constantly refers, J.P. hates youth because, no longer troubled by a thirst for the absolute, it lives untouched in unshakeable certainty and self-adoration. In one of *Déjàvu*'s most arresting passages, a field of waving young arms at a rock concert fades into the choreographed mass movements of Nazi rallies in Nuremberg before turning into a deadly sea of conformity, poisoning all individual hope and aspiration:

Are you going to your concert, your gig, tonight? . . . Are you going to *wave?*
Have you noticed . . . how they wave, like fields of rape, have you watched,
they sway, like multitudinous stalks, they wave, limp and twitching like
bleary puppies. Watch me, wave, wave and sway, come . . . wave and sway.
O wave new world, proud and sound, brave, young fearless, numb and gorm-
less, they wave, side to side, arms stretched up, worshipping, side to side,
fixed on the choreographic grunt, so tangible in the fullness of its torpor.
Nuremberg was never so fine, so fluent. They are young, their hard baby fists
softly flailing at the air, remote, in their thrumping, plaintive battering uni-
son, boning fields, landscapes of them, a prairie of Babel, waving and smashing, waving, fingers fluttering, beating, supplicant wings to what we know
not, wave, sway stare gaze, wave, wave . . . deafening, submerging, deadly,
sea plants limp and poisonous, wading . . . (I, 35)

In contrast, haunted by a mythical past, J.P. remains a loner and an outsider, unable ever to fit into the present. Compared to that image of the past,
the present is either too depressingly the same or too regrettably different. This
indeed is the vision that *Look Back* developed from its opening lines: "Why
do I do this every Sunday? Even the book reviews seem to be the same as last
week's. Different books—same reviews" (I, 10). The book reviews, of course,
only appeared to be the same. *Look Back* is built around a number of deceptive repetitions, most obviously in the mirroring of Acts I and III, starting with
a woman ironing while the men lounge in their chairs and bury themselves
under the papers. Jimmy, once again, sighs, "Why do I spend half of Sunday
reading the papers?" (III, i, 75). Again, Jimmy asks Cliff to take off a garment
so as to have it ironed on the spot. Again the woman must defend her ironing
board as the men tumble about the place, but as Cliff remarks privately to
Jimmy, "it's not the same, is it?" Jimmy bursts out, "No, of course it's not the
same, you idiot! It never is! Today's meal is always different from yesterday's
and the last woman isn't the same as the one before. If you can't accept that,
you're going to be pretty unhappy, my boy" (III, i, 83).

The unhappy boy, however, is Jimmy, who is clearly less troubled by repetition than by the realization that nothing can be quite the way it was before.
Time brings inexorable loss. Alison is gone, and though Jimmy continues his
life in the usual way, doing the usual things, but with Helena at his side now,
he cannot find rest. Would it not be better then to accept the impossibility of
repetition and start something completely new? When Cliff decides to leave,
Jimmy is ready to do exactly that: "I'll close that damned sweet-stall," he tells
Helena, "and we'll start everything from scratch" (III, i, 86). Ironically, as soon
as he decides to change his life drastically, Alison walks into the room, and his
old life catches up with him. If one cannot repeat the old life, one can never
quite start anew either. One is stuck between the old and the new, unable to
return, unable to proceed—an absurdist-existentialist message obscured by
Look Back's down-to-earth realism and welter of allusions to contemporary

politics. French productions, on the other hand, by cleverly re-titling the play *La paix du dimanche,* emphasized the link between ennui and despair.

"Why do I do this every Sunday?" J.P. wonders yet again in the opening scene of *Déjàvu.* "I keep thinking it's Friday."

> CLIFF: Well, it's Sunday.
> J.P.: La paix du dimanche.
> CLIFF: What's that?
> J.P.: Some cunning French play I expect. All bombast and logic and no balls.
> (I, 3)

In *Look Back,* the passion (the balls) hid the logic, but in returning to that play *Déjàvu* emphasizes the latter in a way quite unusual for Osborne. *Déjàvu* relates to *Look Back* as the latter play's third act relates to its first—namely, as a deceptive repetition and therefore as an equally deceptive closure. "The original character of J.P. was widely misunderstood," Osborne states in an Author's Note, "largely because of the emphasis on the element of 'anger' and the newspaper invention of 'angry young man'." Apparently, Osborne wrote *Déjàvu* to save *Look Back* from those "dubious and partisan 'academics'" whose "wearisome theories about J.P.'s sadism, anti-feminism, even closet homosexuality are still peddled to gullible students." If those were indeed his intentions, then Osborne used a peculiar method of realizing them, since J.P.'s behavior is only bound to increase the original misunderstanding being no less sadistic, misogynistic, or campy than Jimmy's supposedly was.

On the level of production, by calling *Déjàvu Look Back II,* Osborne wants the audience to believe that the character it sees is the Jimmy Porter of *Look Back,* only thirty-six years older. If the audience allows J.P. to re-appropriate *Look Back,* by taking his interpretation of the youthful Jimmy as the final and authentic one, then it simultaneously allows Osborne to re-appropriate his play from the critics. The play then, so to speak, folds back into its maker. Yet a point that *Déjàvu* most eloquently argues is that repetition never involves recovery, that the past is inexorably, always already, lost. This is why, in the final instance, "J.P. is a comic character," as Osborne continues his explanation in the Author's Note. "He generates energy but, also, . . . an inescapable melancholy" (vii). The comic element lies in an expenditure of energy which is necessarily futile and therefore creates a melancholy that is inescapable. In other words, J.P. is a comic character but only in a tragic sense, in the way of Vladimir and Estragon in Beckett's *Waiting for Godot* (1953) who cannot go on, yet must go on.

This nostalgia for a past that can no longer be recuperated is at the heart of Osborne's work, and in *Look Back* most strikingly present in Jimmy's sympathy for Alison's father, Colonel Redfern, who represents the comfortable certainties of the Edwardian era. It was then already clear that Jimmy realized that memories of the past are nearly by definition false, colored, as they are, by our unhappiness with the present:

> The old Edwardian brigade do make their brief little world look pretty tempting. All home-made cakes and croquet, bright ideas, bright uniforms. Always the same picture: high summer, the long days in the sun, slim volumes of verse, crisp linen, the smell of starch. What a romantic picture. Phoney too, of course. It must have rained sometimes. Still, even I regret it somehow, phoney or not. If you've no world of your own, it's rather pleasant to regret the passing of someone else's. (I, 17)

Regret, the sense of loss, is built on a fantasy of a perhaps never existing fullness of being. Yet Osborne never questions the importance of longing for a past, whether "phoney or not." Thirty-six years later, J.P. returns to that moment:

> The *on dit* is that there never were long days in the sun, the slim volumes of verse. If the linen was crisp, some laundry maid's cracked hands had paid the price for it. As for the smell of starch, it was quite possibly poisonous and nothing so special. No, not only did we, did I at least, footlingly regret the passing of other people's worlds, they were ones we'd just confected for our vulgar comfort." (I, 32)

This is clearly only mockingly an admission of error to those who have missed the whole point of dreaming about a non-existing past. J.P. returns yet again to this point in a cloyingly sentimental song, "In a Little Gypsy Tea Room." A bout of inclement weather drives two people into a tea shop where a fortune teller predicts to one of them that "someone in the tea room,/ Would steal my heart away." "Do you suppose there ever was such a thing as a gypsy tea room?" J.P. asks, mockingly referring to his misrepresentation of the Edwardian Age. In a few lines then, he explains what draws him to the song:

> J.P.: I can see the girl in it. I can certainly see myself. (*Sings:*) 'You made a dream come true.'
> CLIFF: 'It made me feel quite gay.' Pretty poor tea, I should think.
> J.P.: Oh, I don't know. Hot buttered toast, oozing with cholesterol. Some dainty cakes. Of course, the Gypsy Tea Room, if it existed, which it didn't, wasn't Edwardian, so it wouldn't have been too robust, even in the imagination. I think I'd have been a small boy in the corner, watching the man and the girl come in from the rain, thinking of myself as him. (I, 34)

So J.P. thinks of himself as the girl but also as a little boy who sees himself in the man who sees the girl through the fortuneteller's eyes. It is only after the fortuneteller sees this love reflected in tea leaves that the man finds his love in the girl who has accompanied him inside to shelter from the rain. The girl in the song indeed "made a dream come true": a dream preceded reality.

This idea, finally, is embodied in the play itself. *Déjàvu* is a fiction based on another fiction, and J.P. is a fictional character aware of and suffering from his own fictionality. He sometimes admits he "was quoting, actually" and is accused by Cliff of "plagiarizing" himself (II, ii, 68). J.P. therefore has reason to feel "very Dayzhar Voo." Meta-fictionality, the belief of being an offspring of a fiction, is at once the natural, realistic way of being. People thought I was already déjàvu, when I first appeared on the scene in *Look Back,* J.P. explains, referring to reviewers' constant taunts that they had seen it all before, done elsewhere, and usually better. The whole question of originality is quite mistakenly put in such terms: "Let me explain if I can penetrate the mists of your radical squalor," J.P. begins:

> Our furry friend Teddy is *not déjàvu,* as you, and a million other clockwork cunts, would have it. Very simply because he is *not* something which you have 'already seen'—literal translation from a forever foreign tongue. Thus, *déjàvu.* The meaning of which is quite simply the sensation of apparently recognizing some person or event which you could not possibly have ever witnessed. In other words, a deluded sense of recall, a *recherché* experience which could not have ever possibly taken place and most certainly not privy to the likes of canting pillocks like yourself. (I, 19–20)

In this view of a necessarily "deluded sense of recall," J.P. now firmly embeds his philosophy of anger. In 1956, scores of reviewers wondered what Jimmy was so angry about. *Déjàvu* offers a correction and an answer:

> Anger is not *about* ... It is mourning the unknown, the loss of what went before without you, it's the love another time but not this might have sprung on you, and greatest loss of all, the deprivation of what, even as a child, seemed to be irrevocably your own, your country, your birthplace, that, at least, is as tangible as death. (I, 36)

Out of longing, in other words, grows an unbearable dissatisfaction that speaks with the voice of anger, which is, however, at once the voice of grief. This is the philosophy, arguably the neurosis, that colored all Osborne's work and that he most faithfully adhered to, even when it interfered with the ostensibly political message of his plays. In the final instance, he is to be commended for having had the courage to fail. Even if only for its willful perversity, Osborne's work will endure as an inexhaustible subject of analysis and discussion.

A Note on Further Reading

A good way to start the study of Osborne's work and reception is to read the following monographs: Martin Banham, *Osborne* (Edinburgh: Oliver and Boyd, 1969); Alan Carter, *John Osborne* (Edinburgh: Oliver and Boyd, 1969); Ronald Hayman, *Contemporary Playwrights: John Osborne* (London: Heinemann, 1969); Simon Trussler, *John Osborne* (British Council, 1969); Harold Ferrar, *John Osborne* (New York and London: Columbia UP, 1973); Herbert Goldstone, *The Achievement of John Osborne* (University Press of America, 1982); Arnold P. Hinchliffe's *John Osborne* (Boston: Twayne, 1984); Eugene Prater, *An Existential View of John Osborne* (Pine Hill: Freeman, 1993). John Russell Taylor edited a useful collection of critical essays on *Look Back in Anger,* published in Macmillan's casebook series (London, 1969), and Malcolm Page compiled short critical reviews in *File on Osborne* (London: Methuen, 1988). The most recent and complete bibliography on Osborne can be found in Patricia Denison's *John Osborne: A Casebook* (New York and London: Garland, 1997) that also contains a handy chronology of Osborne's life and work and ends with a list of ten additional bibliographies.

Notes

CHAPTER 1

1. "John Osborne in Conversation with Dilys Powell," transcript of a 1976 interview, British Council Literature Study Aids, 1977.
2. Hunter Davies, "I Need To Be Reminded I Was Once Alive," *The Independent*, 26 April 1994.
3. David Hare, "A Lifelong Satirist of Prigs and Puritans," *The Spectator*, 10 June 1995: 24.
4. John Osborne, "They Call It Cricket," *Declaration,* ed. Tom Maschler (London: MacGibbon & Kee, 1957) 76.
5. Irving Wardle, "Revolt Against the West End," *Horizon* 5 (Jan. 1963): 26–33. "John Osborne's Views Not Shared," *Evening News*, 15 October 1957 reported that chairman of the English Stage Company Neville Blond distanced himself from Osborne's views on the monarchy. At the last minute, the English Stage Company canceled the RCT party for the publication of *Declaration,* in which Osborne's views on the monarchy were expressed.
6. John Osborne, "They Call it Cricket" 83.
7. John Osborne, "They Call It Cricket" 67.
8. John Osborne, "Playwrights and South Africa," *The Times*, 16 May 1968. Repr. *Damn You, England.* 218–219.
9. John Osborne, "Fighting Talk," *Reynold News*, 17 February 1957. Repr. in *Damn You, England* 187–190.
10. Kenneth Tynan, "The Men of Anger," *Holiday* 23 (1958) 179.
11. John Osborne, "A Letter to My Fellow Countrymen," *Tribune*, 18 August 1961. Repr. *Damn You, England* 193–94.
12. Lionel Clay, "With Osborne and the Nudists on the Riviera," *The Daily Mail*, 19 August 1961.
13. *A Full Life: John Osborne in Conversation with Jill Cohrane,* Producer Anthony Howard, Executive producer John Miller, Research Bill Thomson.
14. Walter Wager, ed., "John Osborne," *The Playwrights Speak* (New York: Dell, 1967) 107–08.
15. Polly Devlin, "John Osborne," *Vogue* June 1964: 99.
16. John Osborne, "They Call It Cricket" 78.
17. "John Osborne Talks to Kenneth Tynan—Candidly," *Atlas* September 1968: 57.
18. "John Osborne Talks to Kenneth Tynan—Candidly," *Atlas* September 1968: 56.
19. John Osborne, "Voting Pattern," *Observer*, 6 October 1974. Repr. in *Damn You, Eng-*

land 197–198. In "John Osborne Talks to Kenneth Tynan—Candidly," *Atlas* September 1968: 57, however, Osborne claimed not to have voted "since 1951."

20. In 1967, Osborne had the following to say about his 1961 participation in the anti-nuclear sit-down at Trafalgar Square and about left-wing activism in general: "I resolved then that I should never engage in this kind of concerted affair again unless some unforeseeable situation should arise. . . . There is an odour of psychopathic self-righteousness about many of the hardy annual protesters which I find ludicrous and distasteful. . . . . The same principle applies to the Vietnam War, the very name of which has become a synonym for left-wing sanctimony. I have not been able to come to a clear resolution over this or many other political dilemmas. I do know that I see little to choose between Communist police terrorism and shoddy American power politics. Except that I find the latter minimally less repugnant." (John Osborne, "Supporting the Cause," *Encounter* September 1967. Repr. in *Damn You, England* 196–97: 196.

21. John Osborne, "Dear Diary," *Spectator*, 20 June 1992. Repr. in *Damn You, England* 203–206: 205.

22. John Osborne, "Smokeless Zone," *The Times*, 26 December 1991. Repr. in *Damn You, England* 220–221.

23. John Osborne, "Treason of the Clerics," *The Oldie*, 11 December 1992. Repr. in *Damn You, England* 233–234.

24. Robert Chesshyre, " 'Fifty is a young age' for an angry man," *The Observer*, 18 November 1979.

25. *A Full Life: John Osborne in Conversation with Jill Cohrane,* Producer Anthony Howard, Executive producer John Miller, Research Bill Thomson.

26. In "The Lord Thy God is an Angry God" (typescript available at the Harry Ransom Humanities Research Center, Austin, Texas, John Osborne Collection, File 25.18:3–4), Osborne distances himself from politicians on the extreme right and left, as well as from PM Margaret Thatcher as from union leader Arthur Scargill.

27. Georgiana Howell, "Look Back in Candour," *The Sunday Times*, 13 October 1991.

28. In his "Dear Diary" *Spectator* column of 20 June 1992 (repr. in *Damn You, England* 203–206: 204), Osborne points out that he had always been politically incorrect, from his very first play onwards. He admits that he once believed he was a socialist, yet insists that later on, when he was being accused of being reactionary, he was no longer committed to any political party.

29. In broad terms this is also Kingsley Amis' argument in "Why Lucky Jim Turned Right," *What Became of Jane Austen? And Other Questions* (New York: Harcourt Brace Jovanovich, 1971) 200–211.

30. David Hare, "A Lifelong Satirist of Prigs and Puritans," *The Spectator*, 10 June 1995.

31. Lynn Barber, "Bad Behaviour," *The Independent*, 2 February 1992.

32. "Earlier this year he successfully sued the *Daily Mail* when a columnist, quoting an epithet that first appeared in the *Sunday Express,* used the phrase 'original teddy boy.' He didn't claim damages." "John Osborne," *The Observer*, 17 May 1959.

33. Hunter Davies, "I Need to be Reminded I Was Once Alive," *The Independent*, 26 April 1994.

34. The letter can be found in the Harry Ransom Humanities Research Center, at Austin, Texas, John Osborne Collection, 43.1 Correspondence Fans and Friends 1965–82.

35. Melvyn Bragg, "A Line-Up of One-Liners," *Observer*, 8 June 1986.

36. Hunter Davies, "I Need to be Reminded I Was Once Alive," *The Independent*, 26 April 1994.

37. For similar descriptions of the effect Osborne's appearance made on an interviewer, see, for instance, "Good-Natured Man," *New Yorker*, 26 October 1957 and Polly Devlin, "John Osborne," *Vogue*, June 1964: 98–99, 152, 168. Hunter Davies in "I Need to be Reminded I Was Once Alive," *The Independent*, 26 April 1994, also remarks on Osborne "doing his Noel Coward bit." Lynn Barber in "Bad Behaviour,"

The Independent, 2 February 1992, describes Osborne's "dandified clothes, silk scarves and signet rings" and also notes that he "adopts many of the theatrical affectations of a bygone age."

38. Lynda Lee-Potter, "He Made Me Realise That Loving Someone Is the Best Way to Live," *Daily Mail*, 27 January 1995: 20–21.

39. Barbie Dutter, "Osborne Looks Back in Anger," *Guardian*, 3 June 1995.

40. See, for instance, J.P.'s words in *Déjàvu* I, 31: "I did think . . . that those with what you might call privilege . . . [were] unteachable. But I was wrong. No, it was the people I'd thought of as being oppressed or ignored by [the privileged class] . . . who were unteachable. They are avid and malign."

41. In his "Dear Diary" column (*The Spectator*, 17–24 December 1994), Osborne complained that championing homosexual causes can be equally irritating as denouncing them.

42. Article reprinted in *Damn You, England* 255–258.

43. John Osborne, *Almost a Gentleman* 235.

44. Stephen Williams in *The Evening News*, qtd. in *John Osborne: Look Back in Anger, A Casebook*, ed. John Russell Taylor (London: Macmillan, 1968) 43.

45. John Osborne, "Laurence Olivier," rev. of Donald Spoto, *Laurence Olivier, Spectator*, 19 October 1991. Repr. in *Damn You, England* 127.

46. Lynn Barber, "Bad Behaviour," *The Independent*, 2 February 1992. For Osborne's own account of his encounter with Noel Coward, see *Almost a Gentleman* 271.

47. Walter Wager, ed., "John Osborne," *The Playwrights Speak* (New York: Dell, 1967) 92.

48. Anthony Page, "Inadmissible Epitaph," *Weekend Guardian*, 6–7 June 1992.

49. Nicholas de Jongh, "The Secret Gay Love of John Osborne," *Evening Standard*, 24 January 1995: 12.

50. John Osborne, "Dear Diary," *Spectator*, 30 May 1992. Repr. in *Damn You, England* 128–31. In a four-page, single-spaced private letter to Tony Richardson, dated 10 May 1967, signalling the breakup of their fruitful collaboration, Osborne presented the case differently. Pursuing the fiction of Tony's heterosexuality, he claimed, had posed an unbearable strain on friendships. It is not the reticence he attacked, however, but the use of it to force others into compliance. John Osborne Collection, Harry Ransom Humanities Research Center, Austin, Texas.

51. David Nathan, "John Osborne—Is His Anger Simmering?" *The Curtain Rises: An Anthology of the International Theater* (London: Leslie Frewin, 1966) 244–247: 246.

52. John Osborne, "Max Miller," *Observer*, 19 September 1965. Repr. in *Damn You, England* 115–118: 117.

53. John Osborne, *A Better Class of Person* 210 and *Almost a Gentleman* 168.

54. John Osborne, *Better Class* 226.

55. John Osborne, *Better Class* 224, 232.

56. "But if one can't have friendliness, acrimony is preferable to indifference. Indifference is awful." Helena Matheopoulos, "This is what I expect of a woman . . ." no bibl info.

57. Longfellow, "In Memory of Mrs Fanny Kemble's Readings of Shakespeare, 1847–49."

58. Critics who engage in "pedantic, literal-minded flap over inessentials" are targeted in Osborne's article on Tennessee Williams, published in the *Observer* on 20 January 1957. Reprinted in *Damn You, England* 66–68.

59. Robert Chesshyre, " 'Fifty Is a Young Age' For an Angry Man," *The Observer* 18 November 1979.

60. Osborne uses the analogy between penis and pen to good effect in his essay on Joe Orton who "enjoyed the cut and thrust of both hugely, voraciously and ruthlessly." *Spectator* 29, November 1986. Reprinted in *Damn You, England* 76.

61. John Osborne, "Schoolmen of the Left," *Observer*, 30 October 1960. Repr. in *Damn You, England* 14.
62. Walter Wager, ed., "John Osborne," *The Playwrights Speak* 98.
63. Grandfather Grove had a rather more intimate relationship with the theatre. He was rumored to have slept with the music hall artiste Mary Lloyd, an anecdote that John Osborne never tired of repeating. See John Osborne, "They Call It Cricket," *Declaration* 81–82. See also, "Osborne the Romantic," *Times*, 28 August 1970.
64. See the following statement from Michael Billington's obituary of John Osborne: "From the start, he was always a rebel. When a master struck the 16-year-old Osborne at school, he responded by striking back" ("A Prisoner of Dissent," *The Guardian*, 27 December 1984.) See also, Kenneth Tynan, "The Men of Anger," *Holiday* 23 (1958): 179 and "Profile: John Osborne," *The Observer* 17 May 1959.
65. John Osborne, *A Better Class of Person* 55.
66. John Osborne, *Better Class* 101.
67. John Osborne, *Better Class* 271.
68. John Osborne, *Better Class* 100.
69. John Osborne, *Better Class* 109.
70. John Osborne, *Better Class* 104.
71. John Osborne, *Better Class* 127.
72. John Osborne, *Better Class* 141.
73. John Osborne, "Ensemble Performance," *Sunday Times*, 30 September 1956. Repr. in *Damn You, England* 5.
74. John Osborne, *Almost a Gentleman* 31.
75. "John Osborne Talks to Kenneth Tynan—Candidly," *Atlas* September 1968: 56.
76. "John Osborne in Conversation with Iain Johnstone," *The Listener*, 3 July 1969.
77. W.J. Weatherby, "Middle Age of the Angry Young Men," *Sunday Times Magazine*, 1 March 1981.
78. One of these statements, which I am unhappily not allowed to quote verbatim, defines the Welfare State as a society of sulking people, constantly pressured by social obligations. Notebook 1954, qtd. in *Better Class*, 262.
79. Ivor Brown, "The High Froth," *Drama*, 98 (1967) 32–34.
80. "John Osborne Talks to Kenneth Tynan—Candidly," *Atlas*, September 1968: 56.
81. Georgiana Howell, "Look Back in Candour," *The Sunday Times* 13 October 1991.
82. John Osborne, "Dear Diary," *Spectator*, 24 April 1993. Repr. in *Damn You, England* 236–37.
83. John Osborne, "Max Miller," *Observer*, 19 September 1965. Repr. in *Damn You, England* 115.
84. Qtd. by David Hare in "A Lifelong Satirist of Prigs and Puritans," *The Spectator*, 10 June 1995: 27.
85. John Osborne, *A Better Class of Person* 142.
86. John Osborne, "A Letter to My Fellow Countrymen," *Tribune*, 18 August 1961. Repr. in *Damn You, England* 193.

CHAPTER 2

1. *Evening News*, 19 November 1955.
2. Kenneth Pearson, "George Devine Wraps Up a Dream," *The Curtain Rises: An Anthology of the International Theater* (London: Leslie Frewin, 1966) 187.
3. David Rabe, afterword, *Hurlyburly* (New York: Grove, 1985).
4. John Osborne, "All Words and No Performance," *The Times,* 14 October 1967. Repr. in *Damn You, England* 17–21: 20–21.
5. Carl Hare, "Creativity and Commitment in Contemporary British Theatre," *Humanities Association Bulletin* 16 (1965) 21–28.
6. Angus Wilson, "New Playwrights," *Partisan Review* 25 (1959) 632.

7. Gareth Lloyd Evans, *The Language of Modern Drama* (Dent, London, Melbourne and Toronto: Rowman and Littlefield, 1977) 228, 236–7.

8. Examples are Alan Bates, Michael Caine, Chris Harris, Albert Finney. Gordon Rogoff, "Richard's Himself Again: Journey to an Actor's Theatre," *Tulane Drama Review* 11 (1966) 29–40: 33.

9. "Osborne's Royal Fairy-Tale," *The Sunday Times*, 29 April 1962.

10. The blurb on the dust jacket of the script's printed edition reinforces this idea, stating that "few could have foreseen that it would become the most discussed and widely viewed film of the year and winner of a score of awards."

11. Page numbers refer to Robert Hughes, ed, *Tom Jones: A Film Script by John Osborne* (New York: Grove Press, 1964). The film script was published first by Faber and Faber in London. Robert Hughes' American edition features over 200 stills and follows the movie much more closely than the English edition does. An attempt has also been made to make the script more readable, to turn it into a "photo-roman."

12. "I have done lots of film scripts that never saw the light of day—*The Hostage, The Secret Agent*—for enormous sums of money, to pay off the Inland Revenue," says Osborne in W.J. Weatherby, "Middle Age of the Angry Young Men," *Sunday Times Magazine*, 1 March 1981.

13. The script was finely finished by Osborne's friend Charles Wood.

14. Milton Shulman, "It's the Osborne Mixture Again," *Evening Standard*, 12 February 1958.

15. Kenneth Tynan, "A Phony or a Genius?" *Observer*, 16 February 1958.

16. Harold Hobson, "Light From Spain," *Sunday Times*, 16 February 1958.

17. Charles Hussey, "Osborne Looks Forward in Anger," *New York Times Magazine*, 25 October 1964.

18. Hunter Davies, "I Need to be Reminded I Was Once Alive," *The Independent*, 26 April 1994.

19. Harold Clurman, "The World of John Osborne," *The Observer*, 10 May 1959.

20. W.J. Weatherby, "Middle Age of the Angry Young Men," *Sunday Times Magazine*, 1 March 1981.

21. Charles Hussey, "Osborne Looks Forward in Anger," *New York Times Magazine*, 25 October 1964.

22. Milton Shulman, "Osborne Misses With Both Barrels," *Evening Standard*, 20 July 1962.

23. W.A. Darlington, "More Lines For England," *Daily Times*, 20 July 1962.

24. "First of the Angry Young Men: Phrase-maker's 'Shame'," *Daily Telegraph*, 2 October 1957: George Fearon, claiming authorship of the term in a letter to the editor, complains of its exaggeratedly widespread use.

25. Angela Hague, "Picaresque Structure and the Angry Young Novel," *Twentieth-Century Literature* 32.2 (1986): 209–220.

26. John Barber, "The Big Hates of an Angry Young Man," *Daily Express*, 14 October 1957.

27. Some of them, however, were truly very young. Michael Hastings was eighteen when his play *Don't Destroy Me* was produced in 1957, Jane Gaskell sixteen at the publication of her novel *Strange Evil* that same year. Shelagh Delaney, "the Françoise Sagan of Salford," was nineteen when in 1958 Joan Littlewood's Theatre Workshop produced her play *A Taste of Honey*. An instant success, it transferred to the West End shortly after. After the relative failure of her next play *Lion in Love* (1961), Delaney disappeared from the public eye to pursue a quieter career, writing for radio and television.

28. Morton Kroll, "The Politics of Britain's Angry Young Men," *Western Political Quarterly* 12 (1959) 555–557.

29. Harry Ritchie, *Success Stories: Literature and the Media in England, 1950–1959* (London: Faber, 1988) 27.

CHAPTER 3

1. David Nathan, "John Osborne: Is His Anger Simmering?" *The Curtain Rises: An Anthology of the International Theater* (London: Leslie Frewin, 1966) 244. To Georgiana Howell ("Look Back in Candour," *The Sunday Times*, 13 October 1991), he put it still differently: "They buy up your life and turn you into a milch cow."

2. Lesley White, "John Osborne: More in Sorrow Than in Anger," *The Sunday Times*, 7 June 1992:6. Osborne's income rose dramatically after the play, as it would, once again, after *The Entertainer.* In May 1956, when *Look Back in Anger* premiered, Osborne had been an unemployed actor. On 11 October 1957, the *Daily Mail* estimated that the then 27-year old playwright earned approximately £ 20,000 a year ("We're All Out of Step but Mr. J. Osborne"), twice the rate of the prime minister, as Kenneth Allsop observed in *The Angry Decade* (London: Peter Owen, 1964) 107. Figures, however, change rather dramatically according to the source. *Look Back* would continue to pay off all through Osborne's career. To Valerie Grove ("No Mistake, the View is Still Unmellowed," *The Sunday Times*, 30 July 1989), an older Osborne claimed that "*Look Back in Anger* is performed somewhere in the world every night of the year." Elsewhere he proudly stated that "there's going to be a video production of *Look Back* in New York and I get something like $ 50,000 as a start, a wonderful bonus. It's rather like real estate. You get a return not through more work, but through a change in values" (W.J. Weatherby, "Middle Age of the Angry Young Men," *Sunday Times Magazine*, 1 March 1981).

3. Polly Devlin, "John Osborne," *Vogue* June 1964.

4. "People nowadays think *Look Back* was an overnight success, but it took a long time to take off. At the Royal Court the first three months, it never took more than £ 1300. But then there was the famous TV excerpt and over six million people watched. That may be nothing now, but it seemed a lot then. Business went right up." Osborne in W.J. Weatherby, "Middle Age of the Angry Young Men," *Sunday Times Magazine*, 1 March 1981.

5. Tynan's article can be found in John Russell Taylor's *John Osborne: Look Back in Anger:A Selection of Critical Essays,* Casebook Series (London: Macmillan, 1968) 50–51.

6. David Dempsey, "Most Angry Fella," *New York Times,* 20 October 1957: 22.

7. Osborne himself acknowledged indebtedness especially to Arthur Miller and Tennessee Williams, emphasizing the role their drama played in facilitating his reception in Britain. "These men conditioned English audiences emotionally for the kind of plays I am writing." Qtd. in David Dempsey, "Most Angry Fella," *New York Times*, 20 October 1957: 26.

8. "New York Critics Like 'Look Back,'" *Evening Argus Brighton,* 2 October 1957.

9. Lewis Funke, "John Osborne," interview 1968, *Playwrights Talk About Writing* (Chicago: Dramatic Publishing Co, 1975) 200.

10. Arnold Wesker, "Center 42: The Secret Reins," *Encounter* 25 (1962) 3.

11. On 2 November 1957, when *Look Back in Anger* was being produced on Broadway, T.S. Williams from the *Yorkshire Evening Press* ("Osborne Play at York Rep. Soon") reported that the play had already been seen in France, Germany, Italy, Poland, Yugoslavia, Sweden, and Russia.

12. "Weaned by the Welfare State: Play Voices Problems of 'Angry Young Man'," *East Anglian Daily Times,* 20 August 1957.

13. "Anger Without Cause," *Surrey Times*, 12 October 1957.

14. Kenneth Haigh qtd. by Michael Billington, "A Prisoner of Dissent," *The Guardian*, 27 December 1984.

15. Alistair Cooke, "British Play a Hit on Broadway: 'Look Back in Anger' Will be Barking Till Spring," *Glasgow Herald,* 3 October 1957. Also in the *Manchester Guardian,* 3 October 1957.

16. H.R., "Brilliance by Original A.Y.M.," *Dagenham Post*, 23 October 1957.
17. " 'Look Back in Anger' is Electrifying," *Salisbury Times*, 1 November 1957.
18. Richard Findlater, "The Angry Young Man: Britain's Fiery New Dramatist," *The New York Times*, 29 September 1957:1.
19. "Sir Pat Walked Out in Anger," *Press and Journal*, 15 March 1958.
20. "The 'Scum' and I," *Sunday Dispatch*, 6 October 1957.
21. "The language was in effect provided for one voice only—Jimmy Porter's. The characterisation of the minor parts is only sketchily drawn, the other characters have little independent life at all, they are merely 'typical': Alison, the long-suffering wife; the Colonel, an Edwardian relic; Cliff, the faithful friend; and Helena, a bitchy actress. They exist only in relation to Jimmy. It is in Jimmy's character and in his words that the power of the play lies. Other characters have but 'fill-in' dialogue, only Jimmy is allowed to explore the field of ideas." Alan Carter, *John Osborne,* Biography and Criticism 14 (Edinburgh: Oliver and Boyd, 1969) 53.
22. A. Alvarez refers to its language as "slangy, gay, messy and irreverent" in "Anti-Establishment Drama," *Partisan Review* 26 (1959) 610.
23. Anne Karpf in *The Listener,* 15 April 1982. Qtd. in Malcolm Page, ed., *File on Osborne* (London and New York: Methuen, 1988) 15.
24. Peter Marks, "At Mid-Century, Choking on the Class System," *The New York Times*, 18 October 1999: B5.
25. A 1999 London production at the National Theatre, with Michael Sheen as Jimmy Porter, was fairly well received (see Matt Wolf, "Angry Again: Osborne's Jimmy Porter Returns in a Vibrant New Incarnation," *American Theatre,* October 1999: 102–03. Osborne himself approved of Judi Dench's 1989 production with Kenneth Branagh and Emma Thompson.
26. "Even now I have a lot of difficulty with actors who say quite obvious things like 'Why do I say this because he's just said that and it's not an answer?' " Mark Amory, "Jester Fleas the Court," *Sunday Times*, 24 November 1974: 34.
27. Negative space was to be popularized in the mid-sixties by the American visual artist Bruce Nauman, who intimated an object's presence by filling in the space around it.
28. John Osborne, "They Call It Cricket," *Declaration,* ed. Tom Maschler" (London: MacGibbon & Kee) 69.
29. Terry Coleman, "Osborne Without Anger," *The Guardian* August 1971.
30. John Osborne, "They Call It Cricket" 69.
31. Qtd. in François Bédarida, *A Social History of England 1851–1975,* transl. A. S. Forster (London and New York: Methuen, 1979) 197.
32. See, for instance, C.A.R. Crosland, *The Future of Socialism* (London: Jonathan Cape, 1956); John Strachey, *Contemporary Capitalism* (New York: Random House, 1956); and Bryan Magee, *The New Radicalism* (New York: St. Martin's Press, 1963).
33. Jürgen Habermas, *Legitimation Crisis,* trans. Thomas McCarthy (Boston: Beacon, 1975), Herbert Marcuse, *Eros and Civilization* (Boston: Beacon Press, 1955) and *One Dimensional Man* (Boston: Beacon Press, 1964).
34. Harry Hopkins, *The New Look: A Social History of the Forties and Fifties in Britain* (London: Secker and Warburg, 1963) 372.
35. Herbert Marcuse, "Repressive Tolerance," in Robert Paul Wolff, Barrington Moore, Jr., and Marcuse, *A Critique of Pure Tolerance* (Boston, 1965): 82.
36. Doris Lessing, *The Four-Gated City* (New York: Knopf, 1969) 511–512.
37. Situating Osborne in a literary tradition which includes Strindberg, D.H. Lawrence, and Thurber, Kenneth Allsop refers more colorfully to "the warring of desire against resentment that a woman, by apparently lying submissively on her back, can so humble and exhaust a man." *The Angry Decade: A Survey of the Cultural Revolt of the Nineteen-Fifties,* 4th ed. (London: Lowe & Brydone, 1969) 118.
38. Paul Watzlawick, Janet H. Beavin, and Don D. Jackson, *Pragmatics of Human Com-*

munication: A Study of Interactional Patterns, Pathologies, and Paradoxes, Mental Research Institute at Palo Alto, California (London: Faber, 1968).

39. Also qtd. in Carlos E Sluzki and Donald C. Ransom, ed., *Double Bind: The Foundation of the Communicational Approach to the Family* (New York: Grune & Stratton, 1976) 192.

40. Matt Wolf, "Angry Again," *American Theatre* October 1999: 102.

CHAPTER 4

1. George Scott, "Angry Young Theatre," *Everybody's,* 29 August 1957.

2. "Sir Larry Takes a Pay Cut for the Angry Young Man," *Daily Mail,* 13 March 1957. George Scott in the *Everybody's* ("Angry Young Theatre" 29 August 1957) comes up with different figures: "Laurence received about £ 90 a week, instead of the £ 400 or £ 500 a week he could have been earning at a West End theatre."

3. Derek Monsey, "Who Calls Sir Larry a Square?" *Sunday Express,* 14 April 1957.

4. Harry Hopkins, *The New Look: A Social History of the Forties and Fifties in Britain* (London: Secker & Warburg, 1963) 445–46, 448.

5. John Osborne, "They Call it Cricket," *Declaration,* ed. Tom Maschler (London: MacGibbon & Kee, 1957) 76.

6. Rev. of *The Entertainer, Evening Standard,* 11 April 1957.

7. "Money Spinner," *Evening News,* 7 September 1957. "I didn't start to make a lot of money until *The Entertainer* was put on at the Palace Theatre. I got £900 a week, a great deal then." "How much money had I made since 1956? Something like £254,000. How much had I spent? £ 365,000. It's been like that ever since. John Osborne qtd. in W.J. Weatherby, "Middle Age of the Angry Young Men," *Sunday Times Magazine,* 1 March 1981.

8. Kenneth Tynan, "The Men of Anger," *Holiday,* 23 (1958): 93–184. Reprinted as "The Angry Young Movement," *Tynan on Theatre* 184.

9. Milton Shulman, "Olivier: The Master of Pathos and Scorn," *Evening Standard,* 11 April 1957. Derek Monsey in the *Sunday Express* calls it "slackly written, slow and boring" (14 April 1957). Kenneth Tynan also referred to the "sloth of the first act" and the "over-compression of the third" ("A Whale of a Week," *The Observer,* 14 April 1957). *Punch* called it "rambling and repetitive" (17 April 1957).

10. Kenneth Tynan, "A Whale of a Week," *The Observer,* 14 April 1957.

11. Dated 11 September 1957. Philip Hope-Wallace of the *Manchester Guardian* also described the play as "maudlin and only partly successful" (12 April 1957).

12. *Evening Standard,* 11 April 1957.

13. *Daily Mail,* 13 March 1957.

14. George Scott, "Angry Young Theatre," *Everybody's,* 29 August 1957.

15. 11 September 1959.

16. Gerard Fay, "The Books of the Plays," *Manchester Guardian,* 15 October 1957.

17. In an interview with Logan Gourlay, Osborne admitted that Olivier to some extent "did throw [the play] out of balance. The production did suffer in a way, not because of his performance, which was brilliant, but because of the attitude and interpretation of the public, who regarded it as a vehicle for Olivier. The emphasis was too much on him and the other people in the cast, particularly Brenda de Banzie and George Relph, who were outstandingly good, were somewhat overlooked." Logan Gourlay, ed, *Olivier* (New York: Skin & Day, 1974) 149.

18. John Osborne, *Almost a Gentleman: Autobiography 1955–1966* (London: Faber, 1991) 41.

19. Ronald Bryden, rev. of *The Entertainer, Plays and Players,* February 1975: 23.

20. This distrust of the welfare state should not come as a surprise. Discussing the Angry Young Men's political attitudes, A. Alvarez said, "they are not so much pro-Labour as anti-establishment. . . . This means that their most lively political experience has very

little to do with mass unemployment, strikes and union-busting, and a great deal to do with the forlorn sight of the Welfare State sinking under the paralyzing weight of the bureaucrats until it achieved what J.W. Aldridge has called Welfare Stasis. Their political ideas are probably less defined by enthusiasms and causes than by irritation." A. Alvarez, "Anti-Establishment Drama," *Partisan Review* 26 (1959): 609.

21. Qtd. by Ronald Mavor, " 'The Entertainer': What is a Tragedy," *The Scotsman*, 22 November 1957.
22. John Osborne, "They Call It Cricket," *Declaration,* ed. Tom Maschler (London: MacGibbon & Kee, 1957) 80–81.
23. Frank Granville Barker, "Knight at the Music-Hall," *Plays and Players* October 1957.
24. Manfred Pfister, "Music Hall und Modernes Drama: Populäre Komik als Medium und Thema im zeitgenössischen englischen Theater," *Anglistendag 1980* (Giessen: Hoffman-Verlag, 1981) 127.
25. John Osborne, "On the Halls," *Observer*, 20 April 1975. Repr. in *Damn You, England* 121.
26. Harold Hobson, "An Author and Two Players," *Sunday Times*, 15 September 1957.
27. Ronald Mavor, "Osborne Has Written a Beautiful Play: 'The Entertainer' Full of Light," *The Scotsman*, 13 November 1957.
28. Harold Hobson, "An Author and Two Players," *Sunday Times*, 15 September 1957.
29. John Osborne, "They Call It Cricket," *Declaration* 82.
30. Ronald Mavor, " 'The Entertainer' Full of Light," *The Scotsman*, 13 November 1957.
31. John E. Booth, "Rebel Playwright," *The New York Times*, 2 November 1958.
32. Polly Devlin, "John Osborne," *Vogue* June 1964: 98.
33. Derek Monsey, "Who Calls Sir Larry a Square?" *Sunday Express*, 14 April 1957.
34. Raymond Marriott, "New Plays: 'The Entertainer'," *Plays and Players*, October 1957.
35. Ronald Mavor, "Osborne Has Written a Beautiful Play: 'The Entertainer' Full of Light," *The Scotsman*, 13 November 1957.
36. John Raymond, "Books in General: Mid-Century Blues," *New Statesman*, 12 October 1957.
37. Christopher Chateway, M.P., "Challenge to Prosperity," *The Listener*, 5 Jan 1961: 4–5.
38. John Osborne, "Royalty Accounts," *Spectator*, 5 June 1993. Repr. in *Damn You, England* 199.
39. "Anger: The Young Men As the Target," *Daily Express*, 15 October 1957.
40. The Queen's Cousin Bars those Angry Young Men,"*The Daily Mail*, 15 October 1957.
41. "A.Y.M. Are Put Out of Court: Theatre's Council Bans a Party," *News Chronicle*, 15 October 1957.
42. Paul Wheeler, "Olivier Plays Osborne: 'The Entertainer' Reviewed," *Chenwell*, 23 November 1957.
43. Georgiana Howell, "Look Back in Candour," *The Sunday Times*, 13 October 1991. When Olivier died, Osborne complained that "Larry" had not been given the funeral he deserved. He should have been buried in Westminster Abbey, he thought, like Garrick. Valerie Grove, "No Mistake, the View is Still Unmellowed," *The Sunday Times*, 30 July 1989.
44. See also Robert Gordon, "*The Entertainer* as a Text for Performance," *John Osborne: A Casebook,* ed. Patricia D. Denison (New York and London: Garland, 1997) 92.
45. "Angry Again," *Daily Mail*, 9 September 1957.

CHAPTER 5

1. John Osborne, *Almost a Gentleman* (London: Faber, 1991) 127.
2. William Gaskill, "Farewell to a Passionate Man," *Financial Times*, 31 December

1994. The "bodyguard" was the actor Robert Webber. His black tailor was Arthur Maguy.

3. "John Osborne," *The Observer*, 17 May 1959.

4. Richard Findlater,"Angry Young Monk," rev. of *Luther, Time and Tide*, 10 August 1961.

5. Penelope Gilliatt, "A Great Play," *The Queen*, 2 August 1961: "For a long time one has been hearing people ask, in an unsettled voice, whether John Osborne has taken to religion. *Luther* upsets their notion of their pet rebel, who is expected to be anti-God rather as it is now accepted that he will be anti-Queen."

6. Stephen Watts, "Playwright J. Osborne Looks Back—and Not in Anger," *New York Times*, 22 September 1963.

7. Martin Luther, *The Bondage of the Will: Being his Reply to Erasmus,* transl. Henry Cole (Grand Rapids, MI: WM. B. Eerdmans; London: Sovereign Grace Union, 1931) 18–19, 23.

8. Compare, for instance, Osborne's description of the indulgence salesman John Tetzel with that of Heinrich Boehmer, *Martin Luther: Road to Reformation,* transl. John W. Doberstein and Theodore G. Tappert (New York: Meridian, 1957) 180 and following.

9. For examples of Bainton's influence on Osborne's work, see Niloufer Harben, *Twentieth Century History Plays* (Totowa, NJ: Barnes & Noble, 1988) 199–202.

10. "I am like ripe shit and the world is a gigantic ass-hole. We probably will let go of each other soon." Luther's *Tischreden* (Weimarer Ausgaben) V, No. 5537. Qtd. in Erik H. Erikson, *Young Man Luther: A Study in Psychoanalysis and History* (New York: W.W. Norton, 1958) 206.

11. *Luther* was presented virtually "intact," Niloufer Harben states in *Twentieth Century English History Plays* (Totowa, NJ: Barnes & Noble, 1988) 188.

12. "Luther: The Powerful Portrait of a Rebel," *Shields Gazette*, 2 August 1961; "Albert Finney," *The Observer*, 6 August 1961.

13. Alan Brien, "John Osborne," *Sunday Telegraph*, 9 July 1961. Martin Esslin ("Brecht and the English Theatre," *Tulane Drama Review*, 11 (1966) 66) repeated the same sentiment five years later: "References to the jakes continue until they amount to a snigger. And nothing is done to convey the idea that quite half of the great reformer's armament was in his head." Simon Trussler called the play "an exercise in scatology."

14. Kenneth Tynan, "Rebel Writer On a Rebel Priest," *The Observer*, 9 July 1961.

15. "The method is Shakespeare's, Osborne said, "or almost anyone else's you can think of." Qtd. in Niloufer Harben, *Twentieth Century English History Plays* (Totowa, N.J.: Barnes & Noble, 1988) 190.

16. An example of this can be found in Martin Esslin, "Brecht and the English Theatre," *Tulane Drama Review* 11 (1966) 63–70, and *Reflections: Essays on Modern Theatre* (Garden City, NY: Doubleday, 1969) 84. Also in Charles Marowitz, "The Ascension of John Osborne," *Modern British Dramatists,* A Collection of Critical Essays, ed. John Russell Brown (Englewood Cliffs, N.Y., 1968) 119, and in Max Spalter, "Five Examples of How to Write a Brechtian Play That is Not Really Brechtian," *Educational Theatre Jounral*, 27 May 1975: 231.

17. W. A. Mitchell, "Theatre: Osborne Isn't Angry in *Luther,*" *Press and Journal*, 5 August 1961.

18. V.S. Pritchett in *New Statesman*, 4 August 1961.

19. Robert Brustein, "The Backwards Birds," *Seasons of Discontent: Dramatic Opinions 1959–1965* (New York: Simon & Schuster, 1965) 198.

20. Philip Hope-Wallace, "A Masterpiece With Flaws," *The Guardian*, 29 July 1961.

21. Milton Shulman, "Theatrically, Full Marks, But There the Kissing Stops," *Evening Standard*, 28 July 1961.

22. W.A. Darlington, "First Night: Finney Gives a Fine Study," *Daily Telegraph*, 28 July 1961.

23. Penelope Gilliatt, "A Great Play," *The Queen*, 2 August 1961.

24. Richard Findlater, "Angry Young Monk," rev. of *Luther, Time and Tide*, 10 August 1961.

25. Michael Foot, "Osborne's *Luther*," *The Tribune*, 4 August 1961.

26. It is surprising that *Luther,* despite its use of psycho-analytically relevant imagery, has attracted so few psychoanalytic readings of any importance. A limited study may be found in Vera D. Denty, "The Psychology of Martin Luther," *Catholic World* 194 (1961) 99–105. More relevant is Hildegard Hammerschmidt, *Das Historische Drama in England (1956–1971): Erscheinungsformen und Entwicklungstendenzen* (Frankfurt: Humanitas Verlag, 1972).

27. Martin Luther, *The Bondage of the Will: Being his Reply to Erasmus,* transl. Henry Cole (Grand Rapids, Mi: WM. B. Eerdmans; London: Sovereign Grace Union, 1931) 14.

28. John Osborne, "Dear Diary," *Spectator*, 24 April 1993. Repr. in *Damn You, England* 236.

29. 20.4 Miscellaneous holograph notebooks and 20.6 Miscellaneous Ms. fragments, John Osborne Collection, Harry Ransom Humanities Research Center, Austin, Texas.

30. "The Single Image," *Sunday Telegraph*, 30 July 1961.

31. Hunter Davies, "I Need to be Reminded I was Once Alive," *The Independent* 26, April 1994: 21.

32. Osborne admitted to not having a "highly developed visual sense," which is probably why he rarely experimented with the kind of visual metaphors he employed to such good effect in *Luther.* Iain Johnstone, "John Osborne . . . Takes a Black View of Film Work," *The Listener*, 3 July 1969.

33. Erik H. Erikson, *Young Man Luther* (New York: Norton, 1958) 174.

34. "John Osborne Talks to Kenneth Tynan—Candidly," *Atlas* 16 (1968) 55.

35. See also Hortense Calisher, "Will We Get There By Candlelight?," *Reporter*, 4 November 1965: 39. "Somewhere, though perhaps unphrased to himself—and perhaps best so except as in the work itself—[the playwright] must *seem* to know, if only in metaphor or with an imprecision that reflects the inexactitude of life; he must control some of the boundaries of what he is after."

36. Erik H. Erikson, *Young Man Luther: A Study in Psychoanalysis and History* (New York: W.W. Norton, 1958) 72.

37. Erik H. Erikson, *Young Man Luther* (New York: Norton, 1958) 72.

38. Erikson, *Young Man Luther* 204. Otto Scheel, *Dokumente zu Luthers Entwicklung* (Tuebingen: J.C.B. Mohr, 1929): No. 238.

39. Erikson, *Young Man Luther* 205.

40. Lucien Goldman, *The Hidden God*, trans. Philip Thody (London: Routledge Kegan Paul, 1964) 50.

41. "Drama was inherent in Luther, Osborne believes. . . . 'He carried crisis on his back, as it were.'" Stephen Watts, "Playwright John Osborne Looks Back—And Not in Anger," *New York Times*, 22 September 1963.

42. Gordon E. Rupp, "John Osborne and the Historical Luther," *The Expository Times* 73 (1962) 147–151. Charles H. O'Brien, "Osborne's *Luther* and the Humanistic Tradition," *Renascence* 21 (1969) 59–63.

43. Evelyn Waugh, "Wilful Monk," *Sunday Telegraph*, 27 August 1961.

44. Paul Tillich, *A History of Christian Thought*, ed. Carl E. Braaten (New York: Harper and Row, 1968).

45. In "The Pagan Servitude of the Church," Luther had the following to say about the most important representative of the "way of remotion," Dionysius the Areopagite: "All the fruits of his meditations seem very much like dreams. . . . In sum, I myself do not want any believer to give the least weight to these books. So far indeed from learning about Christ in them, you will be led to lose what you know. . . . [Dionysius] plays with his allegories, but this does not make them realities" (*Martin Luther: Selections from his Writings,* ed. John Dillenberger (New York: Doubleday, 1961) 343). The anti-

dote to Dionysius is St. Paul and his straightforward teachings of Jesus Christ and the crucifixion, he says in the same passage. Luther held Dionysius responsible for many of the mystifications of the faith, misused by popes to deceive honest Christians.

46. Paul Tillich, *Systematic Theology,* vol. 3 (Chicago: Chicago UP, 1963) 403–404.
47. Charles Marowitz, "The Ascension of John Osborne," *Tulane Drama Review* 7 (1962): 178.
48. John Whiting, "Theatre: *Luther,*" *The London Magazine* October 1961: 58.
49. Stephen Watts, "Not in Anger," *New York Times,* 22 September 1963.
50. Simon Kavanaugh, "Profile," *Oldham Evening Chronicle & Standard,* 13 September 1961.
51. W.J. Weatherby, "Middle Age of the Angry Young Men," *Sunday Times Magazine* 1 March 1981.
52. Polly Devlin, "John Osborne," *Vogue* June 1964: 99.
53. "I can't understand anybody who doesn't feel self-loathing. But the world is full of people who fell in love with themselves at an early age, and have remained faithful to themselves ever since." Georgiana Howell, "Look Back in Candour," *The Sunday Times,* 13 October 1991.
54. Georgiana Howell, "Look Back in Candour," *The Sunday Times,* 13 October 1991.
55. Jocelyn Herbert qtd. in Michael Billington, "A Prisoner of Dissent," *The Guardian,* 27 December 1984.
56. John Osborne, "Dear Diary," *Spectator,* 20 June 1992. Repr. in *Damn You, England* 203–206: 203.
57. Hunter Davies, "I Need to be Reminded I Was Once Alive," *The Independent,* 26 April 1994: 21.

CHAPTER 6

1. Irving Wardle, "Looking Back at Osborne's Anger," *New Society,* 1 July 1965: 22.
2. John Osborne, "Land of the Free?" *TV Times,* 31 May 1963. Repr. in *Damn You, England* 162.
3. "Admissible Evidence," from *Report of the Joint Committee on Censorship of the Theatre* (1967). Repr. in *Damn You, England* 167.
4. "Obituary of John Osborne," *The Daily Telegraph,* 27 December 1994: 23.
5. Lindsay Anderson, "Court in the Act," rev. of *Almost a Gentleman,* by John Osborne, *The Spectator,* 9 November 1991: 50.
6. *Die Verfolgung und Ermordung Jean Paul Marats dargestellt durch die Schauspiel-gruppe des Hospizes zu Charenton unter Anleitung des Herrn de Sade (The Persecution and Assassination of Marat as Performed by the Inmates of the Charenton Asylum under the Direction of the Marquis de Sade,* 1964).
7. "John Osborne Talks to Kenneth Tynan—Candidly," *Atlas* September 1958: 56.
8. William Gaskill, "Farewell to a Passionate Man," *Financial Times,* 31 December 1994.
9. Valerie Grove, "A Better Class of Osborne," *The New Standard,* 6 March 1981.
10. W.J. Weatherby, "Middle Age of the Angry Young Men," *Sunday Times Magazine,* 1 March 1981.
11. Caryl Brahms, "The Vein of Anger is Still There," *The Guardian Weekly,* 24 August 1974.
12. Polly Devlin, "John Osborne," *Vogue* June 1964: 168.
13. John Osborne, *Tribune,* 12 October 1967. Repr. in *Damn You, England* 215.
14. John Osborne, *The Times,* 16 May 1968. Repr. in *Damn You, England* 218–19.
15. "John Osborne Talks to Kenneth Tynan—Candidly," *Atlas* 16 (1968) 56.
16. "Fossils and Ferment," *Queen,* 11 September 1968.
17. Iris Burton, "The One Regret of Jill Bennett," *Woman's Own,* 16 November 1968.
18. *Westminster and Pimlico News,* 28 June 1968.

19. In "Inadmissible Epitaph" (*Weekend Guardian* 6–7 June 1992), Anthony Page, who directed the play, recalls that Tony Richardson, Osborne's friend until the quarrel over *The Charge of the Light Brigade* (1968), had been furious at recognizing Osborne's opinion of himself in this description of the film mogul.
20. Arthur Thirkell, "Night of Being Nasty," *Daily Mirror*, 18 August 1971.
21. Alan Brien, "You Have to Go Back," *Sunday Telegraph*, 12 June 1966.
22. Daniel Rogers, " 'Not for insolence, but seriously': John Osborne's adaptation of *La fianza satisfecha,*" *The Durham University Journal* 29 (1968) 169, 156.
23. Ronald Bryden, "John Osborne's Perfect Hero," *Observer*, 12 June 1966.
24. "Both plays set new standards in stage violence, and were severely mauled in the overnight press." Irving Wardle, "Osborne and the Critics," *New Society*, 16 June 1966.
25. Qtd. by Irving Wardle, "Osborne and the Critics," *New Society*, 16 June 1966. Wardle received a four-page telegram with more personal insults from Osborne.
26. Benedict Nightingale, "Creative Process?" *Plays and Players* September 1968.
27. Anne Chisholm, "Writing For Television Is Like Writing Short Stories," *Radio Times*, 8 October 1970.

CHAPTER 7

1. To Lynn Barber he admitted writing *Inadmissible Evidence* while drunk on champagne ("Bad Behaviour," *The Independent*, 2 February 1992). On 7 April 1964, Osborne announces in his notebook that, after one last night of feverish writing under the influence of champagne, he has finally left Bill Maitland behind. His wife Penelope Gilliatt, he adds, is impressed and solicitous, although in a patronizing way typical of her (*Almost a Gentleman: An Autobiography* (1955–1966) (London: Faber, 1991) 244).
2. Alan Brien, "Osborne Sets His Seal," *The Sunday Telegraph*, 21 March 1965.
3. Graham Samuel, "Osborne—A Compulsive Blimp of the Left," *Western Mail*, 12 September 1964.
4. Anthony Burgess, "Lawful Ambitions," *Spectator*, 26 March 1965.
5. John Peter, "Hateful Stuff," *The Sunday Times*, 27 June 1993.
6. John Osborne, *Almost a Gentleman* 244.
7. John Osborne, *Almost a Gentleman* 242. Qtd. in program note for the 17 June 1993 production of the play at The Lyttelton Theatre.
8. Jack Tiner, "A Law Bore Condemning Us With Long, Long Sentences," *Daily Mail*, 18 June 1993.
9. J. C. Trewin, "Sound and Fury," *The Illustrated London News*, 26 September 1964.
10. "I admit to being put off by Maitland's opinions," said Mervyn Jones. "I found more ·of a heart in the angry young man than in this petulant middle-aged man incapable of true anger, who rails, not at chauvinism and privilege, but at progress, idealism, and people who believe in 'natural childbirth and CND.'. . . . From a man like him, to accuse young people of being unequal to love and kindness is certainly a charge that invites, but never gets, a retort" ("Middle-Aged Petulance," *Tribune*, 18 September 1964).
11. Graham Samuel, "Osborne—A Compulsive Blimp of the Left," *Western Mail*, 12 September 1964.
12. Felix Barker, "Now Osborne Looks Forward in Anguish," *Evening News*, 10 September 1964.
13. Ronald Bryden in "Everyosborne," *New Statesman*, 18 September 1964, called it "unflaggingly vigorous and inventive, with a sweep and personal force no other of our playwrights can match."
14. Milton Shulman, "Osborne Goes Striding On," *Evening Standard*, 10 September 1964.

15. Eric Shorter, "Triumph in a Rich Osborne Creation," *Daily Telegraph*, 18 March 1965.
16. Brigid Chapman, "It's Boring, This Wordy Sermon On Sex," *Brighton and Hove Herald*, 12 March 1965.
17. "Osborne's Epic of One Man and a Grudge," *Evening Standard*, 18 March 1965.
18. Philip Hope-Wallace, rev. of *Inadmissible Evidence, Guardian*, 10 September 1964.
19. "Character's Humiliating Ugliness," *Times*, 18 March 1965.
20. John Osborne, *Almost a Gentleman* 245.
21. John Osborne, *Almost a Gentleman* 245.
22. Peter Lewis, "Enter the Rebel Who Slams Doors on Success," *Daily Mail*, 21 September 1964.
23. Alan Brien, "Osborne Sets His Seal," *The Sunday Telegraph*, 21 March 1965.
24. Ronald Bryden, "Everyosborne," *New Statesman*, 18 September 1964.
25. Robert Butler, "Gone to Ground," *The Independent on Sunday*, 6 June 1993: 21.
26. "Noisy, So West End Star Halts Play," *Daily Mail*, 7 May 1965.
27. Tom Brown, "Actor Makes Protest From Stage," *Daily Express*, 21 May 1965. "I think this play is terribly, terribly difficult. It is shattering to have to do it six nights a week, let alone two matinees." William Marshall, "Star Lashes Out in Theatre," *Daily Mirror*, 21 July 1965.
28. For an excellent study of this production, see Mark Hawkins-Dady, "From Out of the Shadow of Nicol Williamson," *John Osborne: A Casebook,* ed. Patricia Denison (New York and London: Garland, 1997) 127–146.
29. Nicholas de Jongh, "Osborne's Lament Looks Back More in Sorrow than in Anger," *Evening Standard*, 18 June 1993: 7.
30. Neil Smith, "Insolence of Office," *What's On*, 23 June 1993. Roy Shaw, "Theatre," *The Tablet*, 3 July 1993.
31. Ronald Bryden, "Everyosborne," *New Statesman*, 19 September 1964.
32. Maureen Patton, "Jurassic Justice," *Daily Express*, 18 June 1993. The nameless reviewer for the *Hampstead & Highgate Express* (28 June 1993) expressed similar surprise at hearing such "scabrous misogyny" directed by a woman: she "must have been sitting fist in mouth throughout rehearsals."
33. Paul Taylor, "One Angry Man," *Independent*, 19 June 1993.
34. Kate Kellaway, "Bitter Ages of Woman," *Observer*, 12 June 1993.
35. Patrick Marmion, "Resting Her Case," *What's On*, 16 June 1993. "We thought a woman should direct it because of all the misogyny in the play, which needs properly investigating," said Trevor Eve, recalling how Richard Eyre, director of the National Theatre, had offered him the role. Michael Owen, "The Truth About Me and Johnny O," *Evening Standard*, 10 June 1993.
36. Peter Kemp, "The Mirror and the Lump," *TLS*, 2 July 1993.
37. Michael Coveney, "A Stiff Line in Vulgarity," *The Observer*, 20 June 1993.
38. Michael Billington, rev. of *Inadmissible Evidence, Country Life*, 1 July 1993.
39. Jane Edwardes, "All About Eve," *Time Out*, 16 June 1993. My emphasis.
40. John Osborne, "Tennessee Williams," *Observer*, 20 January 1957. Repr. in John Osborne, *Damn You, England: Collected Prose* (London: Faber, 1994) 66.
41. Michael Owen, "The Truth About Me and Johnny O," *Evening Standard*, 10 June 1993; "Inadmissible Osborne," *Daily Mail*, 3 June 1993.
42. Craig Brown, "Driven Mad By a Back-SeatDriver," *Evening Standard*, 7 June 1993.
43. John Osborne qtd. in Arnold Wesker, *As Much as I Dare: An Autobiography (1932–1959)* (London: Century, 1994) 397.
44. Clive Barnes, "Play's The Thing, Luv," *New York Post Entertainment*, 4 September 1993.
45. Jack Tiner, "A Law Bore Condemning Us With Long, Long Sentences," *Daily Mail*, 18 June 1993.
46. Steve Grant, *Time Out*, 23 June 1993; Martin Spence, *Midweek*, 1–5 July 1993.

47. Charles Spencer, "A Fitful Blaze," *Daily Telegraph*, 21 June 1993. "It is a pity that so much effort has been put into a play that has become dated way before its time," said Adam Goldstein ("An Evening Where No Questions Were Asked and None Were Answered," *Morning Star*, 9 July 1993). Aleks Sierz ("Endless Stream of Tirades," *Tribune*, 25 June 1993) thought the play was dated, except perhaps in its attacks on youth.
48. John Gross, "White-Hot Turns in the Tundra," *Sunday Telegraph*, 20 June 1993.
49. Robert Butler, "True Blue, and Over the Top," *Independent on Sunday*, 20 June 1993.
50. I am indebted for this insight to Sarah Grover.
51. Mark Hawkins-Dady, "From Out of the Shadow of Nicol Williamson," *John Osborne: A Casebook,* ed. Patricia Denison (New York and London: Garland, 1997) 138: "Maitland's assault reveals as much his weaknesses as his aggression, his daughter's silence as much her quiet confidence as her passiveness. . . . At his most aggressive, he spat his accusations out, prowling around the stationary Jane like an interrogator; at his tenderest, he embraced her from behind and swayed his body with hers."

CHAPTER 8

1. This is also Benedict Nightingale's assessment in "The Lost Refuge of a Scoundrel," *Times*, 11 October 1995.
2. This is probably the book Osborne refers to when he says "I found a bad biography by someone" (A. Alvarez, "John Osborne and the Boys at the Ball," *New York Times*, 28 September 1969.
3. The last name in what was in fact a group of four famous spies, was Sir Anthony Blunt. Incidentally, he too was homosexual. But John Clum in *Acting Gay: Male Homosexuality in Modern Drama* (New York: Columbia UP, 1992) is wrong to list him as a possible parallel for Redl because the role he played in what was Britain's worse spy scandal was only revealed in 1979.
4. In that respect it is interesting that Peter Gill, who was director Anthony Page's assistant for the production of *Inadmissible Evidence* and who directed the 1995 RSC revival of *A Patriot for Me,* claims that "there's a lot of evidence to show that [Osborne] wrote [*Inadmissible Evidence* and *A Patriot for Me*] in tandem." Michael Arditti, interview with Peter Gill, *Independent*, 18 October 1995.
5. Michael Ardetti, interview with Peter Gill, *Independent* 18 October 1995.
6. Turning the theatre into a Club had been done before at the Royal Court Theatre for the production of Edward Bond's *Saved*. For *A Patriot for Me* membership immediately rose "from 1,600 to almost 4,000." Nicholas de Jongh, "A Patriot in the Closet," *Weekend Guardian*, 28–29 March 1992. Incidentally, these figures differ substantially from the ones quoted by Terry Browne in *Playwrights' Theatre: The English Stage Company at the Royal Court Theatre* (London: Pitman, 1975). Browne states that membership of the English Stage Company jumped to "over 10,000" after it became known that Osborne's play could only be seen as club production.
7. According to Osborne's testimony in front of the House of Lords Committee on 29 November 1966 (Report of the Joint Committee on Censorship of the Theatre (1967)), the Lord Chamberlain's decision to refuse the play a license for public performance cost him and the Royal Court Theatre each £ 7,500. Repr. as "Admissible Evidence," *Damn You, England* (London: Faber, 1994) 176, 178. Figures confirmed by Terry Browne in *Playwrights' Theatre: The English Stage Company at the Royal court Theatre* (London: Pitman, 1975).
8. Some of these examples are mentioned in J. Roger Baker's review of *A Patriot for Me, London Life* 24 January 1966.
9. Bryan Robertson in "The Critics," BBC-homeservice, summarized in the *Listener*, 15 July 1965.
10. Walter Wager, ed. *The Playwrights Speak,* "John Osborne (New York: Dell, 1967) 92.

11. Nicholas de Jongh reports that "by 1966, out of ten Osborne plays staged in London 'only one was licensed without any requests for cuts and changes'." "A Patriot in the Closet," *Weekend Guardian*, 28–29 March 1992.

12. John Osborne, *Evening Standard*, 25 October 1956. Repr. "Grim Chamberlain," *Damn You, England* 162.

13. She suspects him in fact of having "dark, unnatural instincts" that, if she could only get sufficient proof, would get him into the *News of the World* (II, i, 52).

14. Nicholas de Jongh, " A Patriot in the Closet," *Weekend Guardian*, 28–29 March 1992. This is an edited extract from Nicholas de Jongh's *Not in Front of the Audience: Homosexuality on Stage* (London: Routledge 1992). An article similarly based on Nicholas de Jongh's book, Michael Arditti's "The Day London Theatre Grew Up," appeared in the *Evening Standard* on 19 October 1995 on the occasion of a posthumous revival of Osborne's *A Patriot for Me*.

15. Nicholas de Jongh, "The Day London Theatre Grew Up," *Evening Standard*, 19 October 1995.

16. Nicholas de Jongh, *Not in Front of the Audience: Homosexuality on Stage* (London: Routledge, 1992) 110. de Jongh reports that Maximilian Schell did have some scruples and objections. He insisted on wearing long Johns during bed scenes and was of the opinion that Redl turned to sex with men only because he had been disappointed in his love for women.

17. Milton Shulman, "First Night," rev. of *A Patriot for Me, Evening Standard*, 1 July 1965.

18. W.A. Darlington, rev. of *A Patriot for Me, Daily Telegraph*, 1 July 1965.

19. Bernard Levin, rev. of *A Patriot for Me, Daily Mail*, 1 July 1965.

20. Bernard Levin, rev. of *A Patriot for Me, Daily Mail*, 1 July 1965.

21. Felix Barker, "If Only Osborne's Hero Deserved Our Sympathy," rev. of *A Patriot for Me, Evening News*, 1 July 1965.

22. Felix Barker, "If Only Osborne's Hero Deserved Our Sympathy," *Evening News*, 1 July 1965.

23. Harold Hobson, "The Casting Out of Lieutenant Redl," *The Sunday Times*, 4 July 1965.

24. Harold Hobson in "The Critics," an interview with Hobson, Iain Hamilton, and Bryan Robertson about *A Patriot for Me* for the Home Service of the BBC, under the chairmanship of Walter Allen, published in *Listener*, 15 July 1965.

25. Qtd. by Nicholas de Jongh, *Not in Front of the Audience: Homosexuality on Stage* (London: Routledge, 1992) 107.

26. Trixabelle del Mar, "How Osborne Played the Patriot Game," *Gay Gazette*, 25 October 1995.

27. Michael Arditti, Interview with Peter Gill, *Independent*, 18 October 1995.

28. Georges Bas, "Alfred Redl, le juif galicien: Thématique et technique dans *A Patriot for Me* de John Osborne," *Etudes Anglaises* 30 (1977): 440.

29. Bernard Levin, rev. of *A Patriot for Me, Daily Mail*, 1 July 1965.

30. Ronald Bryden, "Fulfillments," *New Statesman*, 31 December 1965.

31. Michael Ardetti, interview with Peter Gill, *Independent*, 18 October 1995.

32. Personal letter to the author.

33. John M. Clum, *Acting Gay: Male Homosexuality in Modern Drama* (New York: Columbia UP, 1992) 211.

34. Redl's categorical unwillingness or inability to identify with women, and thus, according to the definition of the gaze in this play, to "see" them is demonstrated on several occasions. At a reception at the Hofburg, Redl is seen dancing with a beautiful young woman. When Hötzendorf asks him who the pretty young lady was, Redl asks "which one?" (I, vi). The officers laugh at what could be an example of swaggering masculine self-assurance, but Redl in this case may well be just honest. Because he does not desire women, he does not really "see" them and therefore finds it hard to

distinguish between them. Later the Countess will claim that Redl has met her on three previous occasions and yet does not remember her (I, vi, 47).

35. This is a curiously recurring obsession in Osborne, as can be seen for instance by the many dubious jokes about "anal dilatation" in *Déjàvu*. In general terms, it expresses a fear that the body may finally fix an identity upon oneself.

36. "I had for years been wanting to write a play about homosexuality and the whole ambiguity of it," Osborne said in an interview. And he wanted to see this ambiguity realized in a daring drag ball scene where the audience would at least for a moment be led to believe that there were actual women among the participants. A. Alvarez, "Osborne and the Boys at the Ball," *New York Times,* 28 September 1969: section 2, p. 5.

37. When Redl talks about officers as an elite that often clash with one another, Countess Delyanoff, well informed about his humble origins, teases him by saying that he has "spoken like a true aristocrat" (51).

CHAPTER 9

1. Michael Owen, "Contented Old Man," *Evening Standard*, 13 October 1988.
2. Michael Billington, "The Carton Image is a Potential Angry Brigade Member," *The Guardian*, 18 December 1973.
3. Michael Billington, "A Major Talent for Crucifixion," *The Guardian*, 25 January 1994.
4. Mark Ravenhill, "Looking Back Warily at a Heterosexual Classic," *New York Times*, 17 October 1999; Fiachra Gibbons, "Angry Young Men under Fire from Gay Writer Mark Ravenhill . . .," *Guardian*, 8 November 1999.
5. Robert Chesshyre, "Fifty is a Young Age for an Angry Man," *The Observer*, 18 November 1979.
6. See letter written by John Dexter, dated 27 May 1975. [John Osborne Collection at the Harry Ransom Humanities Research Center in Austin, Texas. File 35.3 Correspondence J.O. Personal C-J (1958–1976)]. In 1973, Osborne was tried for driving while intoxicated.
7. John Osborne Collection at the Harry Ransom Humanities Research Center File 38. 1–2 Correspondence, Gilliatt, Penelope and Nolan Osborne, 1967–76.
8. Lynn Barber, "Bad Behaviour," *The Independent*, 2 February 1992.
9. Letter from Kenneth Marsh, from BUPA Medical Centre, dated 10 June 1982 [John Osborne Collection at the Harry Ransom Humanities Research Center in Austin, Texas. File 43.1: Correspondence Fans and Friends 1965–82].
10. Since the end of the seventies, his income had sometimes dropped to £ 15,000 a year, most of it coming from royalties from performances abroad. In 1993, the Royal Literary Fund offered him £6,700 to cover his dentist bill. See, Lynn Barber, "Bad Behaviour," *The Independent* 2 February 1992. See also, letter from The Royal Literary Fund, dated 15 July 1993, in the John Osborne Collection of the Harry Ransom Humanities Research Center at Austin, Texas, "Correspondence from expanding file 1958–1992 M-S."
11. John Osborne Collection, Harry Ransom Humanities Research Center, Austin, Texas. File 35.1 Correspondence J.O. Personal A (1967–78).
12. Rebecca Hardy, "Look Back in Remorse," *Daily Mail*, 29 September 1992.
13. John Osborne, "Looking Back on the Week's TV," *Mail on Sunday*, 20 June 1982.
14. John Osborne, "Looking Back on the Week's TV," *Mail on Sunday*, 6 June 1982: 37.
15. Letter to Michael Boss, dated 14 March 1974. John Osborne Collection at the Harry Ransom Humanities Research Center in Austin, Texas: File 43.3 Correspondence Fans, General Enquiries, and Lunatics 1972–77.
16. John Osborne Collection, Harry Ransom Humanities Research Center at Austin,

Texas: File 25.24 and 25.25 British Playwrights Mafia 1977; File 44.4 Correspondence from expanding file 1958–1992 T-Z.

17. Michael Billington, "A Talent for Dissent," *The Guardian*, 18 December 1973:10.
18. Michael Owen, "Contented Old Man," *Evening Standard*, 13 October 1988.
19. Janet Gorman, rev. of *The Father, Openmind* 36 (December 1988/January 1989); Carl Miller, rev. of *The Father, City Limits*, 3 November 1988.
20. Jack Tinker, "Come On In, the Red Herrings Are Lovely!" *Daily Mail*, 17 January 1975.
21. "The Author on the Play," part of an interview Osborne gave to *Cue* in 1975, quoted in the program note to the play.
22. Irving Wardle, "Osborne Exercise in Penthouse Manner," *The Times*, 17 January 1975; Robert Cushman, "True Love Conquers," *Observer*, 19 January 1975.
23. Qtd. in Richard Morrison, Obituary: John Osborne, *Times*, 31 December 1994.
24. Lynn Barber, "Let's Hear It For the Great John Osborne," *The Independent*, 4 October 1992.
25. Jeremy Treglown, "Fouling the Nest," *TLS*, 15 November 1991:21.
26. Lindsay Anderson was one of many former Osborne friends who were deeply shocked by such and similar attacks on former spouses and friends ("Court in the Act," rev. of *Almost a Gentleman,* by John Osborne, *The Spectator*, 9 November 1991: 50–51.) Osborne called Jill Bennett Adolf. Correspondence from Expanding File 1958–1192 T-Z in the Harry Ransom Humanities Research Center at the University of Texas, Austin, contains several yellowing photographs of Jill Bennett adorned with Adolf Hitler mustache and surrounded by dollar signs. On top are scribbled various German phrases, signed Adolf, supposedly indicative of Jill Bennett's imperiousness and greed.

CHAPTER 10

1. Sheridan Morley, "On the Theatre," rev. of A *Sense of Detachment, The Tatler* February 1973.
2. Michael Billington, rev. of *A Sense of Detachment, Guardian*, 5 December 1972. Ronald Hayman in "Arts Commentary" on BBC Radio 3 (8 December 1972) called it technically "a step forward for him" as well. Because they did give his plays an occasional negative review, Osborne would not have called Billington and Hobson his "staunch supporters." In 1977, he in fact lumped them together with a host of other London critics (Morley, Shulman, Levin, Hope-Wallace . . .) he heartily disapproved of and derided in a satirical article published in *The Evening Standard* on October 14, 1977.
3. John Elsom, "Supporting Stoke," *The Listener*, 14 December 1972.
4. *Sunday Times,* rev. of *A Sense of Detachment*, 28 January 1973.
5. Kenneth Hurren, "Osborne and Arden," *Spectator*, 9 December 1972.
6. Benedict Nightingale, "Osborne in Disintegration," *New Statesman*, 8 December 1972.
7. John Osborne, *A Better Class of Person: An Autobiography 1929–1956* (London: Faber, 1981) 276.
8. Osborne, *A Better Class of Person* 276.
9. Arnold P. Hinchliffe, "Whatever Happened to John Osborne?" *Contemporary English Drama*, ed. C.W.E. Bigsby, Stratford-upon-Avon Studies 19 (London: Arnold, 1981) 59; Ronald Hayman in "Arts Commentary," BBC Radio 3 8 December 1972. John Elsom in "Supporting Stoke," *The Listener* 14 December 1972, attributes *Insulting the Audience* wrongly to Fassbender [sic].
10. Peter Handke, *Offending the Audience, Kaspar and Other Plays,* trans. Michael Roloff (New York: Hill and Wang, 1969) 1–32.

11. Luigi Pirandello, Preface to *Six Characters in Search of an Author,* Appendix 1, *Naked Masks,* ed. Eric Bentley (New York: Penguin, 1952) 363–375.

12. In Freudian psychoanalysis, neurosis is inevitable because, however emancipated we may be in the expression of our desires, the libido can never be adequately expressed. That which precedes Form always exceeds it. These three thinkers are united in their tragic Hegelianism: Some blind life force seeks to realize itself in the material world but never completely succeeds because of the inherent insufficiency of matter.

13. For another discussion of the play along similar lines, see Francis Fergusson, *The Idea of a Theater: The Art of Drama in Changing Perspective* (Garden City, N.Y.: Double-day, 1949) 198–206.

14. Rev. of *A Sense of Detachment, Sunday Times,* 10 December 1972.

15. Ronald Hastings, "Plays and Players: As the Audience Wishes," *Daily Telegraph* 25 November 1972.

16. Hastings, "Plays and Players: As the Audience Wishes."

17. Rev. of *A Sense of Detachment, Yorkshire Evening* and *Shropshire Star,* 27 January 1973.

18. "Hecklers Say Sorry to Miss Kempson," *Daily Telegraph,* 25 January 1973.

19. Philip Oakes and Lesley Garner, "Coming On: Court Circular," *Sunday Times,* 26 November 1972.

20. Oakes and Garner, "Coming On: Court Circular."

21. "Arts Commentary," BBC-Radio 3 8 December 1972.

22. Benedict Nightingale, "Osborne in Disintegration," *New Statesman,* 8 December 1972.

23. Letter to Alan Bates, 31 July 1973. John Osborne Collection. Harry Ransom Humanities Research Center, Austin, Texas.

24. These letters can be found in the Osborne collection at the Harry Ransom Humanities Research Center at the University of Texas in Austin.

CHAPTER 11

1. *New Standard,* 7 April 1981. Reprinted as "Devine and Fall," *At the Royal Court,* Richard Findlater. Also reprinted in John Osborne, *Damn You, England: Collected Prose* (London and Boston: Faber, 1994) 26–28.

2. Qtd by Arnold P. Hinchliffe, *John Osborne,* Twayne's English Authors Series (Boston: Twayne, 1984) 114–15.

3. *Daily Telegraph,* 13 August 1964. Reprinted in *Damn You, England* 227–228.

4. *Daily Telegraph,* 19 August 1964. Reprinted in *Damn You, England* 228.

5. *Daily Express,* 2 December 1959. Repr. in *Damn You, England* 193.

6. *The Times,* 14 October 1967. *Damn You, England* 20.

7. See also Kimball King, "John Osborne, Summer 1993," *John Osborne: A Casebook,* ed. Patricia Denison (New York: Garland, 1997) 178.

8. "I long for space. I'd like to live in a place as big as a railway station. But I don't think I'd buy a jet plane or anything like that because I never want to go anywhere very much." Kenneth Tynan, "Osborne," *The Observer,* 7 July 1968.

9. See, for instance, Ronald Bryden, "The House that Jimmy Built," *John Osborne: A Casebook,* ed. Patricia Denison 3–20.

10. John Osborne, "Something Concrete," *The National: A Dream Made Concrete,* Peter Lewis. Also in *Spectator,* 5 January 1991, and reprinted in *Damn You, England* 28.

CHAPTER 12

1. Lesley White, "More in Sorrow than in Anger," *The Sunday Times,* 7 June 1992.

2. Rev. of *Déjàvu, Weekend Telegraph,* 20 June 1992.

3. Rev. of *Déjàvu, Weekend Telegraph,* 20 June 1992.

4. Lynn Barber, "Bad Behaviour," *The Independent,* 2 February 1992.

5. "Noises Off," *Standard*, 3 July 1992.
6. Rev. of *Déjàvu, Weekend Telegraph*, 20 June 1992.
7. Alf Garnett is the creation of socialist writer Johnny Speight. The character featured first in the 1964 BBCseries, "Till Death Do Us Part" and appeared in 1992 again in the series "In Sickness and in Health."
8. Georgina Brown, "Beside Himself," *Independent*, 10 June 1992.
9. Malcolm Rutherford, "*Déjàvu* Revisited," *Financial Times*, 15 June 1992.
10. Shaun Usher, "Last Night's First Night," *Daily Mail*, 11 June 1992.
11. Jane Edwardes, rev. of *Déjàvu, Time Out*, 17–24 June 1992.
12. Di Parker, rev. of *Déjàvu, MS London*, 29 June 1992.
13. Malcolm Rutherford, "*Déjàvu* Revisited," *Financial Times*, 15 June 1992.
14. Emma Lilly, rev. of *Déjàvu, Good Times*, 18 June 1992.
15. Di Parker, rev. of *Déjàvu, MS London*, 29 June 1992.
16. Charles Spencer, "John Osborne: Still Looking Back in Anger," *The Daily Telegraph*, 11 June 1992.
17. Ian Shuttleworth, rev. of *Déjàvu, City Limits*, 18–25 June 1992.
18. Lewis Funke, *Playwrights Talk About Writing* (Chicago: Dramatic Publishing, 1975) 212.
19. John Osborne, "Workers wives and women," *Evening Standard*, April 29 1980:15.
20. http://www.mmnewsstand.com/trivia/biography/index.html
21. T.O. Lloyd, *Empire, Welfare State, Europe: English History (1906–1992)*, 4th ed. (Oxford: Oxford UP, 1993) 515.
22. Melvyn Bragg, "A Line-Up of One-Liners," *Observer*, 8 June 1986.
23. A similar view can be found in Régis Debray, "A Modest Contribution to the Rites and Ceremonies of the Tenth Anniversary," *New Left Review* 115 (1979): 45–66; Gilles Lipovetsky, *L'ère du vide: essais sur l'individualisme contemporain*, Les Essais CCXXV (Paris: Gallimard, 1983); Luc Ferry and Alain Renaut, *La pensée 68: Essai sur l'anti-humanisme contemporain*, Le monde actuel (Paris: Gallimard, 1985).
24. Daniel Bell, *The End of Ideology* (New York: Free Press, 1962).
25. *Guardian,* 27 Oct. 1992.
26. John Osborne, "Schoolmen of the Left," *Observer,* 30 October 1960. Repr. in *Damn You, England* 13.
27. George Orwell, "The Principles of Newspeak," Appendix *Nineteen Eighty-Four, The Penguin Complete Novels of George Orwell* (Harmondsworth and New York: Penguin, 1983) 924.
28. John Osborne, "Unacceptable Alternative," *The Times,* 20 June 1980. Repr. in *Damn You, England* 232–233.
29. John Osborne, "Treason of the Clerics," *The Oldie,* 11 December 1992. Repr. in Damn You, England 233–234.
30. John Osborne, "Jeffrey Bernard," foreword to Jeffrey Barnard, *Low Life* (Duckworth, 1986). Repr. in. *Damn You, England* 253.
31. Osborne's last work for television, *England, My England,* about the life and music of Henry Purcell, directed, again, by Tony Palmer, was shown on Channel 4 on December 1995—that is, one year after Osborne's death.

Index

Absurdism, 23, 30–31, 110
Adamov, Arthur, 30
Addison, John, 34, 87
After Haggerty (David Mercer), 168
Agit-Prop, 110
aggro-effect, 110
Albee, Edward, 184, 196, 200, 203
Aldridge, J.W., 242–43n.20
Aldwych (theatre), 110
alienation technique, 22
All My Sons (Arthur Miller), 32
Allsop, Kenneth, 241n.37
Amis, Kingsley, 44, 53
Anderson, Lindsay, 109, 111, 252n.26
anger, 33, 44;
  and creativity, 89, 105–106;
  in *Déjàvu*, 233; in *Luther,* 103–106
Angry Young Man, 43–44, 125, 242–43n.20
Annan, Lord, 145
Anouilh, Jean, 30, 89
anti-psychiatry, 57–58
anti-theatre, 178–83
Any Woman Can (Jill Posener), 164
Archer, William, 119
Arden, John, 32
Armstrong, Alun, 172
Arnold, Matthew, 10
Artaud, Antonin, 110, 180
Asprey, Robert, 141
Atkins, Eileen, 176

Bainton, Ronald H., 86
The Balcony (Jean Genet), 143
Ballester, Gonzalo Torrente, 37
Banks, Lynn Reid, 15, 44, 53
Banzie, Brenda de, 77, 242n.17
Barber, Lynn, 13, 216

Barker-Vedrenne, 30
Barnes, Clive, 128
Bas, George, 146
Bates, Alan, 121, 170
beat generation, 44
Beatles, 124
Beaumont, Binkie, 30
Becket (Jean Anouilh), 89
Beckett, Samuel, 23, 30–31, 177, 184, 193, 231
Behan, Brendan, 189
Beissel, Henry, 119
Belcher's Luck (David Mercer), 168
Bennett, Jill, 112, 165;
  in *Almost a Gentleman,* 176, 252n.26; in *The End of Me Old Cigar,* 173; in *Hedda Gabler,* 120; in *Jill and Jack,* 172; in *Time Present,* 114, 215
Bent (Martin Sherman), 164
Benthall, Michael, 33
Bergson, Henri, 183
Berliner Ensemble, 21, 31, 88
Berman, Charles, 166
Bernard, Jeffrey, 24, 226
Bertolucci, Bernardo, 166
Bessborough, Earl of, 83
Beyond the Fringe, 43
Billington, Michael, 128, 164, 170, 177, 217, 252n.2
Billy Liar (Keith Waterhouse), 87
The Birthday Party (Harold Pinter), 31
Bjökman, Edgar, 171
Black Comedy (Peter Shaffer), 117
Blacksell, J.E., 29
Blond, Neville, 29, 83, 235n.5
Blunt, Sir Anthony, 249n.3
Boehmer, Heinrich, 86

Boeing-Boeing (Marc Camoletti), 143
Bolt, Robert, 32, 89, 114
Bond, Edward, 23, 32, 110, 166, 249n.6
Bond, Philip, 120
Bondage of the Will (Martin Luther), 24, 86, 87, 89
Booth, John, 82
Braine, John, 44, 53
Branagh, Kenneth, 241n.25
Brandauer, Klaus Maria, 158–9
Brando, Marlon, 44, 144
Brecht, Bertolt, 21, 31, 88, 178, 180
Brenton, Howard, 110
Brett, Jeremy, 170
Breughel, 15, 17
Briefing for a Descent into Hell (Doris Lessing), 53
Brien, Alan, 88, 126, 194, 206
British Playwright Mafia, 167
Brook, Peter, 33, 110, 117, 143, 185
Bryden, Ronald, 66, 126
Burgess, Anthony, 53, 123
Burgess, Guy, 141
Burton, Richard, 42, 85, 87, 144, 215
Butler, Robert, 129

Cage, John, 177
Camoletti, Marc, 143
La Cantatrice Chauve (Eugène Ionesco), 30
Cards of Identity (Nigel Dennis), 32
Care and Control (Michelene Wandor), 163
Cat on a Hot Tin Roof (Tennessee Williams), 32
The Caucasian Chalk Circle (Bertolt Brecht), 31

censorship, 32, 109–110;
  abolishment of, 142–43; in
  Luther, 87; in *A Patriot for
  Me,* 144, 145
Les Chaises (Eugène Ionesco),
  30
Chapman, Brigid, 125
*The Charge of the Light
  Brigade,* 36, 112, 167, 215,
  247n.19
Chekhov, Anton, 114
Chesshyre, Robert, 16
Chicken Soup with Barley
  (Arnold Wesker), 32
Churchill, Caryl, 163, 220
Circle (Somerset Maugham), 30
Clark, Max Stafford, 173
Cleland, John, 124
A Clockwork Orange (Anthony
  Burgess), 53
Clurman, Harold, 41
Cobbold, Lord, 144
The Cocktail Party (T.S. Eliot),
  30
Coffey, Denise, 193
Comedy Theatre, 216
Confessions (Jean Jacques
  Rousseau), 176
The Confidential Clerk (T.S.
  Eliot), 30
The Constant Wife (Somerset
  Maugham), 30
Coriolanus (William
  Shakespeare), 168–170
Coward, Noel, 8, 13, 30, 144,
  166
Cranmer, Thomas, 222–23
Creighton, Anthony, 13, 20, 29,
  37, 144, 146
The Crucible (Arthur Miller), 32
Cunliffe, David, 120
Cushman, Robert, 174

Daniels, Sarah, 163
Davis, Desmond, 33
Dawson, Helen, 147, 165
Dean, James, 44
Death of a Salesman (Arthur
  Miller), 32, 81–82
The Death of Satan (Ronald
  Duncan), 32
Declaration (Tom Maschler),
  43–44, 64, 84
The Deep Blue Sea (Terence
  Rattigan), 30
Delaney, Shelagh, 32, 33, 44,
  53, 63, 239n.27
del Mar, Trixabelle, 146
Dench, Judi, 241n.25
Dennis, Nigel, 32
Devine, George, 29–30, 32, 45,
  111, 144, 145, 176
Dexter, John, 33, 43, 117

Dionysius, the Pseudo-
  Areopagite, 103, 245–46n.45
A Doctor's Dilemma (Bernard
  Shaw), 37
Don't Destroy Me (Michael
  Hastings), 239n.27
double bind, 56–58
Drabble, Margaret, 53
Draper, Peter, 112
The Dumbwaiter (Harold
  Pinter), 31
Duncan, Ronald, 29, 32
Dunlop, Frank, 192–93
Dyer, Charles, 143

Eagleton, Terry, 222
East of Eden, 44
Easy Money (Caryl Churchill),
  220
Edgar, David, 5, 110
Egan, Peter, 215–16
Eliot, T.S., 30
Elizabeth, Queen, 64
En Attendant Godot (Samuel
  Beckett), 30–31
English Stage Company, 29, 32,
  33
Entertaining Mr. Sloane (Joe
  Orton), 143
Erasmus, Desiderius, 24, 86
Erikson, Erik H., 87, 95, 98
Eros Denied (Wayland Young),
  143
Evans, Edith, 36
Evans, Gareth Lloyd, 32
Eve, Trevor, 128, 248n.35
Everyman, 127
existentialism, 98, 101
Eyre, Richard, 214, 248n.35

Falkland Islands, 219–20
Fanny Hill (John Cleland), 124
Farnsbarns, Charles, 184
Fearon, George, 43
Festival of Britain, 30
La fianza satisfecha (Lope de
  Vega), 117
Fielding, Henry, 24, 34
Finney, Albert, 36, 87, 88, 144,
  215
Firth, Peter, 170
Fleetwood, Susan, 172
Flint (David Mercer), 168
Foco Novo, 164
Foot, Michael, 89, 166
Forster, E.M., 146
The Four-Gated City (Doris
  Lessing), 53
Frankfurt School, 52
Freud, Sigmund, 91, 183,
  253n.12
Fringe theatre, 111
From Russia with Love, 124

Fry, Christopher, 30
Funke, Lewis, 220

Gaitskell, Hugh, 3, 52
Galileo (Bertolt Brecht), 88
Gambon, Michael, 66
Gaskell, Jane, 239n.27
Gaskill, William, 33, 111
Gaulle, Charles de, 111
Gay Sweatshop, 164
Gems, Pam, 163
Genet, Jean, 43, 143
Gielgud, John, 144, 170
Gill, Peter, 142, 146, 147, 249n.4
Gilliatt, Penelope, 112, 165,
  208, 247n.1
The Girl with Green Eyes (Edna
  O'Brien), 33
glasnost, 221
The Glass Menagerie
  (Tennessee Williams), 32
Goldfinger, 124
Goldman, Lucien, 102
Gorbachev, Mikhail, 221
Gorman, Janet, 170
Gosse, Edmund, 119
Grant, Steve, 129
Greene, Graham, 30
Greenwich Theatre, 170, 173
Greenwood, Joan, 36
Griffith, Hugh, 36
Griffith, Trevor, 110
The Grimm Sisters (Liz Loch-
  head), 163
Grove, Nellie Beatrice, 18–20
Guiness, Sir Alec, 122, 215
Gustafson, Jonas, 171

Habermas, Jurgen, 52
Hall, Peter, 9, 33, 170
Hamlet (William Shakespeare),
  22, 149, 217
Hampton, Christopher, 111,
  119, 184
Handel, George Frederick,
  174–75, 215
Hare, David, 1, 7, 110, 111
Handke, Peter, 178–86, 192,
  194, 196
Harewood, Earl of, 29, 83–84
Hastings, Michael, 239n.27
Hay Fever (Noel Coward), 30
Heath, Edward, 112
Hegelianism, 183, 253n.12
Hellman, Lillian, 31–32
Herbert, Jocelyn, 87
Here I Stand (Ronald H.
  Bainton), 86
Heriot, Charles, 144
Hobson, Harold, 37, 77, 78,
  143, 145, 177, 252n.2
The Homecoming (Harold
  Pinter), 143

homosexuality, see Osborne, John
Hooper, Sir Frederic, 83
Hopkins, Bill, 44
Hopkins, Harry, 52–53
Hughes, Robert, 34
Huis-Clos (Jean-Paul Sartre), 30
Hurry On Down (John Wain), 44
Hussey, Charles, 40, 42

Ibsen, Henrik, 116, 119–20, 171
The Iceman Cometh (Eugene O'Neill), 123
Ikoli, Tunde, 164
In Memoriam (Alfred Tennyson), 227
International Theatre Festival (1961), 87
L'Invitation au château (Jean Anouilh), 30
Ionesco, Eugène, 30
Irving, Sir Henry, 113
It's Only Us (Peter Draper), 112

Jellicoe, Ann, 44
Johnson, Samuel (Dr. Johnson), 8, 23, 24
Jongh, Nicholas de, 13, 127, 250n.11
Justine (Marquis de Sade), 124

Kant, Immanuel, 183
Kaspar (Peter Handke), 180
Kavanaugh, Simon, 104–105
Kemp, Peter, 217
Kempson, Rachel, 193
Kerouac, Jack, 44
Kerr, Walter, 46
The Killing of Sister George (Frank Marcus), 143
King, Francis, 7
The Kitchen (Arnold Wesker), 32
kitchen-sink realism, 32
Knots (R.D. Laing), 57
Kops, Bernard, 32
Lady Chatterley's Lover (D.H. Lawrence), 124, 143
Lady Frederick (Somerset Maugham), 30
The Lady's Not For Burning (Christopher Fry), 30
Laing, R.D., 57
Lane, Pamela, 13, 85
Lassally, Walter, 36
Last Tango in Paris, 166
La Leçon (Eugène Ionesco), 30
Lawrence, D.H., 124, 143, 224, 241n.37
Le Gallienne, Eva, 119
Leigh, Vivien, 65
Lessing, Doris, 44, 53

Leveaux, David, 172
libido, 183, 253n.12
Lill, Denis, 120
Lilly, Emma, 217
Linden, Stella, 29
Lion in Love (Shelagh Delaney), 239n.27
The Little Foxes (Lillian Hellman), 31
Littlewood, Joan, 185
Live Like Pigs (John Arden), 32
Liverpool Playhouse, 215
The Living Room (Graham Greene), 30
Livings, Henry, 32
Lloyd, Mary, 238n.63
Lochhead, Liz, 163
The Loneliness of the Long Distance Runner (Alan Sillitoe), 53
The Long Revolution (Raymond Williams), 76
Lotis, Dennis, 40
The L-Shaped Room (Lynn Reid Banks), 15, 53
Lucky Jim (Kingsley Amis), 44, 53
Luther, Martin, 24, 85–86, 89, 103, 142
Lysistrata, 172

Maclean, Donald, 141
Macmillan, Harold, 3
Magee, Bryan, 52
Magritte, René, 181
Maguy, Arthur, 243n.2
Major, John, 6
The Making of Moo (Nigel Dennis), 32
A Man for All Seasons (Robert Bolt), 89, 114
Marat/Sade (Peter Weiss), 110, 117
Marcus, Frank, 143
Marcuse, Herbert, 52, 53
Margaret, Princess, 114
Marks, Elaine, 83
Marowitz, Charles, 104, 119
Marriott, Raymond, 82
Martin Luther: Road to Reformation (Heinrich Boehmer), 86
Maschler, Tom, 18, 43–44, 64
Mason, Angela, 146
Masterpieces (Sarah Daniels), 163
The Matchmaker (Thornton Wilder), 32
Matheopoulos, Helena, 11
Matura, Mustapha, 164
Maugham, Somerset, 30, 47
Maurice (E.M. Forster), 146
Mavor, Ronald, 78, 82

Maxwell, Robert, 221
Maydays (David Edgar), 5
McKellen, Ian, 14, 164
Meals on Wheels (Charles Wood), 167
Men's Movement, 129
Mercer, David, 168
Merchant-Ivory Productions, 146
Miller, Arthur, 32, 46, 63, 81, 140, 240n.7
Miller, Carl, 170
Miller, Jonathan, 43
Miller, Max, 14, 24
The Millstone (Margaret Drabble), 53
The Misanthrope (Molière), 6
Miss Julie (August Strindberg), 171
Mister X (Gay Sweatshop), 164
Molière, 6, 200
Monsey, Derek, 64
Monstrous Regiment, 163
Morley, Sheridan, 177 190, 252n.2
Mortimer, John, 1, 32
Mother Courage (Bertolt Brecht), 21–22, 31
Les Mouches (Jean-Paul Sartre), 30
The Mulberry Bush (Angus Wilson), 32
Murder in the Cathedral (T.S. Eliot), 30
Murdoch, Iris, 44, 143
Murdoch, Rupert, 220
music hall, 71, 75–76

Nasser, Gamal Abdel, 64
Nauman, Bruce, 241n.27
La nausée (Jean-Paul Sartre), 78
negative space, 50, 241n.27
Nekrassov (Jean-Paul Sartre), 30
Newell, Mike, 122, 172
The New Look (Harry Hopkins), 52–53
Newman, John Henry, 176, 220
The New Radicalism (Bryan Magee), 52
Nightingale, Benedict, 119, 167, 178, 194

Oberst Redl, 158
Obrecht, Jakob, 87
O'Brien, Edna, 33, 184
Obscene Publications Act, 166
Odets, Clifford, 46
Offending the Audience (Peter Handke), 178–82, 192
Old Vic (theatre), 33, 117, 198

Olivier, Laurence
    and *The Entertainer,* 63–66,
      84, 144, 215, 242n.2, 17; and
      Luther, 125; and music hall,
      75; and Osborne, 15,
      243n.43; and *A Patriot for
      Me,* 142;
One for the Pot, 164
O'Neill, Eugene, 46, 123
One Way Pendulum
    (F.N.Simpson), 31
Orton, Joe, 143
Orwell, George, 222
Osborne, John
    general:
    and actors, 215, 193–94; aes-
      thetics of, 4, 6; aesthetics of
      economy and excess, 197,
      199, 207–208; aesthetics of
      loss and failure, 194–95, 196,
      199, 233; and Alternative
      Service Book, 6, 222–23,
      224; and anger, 18, 20, 21,
      25; and Angry Young Men,
      43–44, 45; and apartheid, 6,
      166; and audience, 23, 25–26,
      40, 41–42, 105, 197, 211; and
      audience participation, 185,
      193; and authenticity, 38–40,
      197, 199, 206–207, 210–11;
      awards given to, 34, 109, 166;
      and Berlin Crisis, 2–4; and
      censorship, 13, 109, 124, 142,
      144, 208, 249n.7, 250n.11;
      and CND, 236n.20; and con-
      servatism, 5, 6, 12, 112–13,
      125, 166, 236n.26; and cre-
      ativity, 24–25, 92, 104–106;
      and critics, 7, 15–17, 50–51,
      118–19, 167–68, 194, 208;
      and despair, 81–84; and
      detachment, 76–77; and
      enthusiasm, 23, 77, 82; and
      European Community, 6, 35,
      111–12, 166, 190, 218; and
      failure, 25, 37, 38–40, 41; and
      feelings, 6, 23, 25, 76, 84, 86;
      and feminism, 172, 190; and
      film, 41, 239n.12; and gender,
      11–21, 23, 41, 48, 55,
      237n.60, 241n.37; health
      problems of, 165; history
      plays, 141; and homo-
      sexuality, 10, 13–14, 144,
      145–47, 150, 157–58,
      166–67 224, 251n.36; homo-
      phobia of, 237n.41; and
      humanism, 171; and improvi-
      sation, 193, 199; and journal-
      ism, 218; and language, 10,
      11, 24, 48, 110, 206, 222–24;
      and liberalism, 124, 189, 190,
      221–22; life-art relationship,

9, 23–24, 37, 104–105, 187,
      195, 208, 209, 216; lifestyle
      of, 2, 3, 85, 164, 216, 240n.2,
      242n.7, 251n.10; misogyny
      of, 127, 170–71, 172,
      189–90, 248n.32, 35; and
      modernity, 125, 187,
      209–210; and monarchy, 64,
      244n.5; and music hall, 75,
      76–77, 196; and patriotism,
      35; pet peeves of, 9–10, 224;
      and philistinism, 4, 7, 10, 14,
      25, 26, 166–67, 207–208,
      213–14, 223, 225; and politi-
      cal correctness, 6, 7, 216,
      221–23, 236n.28; and poli-
      tics, 6, 236n.20; puritanism
      of, 105; and religion, 165,
      244n.5; and satire, 7; self-
      image of, 18, 111, 238n.64;
      and socialism, 2, 5, 236n.28;
      and style, 11, 22–25; and
      symbols, 92, 94, 95; as a the-
      atrical personality, 8–9,
      236–37n.37; and Vietnam
      War, 236n.20; and vitupera-
      tion, 15, 22–23, 24, 216–17;
      and welfare state, 2, 10, 12,
      24; and well-made play, 199;
      youth of, 18–21, 29; and
      youth cult, 125, 170
Osborne, John
    works:
    Almost a Gentleman, 36, 176,
      218
    Almost a Vision, 173
    A Better Class of Person,
      18–21 passim, 176, 218
    The Blood of the Bambergs,
      43, 144
    A Bond Honoured (adapted
      from Lope de Vega),
      116–19, 167
    "Damn You, England," 2–4
    Déjàvu, 9, 10, 105, 168, 175,
      178, 213–33;
    The Devil Inside (with Stella
      Linden), 29
    The End of Me Old Cigar, 12,
      17, 19, 153, 168, 172–74
    England, My England!
      174–75, 254n.31
    The Entertainer, 25, 29, 36,
      63–84, 125, 170;
      and aesthetics of loss, 195;
      and Brecht, 22, 178; and
      Tony Richardson, 33
    Epitaph for George Dillon
      (with Anthony Creighton),
      21, 29, 36–40, 163
    The Father (adapted from
      August Strindberg), 168,
      170–72, 218

The Gift of Friendship, 117,
      122
God Rot Tunbridge Wells!
      141, 168, 174–75, 215, 218
Hedda Gabler (adapted from
      Henrik Ibsen), 116,
      119–20, 171
The Hotel in Amsterdam, 21,
      111, 114–15
Inadmissible Evidence,
      123–40;
      film version of, 33; major
      themes of, 42, 112, 122;
      and Osborne's life, 165,
      167; tragic aspects of, 25,
      141–42, 163
Jill and Jack, 168, 172
"Letter to My Fellow
Countrymen," 2, 143
Look Back in Anger, 45–62;
      and aesthetics of loss, 195;
      and America, 40, 44; and
      Angry Young Man, 44;
      autobiographical elements
      in, 19, 37; and *Déjàvu,*
      227–28, 230–32; financial
      effects of, 33, 240n.4; gen-
      der in, 12–13; 16–17,
      46–47; homosexuality in,
      14; as innovative theatre,
      31, 32, 46; and *Luther,* 89;
      and melodrama, 23; music
      and language in, 49, 50,
      60–62; and nostalgia, 35;
      and Osborne's public
      image, 45; as play for one
      voice, 241n.21; and Royal
      Court Theatre, 33; and
      success abroad, 240n.2,
      11; tragic aspects of, 25;
      values in, 10; and welfare
      state, 46; and well-made
      play, 22, 47
Luther, 85–106;
      and anger, 21; and Brecht,
      22, 178; as an actor's vehi-
      cle, 125; financial effects
      of, 3, 33; as a history play,
      141; and Osborne's public
      image, 9; and public voice,
      42; tragic aspects of, 25
A Patriot for Me, 9, 13, 21,
      32, 111, 124, 141–59, 195
Personal Enemy (with
      Anthony Creighton), 29,
      37, 144
The Picture of Dorian Gray
      (adapted from Oscar
      Wilde), 168, 170
A Place Calling Itself Rome
      (adapted from Shakes-
      peare's *Coriolanus),*
      168–70

Plays for England, 42–43, 143–44

The Right Prospectus, 117, 120–21, 163

A Sense of Detachment, 25, 26, 168, 176, 177–96

A Subject of Scandal and Concern, 41–42, 85, 141

"They Call It Cricket," 4, 18

Time Present, 111, 112–14

Tom Jones (adapted from Henry Fielding), 33–36

Try a Little Tenderness, 168, 174, 218

"Turning the Tables: Kicking Against the Pricks," 167

Under Plain Cover, 43, 144

Very Like a Whale, 117, 121–22, 163, 166

Watch It Come Down, 25, 167, 168, 170, 173, 178, 197–211, 218

West of Suez, 111, 115–16, 195

The World of Paul Slickey, 25, 40–41, 85, 118, 167, 178

You're Not Watching Me, Mummy, 168, 174, 218

Osborne, Nolan, 165

Osborne, Thomas Godfrey, 18–20

O'Toole, Peter, 144, 215

Our Country's Good (Timberlake Wertenbaker), 163

The Outsider (Colin Wilson), 44

outsider motive, 142

Owners (Caryl Churchill), 163

Page, Anthony, 13, 33, 111, 125, 144, 247n.19

Palace Theatre, 41, 64

Palmer, Tony, 175, 215, 254n.31

The Panther's Feast (Robert Asprey), 141

Les Paravents (Jean Genet), 143

Parker, Di, 217

Pascal, Blaise, 102

Pavilion Theatre, 40

perestroika, 221

Peter, John, 124

Pinero, Sir Arthur Wing, 31

Le Ping-Pong (Arthur Adamov), 30

Pinter, Harold, 24, 31, 32, 119, 143, 184

Pirandello, Luigi, 178–186, 194, 196

Piscator, Erwin, 185

Plowright, Joan, 170, 216

The Politics of Experience (R.D. Laing), 57

The Pope's Wedding (Edward Bond), 32

Portable Theatre, 111

Posener, Jill, 164

postcolonial theatre, 164

postmodernism, 6–7, 11

Pres, Josquin de, 87

Priestley, J.B., 30, 143, 166

Private Lives (Noel Coward), 30

Le Professeur Taranne (Arthur Adamov), 30

psychoanalysis, 87, 94

Purcell, Henry, 174, 175, 176, 254n.31

Queen Christina (Pam Gems) 163

Rabe, David, 31

Rattigan, Terence, 30, 38, 88, 196

Ravenhill, Mark, 164

Raymond, John, 83

Raymond, Williams, 76

Rebel Without A Cause, 44

Redgrave, Michael, 193

Redgrave, Vanessa, 12, 113

Reinert, Otto, 119

Relph, George, 77, 242n.17

Renton, Nicholas, 66

repressive tolerance, 53

A Resounding Tinkle (F.N.Simpson), 31

Richardson, Ralph, 115, 215

Richardson, Tony
and *Charge of the Light Brigade,* 36, 215; and *Déjàvu,* 228, 237n.50; and *The Entertainer,* 66; homosexuality of, 13, 14; and *Hotel in Amsterdam,* 247n.19; and *Luther,* 87; and *Subject of Scandal and Concern,* 41; and *Tom Jones,* 33–36; and Woodfall film, 33–34

Rickman, Alan, 166

Rigg, Diana, 120

Ritchie, Harry, 44

Roberts, Rachel, 173

Rogers, Daniel, 117

The Room (Harold Pinter), 31

Room at the Top (John Braine), 44, 53

A Room of One's Own (Virginia Woolf), 11, 106

Ropps, Félicien, 15

Rousseau, Jean Jacques, 176

Royal Court Theatre, 29–30, 32–33;
and Angry Young Man phenomenon, 43; and *Déjàvu,* 214; and *The Entertainer,* 65, 83–84; and *Epitaph for*

George Dillon, 37; and *Hedda Gabler,* 120; and *Inadmissible Evidence,* 125, 126; and John Osborne, 111, 120, 198; and *Look Back in Anger,* 45, 64; and *Luther,* 87; and *A Patriot for Me,* 142; and Theatre Upstairs, 111; and *Time Present,* 114; and *West of Suez,* 115; *The World of Paul Slickey,* 40

Royal National Theatre, 117, 126; Cottesloe, 172; and *Déjàvu,* 214; and *Inadmissible Evidence,* 248n.35; Lyttelton, 126, 170; and *Watch It Come Down,* 198

Royal Shakespeare Company, 33, 146

Rushdie, Salman, 221

Russell, Bertrand, 3

Rutherford, Malcolm, 217

Sade, Marquis de, 124

Samuel, Graham, 125

Sartre, Jean-Paul, 30, 78

Satanic Verses (Salman Rushdie), 221

Saturday Night and Sunday Morning (Alan Sillitoe), 3, 33, 36, 88, 143

Saved (Edward Bond), 32, 249n.6

Scargill, Arthur, 220, 236n.26

Schell, Maximilian, 144, 215, 250n.16

Schopenhauer, Arthur, 183

Scofield, Paul, 114, 215; sentimentalism, 83–84

Separate Tables (Terence Rattigan), 30

A Severed Head (Iris Murdoch), 143

Sexual Offences Act (1967), 143

Shaffer, Peter, 117

Shakespeare, William, 141; and *Déjàvu,* 217, 223; influence on Osborne, 22, 24, 88; and *A Place Calling Itself Rome,* 168–70

Shaw, Bernard, 22, 30, 37

Shaw, Glen Byam, 33

Sherman, Martin, 164

Shopping and Fucking (Mark Ravenhill), 164

Shulman, Milton, 74–75, 125, 145, 252n.2

Shuttleworth, Ian, 218

Sillitoe, Alan, 3, 34, 53, 88, 143

Simpson, F.N., 23, 31

Six Characters in Search of an Author (Luigi Pirandello), 178–79, 182–83

Smith, Maggie, 117
Snowdon, Lord, 114
The Sound of Music, 127
Soyinka, Wole, 164
Speight, Johnny, 254n.7
Spence, Martin, 129
Spencer, Charles, 218
Staircase (Charles Dyer), 143
St. Augustine, 92
Stephens, Robert, 37, 117
St. George, Clive, 29
St. James Theatre (NYC), 89
Stonewall, 146
Storey, David, 44, 111, 184
Strachey, Lytton, 205
Strange Evil (Jane Gaskell),
  239n.27
A Streetcar Named Desire
  (Tennessee Williams), 32
Strindberg, August, 57, 170–72,
  241n.37
The Stronger (August Strind-
  berg), 57
Suez Crisis, 64, 82–83, 84, 220
Sugar Babies, 164
symbolism, 94
Szabó, István, 158

A Taste of Honey (Shelagh
  Delaney), 33, 53, 239n.27
Taylor, Paul, 127
technocracy, 52, 57
Teddy Boy, 7, 236n.32
Tennyson, Alfred, 227
Thatcher, Margaret, 6, 219–21,
  236n.26
That Uncertain Feeling
  (Kingsley Amis), 44
Theatre Act (1968), 142
Théâtre des Nations, 36
Le théâtre et son double
  (Antonin Artaud), 110
Theatre of Antagonism, 179
Theatre of Cruelty, 110, 117
Theatre Royal (Nottingham),
  87
Théâtre Sarah Bernhardt (Paris),
  87

This Sporting Life (David
  Storey), 44
This Way to the Tomb (Ronald
  Duncan), 32
Thompson, Emma, 241n.25
Thorndike Theatre, 216
Thurber, James Grover, 241n.37
Tillich, Paul, 104
Tischreden (Martin Luther), 87
Tous contre tous (Arthur
  Adamov), 30
Trevis, Di, 127–28
Turner, David, 32
Tushingham, Rita, 33
Tynan, Kenneth,
  and *A Bond Honoured,* 117;
  interviewing Osborne, 5,
  112; and *Look Back in Anger,*
  23, 45, 59, 64, 217

Under the Net (Iris Murdoch),
  44
United Artists, 166
Ure, Mary, 85, 187

Vega, Lope de, 116
Via Negativa, 103–104,
  245–46n.45
A View From the Bridge (Arthur
  Miller), 140
Vinegar Tom (Caryl Churchill),
  163
vituperation, 59, 113, 170, 184,
  222, 226

Wager, Walter, 13
Wain, John, 44
Waiting for Godot (Samuel
  Beckett), 231
Walden, Ben, 165
Wall, Max, 66
Wandor, Michelene, 163
Wardle, Irving, 109, 167, 174
Waterhouse, Keith, 87
Watts, Stephen, 105
Waugh, Evelyn, 104
Webber, Robert, 243n.2
Weigel, Helene, 21

Weiss, Peter, 110
welfare state, 44, 242–43n.20;
  in *Déjàvu,* 219; in *The Enter-
  tainer,* 72; in *Inadmissible
  Evidence,* 51, 125; in *Look
  Back in Anger,* 47–48, 51–53
well-made play, 22, 31;
  and *Look Back in Anger,* 47,
  50; and *Luther,* 88
Wertenbaker, Timberlake, 163
Wesker, Arnold, 9, 32, 43, 46,
  128, 184, 196
West Side Story, 40
Whitehead, Ted, 111
Who's Afraid of Virginia Woolf
  (Edward Albee), 200, 203
Wilby, James, 146
Wilde, Oscar, 166, 168
Wilder, Thornton, 32
The Wild Ones, 44
Williams, Hugh and Margaret,
  31
Williams, Raymond, 52, 76
Williams, Tennessee, 32, 46,
  240n.7
Williamson, Nicol, 125–26,
  128, 144, 215
Wilson, Angus, 32
Wilson, Colin, 44, 63, 84
Wilson, Harold, 52, 111, 124, 187
Wilson, Snoo, 110, 219
Wolf, Matt, 59, 227
Wolfenden Report, 143
Wolfit, Sir Donald, 113
Wood, Charles, 112, 167, 184
Wood, Peter, 33
Woodfall Films, 33, 36, 66, 88,
  126;
  and apartheid, 112
Woolf, Virginia, 11, 106

York, Susannah, 36
Young, Leslie, 43
Young Man Luther (Erik H.
  Erikson), 87
Young, Wayland, 143
youth cult, 44, 170
yuppies, 220